VIOLENT SPACE

VIOLENT SPACE

The Jewish Ghetto in Warsaw

ANJA NOWAK

INDIANA UNIVERSITY PRESS

This book is a publication of

Indiana University Press
Office of Scholarly Publishing
Herman B Wells Library 350
1320 East 10th Street
Bloomington, Indiana 47405 USA

iupress.org

Manufactured in the United States of America

First printing 2023

Cataloging information is available from the Library of Congress.

ISBN 978-0-253-06742-5 (hdbk.)
ISBN 978-0-253-06743-2 (pbk.)
ISBN 978-0-253-06744-9 (web PDF)

Maps and figures created with the generous support of the *Hamburger Stiftung zur Förderung von Wissenschaft und Kultur* (Hamburg Foundation for the Advancement of Research and Culture).

CONTENTS

PART IV: CONCLUSION

PREFACE

How We Got Here . . .

This is a book about the Jewish ghetto in German-occupied Warsaw (1939–1943) and the human experience within it. *Violent Space* traces out the trauma that the space of the ghetto brought on Jewish people, the way it alienated, disoriented, hurt, and harmed them. For the Germans, the ghetto was a sociopolitical tool used to bring forward the Nazi anti-Jewish campaign. For the Jews, however, the ghetto became the very center of their lives even though it was a source of immense suffering. *Violent Space* is about these Jews and about the ghetto as a space that shaped Jewish experience of the first phase of the Holocaust.

My understanding of the impact that space had on the experience and fate of the victims was initially formed not in Warsaw but at another central site of the Holocaust: the former Auschwitz-Birkenau concentration and death camp(s). One could thus say that I started the journey from the end. While *Violent Space* focuses on the Warsaw ghetto as a space where, at least for some time, Jewish life still took place, the project's origin is bound to a space where Jewish lives ended. For the majority of those who did not perish in the ghettos or during deportations, Auschwitz II-Birkenau, as one of several death camps the Germans established in occupied Poland between the fall of 1941 and the spring of 1942, became the violent endpoint of their journey. Here, in the context of industrialized mass killing, the oppressive nature of space is quite evident, which is why I introduce the research question of this book by taking an indirect route, spanning almost the entire duration of the Holocaust.

Before I began my research on the Warsaw ghetto, which, for many Jews, embodied the first phase of the Holocaust, I had already spent some time working as an educator and researcher in the field of Holocaust studies. It was in this context that I first developed the ideas that would lead to the conception of *Violent Space*.

I came to the Auschwitz-Birkenau Memorial and Museum as an assistant for
the Witnessing Auschwitz intensive research seminar, spending several weeks
on-site with three consecutive groups of Canadian students in the summers of
2014, 2015, and 2016.[1] Visiting what remained of the Auschwitz camps, I quickly
realized the importance that spatial experience held for my understanding of the
Holocaust. I entered the former camps (Auschwitz I-Stammlager and Auschwitz
II-Birkenau) equipped with the knowledge I had gained from memoirs and literary texts of survivors, such as Halina Birenbaum's *Hope Is the Last to Die*, Seweryna Szmaglewska's *Smoke over Birkenau*, Tadeusz Borowski's *This Way for the
Gas, Ladies and Gentlemen*, and Ruth Klüger's *weiter leben* and *Still Alive*. Their
descriptions framed my first encounter with these sites, and, right away, I was
struck by how much the physical reality of the camps added to my understanding
of the texts I had read and of the experiences their survivor-authors described.
The camps' layout and terrain, distance, perspective, walls, fences, and particular
buildings each gave a concrete appearance to knowledge I previously possessed
only in theory.

As a central site of the Holocaust, the Auschwitz camp complex explicitly
served the Nazis as a space to implement violence. During the time of its operation, it consisted of the Auschwitz I-Stammlager concentration camp, the
Auschwitz II-Birkenau death camp, the Auschwitz III-Monowitz work camp,
and roughly forty smaller subcamps. Each of them had its own structure, architecture, function, and dynamics. While Auschwitz I-Stammlager was established
on the premises of former Polish army barracks and thus largely consisted of solid,
two- or three-story brick buildings, the death camp, Auschwitz II-Birkenau, was
newly built in 1941 for the sole purpose of administering the "Final Solution."
Auschwitz II-Birkenau extended over 171 hectares and consisted mainly of simple
one-story prisoner barracks made of brick or wood and laid out symmetrically
in separate fenced-off sectors.[2] Only these two main camps were preserved as
part of the Auschwitz-Birkenau Memorial and Museum. Although I had read a
fair bit about them, their architectural and territorial differences became much
more palpable when I experienced them firsthand. Walking along the outer fence
of Auschwitz-Birkenau, for example, and realizing the extent of the camp complex not as a theoretical variable but as an actual bodily experience and effort,
created a different sense of the camp's magnitude. It also led me to see the camp
as a space that, in its sheer expansiveness, implied physical exhaustion and was
therefore, for most of the starving and sick prisoners, physically impossible to
master. Walking along the perimeter of the camp several times during my visits,
both under scorching sun and heavy rain that quickly turned the ground into
slippery and "boggy mud" that "sucks in the feet," as Szmaglewska writes, I realized there was a material and bodily dimension to distance that was bound to the

weather conditions, to properties of the ground surface, to temperature, but also to an individual's physical condition, to his or her bodily capacities, to footwear, clothing, diet, and health.[3]

The Germans had set up the Auschwitz camps in the vicinity of the Polish town of Oświęcim, and each year, out of two weeks studying on-site at the Auschwitz-Birkenau Memorial and Museum, Witnessing Auschwitz students and faculty stayed one week in a hotel close to the town's market square. Walking the approximately three kilometers from the town of Oświęcim, where, incidentally, many of the camps' guards had lived, to the grounds of the former Auschwitz I-Stammlager each day taught me much about mechanisms of decoupling personal life and work in the camp—in other words, about dissociation. Standing on top of the watchtowers in both Auschwitz I-Stammlager and Auschwitz II-Birkenau and looking down onto the camps' grounds from the perspective of the SS guards held strong explanatory value in regard to questions of power, hierarchy, and victimization. Likewise, the daily experience of entering and leaving the camp freely through its gates had a similar effect. At the same time, I realized that the space of the camp, as it is today, is very different from the camp the prisoners had experienced. It is now a myriad of things: a memorial, a graveyard, a museum, an archive, a research institution, a workplace, but it is no longer a German concentration and death camp. To help bridge the gap between past and present, I needed the testimonies of those who had been forced to live through the camp during the time of its operation.

Many of the accounts I had read suggested that the camps' prisoners perceived the camps as violent spaces, both in the sense that they were dominated by violence and as spaces that were, in and of themselves, violations of the prisoners' most basic needs (such as, for instance, privacy, safety, personal space, and basic sanitary necessities). This first instilled the notion of space as violence that I would carry over into my analysis of the ghetto, where, as I soon realized, many of the Jewish victims had already been exposed to spatially organized violence before they entered the camps. Starting my work at the point where Jewish experiences of the Holocaust violently culminated, my first paper on a Holocaust space focused on the spatial layout and functioning of the camps but also on the question of how this space was regulated and how it was experienced, in particular exploring questions regarding boundaries and confinement, isolation, and spatial restrictions.[4]

My study of the nexus of space and violence began in the context of the industrialized mass murder perpetrated at Auschwitz, and it was only later that the idea took shape to analyze spaces of an earlier phase of the Holocaust. While my first encounters with the Warsaw ghetto dated back to 2014, I only began to conduct independent research into this topic a year later. My initial approach to the ghetto was to study it as a space that, for many Jews, preceded their deportation to the camps. In addition, I was curious to see how the concept of a violent space would apply to this very different spatial setting. Two aspects became central for my first examination of the space of the former ghetto in Warsaw: first, that it is, in fact, a space that does not exist anymore—that is, that it is indeed a "perished city," as the title of Barbara Engelking and Jacek Leociak's seminal work suggests, and, second, that it was situated in an urban environment, implemented within the capital city of Warsaw's very center. This evoked theoretical understandings I had brought with me from previous research, such as that on Walter Benjamin's *Berliner Chronik* (*Berlin Chronicles*) and his *Berliner Kindheit um Neunzehnhundert* (*Berlin Childhood around 1900*)—which are both, in essence, studies of a space that is ultimately lost—or, for example, research I had done on the literary "construction" of urban space in Alfred Döblin's *Berlin Alexanderplatz*. Reflecting on the urban environment also entailed theoretical concepts with which I had already engaged during my earlier work and that strongly influenced my approach to urban space and, thus, also to the ghetto, right from the beginning. This included, for example, Michel Foucault's concept of "heterotopias" and his decisive linking of space and power; Henri Lefebvre's Marxist theory of the production of (urban) space and his distinction between "perceived space" (*espace perçu*), "conceived space" (*espace conçu*), and "lived space" (*espace veçu*); as well as Michel de Certeau's distinction between "strategy and tactic" (*stratégie/tactique*) and his general notion of the "art of using," which introduced the capacity of the marginalized to subvert dominant structures.[5]

The fact that the physical ghetto—that is, its buildings and streets—does not exist anymore and that in its place a new urban structure, a new city, has been built marks a distinct difference between the ghetto and the Auschwitz camp complex, which has been, at least partially, preserved. The case of the Warsaw ghetto is, in fact, quite unique. While most death camps were, toward the end of their operations, dismantled by the Germans (albeit to varying degrees), there are usually some spatial residues or, otherwise, the voids themselves have been maintained and commemorated through the establishment of museums and memorials after the war. The Nazi ghettos in occupied Poland were all "liquidated" by the fall of 1944—meaning that their inhabitants were murdered on the spot or deported to concentration and death camps and that the physical ghettos were dismantled.[6] As the ghettos were implemented within existing settlement structures, their boundary markers usually disappeared, but the streets and buildings that had been part of the ghetto are still accessible today. The Litzmannstadt ghetto,[7] which was established by the Germans in the Polish city of Łódź,[8] for example, was separated from the "Aryan" side by a fence that does not exist anymore, and the wall of the Kraków ghetto has been torn down save for a few fragments;[9] the streets of these cities, however, have remained almost unchanged. This means that, in both Łódź and Kraków, it is possible to walk along the border streets of the former ghetto with very little interruption. Many buildings from the time of these ghettos' existence have survived as well. In the case of the Warsaw ghetto, however, none of that applies. Having been razed to the ground by the Germans after the defeat of the Ghetto Uprising in 1943, the space of the former ghetto does not coincide at all with the space of the city as it is today.[10] Walking along the ghetto's perimeter requires great effort in terms of orientation, and it is never more than an approximation. Major streets on its former territory have changed their course or ceased to exist altogether. There are very few landmarks or buildings standing today that have witnessed the time of the ghetto.[11]

Still, the physical experience of being on-site added to my understanding of the space of the past. Following the former ghetto's outline, often virtually against the postwar structures of the current urban environment, made me come to a sobering realization of how much was missing and, thus, of the Germans' determination to annihilate not only people but also the spaces associated with them. Walking along the approximated line of the initial ghetto boundary (at the point of its closing, November 1940) also brought to my attention an interesting paradox: compared to the ghetto area itself, especially its first border was, in fact, very long. This was the result of a very dented boundary, excluding certain buildings and passages from the ghetto. My subsequent research confirmed that the ghetto's inhabitants experienced this irregular course of the boundary as extremely disruptive and arduous. But this paradox is also very telling in regard to the hierarchy inherent in the racially coded distribution of space under German rule. Precedence was given to the spatial needs and interests of the "Aryan" side, and this, in turn, produced an inside space that translated the social disenfranchisement and degradation that the Jewish population experienced into spatial coordinates.

During one of the walking tours for the Witnessing Auschwitz students, Professor Jacek Leociak pointed out the fact that the houses of the present-day Muranów district in Warsaw were literally built on the remains of the former ghetto, on rubble and on the mortal remains of those who perished during the Ghetto Uprising. The new quarter is layered on top of the old one, the city's present quite literally built on its past, creating a palimpsest.[12] This changes the current city's three-dimensional space quite drastically, adding a layer of buried history to it, elevating its buildings onto small mounds consisting of the only physical remains that are left of the ghetto. During one of our walks, students were able to witness these layers firsthand, when construction work done on the sewers along Zamenhofa Street exposed the rubble underneath the streets on which we were walking. Again and again, the city of Warsaw confronts us with this type of stratification of past and present.

While the physical remains of the ghetto and the typical experiences of a current-day visitor to the city might be telling in many regards, they cannot grant access to the ghetto that has ceased to exist. Even if we were able to walk the streets of the former ghetto, we would understand very little of it. The ghetto was defined not only by its architectural structure but by social dynamics as well, as it was concurrently shaped by the presence of its inhabitants: huge crowds in the early times of the ghetto's existence, many of whom were destitute and starving; followed in the summer of 1942 by rows of people, terrified and desperate, forced to march to the *Umschlagplatz* to be deported; afterward, individuals hurried, exposed and scared in the now-empty streets of the ghetto, columns of workers marched to their places of work in the ghetto's factories; and in 1943, members of the Jewish Fighting Organization rising up, while noncombatant civilians were desperately seeking shelter in hiding places and underground bunkers. The ghetto was defined by the cultures and behaviors of those forced to inhabit it: by their customs, their religions, their habits, their various attire, their gestures, their pace, their trades, their encounters, their voices, their languages, their memories, their expectations, their hopes and plans, their fears and sorrows, and by traffic, smells, colors, lighting, darkness, surfaces, textures. It was defined by the German anti-Jewish policies and by the violence used against the ghetto inhabitants, by the numerous acts of humiliation they faced, by the confinement and segregation the Germans enforced through the ghetto, by the raids, round-ups, beatings, shootings, and executions that the Germans carried out within its walls, by epidemics, starvation, lack of sanitation, and lack of medical care, and by the fear, loss, and death the ghetto inhabitants experienced due to these conditions. The only way to access these dimensions of the ghetto is through the narratives of those who witnessed it. Ultimately, all theoretical analysis and historical framework aside, this is what this book presents: an evocation of the space of the Warsaw ghetto as seen through the eyes of those who were forced into it. While space as a category might at first seem very technical and not particularly suitable to do justice to the immense suffering and loss experienced within the ghetto, testimonies show it to be an experiential category of great intimacy and particular value to those in the ghetto. Space was closely linked to social relations and personal life; to one's identity, one's sense of belonging; but also to personal freedom, safety, and well-being as well as to the lack thereof. Before it was brutalized and turned deadly, it was, in many ways, a fundamental part of the very delicate and sensitive net that made up a person's individual life. The Nazis' victims thus experienced its disruption and contortion as immensely painful. For those in the ghetto, space and suffering were not antithetic but closely intertwined.

Notes

1. On the initiative of Professor Dr. Bożena Karwowska (University of British Columbia, UBC), since 2014, the Witnessing Auschwitz research seminar is organized in cooperation among UBC (Vancouver), the Auschwitz-Birkenau State Memorial and Museum, the Jewish Historical Institute in Warsaw, and numerous other research institutions in Poland. Each year, students from UBC spend about a month in Poland, studying and working with specialists from the field of Holocaust studies. In 2017, the results of students' research on topics pertaining to the Auschwitz camp complex were published in cooperation with the Auschwitz-Birkenau State Museum's research department and publishing house (Karwowska and Nowak, *The More I Know, The Less I Understand*).

2. The number given here refers to the grounds covered today by the Auschwitz-Birkenau Memorial and Museum. At the time of the camp's construction in the winter of 1941/1942, Birkenau extended over 140 hectares, but it was significantly expanded over time (Auschwitz-Birkenau Memorial and Museum, "Construction of the Camp"). For a comprehensive overview of the history, topography, and operations of the camps, see the Auschwitz-Birkenau Memorial and Museum's website (for example, "History" or "Topography of the Camp"); for more detailed information, see, for example, Cywiński, Setkiewicz, and Lachendro, *Auschwitz from A to Z. An Illustrated History*; Długoborski and Piper, *Auschwitz 1940–1945. Central Issues in the History of the Camp*; or Gutman and Berenbaum, *Anatomy of the Auschwitz Death Camp*.

3. The mud of Birkenau is prevalent in many memoirs. Szmaglewska describes it repeatedly and explains its effect on the exhausted prisoners: "It is thawing. The mud, the special boggy mud of Birkenau, sucks in the feet. The sick women are hardly able to walk in spite of the nurses' assistance. They toil through the mud while the wind roars and tears the blankets off them and whips them with its damp blasts. They have not far to go. But one must know the mud of Birkenau to appreciate how long it takes to walk even this short distance" (*Smoke over Birkenau*, 78).

4. Parts of which were presented in Bialystok in 2015 at the conference *Geograficzne przestrzenie utekstowione* (Narrating Geographic Space), and later published in the conference proceedings under the title "Spatial Configurations of the Concentration Camp: The Inside and the Outside" (Karwowska et al., *Geograficzne przestrzenie utekstowione*, 371–386).

5. Key texts by these three authors include Michel Foucault's influential talk on heterotopias, "Des Espaces Autres/Of Other Spaces" and his interview "Espace, savoir et pouvoir/Space, Power and Knowledge", Henri Lefebvre's *La production de l'espace/The Production of Space*, and Michel de Certeau's much-cited *L'invention du quotidien. Vol. 1, Arts de faire/The Practice of Everyday Life*. For comprehensive introductions to Foucault's, de Certeau's, and Lefebvre's work on space, see, for example, Grbin, "Foucault and Space," Füssel, "Tote Orte und Gelebte Räume," or Zieleniec,

"Henri Lefebvre: The Production of Space." For a more general introduction to theories of social space, see, for example, Dünne and Günzel, *Raumtheorie*, 289–303.

6. Refer to the section "A Note on the Use of Nazi German Terminology" for the use of quotation marks in the text.

7. When talking about the ghettos and camps the Germans established in occupied Poland, I use the German name to denote the Holocaust site and the Polish name when referring to the respective village, town, or city where the site was located.

8. Which was part of the Reich district *Wartheland* and, as such, annexed to the Reich.

9. Which was, just as Warsaw, part of the so-called *Generalgouvernement* and, as such, not annexed to the Reich.

10. For a highly informative map, see Weszpiński, "Present Structure of Streets and Remains of Buildings in March 2001 against the Old Plan of the City."

11. In his paper "Reading the Palimpsest," Konstanty Gebert describes quite extensively how and where these last remnants of the Jewish past protrude into the present city. For a virtual tour bringing into conversation the contemporary city and the last physical traces of the ghetto, see these two documentations prepared for the POLIN museum by Eleonora Bergman and Jozef Hen: "'Following the Markers.' Jewish Warsaw: Past and Present" and "'Walking in a Non-Existent City.' Jewish Warsaw: Past and Present."

12. The idea of a palimpsest can be understood here in several ways: as an architectural palimpsest, with the new quarter of Muranów built on "piles of rubble covered by earth on which stand apartment buildings constructed of cinder blocks made of ground rubble and concrete" (Leociak, "From Żydowska Street to Umschlagplatz," 5)—that is, the new buildings quite literally overwriting and at the same time absorbing their predecessors. In a similar way, as Gebert points out, the city's street network can also be deciphered as a palimpsest: "If one looks down on Warsaw from one of the many high-rises, one sees clearly that the city has two street grids, superimposed on top of one another and coexisting uneasily. Prewar streets, their traces visible through the facades of a few surviving houses, lead nowhere. Modern thoroughfares cut a building in half. The palimpsest is difficult to read" ("Reading the Palimpsest," 230). Closely interlocked with this architectural one is a temporal dimension of the palimpsest, with the ruins and residues of the old quarter being "reincarnations of the past into the present and future" (Meng, "Muranów as a Ruin," 72). Past and present physically and symbolically converge in what Sławomir Kapralski—borrowing from Bakhtin—calls a "chronotope," a "locus in which time has been condensed and concentrated in space" ("Battlefields of Memory," 36). This convergence defines Muranów as a palimpsest of memory, history, and identities, with the history of the now-extinct quarter deeply connected to the identity of the contemporary city, the quarter, and its inhabitants, but also to the identity and commemoration of those who perished. The quarter's "multiple temporalities" include "the prewar history of Jewish life, the wartime history of ghettoization and genocide, and the postwar history of building an amnesiac socialist future" (Meng, "Muranów as a Ruin," 82–83).

ACKNOWLEDGMENTS

For me, writing the acknowledgments to a book is one of the nicest parts of the process. Right at the end, when most of the work is done, you sit down to recall and thank all the people and institutions that helped you along the way. It is, in a way, like going through a series of photographs from a very long and intense trip—one that was strenuous at times but also full of the most wonderful encounters, memories, and lessons learned.

To begin, I would like to thank the person who took me on this journey in the first place (quite literally as well): Professor Dr. Bożena Karwowska, who was the most dedicated and supportive thesis supervisor I could have hoped for. More than once, she saw more in my work than I did, and I owe much to her sharp intellect, vast knowledge, and brilliant feedback. Thank you, Bożena, for everything.

A very special thank-you goes to Professor Dr. Jacek Leociak (Warsaw) for many inspiring conversations and for his willingness to share his ideas and to provide me with material, helpful suggestions, contacts, and advice. His work on the ghetto has been a constant inspiration, and I will never forget his wonderful walking tour of the perimeter of the *Perished City* in Warsaw. A big thank-you also to Harrie Teunissen (Dordrecht) for a lively and inspiring exchange over the years. Thank you to Rabbi Dan Moskovitz of Temple Sholom (Vancouver) and Hannah Hermann (Darmstadt) for their helpful advice.

I am grateful for the time I spent at the Archives of the Jewish Historical Institute (Żydowski Instytut Historyczny) in Warsaw. Special thanks to its former director, Professor Dr. Paweł Śpiewak; to the head of the Archival Department, Agnieszka Reszka, and her team; as well as to Michał Czajka, Marta Janczewska, and Dr. Alicja Mroczkowska for kindly sharing their knowledge with me. Thank you also to the director of the Jewish Cemetery on Okopowa Street, Witold

Wrzosinski, and to Robert Hasselbusch from the Pawiak Museum (Warsaw). Additional thanks go to Dr. Piotr Setkiewicz and Dr. Jacek Lachendro from the Auschwitz-Birkenau Research Department, as well as to the head of the museum's archives, Wojciech Płosa, and his team for their support during an early stage of this project.

For kindly providing the historical maps and photos for this book, I thank the Jewish Historical Institute, Warsaw (in particular, Olga Pieńkowska and Alicja Mroczkowska), Yad Vashem (in particular, Emanuel Saunders), the Ghetto Fighters' House (in particular, Shoshi Norman), the Bundesarchiv Koblenz (in particular, Monika Laschet), the United States Holocaust Memorial Museum, the National Archives and Records Administration, the Warsaw Rising Museum (in particular, Joanna Jastrzębska-Woźniak), the Urban Media Archive of the Center for Urban History, Lviv (in particular, the head of its archives, Oleksandr Makhanets), and the Scientific Library of the Ivan Franko National University of Lviv (in particular, its director, Vasyl Kmet).

A large part of the research for this book was done while I was pursuing my PhD at the Department of Central, Eastern, and Northern European Studies at the University of British Columbia (UBC, Vancouver). A special thank-you to the members of my supervisory committee, Professor Dr. Geoffrey Winthrop-Young and Professor Dr. Markus Hallensleben, and to Colleen O'Connor, Charlene Mc-Combs, Hillary Hurst, and Diane Smyth for all their help. My work would not have been possible without the ongoing financial support I received from both my department and the university. A generous four-year fellowship (2012–2016) and International Tuition Award (2012–2018), as well as a number of larger and smaller scholarships, awards, and grants, allowed me to pursue my graduate studies at UBC and made it possible to travel abroad on numerous occasions to conduct research in Poland and Germany. A special thank-you to the Killam Trust for their generous support of my work (2013–2015).

Thanks to UBC's Go Global and Arts Research Abroad as well as to the Holocaust Education Committee and the participating institutions (in particular, the Jewish Historical Institute and the Auschwitz-Birkenau State Memorial and Museum) for making possible my participation in the Witnessing Auschwitz program in the years 2014, 2015, and 2016. Special thanks to Professor Dr. Bożena Karwowska, Shareen Chin (Vancouver), Alicja Białecka, Marta Berecka, and Adelina Hetnar-Michaldo (Oświęcim). A heartfelt thank-you also to the Honourable Madam Justice Risa E. Levine and Bill Levine (Vancouver) for their generous support of the program.

For a wonderful collaboration, I would like to thank Tilo Schwarz (Mannheim), who worked with me on the visual components of this book—it is a real pleasure to work with you. A huge thank-you also to Corina Fuchs and

Nick Antonich (Weinheim) for the graphic design. Without the three of them—their ideas, patience, and professionalism—none of the maps or images would have made it into this book.

A special thank-you to the Hamburger Stiftung zur Förderung von Wissenschaft und Kultur, who financed this important part of the project. My sincere thanks in particular to Dr. Joachim Kersten for his support.

I was lucky to have my work reviewed with great care and insight by Professor Dr. Tim Cole (Bristol) and Professor Alberto Giordano (San Marcos)—thank you both for the helpful suggestions and remarks!

A huge thank-you goes to Barbara Czepek for helping me with the translations of Polish sources. Without her, a lot of incredibly helpful information would have evaded me. Thank you, Barbara, for many lovely hours of working together. Thank you also to Magdalena Siek, who kindly provided me with translations from Yiddish. I am immensely grateful to Asia Beattie, who generously gave her knowledge and her time in proofreading. Thank you, Asia, for our many conversations—I have learned a lot from your linguistic competence and critical mind. A heartfelt thank-you also to Meredith Shaw for her tireless support and skillful proofreading.

Thank you very much to the wonderful team at Indiana University Press, who helped make this book into what it is today. A special thank you to my acquisitions editor, Bethany Mowry, and to assistant acquisitions editor, Sophia Hebert, for taking such good care of me and my project. Thank you also to Jennika Baines who guided me through the first phase of this book's publication. Thank you also to David Miller, Brenna Hosman, Kathryn Huggins, Stephen Williams, Pamela Rude and Vinodhini Kumarasamy for all their help.

I am infinitely grateful for the support of my mother, Eva Dippmann, who was a tireless reader of my work. Thank you for your genuine interest, for your love, and for always being there for me. Thank you also to my friends, who kept me company during these intense years of research and writing—thank you for taking my mind off work (at least occasionally)! Special thanks to Stefan Beyer, Mira Bussemer, Judith Czepek, Anna Deutschmann, Christine Euler, Carolina Franzen, Isabelle Hackenberg, Valentina Lauer, Eva Meininger, Tilo Schwarz, and Meredith Shaw for always looking out for me.

Thank you, Messer, for being there every step of the way.

A NOTE ON THE USE OF NAZI GERMAN TERMINOLOGY

The Nazis' language and their semiotic twisting of words—such as *"Endlösung"* (Final Solution), *"Sonderbehandlung"* (special treatment), *"Vernichtung"* (extermination), and *"Liquidierung"* (liquidation)—have become part of both the academic and popular discourse about the Holocaust. This is particularly true in the English usage as much of the terminology is a direct translation from the original German. As part of the *"Lingua Tertii Imperii,"* as Victor Klemperer has called "the language of the Third Reich," these words became terms deeply saturated with the Nazis' ideology and propaganda and reflect the Nazis' dehumanizing and genocidal worldview (and practices). As such, these words should be used with caution, which means that it should always be clear that they carry antisemitic and genocidal implications. In some instances, a term such as "liquidation" might seem like the most apt choice of words, because it communicates dimensions of the Nazis' politics and their crimes that might otherwise go unnoticed (in the case of "liquidation"—*"Liquidierung"* or *"Liquidation"* in German—this concerns, for example, the economic dimension of many of the German anti-Jewish measures as the term is derived from a business context and implies the final conversion of a business's assets into monetary gain in the process of winding it up). Precisely because they are ideologically charged, the Nazis' own terms often also express important aspects of the historical reality. Terms such as "Final Solution" were, in a sense, performative in nature, creating reality and "fundamentally affect[ing] the situation and treatment of the people to whom they applied" (Paulsson, *Secret City*, ix). In some instances, Gunnar S. Paulsson points out, it is difficult to understand the Nazi system without resorting to the terminology they used and capturing distinctions they introduced (such is the case, for example, with the ideological distinction between "Aryan" and "non-Aryan," which was widely adopted at the time and formative for the structuring of social and spatial relations under German rule [Paulsson, *Secret City*, ix]). Whenever the use of a German term does not add to the understanding of the historical process or its ideological background, however, I use instead terminology that is free of the ideological connotation and substitute dehumanizing expressions such as "extermination" (which linguistically transfers the semantics of practices from the context of pest control to the treatment of people) with descriptions that are more reflective of the contemporary perspective on the Nazi crimes—in this case, for example, "genocide," "mass killings," or "mass murder." In cases where I still use German terms with a particularly strong ideological undercurrent, I mark them by putting them in quotation marks.

Unfortunately, it is not possible to speak about Jews as the group targeted by the Nazis without repeating the gesture of the perpetrators—that is, grouping individuals, whose identities consisted of numerous "permeable" and "diverse... identifications" that were constantly negotiated (Dynner and Guesnett, "Introduction," 3) under a sole denominator, one that is not necessarily reflective of their sense of self but externally ascribed. They, however, were targeted by the Nazis not as individual people but as "Jews"; thus, using this term is practically unavoidable, and for reasons of readability, I will not use quotation marks in this case.

VIOLENT SPACE

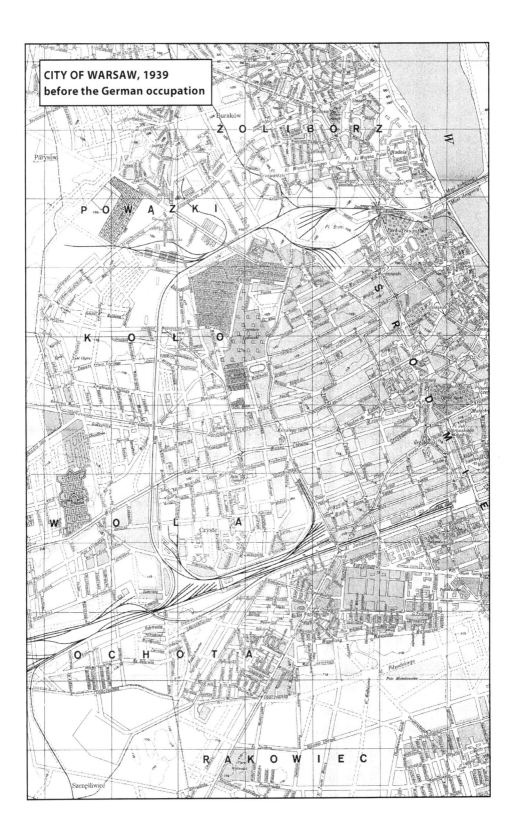

CITY OF WARSAW, 1939
before the German occupation

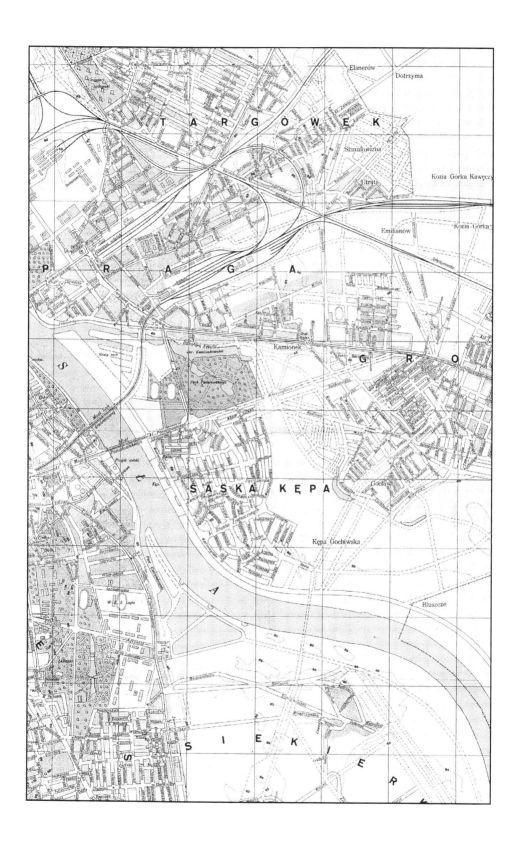

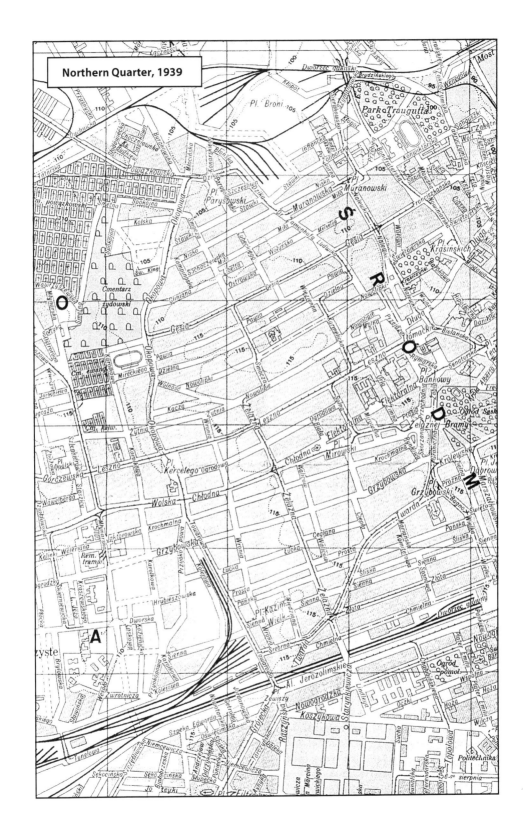

Northern Quarter, 1939

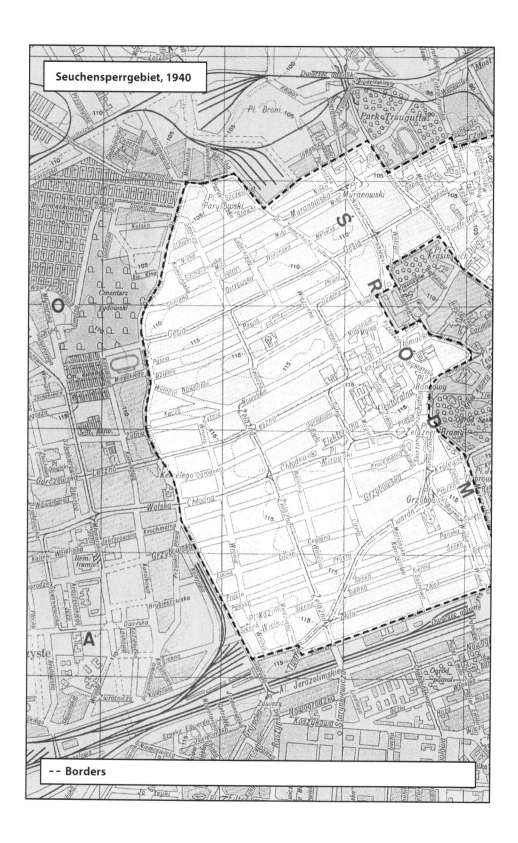

Seuchensperrgebiet, 1940

-- Borders

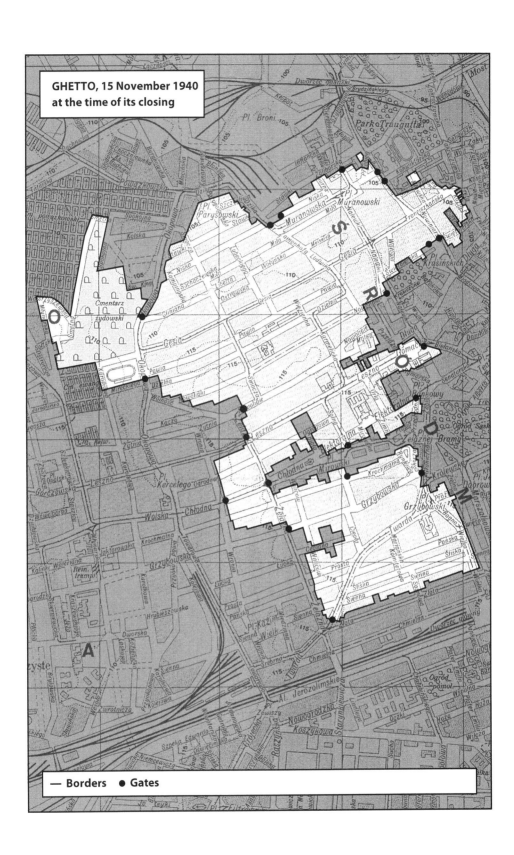

GHETTO, 15 November 1940
at the time of its closing

— Borders ● Gates

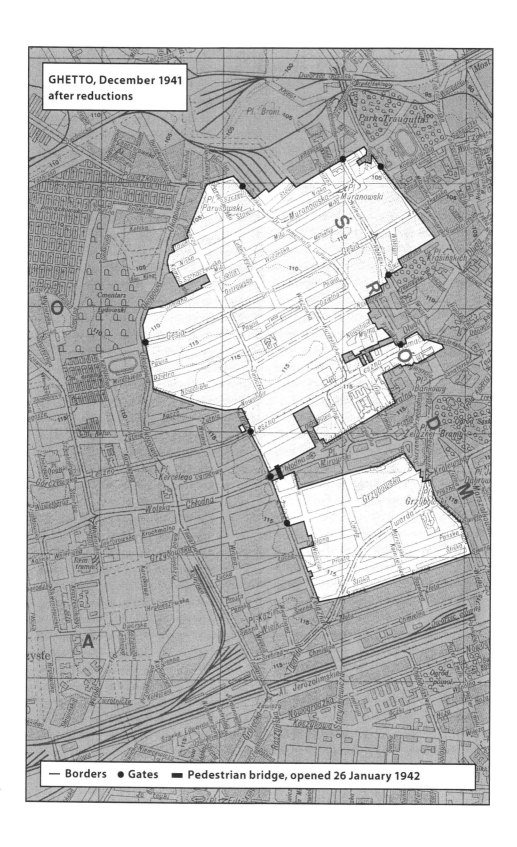

GHETTO, December 1941
after reductions

— Borders ● Gates ▬ Pedestrian bridge, opened 26 January 1942

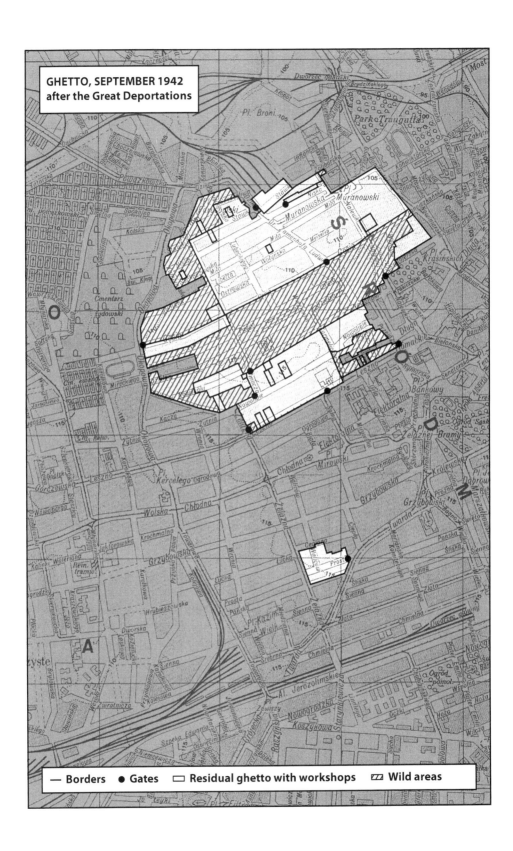

GHETTO, SEPTEMBER 1942
after the Great Deportations

— Borders • Gates ▭ Residual ghetto with workshops ▨ Wild areas

GHETTO AREA, DECEMBER 1944

PART I

LOCALIZATION

Introduction

Localization

Key thinkers of the spatial turn such as Henri Lefebvre, Michel de Certeau, and Michel Foucault established the conception of space as a social product. Moreover, space not only reflects existing social relations but also impacts them and, thus, itself becomes a social agent.[1] Space underlies historical changes and differs in relation to society. According to Lefebvre's *The Production of Space*, in fact, every society produces a distinctive space that, in turn, warrants analysis.[2] This theoretical approach is of particular interest for Holocaust studies because the National Socialists produced very extreme spaces, in both Germany and all occupied countries, and they did so in very drastic ways, fueled by an ideology that, itself, was in many regards concerned with questions of space.

Their grand architectural plans for German cities, the pompous staging of political rallies and processions, the geographical and urban reorganization projected for the occupied territories, the importance of ideological constructs such as *Lebensraum* (living space) or *Blut und Boden* (blood and soil), and the general influence of geopolitical thought on the Nazi project clearly show how obsessed the Nazi leadership was with the concept of space.[3] In fact, as historian Dan Stone suggests, one could see Nazism itself as "a radical geographical project" with the goal of drastically reorganizing all space under the Nazis' control.[4] Nazi Germany intervened in space on all possible levels, from "the scale of the body to the scale of the continent."[5] The implementation of the Nazis' sociopolitical agenda "violently imposed new rules that restructured daily life for victims, perpetrators, and bystanders," as Anne Kelly Knowles, Tim Cole, and Alberto Giordano explain in their introduction to *Geographies of the Holocaust*.[6] For those deemed racially inferior (or politically resistant), the Germans created particularly intense and hostile spatial settings, such as the ghettos and camps. These spaces were active social and political agents used to organize power relations among the perpetrators, their victims, and the bystanders. They heavily impacted the social position of the victims as well as their relationships with each other, affecting the way in which victims experienced themselves, the other, and their environment, and drastically limiting the way people could live (and die).

Consequently, current historical research has put forward the need to analyze the Holocaust as an inherently spatial phenomenon. Studies in the wake of this spatial/geographical refocusing address the aforementioned aspects from numerous spatially oriented perspectives and thus shed light on the particular "spatiality" of the Holocaust, its concrete sites, their inner workings, and the distinct spatial dimension of the victims' experiences.[7] In *Violent Space*, I follow a similar approach, focusing on a very particular spatial configuration: the Jewish ghetto that was established by the German occupiers in Warsaw in 1940. Following Cole's argument that the Holocaust was implemented not only in space but also "through" space,[8] my book addresses two main questions: First, how was the particular space of the ghetto created and organized—that is, which policies, regulations, decisions, practices, and actors (individual or collective) were involved in its creation and defined its inner workings? And second, how did the people who were forced to inhabit this space experience it, and what did it do to them? While the first question involves a study of the ghetto's history, of its planning and implementation, the second inquiry focuses on the "lived" space of the ghetto, on the way it affected people, the way it was perceived, navigated, and appropriated.

To get answers to these questions, it is necessary to first establish the basic postulates and an appropriate theoretical framework with which to work; this is what the first part of the book ("Localization") provides. All phenomena described are, in one way or another, expressions of violence. The ghetto was built by means of violence and was a site where excessive violence took place. It was, however, also in and of itself an act of violence perpetrated against the Jews. It excluded them, exposed them, and victimized them; it ruptured their relationships and created enormous physical and psychological strain; it severely disoriented, disrupted, impeded, and undermined Jewish lives; and it was used by the Germans as a means for indirect mass murder through malnutrition, starvation, and epidemics, and, later, also facilitated the process of direct mass murder by serving as a holding area for the victims before the Germans deported them to the death camp(s). To properly describe the mechanisms by which space itself became a violation, it is necessary to first define what I mean when I speak of violence and what the specifics of a spatially enacted violence are (chap. 1, "Spatial Violence"). This understanding of a space-related form of violence is what the book's analysis is built on, and it is also the main theoretical contribution of *Violent Space*. Building on a set of influential theories of violence (i.e., Popitz, von Trotha, Galtung, Reemtsma, Baberowski), I propose a conceptualization of violence that allows for the simultaneous description of space as shaped by violence (i.e., a space of violence) and space as an act of violence in and of itself (i.e., violent space). Both notions will unlock a novel perspective on the ghetto, making visible dimensions of experience that are seldom covered in historical research on the topic.

Since the Warsaw ghetto is inaccessible today, both physically and temporally, at the core of any study of it lies an act of historical evocation based on the few remnants, documents, accounts, and memories left from the time of its existence. Every decision concerning the selection of these sources, the perspective, focus, and theoretical approach, is formative for the outcome of an academic inquiry—that is, formative for the particular segment of the ghetto that is made visible. As the choice of perspective and material defines what can be seen, it is crucial to make transparent and to critically discuss the basis of the proposed evocation (chap. 2, "Mapping the Ghetto," and chap. 3, "The Archive").

The book at hand focuses mostly on the space of everyday life. This space, the space in which Jewish life unfolded, can be analytically divided into two spheres: the public and the private (which naturally often intersected). Thus, my analysis focuses on two urban structures representative of these spheres: the ghetto's streets and its residential buildings. Before proceeding to an analysis of these spaces as seen and experienced by their inhabitants, a theoretical orientation regarding their various historical, architectural, perceptual, and social dimensions will prove useful (chap. 4, "Streets and Buildings"). Understanding the structures and interdependencies of streets and buildings and the concrete configuration they took within the Warsaw ghetto sharpens the perception of the many details that are, either explicitly or implicitly, mentioned in testimonies and accounts. The expertise of architects, urban planners, (human) geographers, sociologists, and legal scholars provides the terminology and insight needed for an informed interpretation of the material.

On the basis of this theoretical and historical foundation, in the second part of the book ("The Making of a Violent Space"), I set out to answer the question of how the ghetto was created and how it was organized. This question comes with a time index: over the years, the physical layout and social practices changed to such a degree that there was, in fact, not one ghetto but several. Entering the early ghetto of fall/winter 1940, an observer would have encountered an entirely different space than when entering the ghetto less than two years later, after the Great Deportation *Aktion* had taken place in the summer of 1942. But, even in between such major turning points, every German order, every new decree, every street that was excluded, every gate that was closed meant a significant shift in the extremely compressed environment within the walls. These changes had severe implications for those forced into the ghetto. They affected their everyday life, their sociality, and their chances of survival. The chapters of part II thus follow a temporal order and guide the reader through the different phases of the ghetto's history—from the German invasion of Poland in late 1939 to the ghetto's "liquidation" in early 1943. They provide a detailed description of the ghetto's changing physical and social topography, of the changing German agendas, their administrative practices, and the fate of their victims.

When the Germans invaded Poland in September 1939, its capital was home to a thriving, culturally diverse Jewish community, making up roughly 30 percent of the city's population. To understand how these people, and those non-Jewish Poles who were, in many instances, their direct neighbors, experienced the German occupation, the escalating anti-Jewish policies, and, finally, the process of ghettoization and mass killings, it is necessary to first form an understanding of the history of Jewish presence in the city (chap. 5, "Jews in Prewar Warsaw"). This historical background provides context for understanding the relationships that existed between Varsovians (Jewish and non-Jewish) before the German occupiers created new social dynamics by emphatically otherizing the Jews, opening up a whole spectrum of opportunities for non-Jewish Varsovians to act—ranging from providing support to becoming a bystander to profiteering, harassing, or actively persecuting. Outlining where and how Jews had lived in the prewar city also sheds light on patterns of relocation during ghettoization, on the living conditions and the social and economic standing of the victims, as well as their expectations and coping strategies, which were rooted in previous experiences. Moreover, the historical briefing contextualizes the ruptures and changes the victims went through with the onset of the German occupation.

The ghetto established in Warsaw took over a year to complete (chap. 6, "Creation of the Ghetto"). This early phase of the ghetto's history began with the German attack on Poland. The four-week-long siege of Warsaw (including the heavy bombardment during the first days of the war) had the most severe impact of all on the city and its inhabitants. Buildings and infrastructure suffered dramatic damages, and there was a large number of civilian casualties. This, however, was still a shared experience, with Jewish and non-Jewish Poles suffering alongside each other. And yet, administratively and ideologically, the Germans had already set the course for their divisive policies when they entered the city in late September 1939 ("Early Days of the Occupation"). Right away, they began the implementation of anti-Jewish measures, with interventions into the shared urban space. During the first weeks and months, the Germans introduced a new racial/spatial order that marginalized Jewish Varsovians and drove a wedge between them and the Gentile population. In fact, many of the German anti-Jewish measures and policies were implemented on the level of the city, preceding the more drastic segregation that was to follow. Jews were excluded from certain areas of the city: from public spaces, such as squares, parks, and even individual streets, but also from privately owned establishments, such as cafés, restaurants, theaters, cinemas, and shops. With the introduction of compulsory armbands, they themselves were also marked. Collectively, these steps introduced a first, sociospatial form of ghettoization, long before any walls were built. Ghettoization was also a work in progress: before the actual ghetto was created, the Germans had considered several other scenarios for a forced relocation of the Jews, and they had devised and discarded a number of different plans for establishing a ghetto in other sections of the city. In the meantime, they had begun with the erection of fences to enclose the so-called *Seuchenschutz-/Seuchensperrgebiet* (an area "threatened by epidemics"), which ultimately turned out to be a predecessor to the actual ghetto ("Exclusion and Segregation").

In August 1940, the Germans officially announced the establishment of a "Jewish district"—that is, the ghetto. At this point, the Germans tasked the *Judenrat*, which they had installed in October 1939, with replacing fences with walls to cordon off a territory that was significantly smaller than the *Seuchensperrgebiet*.[9] This set in motion a huge wave of forced resettlement within the city, affecting a large part of its Jewish population but also Gentiles who had been living in the area that was to become the ghetto. Again, the process was characterized by continuous changes and reconsiderations. The German administration repeatedly redrew the boundaries of the ghetto, which translated into an unsettling sense of uncertainty and instability for the Jews. This indicates a tendency that became typical for the ghetto: from the very beginning, the ghetto space was constantly changing and, most notably, shrinking.

The last step in the creation of the ghetto was marked by its sealing in November 1940. This led to the next stage of decoupling the ghetto and the city and allowed the Germans to control the ghetto space and life inside the walls much more tightly and extensively. To understand the experiences of those who inhabited this early ghetto, it is crucial to be aware of its most minute spatial specifications, as its layout and organization were formative for the first phase of ghettoization ("Ghettoization"). Over the following months, demarcation of the ghetto was continuously tightened and more strictly enforced, which created an ever more strained internal environment and deteriorating living conditions. And yet, at this point, life inside the walls was developed the furthest. Cut off from the outside world, dominated by violence and harrowed by willful neglect on the part of the German administration, the ghetto, in many senses, was a world of its own with its own culture and distinct forms of social life. The arts, entertainment, education, political activities, illegal trade, and social welfare all flourished despite the dire conditions ("Confinement").

The second phase of the ghetto's history, its dissolution, already started shortly after it had officially been established, with the first streets and buildings being extracted the moment the ghetto was announced for the first time (chap. 7, "Dissolution of the Ghetto"). While inside the ghetto, with much resilience and ingenuity, the victims fought to preserve their lives, the perpetrators were driving forth their genocidal agenda with increasing momentum, starting with the gradual elimination of Jewish living space. Right from the beginning, given the high number of people forced into the constricted space of the ghetto, its shrinking had the most severe effects on its inhabitants' living conditions and sociality. Over time, the process of dissolution encompassed a drastic spatial restructuring and was closely tied to the German genocidal practices. Between March and December 1941, the German occupiers pursued the reduction of the ghetto with increasing rigor, excluding the Jewish cemetery on Okopowa Street as well as several streets and buildings, particularly in the southern part of the ghetto. At the same time, borders were restructured and more strictly enforced. The Jewish community desperately fought to retain certain streets for the ghetto, but to no avail. Again, a huge number of people were forced to resettle within the ghetto walls ("Reduction of the Ghetto"). This first concerted reduction of the ghetto preempted the "liquidation" of the "small" southern ghetto in July 1942 as part of the Great Deportation *Aktion*.

After having discussed and abandoned various territorial solutions of the "Jewish question,"[10] the Wannsee Conference in January 1942 marked the decisive point when the Nazi leadership determined their plans for Europe's Jewry. With this, their agenda for the ghetto also changed drastically. It then became, quite literally, the "antechamber to the Final Solution."[11] Violence enacted against Jews increased continuously, culminating in the most drastic step in the process of the ghetto's dissolution: the deportation and murder of the largest part of its inhabitants during the Great Deportation *Aktion*, from July through September 1942 ("Mass Murder"). These events initiated another fundamental change in the ghetto's physical and social space. The ghetto was transformed to the core and was now characterized by a highly fragmented layout and a substantially reconfigured social organization. The Germans divided the former ghetto into workshops on the one hand and, on the other, so-called wild areas, wherein life was technically forbidden. This new order closely tied the right to live to spatial coordinates ("Reshaping of the Ghetto").

Paradoxically, the last phase of the ghetto's history also brought about the most dramatic changes to Jewish autonomy—if only relatively briefly (chap. 8, "Destruction of the Ghetto"). The ultimate destruction of the ghetto was accompanied by a crucial shift in terms of agency and power relations. The emergence of a Jewish armed resistance posed an unprecedented challenge to the German monopoly on violence and their domination of public space. Along with this came a number of changes concerning the ghetto space and its inhabitants' relation to it. During the Ghetto Uprising, both passive and active resistance stood in close relation to the specific characteristics of the ghetto's physical space ("Armed Resistance"). Ultimately, however, the murder of the ghetto's inhabitants and the destruction of their living quarter coincided, and the Germans razed the ghetto to the ground after the defeat of the uprising in May 1943 ("Final Liquidation of the Ghetto").

The third part of the book ("Experiences of a Violent Space") is dedicated to the analysis of the ghetto space from the perspective of its inhabitants. Here, the spatial focus will become the organizing principle, as the chapters themselves are thematically grouped, discussing selected aspects of the ghetto space as experienced and interpreted by its inhabitants. Building on personal accounts, the focus of the book now moves to the subjective space of the victims' experience, while at the same time providing a very concrete and detailed description of the ghetto as seen through the eyes of people who knew every house and every street in Warsaw and who were thus very perceptive of the drastic changes brought about by the occupiers' interventions.

A first factor that had a particularly strong impact on people's experience was that of destruction. The term, in the context at hand, has several layers. During the siege, the city of Warsaw had been "violated" by military presence and by severe war damage. Sources show that the Jewish inhabitants of Warsaw identified very strongly with their city. Correspondingly, many of them described the violation of the city and its people as closely linked. Indeed, the Germans did consciously pursue the destruction of the city and its inhabitants concurrently. Parallel to ghettoization and "extermination," the German urban planners responsible in Warsaw proposed dismantling the Polish capital and creating in its place a "new German city" (chap. 9, "Destruction").[12]

Right from the beginning, the German occupiers specifically targeted Jews and excluded them from the public spaces of the city. By means of decrees, regulations, bans, threats, and physical violence, the Germans forcefully restructured urban space along racial criteria. This created a "decreed space," to use Engelking and Leociak's terminology, which otherized and marginalized the Jewish population very early on. It also introduced right away the principle of racializing space that was so formative for the German agenda in the occupied territories (chap. 10, "Decreed Space"). When looking at the actual physical ghetto, a factor that is crucial for gaining a better understanding of the victims' reality is the typical architectural structure of their living space (i.e., of apartments and residential buildings). As sources indicate, in the violent setting of the ghetto, architecture was of heightened importance for its inhabitants' experience and their fate. In fact, architectural factors often translated into questions of life and death (chap. 11, "Buildings").

The first stage of ghettoization was, for many Jews, connected with the experience of losing their home in the process of forced resettlement. Later, throughout the ghetto's existence, the repeated changes the Germans made to the ghetto's boundaries and its territory forced people to relocate again and again. The loss of one's home was often experienced as highly traumatic and disruptive. It usually also entailed significant material damage and left those affected in highly unstable and precarious domestic circumstances (chap. 12, "Lost Homes"). Generally, any concept of home was challenged as the German policies and violent practices disrupted the Jewish community's sense of security even in their most private spaces. German violence, as represented by the entering of Jewish homes in the form of raids, searches, arrests, and executions, turned "domestic space" itself into a "violated and violent space" (chap. 13, "Violated Homes").[13] The ghetto and its spatial structures also had a strong impact on social relationships. In both the public and private spheres, the immense population density that the Germans had created within the walls turned people against each other. They became a hindrance to each other, impeding movement, creating intense physical and psychological pressure, undermining privacy, but also implying a very concrete health risk. With people living together much more closely than before the German occupation, their social life and their relationships were severely strained and had to be renegotiated (chap. 14, "Overcrowding").

During the first years of the ghetto's existence, the ghetto's streets became the new centers of social life. They took over the function of several prewar institutions and locations and reflected drastically altered social conditions. Social exchange, but also the exchange of information and goods, now took place predominantly in the open (chap. 15, "Life and Death," and chap. 16, "News"). While the public space of the streets held great importance for ghetto life, at the same time, people were yet exposed to unprecedented levels of sickness and death, encountered in plain view. The conditions in the ghetto fundamentally interfered with people's ability to organize the private and public spheres as separate, and thus challenged, for example, notions of piety or shame.

People in the ghetto had to go through a radical process of social reorientation and adaptation. The topography of the ghetto proved equally difficult to master. Ghettoization greatly impaired traffic and communication both inside and outside the walls (chap. 17, "Communication"). In many ways, the new spatial setting defeated both practical and personal logic. Consequently, the inhabitants experienced the space of the ghetto as highly dysfunctional, dangerous, and traumatic. Personal accounts reveal how destabilizing the urban reorganization was for the inhabitants, who saw themselves confronted with a space that was connected to their previous experience and, at the same time, fundamentally alien (chap. 18, "Orientation"). Violence played a crucial role in shaping the Jewish community's relationship to their environment. Its constant presence made becoming a "topographer"[14] and being able to navigate the ever-changing patterns of danger and violence permeating the ghetto necessary for survival (chap. 19, "Topography of Violence"). The many acts of public violence performed by the Germans quite drastically impacted the perception and use of an environment in which all Jews became potential victims. In fact, the humiliations, beatings, and executions had a performative quality to them, which turned them into acts of communication used by the German occupiers to terrorize the ghetto population (chap. 20, "Public Violence").

The Germans created a space that was permeated by violence to a degree that people could not evade it; violence pressed in on them—physically but also aurally. And indeed, many accounts paint a very vivid picture of these aural aspects of the ghetto: of the roaring and humming of the ghetto's streets; of the sounds of fear, pain, and distress; as well as the complex patterns of sound associated with violent assaults, round-ups, raids, and deportations. In many ways, this particular "soundscape"[15] of the ghetto played a central role in its inhabitants' lives and experiences (chap. 21, "Sound of the Ghetto"). While the sounds of the ghetto were bound to the lives of its inhabitants and often accompanied the aggression they experienced, their murder, in contrast, created voids and silences. When people in the ghetto were rounded up and deported, they left behind living space and belongings ravaged by the Germans and their auxiliaries. These physical remainders marked the absence of the people who were violently torn from their lives; quite often, they lingered on as material testimonies to the violence enacted against the deported people. These sites became nonplaces, desecrated and exposed (chap. 22, "Deserted Apartments").

German violence was quite frequently targeted according to spatial coordinates (i.e., directed toward certain sections of the ghetto, certain streets, individual buildings). By this, the Germans created spaces that were, temporarily or more permanently, antithetic to Jewish life. With the new organization of the ghetto after the Great Deportations, the right to space and the right to live began to coincide (chap. 23, "Death Space"). Confronted with a space that, from day one, was hostile to Jewish life, the inhabitants engaged in numerous practices of resistance. Borrowing central concepts from Michel de Certeau's *The Practice of Everyday Life*, it is possible to identify various spaces—or "tactics"—of spiritual, cultural, and physical resistance that the inhabitants of the ghetto created within the increasingly adverse environment (chap. 24, "Spaces of Resistance"). Especially during the last phase of the ghetto's existence, a very concrete means of resistance was the creation of hiding places and alternative passages. These structures became essential for survival. The ghetto's inhabitants were so invested in building them that they turned the ghetto into a veritable "underground city."[16] The network of bunkers, hiding places, tunnels, and passages in cellars and attics created a new multidimensional space that fundamentally altered the urban structure and the logic of its use.[17]

In the closing chapter, I revisit the basic assumptions and analytical concepts of the study to see how they can be complemented and adjusted in light of the analyzed material (part IV, "Conclusion"). Based on the historical analysis, the notion of space as a potent social agent, which affected processes of identity formation, power relations, and victimization, is further explicated. By complementing the conceptualization of spatial violence with concrete insights derived from the study of the historical source material, the concluding chapter further differentiates the central theoretical contribution of this book. The explanatory value of the concept in the context of the Holocaust and other genocidal settings is detailed alongside its relevance for current sociopolitical issues (chap. 25, "Violent Space"). Finally, the book reexamines the value of the interdisciplinary mode of historical inquiry that it has proposed and probes possible areas of application.

In the appendix, *Violent Space* provides additional information to help contextualize the material basis and visual components of the study. Maps und images are meant to create a deeper sense of orientation, both in terms of the ghetto's topography and its appearance. In the appendix, information on the choices made in the process of mapping and on their implications is presented ("Maps"); so is information that helps contextualize the photos ("Images"). In addition, the archival documents that were used in this book are listed, together with information on their translations ("Archival Material"). Finally, the appendix provides biographical information on the people whose words have guided me through the Warsaw ghetto, whose experiences, perceptions, and memories have shaped the image I create in my own work and whose lives and deaths should not be passed without comment ("Biographies"). Due to the precarious circumstances under which their testimonies reached posterity, information on their fate is often fragmentary and incomplete, but these gaps in our knowledge are an integral part of the authors' story as well. The appendix also provides information on the main German agents who were responsible for the Warsaw ghetto. Here also, visibility is a must, but for different reasons: following Zofia Nałkowska's dictum that "people dealt this fate to people,"[18] the German perpetrators have to be held accountable, if only narratively.

Notes

1. Massey, "On Space and the City," 162–163.
2. Lefebvre, *Production of Space*, 31.
3. For some exemplary studies on these various aspects, see Taylor, *Word in Stone*;

Miller Lane, *Architecture and Politics in Germany, 1918–1945*; Hagen, "Parades, Public Space, and Propaganda"; Aly, *Endlösung. Völkerverschiebung und der Mord an den Europäischen Juden*; Heinemann and Wagner, *Wissenschaft—Planung—Vertreibung*; Gutschow, *Ordnungswahn*; Gutschow and Klain, *Vernichtung und Utopie*; Wasser, *Himmlers Raumplanung im Osten*; Mai, "Rasse und Raum"; Lange, "Der Terminus 'Lebensraum' in Hitler's 'Mein Kampf'"; Wolter, "*Volk ohne Raum*"; Rössler, "Applied Geography and Area Research in Nazi Society"; Wolf, "East as Historical Imagination and Germanization Policies of the Third Reich"; Zimmerer, "In Service of Empire"; or Aly and Heim, *Vordenker der Vernichtung*.

    4. Stone, "Holocaust Spaces," 47.

    5. Knowles, Cole, and Giordano, *Geographies of the Holocaust*, 3.

    6. Ibid.

    7. Stone, "Holocaust Spaces," 49–50; Cole, "Ghettoization," 77. See, for example, the papers presented in Paolo Giaccaria and Claudio Minca's groundbreaking volume *Hitler's Geographies*, which addresses the connection of spatial theory and spatial politics in the Third Reich; Anne Kelly Knowles, Tim Cole, and Alberto Giordano's innovative collection of papers emphasizing the potentials that mapping and the use of GIS hold for Holocaust studies, *Geographies of the Holocaust*; or, for that matter, Tim Cole's influential study of the ghetto in Budapest, *Holocaust City*. For some examples of analyses pertaining specifically to the material sites of Nazi German crimes, see Charlesworth, "Topography of Genocide"; Cole, *Holocaust City*, *Holocaust Landscapes*, and *Traces of the Holocaust*; Gigliotti, "Mobile Holocaust?"; Cobel-Tokarska, *Desert Island, Burrow, Grave*; Sofsky, *Ordnung des Terrors*; Wienert, *Das Lager Vorstellen*; Leociak, *Text in the Face of Destruction*, or *Doświadczenia graniczne*.

    8. Cole, *Holocaust City*, 14.

    9. Engelking and Leociak, *Warsaw Ghetto*, 64.

  10. Aly, *Endlösung*, 131, 144.

  11. Engelking and Leociak, *Warsaw Ghetto*, 26.

  12. Gutschow and Klain, *Vernichtung und Utopie*, 13, 16–17, 26.

  13. Miron, "'Lately, Almost Constantly, Everything Seems Small to Me,'" 140.

  14. Boehm, "Introduction," 3.

  15. Birdsall, *Nazi Soundscapes*.

  16. Zuckerman, *Surplus of Memory*, 336.

  17. Leociak, *Text in the Face of Destruction*, 52.

  18. Nałkowska, *Medallions*, 47.

CHAPTER 1

Spatial Violence

Violence was used to create and enforce spaces such as ghettos and camps, and, in most cases, it remained a formative governing principle within them. At the same time, these spaces were a form of violence in and of themselves. Their spatial structures and the practices associated with them exposed, marginalized, hurt, and harmed the people who were subjected to them. To distinguish this spatial violence from the direct violence of the Nazi mass murder (i.e., the "Holocaust by bullets"[1] or the mass "extermination" in the gas chambers of concentration and death camps), I will refer to violence that was exercised through the organization of space as "indirect" violence.[2]

Although there has been a growing interest among researchers in studying violence within the theoretical framework of the spatial turn and, along with this, an "increased sensitivity for the multiple forms of violence and their geographical dimensions,"[3] specific and consistent terminology to describe such spatialized forms of violence has not yet been developed. To this end, I combine and expand existing theories of violence in a way that allows for an apt description of the phenomenon. Two very different theoretical approaches to violence prove useful here: one advocated by Heinrich Popitz and Trutz von Trotha, and one by Johan Galtung. While the first is relatively narrow and precise and allows me to capture the existential threat that was always inherent to violence during the Holocaust, the second is less positivist and much broader, formulated to include a much larger number of manifestations. This is particularly helpful when it comes to exploring the indirect nature of spatial violence.

Popitz and von Trotha both argue for a definition of violence that focuses almost exclusively on physical harm to another person's body.[4] Their concept of violence is closely tied to the physical reality of the victim, to bodily harm or the threat thereof. This narrow definition holds value for the following analysis because it helps to emphasize that, ultimately, German violence in the ghetto always pointed toward the potential to kill the other.[5] In fact, in accordance with Nazi ideology, anti-Jewish violence during the Holocaust always ultimately aimed at annihilation. *Violent Space* also shares with the work of von Trotha a clear focus on the reality of the victim and a phenomenological approach aiming at an antireductionist (*antireduktionistisch*) and precise description of the victims' realities.[6] A particular strength of Popitz's work on violence is that it highlights that violence is a form of exercising power. Popitz describes violence as a specific manifestation of what he calls "power of action" (*Aktionsmacht*), a power that is ultimately equivalent to the power to hurt one another.[7] Popitz differentiates three variants of this "power of action": one related to social exclusion, the second to material damage, and the third targeting the human body.[8] It is only this last one, which directly harms a person's body, that Popitz himself refers to as violence.

Johan Galtung, in his 1969 article "Violence, Peace, and Peace Research," advocates an "extended concept of violence."[9] He sees violence as anything that hinders the realization of a possible, more positive state: "*Violence is here defined as the cause of the difference between the potential and the actual*, between what could have been and what is. Violence is that which increases the distance between the potential and the actual, and that which impedes the decrease of this distance."[10] It is important to understand that for Galtung violence takes place only when a negative difference between "the potential and the actual" is avoidable. Galtung explains, "Thus, if a person died from tuberculosis in the eighteenth century it would be hard to conceive of this as violence since it might have been quite unavoidable, but if he dies from it today, despite all the medical resources in the world, then violence is present according to our definition."[11] In the context of the Holocaust, it is particularly useful that this definition allows the inclusion of acts of neglect, or of "omission,"[12] as forms of violence.

What makes Galtung's concept very useful for the analysis of spatial violence, as well, is that it covers a very broad range of phenomena. Yves Winter, who approaches the question from the perspective of political theory, elaborates, "The virtue of Galtung's concept of structural violence is that it opens up the category of violence so as to include poverty, hunger, subordination, and social exclusion. It makes it possible to theorize differential access to power and resources as a form of violence, shifting the category of violence away from surface phenomena toward a broad set of social relations."[13] At the same time, as both Winter and von Trotha argue, this is also the theory's weak point, in that the concept of violence that it elaborates runs the risk of becoming somewhat blurred.[14] Regardless of this criticism, in the context of the particular spatial settings created by the Germans, Galtung's approach (and the more current research in his tradition)[15] is helpful for its inclusion of phenomena not covered by Popitz's theory but relevant to analysis of the indirect violence wielded through such spaces.

In combining the acuteness of Popitz's and von Trotha's views of violence focused on physical harm with the broadness of Galtung's definition, the concept of indirect spatial violence allows us to describe the situation within the ghetto, where violence that did not directly target the physical body still had drastic effects. For example, assaults on resources and on social participation—that is, "causing material harm" and "diminishing social participation" in Popitz's terminology[16]—were so extreme as to eventually turn into, or be directly accompanied by, physical harm. Therefore, contrary to Popitz but following Galtung, I classify such material and social assaults as a form of violence as well. This form of violence did not necessarily target the victims' bodies immediately and directly—as did beatings and killings—but nevertheless had a fatal (deadly) effect on them. Accordingly, the concept of indirect violence also allows us to define as a form of violence the creation of an environment—such as the ghetto—that is detrimental to its inhabitants. Hunger, sickness, and death caused by the ghetto setting are, in this context, indirect violence exerted against the victims through the organization of space. Consequently, the ghetto, as it was created and managed by the Germans, was an assault on the victims' living conditions, depriving them of their resources and social support and creating conditions that were highly detrimental to their physical, social, and psychological well-being. Following Galtung's approach, the category of violence will also apply to cases when personal well-being, identity formation, or cultural and social inclusion were affected but no direct physical effect can be determined.

One major point on which *Violent Space* will depart from Galtung's approach is that I will always assume a direct link between violence and a particular group of perpetrators who are to be held accountable for it.[17] While Galtung's concept of "structural" violence specifically allows for addressing violence that is "not immediately attributable to an acting subject"[18] but "built into structure,"[19] violence during the Holocaust can always be linked to Nazi ideology and politics. It was targeted and actively implemented. This means that in this book the term *indirect* will apply to the means, not to the actors. *Violent Space* will expand the forms of violence under scrutiny to include the "inequality of power, resources, and life opportunities,"[20] but I will always assume a general "subject-object relation" regarding culpability.[21] Although this book also includes reflections on effects of the ghetto's spatial setup that cannot be attributed to an individual actor—nor can a clear intention necessarily be established for every single effect—it is clear that all detrimental consequences were in line with the perpetrators' motivations or were at least approved by them. In the context of the Warsaw ghetto, intent and effect were not necessarily always congruent, but they were interlocked. The violence that was "spatialized" in the ghetto can always be linked to a will to neglect or to harm. With time, such spatialized violence became a means of genocide.

While the concept of indirect violence helps to explain the spatial measures implemented by the Germans as manifestations (and means) of violence, direct violence also played a formative role in shaping the ghetto space. Most of the violence enacted by the Germans falls into the categories of what Jan Philipp Reemtsma calls "locative" and "autotelic" violence. Reemtsma describes the former as violence that "treats the other's body as a mass to be allocated,"[22] a violence that determines the location of a body.[23] He further specifies, "It issues the command 'Move away from here!' or 'Move over there!'"; as such, "locative violence does not center on the body qua body but qua displaceable entity—something in the way, something to be moved as needed."[24] Locative violence is therefore, according to Reemtsma, ultimately a violence that is aimed at "something other than the body,"[25] a violence that is instrumental in the sense that it aims at achieving a certain goal different from inflicting damage.[26] Reemtsma further differentiates this category into "captive" and "dislocative" violence, describing the first as violence that confines a body and the second as violence that removes or eliminates it.[27] Using this subdivision, the ghetto itself, as well as many measures within it (for example, imprisonment, the implementation of a curfew, forced quarantines, *Blockaden*, the waiting area at the *Umschlagplatz*) can be described as a form of captive violence, with the purpose of keeping, as Reemtsma phrases it, a huge number of bodies "in a designated place."[28] The concept of dislocative violence—a violence that removes or eliminates—helps to explain and categorize as violence the act of resettlement, the forceful reorganization of the urban space by racial criteria, as well as the very process of ghettoization or deportations.

The concept of autotelic violence, in contrast, describes that which "seeks to damage or destroy the body."[29] It refers not to instrumental violence— instrumental in the sense of being used to achieve something other than destruction—but, rather, to violence for which destruction is, in fact, an end in and of itself.[30] Reemtsma differentiates between the two categories on the grounds that while locative violence might entail physical harm to the body, the destruction of the body (and thus the other) is not its primary goal. In the case of autotelic violence, however, "*the body's destruction is not merely a possible consequence, it's the point.*"[31] Incidents of individual or mass violence driven by ideological hatred can be counted as a manifestation of this latter type of violence. But the distinction between locative and autotelic violence is by no means unambiguous. Nazi German policies were usually fueled by both instrumental and noninstrumental impulses, albeit to varying degrees. It is, for example, possible to interpret the mass murder of the European Jewry as the endpoint of a process of locative violence, in that it would rid a certain territory of its Jewish population, but, at the same time, one can see it as a case of autotelic violence, aimed at destruction for destruction's sake. Indeed, both types of violence tended to be mutually dependent, directing and furthering one another.

Reemtsma introduces locative violence as "a paradigm of instrumental violence," because its purpose "lies outside itself."[32] This leads me to another basic distinction that holds important explanatory value in the context of the Holocaust: according to Popitz, instrumental violence either serves as a means to exercise power for the purpose of achieving a particular objective or is used to establish control over people or a territory.[33] Corresponding to this distinction, Popitz differentiates between what he calls "pure power of action" (bloße Aktionsmacht) and "binding power of action" (bindende Aktionsmacht)—that is, power that exhausts itself in one singular act as opposed to power that is used to establish a more stable relation.[34] It is the latter, in the form of a convincing threat, that can be used to establish permanent rule over a person (or a territory).[35] Popitz explains, "Durable power relations are based on binding power of action. This becomes binding when it is exercised, or the plausible assumption of its exercise can be transformed into threats.... Finally, inflicting harm on the weaker party even without a specific reason can stabilize the power relation in terms of demonstrating 'symbolically' the capacity of ego to control the situation."[36]

In the context of the ghetto, the Nazis' violence, often used in the pursuit of pragmatic goals, such as the confiscation of goods or the exploitation of a workforce, also always served as a means to establish and maintain German control over people in the ghetto and the occupied territories at large. With the invasion of Poland, the Germans suspended the previous state order—in fact, running counter to the principles of international law, the Germans assumed the "extinction" of the Polish state[37]—and seized the monopoly on violence previously held by the Polish state.[38] The nature of monopolized violence, however, changed drastically under German rule. As conceptualized in both Thomas Hobbes's and Jean-Jacques Rousseau's theories of a "social contract," the state monopoly on violence is endowed with a responsibility to protect.[39] But under German rule, with respect to the majority of the population (further differentiated according to the Nazis' racial hierarchy), the monopoly was no longer predominately used to control violence and to guarantee safety (in fact, noninstitutional violence against Jews was even encouraged); instead, violence in all its forms and meanings was acted out ruthlessly and with few restraints by the state itself. In practice, the Germans turned violence into a means of governing.[40]

Although a juridical system was still in operation in the Generalgouvernement,[41] ultimately police and SS forces acted on most matters pertaining to Jews without involving the judiciary (or the civil administration, for that matter).[42] Soon, the most common penalty for any offense, regardless of age or gender, was a death sentence that was usually carried out without a trial.[43] Jews had "lost the status of legal entities,"[44] and their factual situation was that of a "state of exception" in Giorgio Agamben's sense. The establishment of the ghetto was not based on the principle of *Schutzhaft* (protective custody); the pretext of a "sanitary protection" of the "Aryan" society, however, permitted a similar form of ostensibly preventive detainment.[45] Just as in the situation of the camp, the ghetto delimited "a space in which, for all intents and purposes, the normal rule of law is suspended and in which the fact that atrocities may or may not be committed does not depend on the law but rather on the civility and ethical sense of the police that act temporarily as sovereign."[46]

With the suspension of any rights for the Jews, the ghetto became an example of what Jörg Baberowski, in his book of the same title, calls *Räume der Gewalt*—spaces of violence. The ghetto, as a space that segregated and vigorously otherized the Jews, enabled ("*ermöglichen*"[47]), fostered, and enforced violence against them. Moreover, the Germans instituted conditions that changed the existing relationships between Jewish and non-Jewish people, undermining support and positive exchange, creating in its place a myriad of opportunities for both Germans and Poles to economically exploit and take advantage of the Jews.

Notes

1. A concept coined by Patrick Desbois in his book *Holocaust by Bullets*.

2. This use of the term does not coincide with Galtung's coining of this term, which he introduced to describe the difference between violence that can be attributed to a particular actor ("personal or direct" violence) and violence that is systemic ("structural or indirect" violence) ("Violence, Peace, and Peace Research," 170). While highly influential and relevant, this distinction does not hold much explanatory value in the context of the ghetto simply because, in the case of the ghetto, violence can always be traced back to a perpetrator (or a group of perpetrators)—that is, violence is enacted, instigated, or approved by the Germans. Consequently, in this study, the term will refer to the means, not the actors.

3. Springer and Le Billon, "Violence and Space," 1, 2.

4. Popitz, *Phänomene der Macht*, 44, 48; von Trotha, "Zur Soziologie der Gewalt," 14. This study generally refers to the German original of Popitz's study. All English terminology and direct quotations, however, are taken from the 2017 translation *Phenomena of Power: Authority, Domination, and Violence*.

5. See also von Trotha, "Zur Soziologie der Gewalt," 12; Popitz, *Phänomene der Macht*, 52–53, 56.

6. Von Trotha, "Zur Soziologie der Gewalt," 20–21.

7. Popitz, *Phänomene der Macht*, 43.

8. Ibid., 44.

9. Galtung, "Violence, Peace, and Peace Research," 168.

10. Ibid., 168 (emphasis in the original).

11. Ibid., 168.

12. Winter, "Violence and Visibility," 198.

13. Ibid., 195.

14. Ibid.; von Trotha, "Zur Soziologie der Gewalt," 14.

15. See, for example, Dilts, "Revisiting Johan Galtung's Concept of Structural Violence" or Winter, "Violence and Visibility."

16. Popitz, *Phenomena of Power*, 26.

17. Von Trotha, "Zur Soziologie der Gewalt," 31.

18. Winter, "Violence and Visibility," 195.

19. Galtung, "Violence, Peace, and Peace Research," 171; Winter, "Violence and Visibility," 195.

20. Winter, "Violence and Visibility," 195.

21. Galtung, "Violence, Peace, and Peace Research," 171–172.

22. Reemtsma, *Trust and Violence*, 56.

23. Ibid., 57.

24. Ibid., 56.

25. Ibid., 57.

26. Ibid., 62.

27. Ibid., 57.

28. Ibid.

29. Ibid., 56.

30. Ibid., 62.

31. Ibid., 62 (emphasis in the original).

32. Ibid., 62.

33. Popitz, *Phänomene der Macht*, 47, 79.

34. Ibid., 46–47.

35. Threats were indeed one of the basic principles of German-Jewish relations and were formative in the negotiations between the *Judenrat* and the German administration.

36. Popitz, *Phenomena of Power*, 28 (emphasis in the original).

37. Majer, *"Non-Germans" under the Third Reich*, 265; Broszat, *Nationalsozialistische Polenpolitik*, 9. At the same time, Polish citizenship was dissolved (Majer, *"Non-Germans" under the Third Reich*, 308). The Polish government, however, defying the German proclamation, resumed its work in exile and continued to operate.

38. Referring here to the state's ability and authority to enforce order in a certain territory through the exertion or threat of violence (Weber, *Politik Als Beruf*, 6; see also Blomley, "Law, Property, and the Geography of Violence," 121; Engel, "What's in a Pogrom?" 27).

39. Krahmann, "State Monopoly on Collective Violence," 22; see also Baberowski, *Räume der Gewalt*, 78, 94.

40. See, for example, Broszat, *Nationalsozialistische Polenpolitik*, 51, 177–178, 183; Majer, *"Non-Germans" under the Third Reich*, 321.

41. It was based on the parallel introduction of German law, applied "in the realms of police, criminal, and labor law" (Majer, *"Non-Germans" under the Third Reich*, 271, see also 487) and the preservation of a "native jurisdiction" (ibid., 262) applied in cases "where German security or economic interests" were not affected (ibid., 271). In practice, this meant that "Polish jurisdiction was stripped of all important responsibilities and subordinated to the German system" (ibid., 490). In addition, "special law" was introduced in matters concerning Jews and Poles, implemented mostly in the form of decrees (ibid., 287–288). The legal system under German rule explicitly implemented "*völkisch* inequality before the law" (ibid., 501).

42. Majer, *"Non-Germans" under the Third Reich*, 307, 313–315, 320–321, 512–519; Broszat, *Nationalsozialistische Polenpolitik*, 28, 44.

43. Majer, *"Non-Germans" under the Third Reich*, 321, 500, 508, 518; Szarota, *Warschau unter dem Hakenkreuz*, 18, 21–23.

44. Majer, *"Non-Germans" under the Third Reich*, 316.

45. Arad, Gutman, and Margaliot, *Documents on the Holocaust*, 225; Majer, *"Non-Germans" under the Third Reich*, 313.

46. Agamben, "What Is a Camp?" 41.

47. Baberowski, *Räume der Gewalt*, 32.

CHAPTER

2

Mapping the Ghetto

Space as a theoretical construct has been defined over the centuries in numerous ways, accentuating different aspects and conditioning the way we view it.[1] In the case of Holocaust studies, however, the choice of perspective always carries ethical implications. Who or what we choose to look at, whose voices we choose to listen to, whose fate we recount and whose we omit—our decisions are laden with consequences. Hence, when looking at sites of the Holocaust, such as the Warsaw ghetto, space has to be conceptualized in a way that is ethically responsible. Two factors are particularly relevant here: to allocate responsibility to the perpetrators of the Holocaust and to give room to the victims' individual experiences and voices. As a consequence, space has to be conceptualized in an anthropocentric rather than a technical way. It has to be addressed as something social, made by people and affecting people.

To be sensitive to these dimensions, *Violent Space* adopts a notion of space similar to that of de Certeau, who defines space as "practiced place"[2]—thereby inevitably linking space with people. A spatial setting (or "place") is regarded here as a relatively stable configuration of elements and their relation to one another.[3] In the case of the Warsaw ghetto, this would be the topographical and architectural layout of the section of houses and streets in the northern quarter, cordoned off on German order. Knowledge of the ghetto's spatial setting is crucial for understanding it, but this perspective limits us to the dimension of physical givens. The Warsaw ghetto, as it is analyzed in this book, however, is of interest not primarily as a physical configuration but as a dynamic social entity, which comes into existence only through the practices of the perpetrators (the German agents on site) who forcefully created and governed it and the victims (the Jewish people) who inhabited it. It is their actions that defined the ghetto and that, conceptually and practically, turned it from something inactive and indetermined into something that was socially active. The physical setting of the ghetto was not oppressive or deadly per se; it became so because of the way the German agents on-site practiced it, the ways in which they enforced and managed it. The ghetto became part of the Holocaust processes not primarily because of its topographical or architectural characteristics but because of the genocidal agenda the Nazis realized in (and through) it.[4] At the same time, the ghetto space was also animated by the Jewish people who were forced into it. By making use of the "ensemble of possibilities . . . and interdictions"[5] that the ghetto presented to them, the inhabitants shaped the ghetto, filling it with their lives and their struggles but also undermining and challenging the Nazi agenda through practices of subversion and resistance.

In the case of Warsaw, both the ghetto's topographical and architectural layout and the interplay of conflicting human practices that activated its space are irretrievably lost. To understand the specific space of the ghetto the Germans established in Warsaw, these two dimensions have to be described as accurately as possible. No amount of written detail, however, can capture the past space in all its complexity, as it can never be rebuilt; it can only be approximated, evoked. In *Violent Space*, this evocation relies on two main sources: historical documents attesting to the Nazi crimes on the one hand, and the subjective perceptions and memories of the people who experienced the ghetto on the other. Bringing this material into a theoretically informed and meaningful constellation does not re-create the ghetto as it was but rather evokes an imaginary space, built from words, making visible only what the chosen textual testimonies reveal of the past. Because the choice of material defines what can be seen, it is of the utmost importance to clearly frame the material basis of this book (and, in fact, any study on the topic).

Violent Space relies almost exclusively on written sources. It is this written quality of both documents that administered the Holocaust as well as testimonies of the intimate, personal experiences of the people who were victimized by the Nazis that builds the basis for its narrative evocation and its spatial analysis of the Warsaw ghetto. In addition, the book focuses on the space that people inhabited, the *"espace vécu"* so to say.[6] This means that the fringes, the spaces where Jewish lives had already passed over into the sphere of death, are not included in the analysis. Border spaces, such as the *Umschlagplatz*—the holding area before deportations and the boarding ramp for the trains to Treblinka—the ghetto prisons, and the Gestapo headquarters on Aleja Szucha were central sites of violence,[7] but they were, administratively and to some degree also geographically, outside the ghetto and did not constitute a part of its environment. The *Umschlagplatz*, for example, constituted the threshold between the Warsaw ghetto, which, despite the overwhelming presence of death, was still a site of Jewish life, and Treblinka and other death camps, sites of concluded death. As a liminal space, the *Umschlagplatz* hinged between both the inside and outside of the ghetto. Located at the ghetto's borders, it was not accessible to those who were still inhabiting the Warsaw ghetto,[8] but, more importantly, those who passed through it had been excluded from the order of ghettoization and had entered the order of industrialized mass killing. The *Umschlagplatz* was absolutely central for the Warsaw ghetto: it was the abyss toward which the ghetto gravitated, but it was not a space that Jewish people ever inhabited.

Despite *Violent Space* being concerned with violence and, consequently, with death, the book situates itself in the sphere of the living. Therefore, the focus is on two central sites of Jewish life: the ghetto's streets and its residential buildings. These two urban structures were, as Leociak observes, "the two basic social spaces of the ghetto."[9] They were the spaces in which all life took place and are thus particularly well suited to become the object for a study on the lived experience of the ghetto. To access this experience, streets and buildings cannot be treated as abstract concepts or generalized entities. In fact, each building was a microcosm of its own; each street had its individual character and played a unique role in the compressed space of the Warsaw ghetto. Streets and buildings had their own history, too:[10] situated in a specific city, at a specific time—the city of Warsaw during the years 1939–1943—they were part of the grown urban structure of a European city, with its diverse architecture and its particular culture and economic makeup, relics of the prewar years. To the Germans, for whom the ghetto was, above all, a sociopolitical instrument, these dimensions were of very little importance. To the Jews who lived in it, however, the ghetto was not an abstract entity but a very concrete space. It consisted of streets with distinct features, relations, and character—such as Smocza Street, wide and spacious enough for starved children to make an escape when they had snatched some bread from a customer of the nearby street market,[11] or the "poor crowded neighborhood around Krochmalna Street," which in prewar times had been home to "a jumble of backroom shops and courtyard cheders,"[12] or Wołyńska Street with its "dreadful houses," "one of the poorest, shabbiest, filthiest streets in the Warsaw ghetto,"[13] or Komitetowa Street, which Mary Berg describes as a "living graveyard of children devoured by scurvy" and whose inhabitants lived "in long cellar-caves into which no ray of the sun ever reache[d],"[14] or Leszno, with its restaurants, cafés, and confectioneries,[15] so broad one could, without much effort, avoid stepping on the corpses lying on the sidewalk, covered with paper,[16] or Sienna, where Ringelblum observes in the fall of 1941 "fashion [was] in full swing" and "smartly dressed women promenade[d] up and down."[17] The ghetto's houses, too, came in various shapes and sizes, with their own history, their specific architectural features, and residents with different social standings and varying backgrounds and resources. To acknowledge these characteristics and details is crucial for understanding the ghetto reality in all its complexity. Also, in an extreme environment such as the ghetto, each particular feature of the environment encapsulated a range of possible consequences, thereby regulating, for example, the level of danger or safety people were exposed to. The floor a person lived on, for example, could determine whether or not they fell victim to a raid and, subsequent to a raid, whether or not they were deported. The layout of a housing complex could facilitate or impede round-ups, expose or shelter its inhabitants. The fate of a single street or building could carry existential weight, both for individual people and for the ghetto community at large. The exclusion, for example, of Sienna Street in October 1941 was a cause of great distress and posed an existential threat to the people who inhabited it because they lost their homes at a time when the housing situation in the ghetto was at its most disastrous. Sienna had been considered one of the "aristocratic" streets of the ghetto,[18] a "broad street, with good air, little poverty, few beggars, kept clean—literally, an island [of elegance] in the Ghetto."[19] Having its inhabitants evicted caused a disturbance to the intricate equilibrium of the entire ghetto and was also perceived as a threat by those who were not directly affected.

Witnesses who wrote during the ghetto's existence are often incredibly precise in locating their observations, making a noticeable effort to name particular streets, corners, crossings, houses, or landmarks. This minute attention to detail is also visible in many memoirs and shows that these specifics were not circumstantial to the authors but important enough to be diligently noted. Being true to their exactitude is important for this book because, in most cases, knowing the cartographic configuration of the environment is a crucial component for understanding the phenomena that are described. Without having knowledge of the exact course of the border and where exactly it cut the streets running from north to south in the ghetto, for example, one would understand very little of the risks associated with Karmelicka Street—a street the children of the ghetto called the "Forge of Death."[20] In the same way, only precise understanding of the "complicated geography"[21] of the Warsaw ghetto can elucidate the existential dilemma that came in the form of Chłodna Street—the "monstrous Scylla and Charybdis" that could be crossed only if one had the "special aptitude of a short-distance runner," as Stanisław Adler reports.[22] Unlocking these experiences requires knowledge of the numerous different shapes the ghetto took during the time of its existence. The exact physical coordinates of these different ghetto configurations—the course of the border at a given time, the number and location of gates, the layout and location of bridges, the particular way in which the network of streets functioned, the number of cross streets and thoroughfares, possible routes, and neighboring landmarks—provide us with vital information.

on the ghetto inhabitants' lives and experiences within them. For those readers unacquainted with the (past) city, the connections between and relevance
of these physical coordinates do not always reveal themselves through written
sources alone. When carefully read, maps, such as the ones presented in this book,
can be very helpful in this regard. They provide comprehensive information on
the physical topography of the ghetto and serve as an auxiliary line for those who
are not familiar with the city's layout and are thus unable to contextualize information from a witness account alone. Street names, for example, which communicated information on the expanse of the ghetto's territory to the inhabitants of
Warsaw, might need context and visualization to make sense today. Information
on the width, length, or prominence of a particular street that would have been
evident to contemporary inhabitants will have to be actively assessed by future
generations. But maps also signify a change in perspective. They abstractify and
generalize, presenting a "plane projection totalizing observations," as de Certeau
notes.[23] A route or locality described in a diary or memoir, by contrast, will most
often rather provide the reader with an inside perspective, will be processual
and dynamic, an exercise in walking, seeing, experiencing. The maps can add
to this a more general understanding of the environment, of objective distance,
direction, and overall topography. At the same time, maps are reductionist in
nature: projecting the actual spatial phenomenon onto a "plane surface,"[24] they
register street networks, the locations of buildings and landmarks, but they omit
three-dimensional space, the ghetto's architecture, its interiors. More than that,
they do not transmit information on the sensual dimensions of the environment:
smell, sound, surface feel, atmosphere, or lighting. While some maps might depict sociopolitical structures, they rarely communicate other social dimensions
or processes, such as communication, trade, news, the use of space, patterns of
movement, rites, customs, habits, rules, regulations, relationships, cultural meaning, gender differences, or perspectives, to name but a few examples. These dimensions have to be accessed through firsthand accounts. Both sources—the
maps that provide a pictorial representation of the past space and the written
accounts that translate the witnesses' spatial experiences into prose (or poetry)—
contribute to the project of narratively mapping the ghetto. Carefully analyzed
and combined, they allow for a multidimensional evocation of the ghetto space
in the medium of academic text.

When speaking of written accounts, it is important to remember that available
sources on the Warsaw ghetto represent the voices of actual people. As such, they
contain the entirety of their individual experience, their past, their knowledge, their
personal frame of reference. They show what a person saw and felt, how they tried to
make sense of their surroundings, their experiences, their impressions. Depending
on the genre of a text, on the positionality of its author and their perspective, these

individual texts will show very different facets of the ghetto. For each source, the main question will thus always have to be whose text it is that we are reading and, respectively, whose space it is that we see. In a first, very basic sense, this means that we will have to distinguish clearly between the perspective of the perpetrators and the perspective of the victims. Sources authored by members of the German administration, by SS men or Wehrmacht soldiers, render visible very different aspects of the ghetto space than sources written by Jewish people—that is, by those who were forced to inhabit this space. In reality, the ghetto was, of course, all of this at the same time, and the various meanings, functions, and perceptions constantly interfered and interacted with one another. Keeping the different viewpoints apart, however, allows us to define much more clearly the questions that are asked and the scope and validity of the respective answers.

Documents that were written by German administrative agencies and their proxies within the ghetto give testimony to how the Warsaw ghetto was created and organized. These documents were quite frequently performative in nature and defined the ghetto's shape and character as a sociospatial entity—they literally "made" the ghetto. The Germans communicated the ghetto's layout to the Jewish and non-Jewish Varsovians through maps printed in newspapers and through lists of the projected border streets. Public notices and decrees demarcated the Jewish population's scope of movement, defined spatial rights (or the lack thereof), and established new social practices and restrictions. These maps and documents were instruments to exercise territoriality, instruments of power—and we can read them as such.[25] When documents are descriptive (such as a report would be, for example), the German perception of the ghetto often provides both insight into the wider, underlying agenda and the latent political goals, as well as German plans to implement their agenda in concrete ways within the ghetto. All in all, these documents show the ghetto as a sociopolitical act, as an expression of German political intentions and practices. Through these sources, the ghetto is rendered visible as a space that is "part of the Holocaust process."[26] Cole delineates this perspective in contrast to views on the ghetto that focus on the victims: "In short, within Holocaust historiography, the ghetto has been studied not simply—or primarily—as the place of the victim, but as a part of the destruction process implemented by the perpetrator. In these terms, the ghetto has been seen, not primarily as a 'Jewish' place, but as a Holocaust place. And arguably, the tendency within such writing has been less to focus on the ghetto as a place in its own terms and more to examine ghettoization as one element within the implementation of the 'Final Solution of the Jewish Question.'"[27]

Through the documents created by the Germans or on German order, the ghetto is described, to a large extent, from an administrative perspective and appears as a space that is part of the German genocidal project, a space that is closely aligned with and shaped by German ideology, economic interest, and political agenda. It is an administered space, one created by decrees and spatial measures, one that is, at least at first sight, external to the experience of the victims. However, Jewish firsthand accounts, such as memoirs and diaries, can provide information on this side of the ghetto as well. When read not for their experiential dimension but for indications of the Nazis' sociopolitical agenda, they can shed light on everyday practices, dynamics, and details that the German documents omit. Quite frequently, these sources also portray actions by Jewish individuals or organizations that counteracted German intentions and can thus help us decipher the power dynamics at play in the Warsaw ghetto.

The most important quality of texts written by people who lived in the ghetto (or were, in defiance of German orders, hiding on the "Aryan" side of the city), however, is that they show the Warsaw ghetto as it was perceived, experienced, and narrated by the victims. The focus on Jewish perceptions and representations allows for the reconstruction and analysis of a very different space than does the German documentation. Material spatial factors and German policies determined the experiences of the victims, limited their options, and shaped their living conditions as well as the conditions of their deaths, but only the personal, subjective dimensions of the victims' experience can tell us how exactly this sociospatial tool took effect. They tell us not only how the blow was administered but where it hurt, and it is my belief that this understanding is the most important for any analysis of the ghetto.

Personal accounts from the ghetto communicate a profound "transformation" of Jewish lives, of their communities, their identities, and their cultural practices, as well as the affective dimensions of anxiety, loss, terror, uncertainty, and desperation caused by those changes.[28] Amos Goldberg very conclusively describes the segment of Jewish life within the ghetto that these accounts capture—namely, the "experiences of despair, shame, truncation, fundamental upheaval of the self, tremendous anxiety about the future, mourning and terror, radical disorientation, helplessness, unraveling of everyday habits—or *habitus*, as Bourdieu would have called it—and more."[29] As Goldberg observes, "These experiences . . . vividly and tremulously populate every scrap of paper written during that era" but are rarely "made into an object of historical research."[30] Testifying to the ways in which space was experienced and perceived, the subjective depictions found in the victims' accounts reflect not only what the space of the ghetto "was" but what this space—as a social agent—"did."

Differentiating between the perspective of the Germans, who conceptualized and executed the Holocaust, and the perspective of the Jewish victims marks a first, crucial distinction regarding the question of which space we see; further differentiation is required, however. Dalia Ofer and Leonore Weitzman, two pioneers of feminist perspectives in Holocaust studies, underline the importance of realizing that the Holocaust (just as life in the ghetto) was not a homogeneous experience.[31] The space of the Warsaw ghetto was, in many senses, not uniform, and the individual and singular experience that each person went through depended on many different factors. Historian Zoë Waxman emphasizes, "Every witness, experience[d] his or her own ghetto or concentration camp and did so from a very particular perspective."[32]

From the (retrospective) perspective of a researcher, it becomes abundantly clear that time was central in regard to the question of what type of space a person's deixis took up, be it transitory or habitual. As time went on, the ghetto underwent continuous transformation, as did people's hopes and expectations. The passing of time shifted how the victims perceived and interpreted things, what they anticipated and feared, and, consequently, how they acted. This difference also finds expression in the textual genre: a diary or letter written during the time of the ghetto's existence provides access to a very different reality than a memoir, potentially written decades after the war. The main difference, as Leociak points out, concerns the way the author relates to the events: "There is a fundamental opposition between texts written *hic et nunc* and those written *post factum*. It is rooted in extra-textual reality (the caesura of the end of the war, the radical change of external circumstances and the author's existential situation), but it clearly exerts an influence on the structure of the text itself."[33] Texts written *hic et nunc* are written from the perspective of a "reporting witness," by someone who is still engulfed in the course of events,[34] by someone who cannot yet see where they will lead, who is shaken by them, existentially threatened, and whose fate is—both to him- or herself and to the reader—painfully uncertain. These documents reflect their authors' desperate struggle to make sense of the events that transpired around them; they show, in a raw and poignant way, the confusion, instability, misleading hopes, fallible expectations, and loss and pain the authors experienced. Eventually, many of them mark their author's fate in the way their narrative suddenly breaks off. Texts written *post factum*, in contrast, are written from the perspective of the "remembering survivor," who can still be traumatized but who has escaped the imminent danger of the situation.[35] With this, their relation to the events has changed fundamentally. The distance in time also affects the textual form. Memoirs are usually more clearly structured according to compositional rules than are diaries and employ narrative strategies more consciously in order to communicate the authors' experiences.[36] Further, knowledge of the events that the authors did not necessarily possess at the time often finds its way into these texts, shaping the authors' perspective and interpretation. This becomes increasingly important the more time has passed. The text becomes, over time, an examination of the past.[37]

Similarly, a person's location within the ghetto's boundaries had a huge impact on their perspective. Like every urban settlement, the space of the ghetto was socially stratified; there were "better" and "worse" neighborhoods, and living conditions differed from street to street. It also made a significant difference if a person had to move to the ghetto from other parts of the city or could stay in his or her apartment. As Michel Mazor writes in his memoir *The Vanished City* (*La cité engloutie*), "The situation of people in the first group [those who already lived on the territory of the future ghetto] was generally more favorable, for they got to live in their own former apartments and essentially to go about their usual lives; the new arrivals were deprived of all that."[38] People coming to the ghetto as deportees, expelled from rural parts of Poland or from different countries altogether, had a drastically different experience than those who knew the city; those who could hold on to their belongings lived under different conditions than those who could not. Similarly, the language(s) an individual spoke impacted his or her ability to navigate the environment. Foreigners who did not speak Polish were severely handicapped, as they could not communicate with the Gentile population, the Polish police, or the Polish-speaking Jews in the ghetto. Yiddish, on the other hand, provided at least a chance to communicate with some of the other ghetto inhabitants. Knowledge of German (and to some degree also Yiddish) allowed for some exchange with the German agents on-site, for example, at the sentry posts at the ghetto's boundaries.[39] The ability to communicate was crucial for survival as it helped inhabitants understand orders and instructions, to acquire resources, to negotiate, bribe, or plea. Experiences differed along many lines based on different constellations of gender, age, nationality, social and financial background, profession, employment, education, or religious affiliation and practice. The experience of orthodox Jews differed greatly from that of assimilated Jews, just as it differed from the experience of converts who potentially did not even self-identify as Jewish at all.[40] Political activists usually perceived events differently from those not involved in political work; people engaged in Jewish self-help or working for the *Judenrat* (Jewish Council) saw different sections of the ghetto and better understood its inner workings, as did those working in the medical profession or those smuggling food. Peretz Opoczynski, who worked as a ghetto mailman, for instance, saw and experienced a very different ghetto space than a young girl from an affluent family, such as Mary Berg. Generally, women's experience differed significantly from that of men.[41]

It is crucial to acknowledge this multiplicity of experiences; to this end, contextualizing sources is a process of the highest import in understanding the inner differentiation of the ghetto population. While the particular spatial structures investigated in this book affected all ghetto inhabitants, they did not have the same effect on everyone. Generally, the accounts *Violent Space* is based on are, for the most part, written by people with a certain level of education. They are also typically written by people whose scope of movement was comparably wide and who, despite all hardships, were not acutely starving to death. Most authors had lived in Warsaw prior to the German occupation. There are no orthodox Jews among the authors. *Violent Space* also does not specifically reflect the fate of converts, as none of the sources I chose for the book were written by a Christian who was forced by the Germans into the ghetto. There are accounts written by both men and women (some of them young girls at the time), many of whom were either employed in the Jewish administration or worked for the Jewish self-help. Many of the authors were politically active and became part of the Jewish resistance. To make transparent potential factors that shaped the perspective of a witness, *Violent Space* provides in the appendix a short biography of every person who was a part of the events and whose accounts are quoted. The subjective quality of their accounts heavily influences the analysis, which means that only a very particular segment of the ghetto space becomes visible. This, however, should not be considered a flaw. *Violent Space* very consciously aims not for a generalized, "objective" depiction of the Warsaw ghetto but for an evocation of its space as it was lived and experienced. This space, by definition, was intimate, subjective, emotionally charged, and personal.

Notes

1. For a good overview, see, for example, Dünne and Günzel, *Raumtheorie*; Schroer, *Räume, Orte, Grenzen*; or Hubbard, Kitchin, and Valentine, *Key Thinkers on Space and Place*.

2. de Certeau, *Practice of Everyday Life*, 117 (emphasis in the original), see also 118.

3. It is worth noting that this definition of "place" runs counter to other possible conceptualizations, as one would find, for example, in the field of human geography. Here, as Tim Cresswell notes, place is often understood as "a meaningful segment of space," with space being the more "abstract" concept of the two ("Place," 4).

4. In his 1982 interview with Paul Rabinow, Foucault makes an argument that allows for a similar conclusion: while an architectural layout might "ensure a certain allocation of people ... a *canalization* of their circulation, as well as the coding of their reciprocal relations" ("Space, Power and Knowledge," 140 [emphasis in the original]), it is the practice of said space that ultimately defines it. Depending on the practices of a society, Foucault argues, the very same architecture can be either oppressive or liberating (ibid., 135–136). This, again, suggests that the architectural layout alone does not determine space, but people and their practice of said layout do.

5. de Certeau, *Practice of Everyday Life*, 98.

6. Lefebvre, quoted in Miron, "'Lately, Almost Constantly, Everything Seems Small to Me,'" 123.

7. In contrast to the Pawiak prison (located between Dzielna, Pawia, and Więzienna Streets) and the Gęsia Street prison (located at 24 Gęsia Street, with an entrance to 19 Zamenhofa Street), the Gestapo headquarters at 25 Aleja Szucha were de facto located outside the ghetto territory. All three were spaces that offered no room for appropriation, spaces of absolute power (*"absolute Macht"*) in Wolfgang Sofsky's sense (*Ordnung des Terrors*, 22–40).

8. Except for select members of the medical profession and members of the Jewish Police, as well as those few who managed to temporarily buy their way out and/or were smuggled back to the ghetto at the very last minute. But even those very few who were lucky enough to escape the *Umschlagplatz* would, as Marek Edelman illustrates quite urgently, sooner or later return to it and face deportation (Edelman and Sawicka, *Liebe im Ghetto*, 87–89, 91).

9. Leociak, *Text in the Face of Destruction*, 55.

10. A very impressive book on this topic would be Jacek Leociak's *Biografie Ulic*, which presents the history of central Jewish streets in Warsaw that also became part of the ghetto during the occupation (namely, Sienna, Krochmalna, Chłodna, Leszno, Nalewki, Nowolopie, Nowolipki, Karmelicka, Smocza, Miła, Niska, and Stawki Streets).

11. Edelman and Sawicka, *Liebe im Ghetto*, 67–68.

12. Boehm, "Introduction," 4.

13. Bauman, *Winter in the Morning*, 75; see also 499. RING. I/1005.

14. Berg, *Diary*, 80–81.

15. For a map of these localities, see Weszpiński, "Social Life."

16. Berg, *Diary*, 51; Żywulska, *Tanz, Mädchen . . .*, 26; Edelman and Sawicka, *Liebe im Ghetto*, 62–63.

17. Ringelblum, *Notes from the Warsaw Ghetto*, 215.

18. Berg, *Diary*, 122; see also Ring_I_504_Reduction of Ghetto.

19. Ringelblum, *Notes from the Warsaw Ghetto*, 222 (insertion in the original).

20. Ibid., 164.

21. Berg, *Diary*, 122.

22. Adler, *In the Warsaw Ghetto*, 115.

23. de Certeau, *Practice of Everyday Life*, 119.

24. Vasiliev et al., "What Is a Map?," 119–120.

25. For a similar argument concerning other measures of exercising "territoriality," see Cole, "Ghettoization," 82.

26. Ibid., 67.

27. Ibid., 73.

28. Goldberg, "History of the Jews in the Ghetto," 95.

29. Ibid., 84–85.

30. Ibid.

31. Ofer and Weitzman, "Introduction," 2–3.

32. Waxman, "Transcending History?," 148.

33. Leociak, "Literature of the Personal Document," 49.

34. Ibid.

35. Ibid. It is worth noting that while diaries from the ghetto are, by definition, texts that are written *hic et nunc*, memoirs can also potentially fall into this category. Some memoirs were in fact written during the time of the ghetto's existence, often, for example, while the writer was in hiding on the "Aryan" side. These texts "recall events from which they are divided by a few months or, at the most a year or so" (Leociak, *Text in the Face of Destruction*, 16). As Leociak points out, in these cases the time of writing and the time described in the text often converge up to a point where they coincide. An author might start describing events that have passed but writes up to the point where his or her account concerns the present events.

36. Leociak, *Text in the Face of Destruction*, 16.

37. For a very elaborate discussion of this process and its relevance in the context of Holocaust studies, see Waxman, "Transcending History?"

38. Mazor, *Vanished City*, 48; see also Engelking, *Holocaust and Memory*, 87–89.

39. Opoczynski, qtd. in Kassow, "Introduction," *Those Nightmarish Days*, xix.

40. In fact, the Nazis included in their aggressive external definition of Jewishness also people who did not identify as Jewish, alongside many people for whom Jewishness had not necessarily been the sole or even the main denominator of their identity. In the case of the Warsaw ghetto, this translated into "about 2,000 Christians of various denominations" who were "among the total of about 400,000 inhabitants behind the wall" (Engelking and Leociak, *Warsaw Ghetto*, 652). There were also three Catholic churches in the ghetto: the Church of the Birth of the Blessed Virgin Mary on Leszno Street, the Church of All Saints in Grzybowski Square, and the Saint Augustine's Church at Nowolipki Street, which was closed but whose priests remained in the ghetto (ibid., 652). For a very informative study on converts in the ghetto, see Dembowski, *Christians in the Warsaw Ghetto*.

41. For studies of women's experiences during the Holocaust, see, for example, Ofer and Weitzman, *Women in the Holocaust*; Pető, Hecht, and Krasuska, *Women and the Holocaust*; Waxman, *Women in the Holocaust*; Strobl, *Die Angst kam erst danach*; Chalmers, "Jewish Women's Sexual Behaviour and Sexualized Abuse during the Nazi Era"; or Person, "Sexual Violence during the Holocaust."

3

The Archive

The Nazis targeted Jewish lives not only in a physical sense; they also targeted their victims' culture, identities, self-expression, and memory. In this sense, the Holocaust encompassed a process of silencing.[1] That we can know anything about the space of the ghetto as it was lived and experienced should thus not be taken for granted.[2] In fact, it is only due to an impressive act of resistance from within the ghetto that this is possible at all.

Confronted with the aggressive anti-Jewish policies of the German occupiers, in November 1940 *Oneg Shabbat*—a group of Jewish intellectuals who were socially, culturally, religiously, and politically active members of the Jewish community in Warsaw—took up work on a clandestine ghetto archive. Founded by historian and social activist Emanuel Ringelblum, the group was determined to document the occupiers' deeds but also the rich and multifaceted cultural and social life of Jewish communities both in the city and in the provinces. Their work focused on the individual experience and on documenting the here and now of the Holocaust as it unfolded. Their objective was to document not only the "collective catastrophe" but just as much "the individual lives the Germans were about to destroy."[3] The materials collected and preserved by the archive's members testify to an incredible intellectual and personal effort to transmit the experiences of Jews during the Holocaust. Although only parts of the archive survived the war, some documents of which were in poor condition when they were discovered, they are of unparalleled value for any study on the ghetto as they provide an uncensored, autonomous Jewish narrative of the Holocaust and an inside view of the ghetto. *Violent Space* is the first comprehensive study on the ghetto written in English to work closely with the archive's materials.[4]

The archive's collection came to us under extraordinary circumstances, and its history is tied closely to that of the physical space of the ghetto. Endeavoring to preserve their invaluable documentation, the members of the *Oneg Shabbat* group buried parts of their archive in two installments during August 1942 and, most likely, February 1943.[5] David Graber, one of the young *Oneg Shabbat* members responsible for salvaging the documents, left a note with the first portion of the archive: "What we were unable to cry and shriek out to the world, we buried in the ground. I would love to see the moment in which the great treasure will be dug up and scream the truth at the world. So the world may know all.... May the treasure fall into good hands, may it last into better times, may it alarm and alert the world to what happened."[6]

The victims' voices, unheard at the time, were deposited into the ghetto's soil in hopes that they would be preserved and could be held by the hands of future generations. The fate of the archive's collections, however, was precarious. It is a miracle that there was anyone at all who was able to retrace the archive's where-abouts after the war, since, except for three of its members—Rachel Auerbach and Hersz and Bluma Wasser—the entire *Oneg Shabbat* group had perished. Also, as the ghetto was razed to the ground by the Germans in 1943, after the war the spots where the archive had been buried were difficult to locate in the fields of rubble. And yet, in 1946, one part of the material, stored in ten tin boxes, was unearthed with the help of one of the three surviving *Oneg Shabbat* members, Hersz Wasser. The second part, stored in two milk cans, was dug up in 1950 after the cans were accidentally discovered during construction work on the site of their hiding at 68 Nowolipki Street. A third part most likely remains buried alongside the remains of those inhabitants of the ghetto who perished during its "liquidation."[7]

Named after the archive's founding member, Emanuel Ringelblum, the sur-viving parts of the archive (Ringelblum I and II) are currently housed at the Jewish Historical Institute (Żydowski Instytut Historyczny) in Warsaw. They contain about thirty-five thousand pages of documents, interviews, personal accounts, and studies commissioned or written by the group's members.[8] Con-cerned with documenting "the details of everyday life and material history,"[9] the *Oneg Shabbat* group collected a vast variety of materials. Samuel D. Kassow, author of the only comprehensive study on the group's work, describes the scope of the collected documents and sources in his introduction to the archive's *Catalog and Guide* in 2009: "The Oyneg Shabes Archive collected an enormous range of material: the underground press, documents, drawings, candy wrap-pers, tram tickets, ration cards, and theater posters"; the archive's members also filed "invitations to concerts and lectures and took copies of the convoluted doorbell codes for apartments that often contained dozens of tenants." In the archives collection, one can find preserved alongside each other "restaurant menus that advertised roast goose and fine wines and a terse account about a starving mother who had eaten her dead child." The archive preserved "hundreds of postcards from Jews in the provinces, individuals about to be deported to an 'unknown destination,[']" but also "the poetry of Władysław Szlengel, Yitzhak Katzenelson, Kalman Lis, and Joseph Kirman," as well as "the entire script of a popular ghetto comedy, *Love Looks for an Apartment*, and long essays on the ghetto theaters and cafés." In the part unearthed in 1946, there were "many photographs, seventy-six of which more or less survived." In addition, the "Oyneg Shabes filed away hectographed readers used in the ghetto schools and the reports that nurses wrote in the ghetto orphanages." During the weeks of the Great Deportation *Aktion* in the summer of 1942, "the archive collected the German posters that announced the Great Deportation, and those that promised anyone voluntarily reporting for deportation 3 kilograms of bread and a kilogram of marmalade"; it also preserved "frantic appeals for a last-minute rescue from the waiting death trains," smuggled "out of the Umschlagplatz" and written by individuals "whose shaky handwriting betrayed [their] desperation." The archive's documentation also testifies to the armed Jewish resistance that formed in the last months of the ghetto's existence. Kassow concludes, "Among the last documents buried in the second cache were posters calling for armed resistance."[10] The collections also include original or copied German documents, decrees, posters, and correspondence, as well as valuable documentation about the work of the *Judenrat*.

Most of the material in the archive is in Polish, Yiddish, German, or Hebrew.[11] A number of documents and personal accounts are published in English or German translation in collected volumes;[12] others are published in excerpts,[13] are accessible in Polish only, or are not yet published at all. About 272 diaries are also part of another collection at the Jewish Historical Institute Warsaw—*Pamiętniki* (diaries)—excerpts of which have been published in English.[14] Many of the documents from the Ringelblum Collections have not yet been translated into English, however. They were, in fact, for a long time not accessible for research purposes, and—until recently—nigh unavailable for researchers without a sufficient command of the Polish language.

Only in 2003 was a full inventory, covering all material and providing sufficient information on the documents' origin and content, completed in Polish, and it took until 2009 for an English translation of the catalog to become available. According to Tadeusz Epsztein, who led the team of scholars responsible for the new inventory and catalog of the archive, the first attempt at cataloging the material had been undertaken in 1946, but it was far from exhaustive and did not provide much information on the documents.[15] A second inventory was made in 1955, omitting, however, a large number of fragments that are an important part of the collection.[16] Epsztein characterizes the 1955 inventory as follows: "The inventory prepared in 1955 is more of a general list of documents than a real archival inventory. Many of the descriptions were compiled without properly recognizing the contents of the described units and individual documents. The general description provided little data about the real condition of the contents."[17] The Jewish Historical Institute has published materials from the collection in Polish since 1997 (*Archiwum Ringelbluma*, vols. 1–38), and the first five volumes of an English edition appeared in 2017, 2018, 2020, and 2021, respectively.[18] The longtime lack of an English catalog and the scarcity of English translations means that the material has not extensively been used by English-speaking researchers.

For my own research, the new *Catalog and Guide* proved incredibly valuable. The detailed information provided on the content of each document allowed me to evaluate for my particular research interest the importance of sources that were, themselves, written in Polish or Yiddish, to copy them during my visits to the archives, and to work on translations with a Polish native speaker and translator when I was back home. Between 2016 and 2018, several accounts from the archive were translated specifically for this book with the help of Barbara Czepek (Frankfurt).[19] The academic discipline of translation is an integral part of Holocaust scholarship and of particular importance for the nonnative speaker. To work properly with the Polish material, a nonnative speaker needs much more than a mere translation of words. If one cannot rely on published translations, ideally accomplished by trained scholars and translators and validated through a reliable academic publisher, it is thus particularly important to work with someone who is familiar with the cultural knowledge embedded within the language. During the translation process, I learned much not only regarding the idiosyncrasies of individual authors but also on particularities of the Polish language. Many questions that I had were asked from a German cultural perspective that lacked innate understanding of Polish culture and history. Certain questions I discussed with multiple native speakers and Polish academics. Looking for linguistic equivalents in another language often helped with identifying significant details within the texts. For the Yiddish texts, I had the great privilege of working with translations provided by one of the editors of the *Ringelblum Archive* publications, Magdalena Siek from the Jewish Historical Institute (Warsaw).

In addition to the accounts and reports from the ghetto preserved by the *Oneg Shabbat* group, there is also a number of individual diaries smuggled out of the ghetto or hidden during the war and published posthumously (for example, Eugenia Szajn-Lewin's *Aufzeichnungen aus dem Warschauer Ghetto*, Adam

Czerniaków's *Tagebuch* (*Diary*), and Chaim A. Kaplan's *Scroll of Agony*, all of which were translated also into German and/or English.[20] All of them are the result of a highly perilous effort to document life in the ghetto and relied on the physical document or the author to escape the German destruction. In the vast majority of cases, the written testimony ended up being the last trace that remained of the person who recorded it. Even if these diaries started out as personal contemplations, at one point or another they all became an act of documentation, and their authors carefully preserved them to ensure that posterity would learn of their fate and the fate of their families, friends, and community, and of the specifics of their experiences. These accounts, just as those from the *Ringelblum Archive*, were written "*hic et nunc*" as Leociak classifies—that is, during the ghetto's existence—on the premises of the ghetto or in hiding on the "Aryan" side.[21] Their authors noted down their experiences as they were happening or with only a few days' delay. As readers, we see how they were often painfully unaware of what was going to happen next; we observe how they were trying to make sense of the events within the frame of their (oftentimes limited) knowledge, how they interpreted, anticipated, and desperately looked for ways to cope. These diaries are thus not only sources of historical facts or details; they are, above all, testimonies to the very process of living through highly traumatic experiences.

This book also includes memoirs and recollections written by survivors after the liberation, ranging from texts written right after the war to texts written up to fifty or sixty years later (for example, Stanisław Adler's *In the Warsaw Ghetto*, Marek Edelman's *The Ghetto Fights*, Michel Mazor's *The Vanished City*, Halina Birenbaum's *Hope Is the Last to Die*, and Janina Bauman's *Winter in the Morning*)—that is, "*post factum*" in Leociak's terminology.[22] In these texts, the reader hears the survivors speak of their experiences in retrospect. While many of them still struggle to make sense of their experiences, with time, what had been uncertain to them then has since become painful certainty. In contrast to the authors of diaries, these writers know how things developed, and most of them cannot help but add to their memories the knowledge they obtained later. They reinterpret and reorganize their recollections based on what they learned, based on what they now, at the point of writing, know would happen to their past selves, to their families and their communities. Quite often, survivors were also minutely aware of the discourses surrounding their experiences and incorporated (directly or indirectly) parts of academic or popular debates of their time into their writing. The different perspectives drastically shape what the reader can learn from a text, but they all are invaluable sources when it comes to learning about the space of the ghetto.[23]

When studying the Warsaw ghetto, it is crucial to keep in mind that while in comparison to other ghettos there is a comparably large number of documents preserved, the material basis for the reconstruction of its history is still highly fragmentary and incomplete. Research-based studies and secondary texts draw from a limited pool of material, dates and descriptions do not always align, crucial documents and accounts are missing, and many events and experiences have no voice at all. Thus, it is important to understand and accept that not all questions can be answered, not all details filled in. Whenever possible, I will highlight contradictions and conflicting information as such. I do not consider these ruptures in the narrative a flaw but rather a part of the expression of the narrative constructed against the genocidal agenda of the Nazis, an agenda that, in addition to physical genocide, also entailed a silencing of the victims.

Notes

1. For a similar argument, see, for example, Rupnow, "Invisible Crime," 62–63; Stone, "Introduction," 6; Kassow, "Introduction," *Warsaw Ghetto*, xix–xx; or Waxman, "Transcending History?" 147–148.

2. Waxman stresses the unlikeliness of any records of the events of the Holocaust as seen and described by its victims ever reaching posterity: "As we read the texts of these men and women . . . we are seeped with the knowledge that they like the vast majority of the authors who wrote in the ghettos and concentration camps, did not survive. More than this, we are reminded that the vast majority of the victims never wrote anything at all. Each text which survived the Holocaust did so against almost overwhelming odds. . . . It was not enough . . . to find the strength to record what was happening in circumstances that largely militated against the writing of testimony; the authors also had to ensure that their writings would outlive them" ("Transcending History?" 147–148).

3. Kassow, *Who Will Write Our History?* 4, see also 13.

4. A prominent exception would be Engelking and Leociak, *Warsaw Ghetto*, which was translated from Polish. Kassow's influential study on the Oneg Shabbat Archive, *Who Will Write Our History?*, is another of the few examples of historical works drawing widely on the archive's collections.

5. Kassow, *Who Will Write Our History?* 3–5.

6. Qtd. in ibid., 3.

7. Epsztein, "Structure and Organization," 8–9; Kassow, "Introduction," *Warsaw Ghetto*, xv.

8. Epsztein, "Structure and Organization," 1.

9. Kassow, *Who Will Write Our History?* 11.

10. Kassow, "Introduction," *Warsaw Ghetto*, xxi.

11. Shapiro, "Translator's Preface," xiii.

12. Examples would be Kermish, *To Live with Honor and Die with Honor!*; Markowska, *Ringelblum Archive*; or Kazimierski et al., *Ludność Żydowska w Warszawie*.

13. For example, in Leociak's *Text in the Face of Destruction* or in Kassow's *Who Will Write Our History?* both of whom quote extensively from the archive's material.

14. For example, in Grynberg, *Words to Outlive Us*.

15. Epsztein, "Structure and Organization," 9–10.

16. Ibid., 11.

17. Ibid.

18. Volume 1: *Warsaw Ghetto. Everyday Life*, edited by Katarzyna Person (Warsaw: Jewish Historical Institute, 2017); Volume 2: *Accounts from the Borderlands, 1939–1941*, edited by Andrzej Żbikowski (Warsaw: Jewish Historical Institute, 2018); Volume 3: *Oyneg Shabes. People and Works*, edited by Aleksandra Bańkowska and Tadeusz Epsztein (Warsaw: Jewish Historical Institute, 2020); Volume 4: *Children: Clandestine Education in the Warsaw Ghetto*, edited by Ruta Sakowska (Warsaw: Jewish Historical Institute, 2021); and Volume 5: *The Last Stage of Resettlement Is Death. Pomiechówek, Chełmno on the Ner, Treblinka*, edited by Barbara Engelking, Alina Skibińska and Ewa Wiatr (Warsaw: Jewish Historical Institute, 2021). The first three volumes are also available online through the website of the Jewish Historical Institute and the Central Jewish Library.

19. For more information on the corpus of archival texts used in this book, see the section "Archival Material" in the appendix.

20. Oftentimes, both the history of the manuscripts' survival and its publication are extremely convoluted and precarious. Eugenia Szajn-Lewin, for example, stashed her manuscript in a secret space under the floor in the apartment she herself hid in when fleeing to the "Aryan" side shortly before the ghetto's "liquidation." Szajn-Lewin perished during the Warsaw Uprising, and her sister retrieved the manuscript from the apartment after the war. The building had miraculously been spared from the sweeping destruction. In the 1980s, the original manuscript got lost in France. What remained and built the basis for the publication was a copy that Szajn-Lewin's sister had previously made (Line, "Introduction," 7; Siemens, "Die Menschenerniedrigungsmaschine"). Adam Czerniaków's diary (except for one volume, which was probably taken from him during a temporary arrest by the Gestapo) was presumably saved by his wife, Felicja. The manuscript was considered missing for years but reappeared under unexplained circumstances in 1964 in Canada, where it was purchased by Yad Vashem (Kozlowski and Prunitsch, "Czerniaków, Adam," 1–2). Chaim A. Kaplan's diary was smuggled out of the ghetto by a friend of the author in 1942. The notebooks were then kept in a small village at the house of a member of the Polish Underground, Wladyslaw Wojcek, who in 1952 handed parts of the diary over to the Jewish Historical Institute. Others found their way, more or less by coincidence, into the hands of Abraham Isaac Katsh, who became their first editor and translator (Katsh, "Introduction," 13–17). Translating and editing the sources from the ghetto is very challenging and complex scholarly work, and not all early editions withstand the test of time.

21. Leociak, "Literature of the Personal Document," 48.

22. Ibid.

23. The respective category a text belongs to is referenced in the biographical notes on the authors provided in the appendix, where I will also reference the personal

life story of all firsthand witnesses so that the reader can frame the account ("Bi-ographies"). Whenever possible, the appendix also provides information on the type of account, the time span covered, and the publication date. Within my own text, when speaking of a diary, I give the date of the particular entry; the most common verbs I use are "notes," "writes," "states," "observes," and the like. I will identify postwar memoirs as such at the time of their first mention. Typical words associated with them are "recalls," "remembers," "describes," and "reports." This method does not guarantee absolute clarity, but it should help distinguish primary from secondary sources, as well as texts written *hic et nunc* from those written *post factum*.

4

Streets and Buildings

When the territory the Germans designated for the ghetto was walled in and thereby cut off from the city of Warsaw, in many, oftentimes fatal, ways, the northern quarter stopped working as it had when it was still an integral part of the city's macrocosm. And yet, annexing buildings, streets, and infrastructure that previously belonged to the unified whole of prewar Warsaw, the ghetto was made from the city's fabric. Therefore, the city and its space remain a very useful frame of reference for an analysis of the ghetto. Theoretical concepts and approaches from fields of study that address questions related to cities and towns—such as urban studies and urban planning, architecture, and (human) geography, but also cultural anthropology, political theory, and sociology—help us build an understanding of what functions structures, such as streets and residential buildings, have in a working urban environment. Looking at Warsaw's streets and buildings through the lens of these disciplines thereby also sharpens the perception for the various ways in which the German occupiers' decrees, practices, and spatial interventions impacted these functions and affected the ways in which Jews could move through and experience an urban environment that no longer supported them.

The Ghetto's Streets

Written accounts from the Warsaw ghetto show the deep impression the streets of the ghetto made on people. The massive overcrowding of the first phase of the ghetto's existence (from October/November 1940 to July 1942); the resulting noise; the forced proximity; the physical and psychological strain; the constant, visible presence of sickness, hunger, and destitution; the harrowing sight of people begging and dying on the sidewalks (many of whom were children), but also the deeply felt exposure to acts of German violence, were noted by almost everyone who wrote about their experiences inside the ghetto walls. The changes in the streets' appearance and their functioning were "shocking" to the ghetto's inhabitants and "required noting down," as Leociak observes.[1] The fact that the depiction of streets features so very prominently in testimonies from the ghetto reflects the drastic nature of the German spatial politics, but it also attests to the central role streets play in any urban environment. As Vikas Mehta states in his 2013 urban studies book *The Street—A Quintessential Social Public Space*, "Streets play a major role in structuring the form of settlements, particularly urban settlements. A considerable portion of land in cities—one-third to a half—is devoted to streets that serve as the prime infrastructure for movement, access and connectivity, and in carrying and delivering utilities and services."[2] Looking at the city as a "physical relation between buildings and open space"—that is, between "solids" and "voids," as William C. Ellis puts it[3]—it becomes apparent that the particular pattern formed between those two structures fundamentally defines the appearance of the entire cityscape. By extension, because streets enable movement and exchange, their individual layout has a strong impact on inhabitants' spatial experience. In Warsaw's northern quarter, where the Germans ultimately chose to locate the ghetto, the particular configuration of streets and buildings had not been comprehensively planned but had grown over the centuries based on the independent development of several smaller jurisdictions (so-called "*jurydyki*") in the area. In fact, especially in the late eighteenth and early nineteenth centuries, when these jurisdictions were ultimately merged and Warsaw was experiencing a veritable "building boom," the quarter had grown quite chaotically and was mostly unregulated.[4] As a result, the course of the streets was fairly irregular; in addition, many streets included in the ghetto were relatively narrow. Broader streets, such as Nalewki, Zamenhofa, Leszno, Chłodna, Twarda, and Okopowa, harbored in their midst a "tangle of narrow lanes," small streets and alleys, courtyards, and narrow passages.[5] These smaller cross streets often connected two or three parallel streets at most but did not continue. The majority of wider, more prominent streets, which served as channels within the larger street network of the city, ran from east to west,[6] such as Leszno Street, a "major East-West thoroughfare"[7] leading up to Tłomackie, where the Great Synagogue was located; or Chłodna Street, "with its many large modern houses,"[8] traversing the northern quarter in the direction of Iron Gate Square (Plac Żelaznej Bramy) and the Saxon Garden (Ogród Saski).

With the erection of walls to cordon off the ghetto in the fall of 1940, the northern quarter's street network and its functioning were massively disrupted. This affected, in particular, the streets' role as "infrastructure for movement,"

facilitating communication through the "access and connectivity" that they normally provide.[9] Being truncated by walls, streets in the ghetto ceased to function as channels within a wider network of communication. Many of the paths
that people had customarily, occasionally or even just potentially used were now
barred or rerouted.[10] While they still partly fulfilled their role as internal connectors for the ghetto, they did not link the northern quarter to other parts of the city
anymore; the quarter had essentially turned into a maze. As a result, connection
to the world at large—to other cities, towns, villages, and, as a consequence, also
to other countries—had also been cut off. First and foremost, this meant that Jews
were "walled up, locked in," as Berg observes,[11] and that it became very difficult,
if not impossible, for them to escape from the German clutches. In a wider sense,
by cutting off communication, ghettoization ruptured the very essence of urban
spatial organization (i.e., the principle of access and connectivity) and belied
people's deeply ingrained expectations regarding the functioning of their environment. Looking at a map, a modern-day observer might still mistake the streets
of the ghetto for regular streets, but the reality was that all streets of the ghetto
had been turned into dead ends, defeating much of their original purpose.[12] Seeing as communication "every kind of dissemination or exchange, whether it be of
persons, goods, messages or energy, and whether it be transcribed, transported,
or transmitted," as Thomas V. Czarnowski suggests,[13] helps us realize the social
rupture its cutting off had caused. Pedestrians' movement, wheeled traffic (private or public), the transport of goods, the transmission of information, the use
of telephone lines or postal service, and the supply of water and electricity are
all ways in which people connect with each other. Streets play a crucial role in
forging the channels necessary for these connections to take place. All the above
examples mark the variety of ways in which the northern quarter had previously
been an organic part of the rest of the city. With ghettoization, many connections were ruptured, but not all. Telephones and the postal service, for example,
were operational for almost the entire duration of the ghetto's existence—that is,
up until the Ghetto Uprising (and in the case of telephones, at least potentially,
even after).[14] The ghetto also remained connected to the city's central water and
electricity supply—although many households had no access to either or were
cut off at some point.[15] Likewise, the sewer system maintained an intact connection between both parts of the city. While existing utility networks were not cut,
supplies that depended on delivery via the street infrastructure, such as coal and
fuel, were considerably short.[16] With the main arteries of connection discontinued, the remaining ones became significantly more important for the Jews inside
the ghetto. The Jewish underground organizations, in fact, coordinated much of
their clandestine work with members on the "Aryan" side over telephones;[17] the
sewers served as routes for smugglers, and, later, some of the remaining fighters of

the Ghetto Uprising used the sewer system to escape from the burning ghetto.[18] Generally, the desperate and starving Jews made use of every crack in the various barriers between the ghetto and the "Aryan" city, often imperiling their lives.

The Germans limited interpersonal contact between Jews in the ghetto and the non-Jewish inhabitants of the city of Warsaw in the most drastic ways. This included the exchange of goods, services, and utilities; this restriction held severe implications for the ghetto's supplies and thus for the living conditions inside the walls. Goods coming in for the provisioning of people in the ghetto were either regulated by the Germans, who used their control over the ghetto's resources as a means to gradually starve the Jews to death, or had to be acquired through clandestine and thus highly perilous channels. Cutting communication meant that Jews were dissociated from the remaining Polish society and that the people inside the ghetto lost social ties with the non-Jewish population on a large scale.[19] This deeply affected social cohesion within the occupied society and severed important lifelines of support for the ghettoized Jews.

From the perspective of urban studies, streets are divided into different zones that are intended to cater to different functions and to provide different spaces for the manifold physical and social dimensions of their use. Such dimensions of a given street's usage, as well as its layout, are informed by both historical and cultural changes; yet, the street's many structural elements also have the potential to define its use. Architecturally, the very basic elements of the street itself are "roadway, pedestrian way, and flanking buildings."[20] Robert Mantho divides the sidewalk (i.e., the "pedestrian way") further, listing four distinct zones: first, "the transition zone"[21] that is located "immediately adjacent to the building edge" and is "used to move into or out of buildings";[22] second, the "circulation zone,"[23] "in the middle of the sidewalk," which is "predominantly used for movement";[24] third, "the amenities zone"; and "finally the curbside zone, where the sidewalk/ pavement meets the roadway."[25] Mantho elaborates, "The zone against the roadway contains the street furniture and landscape elements. This is the area where light poles, street signs, fire hydrants, telephone poles and other infrastructure items are located, also the zone where many of the public amenities are situated: trees, benches, planters and bus stops."[26]

While, as Mantho points out, these "physical attributes" are by no means fully determinate of the space of a street, they do "have significant impacts on the experience, perception and identity of a specific street."[27] Streets are a central factor in regard to people's daily experiences. Their appearance, their color scheme, the feel of their surface, their physical qualities and proportions, their smells and sounds, their traffic and the temporal patterns of their use, the surrounding architecture, as well as the people a person meets on them are formative to the experience of urban dwellers. Within the ghetto, both the appearance and the use of the streets were significantly altered. The overcrowding, in particular, which prevailed until the summer of 1942, defeated much of the intended differentiation between the zones of the street. The overcrowding was such that the "circulation zone" was usually heavily congested, and people were often pushed onto the roadway, into the vehicular traffic. The composition of vehicular traffic changed as well, as the Germans forbade Jews to own or use motorized vehicles. The only cars in the ghetto were thus German. Most streets in the ghetto were made of cobblestone, and there were tram tracks running along what had been the major traffic arteries of the prewar quarter. The streets of the northern quarter were furnished with a huge variety of "landscape elements." There were ornate iron light poles and electricity pylons, telephone poles, tram wires, hydrant and sewer covers, storm drains, advertising columns, diversely designed curbstones, tram stops, and at the edge of the buildings, there were signboards, displays, basement windows, rainwater downpipes, as well as numerous base pedestals, curb stones, edges, steps, stairs, doorsills, gateways, passages, and entrances, which were soon populated by the ghetto's most destitute population, those begging, starving, and dying on the street. In the curbside as well as the amenities zone, street peddlers put up their stalls.

Streets Reconfigured

Streets play a crucial part in how people perceive and navigate their environment. In an urban setting, streets oftentimes build the grid for people's orientation processes. When describing, imagining, or planning a route, information such as where to turn left or right, how many blocks to walk in a certain direction, or where to cross a certain street is often key. To describe or visualize a route, people rely on what Kevin Lynch describes in *The Image of the City* as a "generalized mental picture of the exterior world."[28] This picture, in turn, is based on a prestructuring of the environment according to certain elements. Lynch lists five of these elements commonly used to form one's image of a city and to help people to "recognize and pattern" their surroundings;[29] these are "paths, edges, districts, nodes and landmarks."[30] According to Lynch, a person's "mental picture" of an environment is formed in a "two-way process" in which "the environment suggests distinctions and relations, and the observer . . . selects, organizes, and endows with meaning what he sees."[31] Streets play a crucial role in this process, as people usually "observe the city while moving through it" and along their way "arrang[e] and relat[e]" the other elements of their environment.[32]

Confronted with a drastically restructured environment, Jews in the ghetto had to go through a painful process of reorientation. Varsovians, who had been well acquainted with the prewar northern quarter, found it profoundly changed as it no longer aligned with their existing mental picture. The Germans excluded landmarks that had been central to the cityscape of Warsaw—and to Jewish culture within it. In fact, many important sites of prewar Jewish life were suddenly out of reach for the ghetto inhabitants. This concerned sites of religious practice that were located in other parts of the city, such as synagogues, private prayer houses, and *mikvehs* (i.e., the ritual baths in which Jews immersed for spiritual cleansing). Numerous private religious schools (*cheders* for younger boys or *yeshivas* for continuing religious education) and secular Jewish elementary, middle, and upper secondary schools all became inaccessible to their staff and students, who were now bound to the confines of the ghetto. Markets and stores in other districts that had been owned and frequented predominantly by Jews were forcibly taken over or closed down. Other central institutions of Warsaw's Jewish community, such as the Jewish Hospital in Czyste or the Janusz Korczak orphanage for Jewish children,[33] had to relocate to buildings inside the ghetto. These localities and institutions had given streets and entire neighborhoods in prewar Warsaw a distinctly Jewish character. Densely populated by Jews, shaped by their community practices, their presence, and their everyday life, these streets and neighborhoods had been considered Jewish by Varsovians, Jewish and non-Jewish alike. In a diary entry on October 17, 1940, shortly after the Germans officially announced the ghetto, Chaim Aron Kaplan notes in disbelief, "They took streets away from us that have been Jewish since ancient times, and which no one imagined would be outside the boundaries of the ghetto."[34]

The walls erected on German order also introduced a whole new set of "linear breaks in continuity" (i.e., "edges" in Lynch's terminology).[35] Where there had been organic connections between the northern quarter and the rest of the city before, there were now barriers that closed the ghetto off from its surroundings.[36] Consequently, previous distinctions between different sections of the city held no practical value for Jewish people anymore, as none of the other quarters was accessible to them. In their place new distinctions emerged: until the fall of 1942, there was the "large" northern ghetto and the "small" southern ghetto, and within them different neighborhoods, often associated with varying degrees of poverty or danger; later, after the Great Deportation *Aktion*, there was the residual ghetto, consisting of the German shops and workers' quarters, and the so-called wild areas,[37] inhabited clandestinely by those who held no official permit to remain in the ghetto (and thus, at least temporarily, stay alive). On the level of the city as a whole, preexisting structures were overwritten by the new, prominent demarcation introduced on German order—that is, between "Jewish" space and "Aryan" space, between the "ghetto" and the "city." In his reflections on the "mental picture" people form of their environment, Lynch also suggests the existence of a "public image" of the city, shared by a "large number of a city's inhabitants,"[38] and, therefore, often formative for, or the expression of, a group identity. With the introduction of this new demarcation line, the image space Varsovians shared before the occupation was shattered. From then on, when thinking about their city, forming new relationships to their environment, and moving through it, Jewish and non-Jewish Poles no longer referenced the same topography. Their perceptions, experiences, and use of the city were decoupled and continued to develop under very different conditions.

Inside the ghetto, "nodes"—as in central junctions, centers of concentration, or "intensive foci," as Lynch explains[39]—had to be renegotiated as well. In view of the new topographical structures and social dynamics, new centers of exchange, trade, communication, and meeting emerged, and, thus, so did new nodal points of intense risk and apprehension. Elements of the urban environment that had held little importance in the prewar city or had not existed at all became pivotal to the ghetto's topography and to life within it. The ghetto prisons, for example, were sites of intense violence, where the Germans executed Jews for the smallest offenses; they also constituted epicenters of German presence in the ghetto, and people thus considered them and their vicinity to be particularly dangerous. Similarly, at the ghetto's gates and bridges encounters with the occupiers often could not be avoided, which turned these locations into sites of impending harassment and violence. Activities such as smuggling, which under the given circumstances was of the utmost importance for the ghetto's survival, brought with them an entirely new topography, based on new needs, impediments, risks, and opportunity structures. A good example would be the border street at Plac Mirowski, where according to Jan Kostański's recollections, about one-third of all smuggled goods "went through" the wall that ran partly along the courtyards of buildings located between Mirowski Square and Krochmalna Street.[40] Due to this particular layout and the general business of the market square, numerous well-disguised opportunities for smuggling were created.[41] From the "Aryan" side, people would occasionally "throw small parcels and loaves of bread across to the ghetto";[42] more elaborate smuggling operations also took place with goods being passed over the wall with the help of ladders and "thick rope[s]" with "iron hook[s]" used to hoist large bags of contraband.[43] To put an end to the smuggling activities in the area, in December 1941, the Germans ordered the Jewish inhabitants of the border buildings to move to the "other side (the odd-numbered side) of Krochmalna Street," thereby creating a "neutral belt where no-one could enter."[44] But, even then, people would devise new ways of moving goods,[45] and Plac Mirowski remained heavily frequented by smugglers. At the same time, Kostański reports the numerous instances of smugglers being beaten, arrested, or shot by German gendarmes or Polish policemen.[46] Just like Plac Mirowski and Krochmalna Street, most border streets and buildings

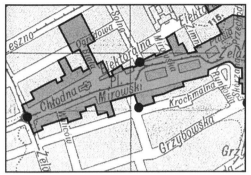

Fig. 4.1a. Borders of the ghetto at Plac Mirowski and Krochmalna Street in November 1940 and after the reductions in December 1941.

became sites of opportunity but also accounted for countless deaths at the hand of German sentry posts.

To master the new environment, people had to adapt and reorganize their relationship to the world around them, and this process had to be accomplished very quickly and under immense existential pressure. Moreover, the process of reorientation never halted, as the ghetto borders were redrawn many times and the ghetto's inhabitants could never settle into any form of stability. For Lynch, the ability to make sense of one's environment is "fundamental to the efficiency and to the very survival for free-moving life,"[47] but, more than that, it is also closely linked to people's "sense of balance and well-being."[48] People's relationship to their environment is not merely practical or functional, as Lynch suggests. When internally structuring their environment, people endow "with meaning" what surrounds them.[49] From the perspective of cultural geography, Karen E. Till takes this observation one step further, emphasizing the existence of "attachments" that form "affective networks that give thick meaning to an inhabitant's experience of place and the city."[50] A person's "mental picture" of the city is thus also shaped by the affective attachments created when they ascribe meaning to certain regions or elements of their environment. The result is an emotive topography that is an expression of the personal and meaningful relationship people develop to the world around them. Many of these attachments were ruptured when the Germans forcefully resettled people to the ghetto. When forced to leave their homes and familiar neighborhoods behind to move to the ghetto, people often lost contact with the grown networks of their personal lives. But, also, those who (at least temporarily) could physically remain where they had lived before found their surroundings so dramatically changed that they could not relate to them anymore.

The violence that people experienced at the hands of the Germans and their auxiliaries generated new layers of meaning and distorted existing relationships to the environment. Attachments that had been, at least predominantly, positive and stabilizing in people's familiar environment were substituted with or transformed into intensely negative and destabilizing attachments. Locations such as the ghetto's refugee centers (the so-called *Punkty*) that the *Judenrat* set up in various locations, from former "synagogues and prayer houses" to "cinemas," "factory buildings," or "housing blocks"[51] and where people lived under terrible hygienic conditions, were sites of unprecedented destitution. Also, the ghetto's sidewalks and doorways became the arena of constant encounters with sickness and death. Central social institutions, such as hospitals and orphanages, shifted their function and meaning in light of the dire conditions and immense shortages the ghetto experienced. Clandestine prayer houses and schools, the various localities of resistance work, as well as hiding places and bunkers were saturated with meaning that transcended the previous realm of experience. Fear, caution, vulnerability, suffering, loss, and trauma became new dominant paradigms for the emotive mapping of people's surroundings.

The Ghetto's Buildings

From an architectural perspective, in an urban environment streets and buildings are interdependent. In contrast to a road, a street is by definition framed by buildings, which define its volume, orientation, and appearance. These buildings, in turn, are connected and made accessible by streets. Moreover, the street itself is always three-dimensional:[52] it consists not only of the "roadway" and "pedestrian way" but also of the "flanking buildings."[53] A street can thus never be fully characterized without including in its examination the building structure that frames it. The layout, spatial distribution, and architectural characteristics of buildings significantly shape the urban environment. In Muranów, the course of the city's streets very clearly ran along building blocks, as architect and urban scholar Guy Shachar observes.[54] Also, in an attempt to meet the housing needs of an ever-growing population, from the late nineteenth century onward, building development in Warsaw's northern quarter was oriented vertically. In fact, in the late nineteenth century, "lower or wooden buildings" had been replaced by multistory tenement houses on a large scale.[55] Peter J. Martyn elaborates,

> A building boom between 1875 and 1890 when nearly 800 tenement houses were put up in Muranów alone was largely responsible for the characteristic late 19th century district existing until 1943. Świętojerska, Przejazd, Niska, Muranowska, Miła, Dzielna, Pawia, Nowolipki, Nowolipie, Gęsia, Kacza

and Karmelicka streets had been largely built up by the end of this boom.
New roads from the late 1870s, such as Miła, Wołyńska, Nowowołyńska and
Sochaczewska were laid out to be almost immediately developed with richly-
decorated three and four storey facadal elevations hiding courtyard warrens.
Such building had already reached the northern and western fringes (Stawki-
Okopowa-Wolność streets) by the 1880s. . . . Wooden one floor and other low
[buildings were] replaced by tenement blocks on the Nalewki, Dzika, Smolna
etc.[56]

Mantho calls attention to the importance that the architectural relation between streets and buildings holds when examining an urban settlement. The
concept of "vertical definition," as he introduces it, relates the height of buildings
to the width of the street and, thus, defines both the volume and the orientation of
the physical and visual space created between streets and buildings.[57] Indeed, the
vertical expansion in the development of prewar Muranów significantly shaped
the appearance of the ghetto's streets. Especially within the "maze of small streets
and alleys" nestled into the larger arteries of the ghetto,[58] the increased height
of the buildings created a very narrow, at times even claustrophobic, impression.
Regulations concerning the building/street ratio also impacted the architectural profile of buildings. Martyn elaborates, "To avoid building higher than the
street's width, mansard roofs accommodating attic apartments became quite
popular; lateral buildings often turned out to be a storey higher than the facade
elevation, or the frontage was actually raised several metres back from the pavement."[59] All in all, the buildings of the prewar northern quarter were architecturally very heterogeneous. Especially in the late nineteenth century, development
was characterized by what Martyn calls "architectural anarchy,"[60] which led to
the coexistence of various different building types and architectural styles. Martyn points out "the chaotic, but picturesque diversity of the Warsaw streets" and,
in particular, the noticeable differences in height, creating what he calls Warsaw's
"characteristica[l] 'toothgap' profile."[61] Using, as an example, two photos of Solna
and Nowolipie Streets, Martyn identifies right next to each other "three building
types from three different eras. One-storey house with attic floor from the 1820s,
regular four-storey tenement housing from the 1880s and high rise (six-storey)
from the turn of the 19th and 20th centuries. Nowolipie Street in 1934 . . . a typical
'tooth-gap' street (Solna 1915) . . . resulting from different periods (late 18th century groundfloor wooden, one-storey brick building from 1820s, two-storey from
1840s and 1850s, three-four storey 1870–1890, five-six storey from 1890–1910)."[62]
    While many one- or two-story buildings had been replaced by multistory
tenement houses in the prewar years, in some parts of the ghetto such low-rise
buildings still existed, often made of wood and marking the northern quarter's

poorer, less developed sections. On the other side of the spectrum, but also associated with pauperization, were the large and crowded tenement houses (*Kamienica* in Polish, literally meaning brick or stone house). Gebert describes two such buildings, which had been part of the run-down and poor neighborhood of Krochmalna Street and which survived World War II: "The buildings on both eastern corners of Krochmalna at Żelazna are jarring. Although badly in need of restoration, they are still inhabited; they are also much taller than the apartment houses on Próżna. These were rent-producing tenements, the bane of penniless renters, and the source of landlords' fortunes."[63] From the 1850s onward, these tenement blocks, which typically consisted of a more representative front building, side wings, and a rear building, enclosing one or several interconnected courtyards, became very much defining for the northern quarter.[64]

In addition to the adjoining buildings' dimensions and orientation (vertical or horizontal), Mantho adds other architectural characteristics that define a street's appearance: "The final component of the street is the street wall, which forms the edge of the room of the street. The fundamental aspects of the street wall to consider are vertical definition, the relationship of the base to the room of the street, the characteristics of the facade above the base and the roofscape created by the top of the street wall."[65] Defining the street as a room—*nota bene*, one without a ceiling—Mantho stresses again the three-dimensional nature of the street and interprets the buildings as the streets' "walls." And indeed, for a pedestrian, the ratios between its different elements and the particular physiognomy of the buildings' facades, in a sense, become the face of the street. Various factors can determine a facade's appearance; it makes a huge difference, for example, if it is "simple, flat" or "highly detailed."[66] The size and distribution of windows, as well as of balconies—that is, the facade's "transparency" or "opacity," according to Mantho's terminology—also strongly influences the outside appearance of a building.[67] Mantho also emphasizes the importance the transitional space between street and buildings—the "base"—holds for a street. This includes, for example, the location of stairs, entrances, gates, doors, and so on, but also the material qualities of this section of the building. Here again, Warsaw's building structure was far from homogeneous; but all architectural diversity aside, the facades of most houses in the northern quarter were highly detailed and "richly decorated,"[68] yet not overly ornate. Close rows of windows and, quite frequently, also balconies (made from cast iron or stone) were typically embedded in a facade that was highly structured both horizontally and vertically, with architectural elements such as stone paneling, particularly in the base but also in the upper levels, cornices, arches, lesenes, pediments, and sometimes risalits shaping the front. There were often wide gates, doors, or passages to the buildings' interiors and yards. Especially in the many commercial streets of the quarter, shops and workshops took up the ground floor, and the dense rows of shop windows with their displays, entrance doors, lattices, and steps leading up to the doors defined the houses' base. This "mixed use of living and commerce" was quite typical for the buildings of the northern quarter and strongly influenced the streets' overall appearance.[69] Many of the ground-floor facades were also full of visual cues, "chockfull with signs" and advertisements in both Yiddish and Polish.[70] As Henryk Nagiel notes in *Tajemnice Nalewek* (*The Mysteries of Nalewki*) regarding the busy and lively Nalewki Street, "You will not be able to find on them a single meter of free wall space: there are shop signs everywhere."[71] Above the base—typically separated from the commercial ground floor by a cornice—a so-called "*bel étage*" was often located. Typical for turn-of-the-century townhouses, these prominent and more luxurious second-floor apartments (first floor by European measures), which provided comfortable street access and were heated indirectly from both above and below, were distinguished from the rest of the building by particularly large windows (reflective of the higher interior ceilings) and balconies, and by additional architectural ornaments such as segment or triangular pediments above the windows. Further up, one or more standard floors were followed by the attic floor—typically set off against the rest of the facade by another cornice—with considerably lower ceilings and smaller windows, intended to house personnel or low-income renters.

Streets and buildings in the ghetto intersected in many transitional spaces in which the inside and outside converged, such as the various passages, gateways, stairs, and doors opening up the buildings toward the streets and vice versa. Most prominently, however, streets and buildings met in the numerous courtyards, which were one of the most distinct architectural and social features of Warsaw's northern quarter and thus, also, the ghetto space. Aerial photos from 1935 clearly show that almost every building in Muranów included an inner yard. Some lay in the center of a single, rectangular building block (these courtyards were very tellingly called "*studnia*" by Varsovians—that is, "wells"); others were interconnected, at times spanning entire blocks—for example, in Nalewki Street.[72] These courtyards were important centers of Jewish Warsaw's sociality, and, as Isaac Bashevis Singer describes in his autobiographical account of prewar Warsaw, *In My Father's Court*, they were small microcosms of their own:

> No. 12 [Krochmalna Street] was like a city. It had three enormous courtyards. The dark entrance always smelled of freshly baked bread, rolls and bagels, caraway seed and smoke. Koppel the baker's yeasty breads were always outside, rising on boards. In No. 12 were also two Hasidic study houses, the Radzymin and Minsk, as well as a synagogue for those who opposed Hasidism. There was also a stall where cows were kept chained to the wall all year round. In some cellars, fruit had been stored by dealers from Mirowski Place; in others,

eggs were preserved in lime. Wagons arrived there from the provinces. No. 12 swarmed with Torah, prayer, commerce, and toil.[73]

Interconnected courtyards, such as the one Singer describes, were a central part of Jewish Warsaw's economic sphere as well, housing various businesses, shops, stalls, and markets, such as, for instance on Bagno Street, where there was a huge market for scrap metal, called *"Pociejów"* by Varsovians, which "spilled into the yard of the house at Bagno 2";[74] or at Nalewki Street, with its several court-yards and passages, harboring, in the case of house No. 20, multiple businesses, including "a hosiery studio, an apron workshop, a travel goods manufacturing workshop, a stocking shop, a yarn and cotton warehouse and a shop selling lace, ribbons and corset accessories."[75] The courtyards, at times, also created pas-sages between different streets, for example, at Zamenhofa and Nalewki Streets, which shared "courtyards with exits to each of the streets. These passages became channels through which flowed the stream of customers of Nalewki, residents of Zamenhofa Street";[76] or at Friedman's passage about which Bernard Singer writes in *Moje Nalewki* (*My Nalewki*), "I admired Friedman's passage in Świętojerska with access to Wałowa street. You could live there without going into the street. There were two houses of prayer, a shrine from Góra Kalwaria for Hasidic Jews, two cheders, a bakery, grocery stores, several eateries and cafes, a hotel and two institutions with a funny name 'furnished rooms.'"[77] The courtyards had their own social dynamics and hierarchies, often reflected in the particular space a person inhabited.[78]

The courtyards are a prime example of the multitude of threshold and transi-tional spaces within urban settlements that are positioned on a broad "spectrum from private to public," as Mantho points out.[79] These spaces exemplify the fact that street and building are by no means completely separated. Mantho, who conceptualizes the private/public divide primarily along the axis of property relations, access, and use, offers a technical categorization: "The terms used for differentiating these zones are: Private (PR), Semi-Private (SPR), Semi-Public (SP) and Public (P). Private space is controlled/owned space which requires permission to enter. Semi-Private space is related to a private space and accessible by a limited group via Private spaces. Semi-Public space is connected to Public space, but has socially discernible boundaries and can be occupied on a casual basis. Public space is shared space which is open to all users."[80]

The ghetto's courtyards created, depending on their use, a large set of addi-tional public, semipublic, and semiprivate spaces, and also, in some cases, offered alternative communication options between buildings and streets. In addition to classifying spaces within the house and its vicinity in terms of their status on the private/public spectrum, Mantho's description also highlights that buildings themselves are divided into zones with different functions to which different rules apply. While the private space of an apartment is space that is inhabited by a defined number of people and "requires permission to enter," other parts of the building, such as the staircase, the yard, or the entrance, are spaces of transition and access. Other spaces, such as attics or cellars used for storage, are commonly shared by the house community. These designations regulate the use of particular spaces within a building and define what kind of practices and sociality are associated with them. Within the ghetto, over time, all these various spaces within the buildings and their vicinity changed their function and use; the rules that used to apply to them were broken—sometimes by force, sometimes by necessity.

Streets and Buildings as Social Spaces

The fact that the Germans forced Jews into the ghetto heavily affected their social relations with the remaining Polish society, but it also had an extreme impact on interpersonal relationships inside the walls. Streets and buildings, which are both central sites of communal life and as such an arena in which a society negotiates its norms, values, and power relations, played a crucial role in this. Both spaces foster different types of relationships, interactions, and practices, and are associated with different paradigms. Consequently, the German spatial politics affected different aspects of sociality on the streets and in buildings.

As the "largest public space" in urban settlements,[81] streets and sidewalks are places of "constant encounter."[82] Streets thus become the arena of a broad spectrum of interactions and exchange, taking place between large numbers of people who are, more often than not, strangers to each other. In the ghetto, especially during the first phase of its existence, the number of people who were on the streets, and thus the amount of contact between strangers, was exponentiated. The northern quarter had been very busy and densely populated before the occupation; Isaac Bashevis Singer describes the lively crowds encountered on its streets in the opening pages of *The Family Moskat*: "The sidewalks were crowded with gaberdined Jews wearing small cloth caps, and bewigged women with shawls over their heads," "street peddlers called out their wares in ear piercing chants," "youngsters, their little lovelocks flapping under octagonal caps, were pouring out of the doors of the Hebrew schools," "the street was a bedlam of sound and activity."[83] This bustling liveliness, however, was nothing compared to the overcrowding the Germans produced within the ghetto walls. People's experience of the ghetto streets was thus first and foremost shaped by the inescapable presence of masses of other people. In his collection "Street Pictures from the Ghetto" written in March 1942, Stanisław Różycki describes what he calls "a sightseeing walk through the main artery" of the ghetto, from "Muranów through Dzika, Dzielna, Karmelicka, Leszno, Żelazna, Grzybowska, and Ciepła as far as Twarda—corner of Sienna," noting, "this is the most busy flume of the quarter through which tens of thousands of passers-by flow daily . . . you find yourself in a beehive or a wasp's nest—the hum, movement, bustle, and crush from all sides";[84] people were every-where, "congested, they tightly cover the whole sidewalk and part of the street."[85] Because there was not enough room, people constantly got in each other's way, and moving through the ghetto became very strenuous. The forced proximity turned the presence of others into a constant nuisance and created a nervous, anxious atmosphere on the streets. Różycki observes, "Virtually anything can trigger an argument, cursing, abuse, insults or violence."[86] Under the conditions of the ghetto, the overcrowding also posed very concrete risks, in terms of both epidemics and street safety. Before the Great Deportation *Aktion* changed the ghetto's layout and sociality to the core, almost all activities of day-to-day life took place on the streets—Różycki notes, the "center of life" moved "to the street."[87] This also meant that all components of the inhabitants' lives and their suffering manifested themselves in plain sight. Under the highly detrimental conditions of the ghetto, this caused a heavy strain on the ghetto society.

As central public spaces, streets play an important role in negotiating a soci-ety's definition of what is private and what is public, and, consequently, in ne-gotiating the question of which parts of life take place in which social sphere. A society's understanding of which behavior is appropriate for display in a pub-lic space, and which behavior is reserved for taking place inside one's own four walls, is clearly reflected on its streets. Stanford Anderson, who approaches the topic from the perspective of an architectural historian, elaborates, "[Streets] are the places where many of our conflicts or resolutions between public and private claims are accessed or actually played out; they are the arenas where the boundaries of conventional and aberrant behavior are frequently redrawn."[88] In the ghetto, due to the immense overcrowding and existential pressure, these boundaries were drastically shifted and renegotiated. The conditions created by the German occupiers were such that they challenged the preexisting norms of what behavior would or would not be acceptable in the public sphere. Hunger and existential need forced the poorest and most destitute people onto the streets and left them with neither the room nor the resources to adhere to previous standards of morality, piety, or shame. Różycki concludes, "A hungry person knows no other feelings except for the need to fulfill the hunger. The more hungry, the weaker their will, the weaker their moral brakes."[89]

Streets are deeply intertwined with social processes and cultural practices, and they are spaces in which individual and group identities are expressed and claims to public space are negotiated. Sig Langegger, as an urban design scholar, argues that streets are an "amalgam of cultural territories," which are "constantly shaped and reshaped by symbolic boundary work."[90] They are thus an arena in which a society negotiates its internal hierarchies and power relations. Streets, while in theory public spaces accessible to everyone, cannot be appropriated by everyone in the same way. In practice, in fact, streets usually reflect the power relations inherent to a society in that the extent to which an individual or group can establish themselves in public space correlates with their social standing and agency. A good example for the way representation in public space is linked with a group's position in a society is enclosed in the doctrine of the "Victorian separation of spheres."[91] The term is used to describe gender relations in Great Britain of the Victorian era, where female identity was relegated to domesticity and male identity linked to activities associated with the public sphere, such as political or economic participation. Malgorzata Fidelis elaborates, "Middle-class men worked for wages and conducted political activity in public, while middle-class women devoted their lives to the family and household."[92] This division entailed different levels of social agency but also defined male/female relations to and presence in the spaces representative of the public sphere, for example, the streets.[93] The Germans very explicitly linked social and spatial disenfranchisement, and their campaign against the Jews also entailed a process of otherizing them spatially. In fact, one of the first anti-Jewish measures the Germans implemented in occupied Warsaw was to actively contest the Jews' right to establish their presence in the public spaces of the city. Thereby, the Germans very clearly translated their racial ideology into spatial terms, as they ousted Jews physically, socially, and symbolically. Inside the ghetto as well, Jews—who were constantly threatened by abuse and acts of violence at the hands of the Germans stationed at the ghetto's walls, gates, and bridges and entering the ghetto to round up people for forced labor, to raid, rob, arrest, or execute them—could never feel entirely safe when moving about in the streets.

While streets are spaces of encounter and exchange,[94] the spaces of the residential building and the apartment are commonly characterized by their physically and culturally established boundaries against the intrusion of other people. Urban design scholar Ali Madanipour explains, "In the discussions about public and private spheres, the private sphere is often represented by private property, which is the historically established, spatial form of an individual's sphere of control. Through the control of its boundaries, individuals regulate their social interactions, and the balance between being on their own and being with others, both in space and in time."[95] Usually, private space accommodates smaller "social units," a "handful of people" living in "a close, intimate relationship," as Madanipour phrases it.[96] The space of the residential building or the apartment is, in this sense, "exclusive."[97] It implies the regulation of access, offering the individual "the ability to be let alone by being protected from the intrusion of others" outside the intimate group of cohabitants.[98] Within the framework of the residential building, individuals or small groups can "regulate the balance of concealment and exposure, the balance of access to oneself and communication with others."[99] The process of regulating access—and thus creating privacy—is repeated inside the living space. Both the house and the apartment are divided into zones of interaction and zones of increased privacy. Cultural boundaries and agreements regulate the relationship between the cohabitants, as well as to those visiting. Sociologist Tony Chapman elaborates, "Within the household, cultural boundaries are carefully preserved. Some are marked off by doors to delineate the 'front region' from the private 'back regions' of the house where people prepare themselves for view in the public front space, or food is prepared for serving in the public rooms."[100] Privately owned spaces thus create the framework for different forms of social interaction than found, for example, in the public space of the streets, following the paradigm of intimacy and privacy rather than that of encounter and exchange.

The home, ideally, protects and shields the individual, but it is also saturated with a person's identity work, their personal and emotional investments, and their self-expression. As a place of belonging, the home is an "affective space," Alison Blunt argues; it is "shaped by everyday practices, lived experiences, social relations, memories and emotions."[101] Therefore, people form strong attachments to it, and it plays an important role in regard to their individual as well as their social identity.[102] Both the affective attachment and the importance for identity formation extend to "houses, gardens, neighborhoods, and towns"[103] but also include the objects assembled in a person's private space. Chapman argues, "The objects of the household represent, at least potentially, the endogenous being of the owner. Although one has little control over the things encountered outside the home, household objects are chosen and could be freely discarded if they produced too much conflict within the self. Thus, household objects constitute an ecology of signs that reflects as well as shapes the pattern of the owner's self."[104]

A home, no matter the standard or form, is thus meaningful both in its function and in its affective attachments. As a result, it is vulnerable to violations on multiple levels, and its disintegration is experienced as highly destabilizing and hurtful.

In the ghetto, the experience of having a "home"—a place reserved for one's intimate relationships, a place to materially and affectively situate one's identity and tokens of one's personal history, a place that promises protection against intrusion—was eroded on multiple levels. Right from the beginning, many Jews lost their homes when the Germans forcefully resettled them to the ghetto. But even people who could (at first) stay where they had lived before were confronted with a new social reality that undermined the experience of privacy and intimacy, as well as their sense of safety and protection. Cultural practices of regulating one's exposure to others—be it protecting oneself against intrusion from outside or regulating contact within the limitations of one's own living space—did not hold anymore. As a consequence of the immense overpopulation that the Germans created within the walls, people who had no intimate relationships with each other (and possibly very little in common) were forced into very close cohabitation. The large number of people compelled to share their living space led to a constant overstepping of one another's boundaries. This was aggravated further by the fact that everyone was facing countless daily hardships and existential threats. Privacy (and thus also intimacy) was essentially made impossible because of the constant presence of people who were not themselves considered part of a person's intimate circle. These (oftentimes temporary) living arrangements held significant potential for conflict. In addition, private space in the ghetto was continuously compromised by encroachments at the hands of the Germans and their auxiliaries, who entered residential buildings to carry out confiscations, raids, arrests, and executions. Disregarding cultural and physical boundaries that would protect an individual from intrusion, their arbitrary entry to people's living spaces shattered any residual notion of safety a person might have associated with the private space of their "home."[105]

Notes

1. Leociak, *Text in the Face of Destruction*, 48.
2. Mehta, *Street*, 1.
3. Ellis, "Spatial Structure of Streets," 115.
4. Martyn, "Undefined Town within a Town," 24–25; see also Grime and Węcławowicz, "Warsaw," 261; Dziewulski and Jankowski, "Reconstruction of Warsaw," 210.
5. Bauman, *Winter in the Morning*, 66, 82.
6. Grime and Węcławowicz, "Warsaw," 262.
7. Martyn, "Undefined Town within a Town," 32.
8. Berg, *Diary*, 122.
9. Mehta, *Street*, 1.
10. Lynch, *Image of the City*, 47.
11. Berg, *Diary*, 117.
12. Mazor, *Vanished City*, 118.
13. Czarnowski, "Street as a Communications Artifact," 207.
14. The postal service was organized by the *Judenrat* and functioned only with restrictions. Communication with the outside world underlay censorship and the service was deemed by the ghetto inhabitants to be expensive and unreliable (Engelking and Leociak, *Warsaw Ghetto*, 367, 369, 378). The scope of the postal service became

very limited after the Great Deportation *Aktion* but was officially kept up until April 1943. Private and business-owned telephones, although not great in number, also remained in operation until the ghetto's "liquidation" (Meed, *On Both Sides of the Wall*, 141). From January 1942 onward, public telephones were mostly disconnected; for the remaining ones, high fees were charged (Engelking and Leociak, *Warsaw Ghetto*, 371–372).

15.   See, for example, Ringelblum, *Notes from the Warsaw Ghetto*, 133; Lewin, *Cup of Tears*, 98. According to Vladka Meed's testimony, the Germans "cut off the supply of water and electricity" during the Ghetto Uprising (*On Both Sides of the Wall*, 151).

16.   Gutman, *Jews of Warsaw*, 26.

17.   See, for example, Meed, *On Both Sides of the Wall*, 96, 101, 141.

18.   See, for example, Lubetkin, *Letzten Tage*, 24–34.

19.   Although it has to be noted that Gentiles also found ways to circumvent the German regulations, quite often, as Opoczynski reveals, out of economic interest. In his reportage "Goyim in the Ghetto," Opoczynski describes the lively trade going on before the sealing of the ghetto with "hordes of goyim descend[ing] on the Jew-ish flea markets, bazaars and business streets," when "trade was booming, and Poles were happy to make deals with Jews" (55). In the transition period, when Jews were already prohibited from leaving the ghetto, but Gentiles could still enter "with special passes" (or by bribing their way in), Opoczynski diagnoses "the goy becomes THE ONLY SOURCE OF A LIVELIHOOD," as Jews themselves for the most part ceased to buy merchandise, but the Gentiles would "exploit the opportunity and buy at rock-bottom prices" (ibid., 59). Especially during the early days of the ghetto, Gentiles would con-tinue to make their way into the ghetto, very simply because the profit margins were extremely high. Economic interest and opportunism fostered social connections, as Opoczynski observes, "If you're looking for some higher value to this buying and selling, then you can find it only in THE BRIDGE that has appeared between the Jew and the Gentile. It is a bridge built out of bad material: speculation. But it has a good purpose: to keep a large part of the Jewish population from starving to death" (ibid., 70). In his groundbreaking study on Jews going into hiding on the "Aryan" side of Warsaw, Paulsson draws attention also to the wide network of connections that had to exist to allow Jews to successfully evade the Germans by hiding on the "Aryan" side of the city. These clandestine networks required a large number of non-Jewish Poles to assist those in hiding, at least temporarily. According to Paulsson's research, the necessary connections between Jews and Gentiles could be roughly categorized in three groups: first, "Jewish assimilants and converts" who "generally had longstand-ing personal, professional and often family contacts with the Polish milieu"; second, Jewish and non-Jewish Poles who "formed their contacts during the ghetto period, mainly through illegal trade"; and last, Jewish and non-Jewish "activists, whose con-nections were mainly institutional, through fraternal political parties or social orga-nizations" (*Secret City*, 26). Some of the connections forged out of economic interest thus also proved useful for the Jewish resistance and helped Jews escape from the

ghetto, as the already established contacts and routes could be used for "smuggling people and arms" (ibid., 61).

20. Ellis, "Spatial Structure of Streets," 117.

21. Mantho, *Urban Section*, 76.

22. Ibid., 57.

23. Ibid., 76.

24. Ibid., 57.

25. Ibid., 76.

26. Ibid., 75.

27. Ibid., 232.

28. Lynch, *Image of the City*, 4.

29. Ibid., 4.

30. Ibid., 8, 46–49.

31. Ibid., 6.

32. Ibid., 47.

33. Janusz Korczak was the pen name of Henryk Goldzmit (Goldszmit), a renowned Jewish writer, pediatrician, and educator. For a short biographical note, see the section "Biographies" in the appendix.

34. Kaplan, *Scroll of Agony*, 210.

35. Lynch, *Image of the City*, 47.

36. Ibid.

37. The term "wild," which is commonly used in secondary sources, goes back to the Polish "*dziki*," which, in the context at hand, can also mean "unlisted" or "unauthorized."

38. Lynch, *Image of the City*, 7.

39. Ibid., 47.

40. Kostański, *Janek*, 21, 32, 37.

41. Ibid., 23. In his reportage "Smuggling in the Warsaw Ghetto" from October 1941, Opoczynski describes a similar spatial setting at Koźla Street, which was part of the ghetto until the Germans excluded it in December 1941. Until then, on the even-numbered side of Koźla, some buildings had been inhabited by Jews, while others had been inhabited by non-Jews. The doors to these "Aryan" buildings had been "walled up" and their entrances were "on the other side of the wall, on Freta Street, meaning outside the ghetto"; the buildings' windows were "secured from top to bottom with wire grates" ("Smuggling in the Warsaw Ghetto," 75). The layout of Koźla, as Opoczynski points out, was a "blessing" for the Jews in the ghetto, because it created opportunities for smuggling (ibid.). Rye was poured down "chutes" from inside the "Aryan" buildings, shooting "through the grate right into the sack held up to the other end of the [wooden] trough by the Jewish smuggler in Koźla alley below" (ibid., 76). "Cereal, millet, sugar, and other foods [were] smuggled in the same way," as Opoczynski explains. "Only flour [got] smuggled in paper bags . . . passed through the windows of the upper floors" and lowered down from the Polish side on a rope (ibid.). Opoczynski reports that even milk is smuggled to the ghetto through

the windows of Koźla street, poured through a "thick tube with a measuring gauge" (ibid., 77).

42. Kostański, *Janek*, 21.
43. Ibid., 23.
44. Ibid., 37.
45. Ibid., 39–42.
46. Ibid., 24–28, 32–33, 35, 39–42.
47. Lynch, *Image of the City*, 3.
48. Ibid., 4.
49. Ibid., 6.
50. Till, "Wounded Cities," 10.
51. Engelking and Leociak, *Warsaw Ghetto*, 315.
52. Mehta, *Street*, 12.
53. Ellis, "Spatial Structure of Streets," 117.
54. Shachar, "Feeling/Filling Void."
55. Martyn, "Undefined Town within a Town," 24.
56. Ibid., 32–33. Toward the south, this process had already started a bit earlier: "Along Chłodna, Elektoralna, Ogrodowa, Grzybowska and the Leszno," development had mostly been concluded by the mid-nineteenth century. "From the 1870s onwards," some of the "older, especially wooden, building[s]" were replaced by tenement blocks; the hitherto "undeveloped Łucka, Sienna, Śliska and Pańska streets received relatively regular three- and four-storey properties in the 1890s." Here also, the vertical development trend could be observed; before World War I, "the number of groundfloor structures (1,500) was barely half the figure recorded in 1882, while three or four storey tenement housing accounted for almost 50 per cent of the total registered property" (Martyn, "Undefined Town within a Town," 35).
57. Mantho, *Urban Section*, 234.
58. Gebert, "Reading the Palimpsest," 227.
59. Martyn, "Undefined Town within a Town," 24.
60. Ibid., 24, 30.
61. Ibid., 25.
62. Ibid. (without pagination).
63. Gebert, "Reading the Palimpsest," 232.
64. Martyn, "Undefined Town within a Town," 24.
65. Mantho, *Urban Section*, 82.
66. Ibid., 239.
67. Ibid.
68. Martyn, "Undefined Town within a Town," 24.
69. Shachar, "Feeling/Filling Void."
70. Gebert, "Reading the Palimpsest," 227; see also Kajczyk, "Nalewki," 33–34.
71. Qtd. in Engelking and Leociak, *Warsaw Ghetto*, 12.
72. Shachar, "Feeling/Filling Void"; Kajczyk, "Nalewki," 31.
73. Singer, *In My Father's Court*, 190–191.

74. Majewski, "Uzbiegu Bagna, Wielkiej, Świętokrzyskiej." Translation by Bożena Karwowska and A. N. The Polish original reads as follows: "*Na podwórko domu przy Bagnie 2 rozlewał się Pociejów.*"

75. Kajczyk, "Nalewki," 31.

76. Zonszajn, "Ulica Dzika-Zamenhofa." Translation by Bożena Karwowska and A. N. The Polish original reads as follows: "*Zamenhofa biegła równolegle do Nalewek, była jej najbliższą sąsiadką. Obie ulice łączyły wspólne podwórka z wyjściami na każdą z nich. Przejścia te stały się kanałami, którymi płynął strumień nalewkowskich klientów, mieszkańców ulicy Zamenhofa.*"

77. Qtd. in "About Nalewki Street talks dr Rafał Żebrowski."

78. Beautiful portraits of prewar Warsaw's courtyards can be found in Abraham Teitelbaum's *Warschauer Innenhöfe*—in the Yiddish original: *Warszewer haif. Mentšn un gešeenišn*.

79. Mantho, *Urban Section*, 236, see also 245.

80. Ibid., 236.

81. Langegger, *Rights to Public Space*, 118; Mehta, *Street*, 8.

82. Mehta, *Street*, 7.

83. Singer, *Family Moskat*, 5–6.

84. "Orientalna egzotyka" ("Oriental Exoticism") 456. RING. I/429. Translation by Bożena Karwowska and A. N. The translation and the following ones are based on the original archival document and on personal transcripts by Jacek Leociak. The Polish original reads as follows: "*Wybrałem sięępiękne południe na spacer krajoznawczy poprzez głównąłarterięrdzielnicy. Od Muranowa przez DzikąziDzielnąziK armelickąarLeszno, ŻelaznąęGrzybowskąrzCiepłąiażżGdTwardej—rogu Siennej—to najruchliwsze koryto dzielnicy, przez które przewala sięicodziennie dziesiątki tysięcy przechodni. Pierwsze wrażenie—to jakbyś sięiznalazł w ulu czy gnieździe os: szum, ruch, rwetes, ściski, ze wszech [s]tron oblepiająbsięidookoła ciebie.*" To specify and facilitate orientation, subchapter headings are given in brackets for each quote. This text is also translated in Person, *Warsaw Ghetto. Everyday Life. The Ringelblum Archive*, Vol. I, 35.

85. Różycki, "Street. July 1942," 61.

86. Ibid., 56.

87. "Orientalna egzotyka" ("Oriental Exoticism") 456. RING. I/429. Translation by Bożena Karwowska and A. N. The Polish original reads as follows: "*przeniesienie punktu ciężkości życia na ulicę.*" This text is also translated in Person, *Warsaw Ghetto. Everyday Life. The Ringelblum Archive*, Vol. I, 35.

88. Anderson, "People in the Physical Environment," 1.

89. "Samosąd" ("Lynching") 456. RING. I/429. Translation by Bożena Karwowska and A. N. The Polish original reads as follows: "*Człowiek głodny nie zna żadnych uczuć poza chęcią zaspokojenia głodu. Im głodniejszy, tym słabsza wola, tym luźniejsze hamulce moralne.*" This text is also translated in Person, *Warsaw Ghetto. Everyday Life. The Ringelblum Archive*, Vol. I, 43.

90. Langegger, *Rights to Public Space*, 126.

91. Fidelis, "'Participation in the Creative Work of the Nation,'" 111.

92. Ibid. While descriptive of a particular historical setting, the "separation of spheres" can be used to describe gendered experiences and access to space in a variety of different societies. Fidelis emphasizes that the private/public divide in Poland was heavily influenced by the country's history of partitions, when the public sphere had been controlled "by a hostile state" (just as it would be again during the German occupation) and the home became the "bastion" for upholding national identity (ibid.); yet, also in Poland, male and female presence on the streets was still shaped by different gender roles and expectations and closely tied to the private/public divide.

93. Gender roles and expectations also impacted people's behavior during the German occupation. In their introduction to *Women in the Holocaust*, Dalia Ofer and Lenore J. Weitzman call attention to the fact that especially in the early days of German occupation, Jewish women were seen much more often in the streets than their male family members. Early on, the Jewish community had developed gender-specific strategies based on the assumption that "the Germans were 'civilized' and would honor traditional gender norms," expecting that they "would not harm women and children" (Ofer and Weitzman, *Women in the Holocaust*, 5). Part of the communities' "anticipatory reactions" involved a focus on men when it came to migration, escape, and hiding (ibid.), but they also applied to questions of safety within the city: "Testimonies and ghetto diaries also attest to the ways in which the anticipation of German behavior shaped everyday life in the cities and ghettos in Eastern Europe. Because Jewish men, especially those with long beards, earlocks, and traditional orthodox clothing, were so easy to identify and target for harassment, many families decided that it was safer for the women to go out in the streets—even before the ghettos were formed" (ibid., 5–6). Initially, the fear of violence was gendered, and due to this, female presence on the street increased. This also led to a new distribution of responsibilities, reinforcing the role of women especially in their interaction with the occupiers (ibid., 6).

94. Mehta, *Street*, 7.

95. Madanipour, *Public and Private Spaces of the City*, 46.

96. Ibid., 62.

97. Ibid., 61; Blomley, "Law, Property, and the Geography of Violence," 130.

98. Madanipour, *Public and Private Spaces of the City*, 61.

99. Ibid.

100. Chapman, "Spoiled Home Identities," 135.

101. Blunt, "Cultural Geography," 506.

102. See, for example, Chapman, "Spoiled Home Identities," 133–134, 137; Duncan and Lambert, "Landscapes of Home," 387.

103. Duncan and Lambert, "Landscapes of Home," 388.

104. Chapman, "Spoiled Home Identities," 135.

105. Interestingly, as Bożena Shallcross points out in her introduction to *Framing the Polish Home: Postwar Cultural Constructions of Hearth, Nation, and Self*, in

the Polish language, the material building and the concept of home even coincide linguistically. She writes, "Home interpreted through its architectural framework is a house—the semantic distinction that is absent in the Polish language, where the single word *dom* signifies both a home and a house: a place where one belongs as well as its material embodiment, a mortar-and-brick building" ("Introduction," 2).

PART II

THE MAKING OF A VIOLENT SPACE

Introduction

The Making of a Violent Space

In his study *Holocaust City: The Making of a Jewish Ghetto*, Cole points out that "ghettoization was, in part at least, an act of urban planning."[1] With this observation, Cole emphasizes that the creation of the ghetto, in addition to being an integral part of the Nazis' genocidal agenda, was also an active and premeditated reorganization of urban space. In the case of Warsaw, by establishing the ghetto right in the middle of the grown, well-functioning structure of the city, the German administration—as an agent of the Nazi state—produced an oppressive and dysfunctional spatial environment that massively impacted the lives of Jews. Ghettoization, in general, was an example of what Guy Miron, in reference to Lefebvre, describes as the "production of space by a hegemonic power" that shapes "the lives of those subordinate to it."[2] The Nazis' interventions drastically changed the functioning of the urban structure of Warsaw but also affected the relationship between Jews and non-Jews and between Jews and their environment. Not only did the German administration "declar[e]—and enforc[e]—where people could and could not go, where and how they could or could not live,"[3] their actions also drastically reorganized how the Jewish population related to the city, to their Gentile neighbors, and to each other, how they were able to organize themselves internally and under what conditions they would live (and die).

Implementing the ghetto was in and of itself a sociospatial practice. It entailed the mapping out of a certain territory, the erection of fences and walls, large-scale resettlement, the regulation of entering and exiting, and the enforcement of the ghetto's boundaries—that is, acts of exercising "territoriality," as Cole suggests.[4] Moreover, ghettoization was driven by a specific agenda concerning space—that is, it was part of a comprehensive, ideologically rooted reorganization of space along racial criteria. The Nazi leadership strived to implement this racial/spatial reorganization both on a macro level (i.e., geopolitically, shifting entire populations) and on a micro level (i.e., locally, on-site). In the case of the Warsaw ghetto, the reshaping of social and spatial coordinates was carried out within the grid of the urban environment. It was based on the principle of racial segregation, following the ideological assumption that living space should be homogeneous according to the Nazis' ideological conceptualization of "race." By outlining a spatially oriented history of the Nazi ghetto in occupied Warsaw, I trace out, in the following chapters, the process by which the German administration introduced and gradually implemented this radical "racialization" of urban space. In doing so, these chapters shed light on the question of how exactly the Germans created the particular space of the ghetto and outline in detail how it was in a continuous state of change due to their evolving anti-Jewish policies and actions, furthering spatial segregation as well as social, cultural, and economic exclusion. These elements are taken as important factors in a ghettoization process that culminated in, but was not limited to, the establishment of a concrete, physical ghetto.

The ghetto's space was produced by two elements (and their interactions): by the characteristics of its physical topography, such as its layout, its size, the course of its borders and streets, the exclusion or inclusion of territory, the condition of its buildings, their architecture, the amount of greenery and open space, and so on, and by social practices, such as the Nazis' overarching ghetto policies and regulations and the behavior and actions of both the ghetto inhabitants and the various Nazi agents on-site. These social practices encompassed both "macro-scale policies" and "everyday routines"[5] and imbued the physical construction that was the ghetto with its particular meaning(s), at the same time defining the ghetto as an instrument of marginalization and violation but also as a space of Jewish "place-making," struggle, and resistance.[6] In particular, the Nazis' escalating anti-Jewish policies and practices strongly affected to what degree (and how) people could actually live in the ghetto. It is for this reason that consolidating and probing into known facts and details on boundary control, on acts of humiliation and physical assault, on round-ups, raids, confiscations, executions, and deportations, as well as information on the general living conditions in the ghetto, is a crucial process for our understanding of the violent space the Germans created for their victims. Making visible the particular configurations of physical space and social practices helps illuminate what kind of space the ghetto was, how it marginalized and victimized its inhabitants, and how, from the very beginning, it was a space adverse to Jewish lives.

Both the functions and the ways in which its inhabitants experienced the Warsaw ghetto changed drastically during the three and a half years of its existence. Firm orientation in its historical development is a key prerequisite to understanding its structures and the experiences of its inhabitants. As Stephan

Lehnstaedt summarizes in his study "Jewish Spaces? Defining Nazi Ghettos Then and Now," "The many 'reasons' to gather Jews transformed during the course of time, and so did the functions, size—that is, their boundaries and the number of their inmates—and conditions of ghettos. . . . Whether these areas were places of exploitation or of forced labor, starving and dying zones, collection areas before deportation, or slave labor institutions after 1942, made all the difference."[7]

The functions the ghetto held for the German occupiers, in turn, strongly affected how space was managed and regulated and thus experienced by those who were forced into it. Following this logic, there was in fact not one ghetto space but, over time, multiple different spaces. Often a shift in the German anti-Jewish agenda or developments in the German war efforts would translate into a very drastic reorganization of the ghetto space, both physically and socially. By rendering visible the various functions and changing configurations of the ghetto space, *Violent Space* illustrates that the ghetto space was not constant but in perpetual flux.

Notes

1. Cole, *Holocaust City*, 2.
2. Miron, "'Lately, Almost Constantly, Everything Seems Small to Me,'" 123.
3. Knowles, Cole, and Giordano, *Geographies of the Holocaust*, 3.
4. Cole, "Ghettoization," 82.
5. Gieseking et al., "Editors' Introduction and Suggestions," 285.
6. Lipphardt, Brauch, and Nocke, "Introduction," 2.
7. Lehnstaedt, "Jewish Spaces?" 49.

CHAPTER

5

Jews in Prewar Warsaw

Before the Germans invaded Warsaw in September 1939, the city had been home to the second-largest Jewish community in the world and had been the richest and most vibrant center of Jewish life in Europe. The city had a long history of Jewish settlement and economic involvement, dating back to the mid-fourteenth century and, by the end of the twentieth century, had become an important artistic and cultural center of the Jewish diaspora, with an "incredibly rich intellectual life reflected in numerous political organizations, religious groups, Yiddish, Hebrew, German and Polish language newspapers, journals, publishing firms and so on."[1] With its culturally, religiously, and politically diverse Jewish population, it was, as Glenn Dynner and François Guesnet put it in their anthology of the same title, a veritable "Jewish metropolis."[2]

An enclosed Jewish quarter, however—as existed, for example, in Kraków[3]— had never developed in Warsaw. While there were parts of Warsaw that were very densely populated by Jewish Poles, these areas largely remained permeable and connected to the rest of the city. The explanation for this lies in the fact that Jewish settlement in Warsaw had been defined by the principle of exclusion rather than confinement. Over the centuries, Jewish presence in particular streets, quarters, or the entire city had been prohibited many times, but there had never been any strict regulations dictating where Jews had to live.

The history of the Jewish community in Warsaw encompasses struggles from the very beginning. Jews were repeatedly expelled from the city—for instance in 1455, 1483, and 1498—marking not only the Gentile's determination to exclude the Jewry but also Jews' habitual return to the city. In 1527, the Catholic inhabitants of Warsaw were granted the privilege *de non tolerandis Judaeis*, and Jews were banished from the city once more. In August 1570, this privilege was renewed again by King Zygmunt, who also "demarcated a two-mile buffer zone around the city that was to be free of Jewish residence and trade."[4] Referring to Hanna Węgrzynek's research, it is possible to see a constant push and pull between two opposing tendencies: while the Gentile population continuously strove to retain the ban on Jewish settlement, "Warsaw Jews, for their part, made consistent efforts to have the law lifted or to evade it one way or another."[5] Even during times when Jewish presence in the city was temporarily allowed or when individual exceptions were made, there were usually restrictions on the areas in which Jewish residency was allowed, and Jews were subjected to special taxes or fees; further, restrictions on trade or the guilds' efforts to limit Jewish economic involvement indirectly limited the scope of the spaces that Jews could use and inhabit. Recurring incidents of anti-Jewish violence made Jews further hesitant to settle among the Gentile population.[6] Still, the Jewish population of Warsaw kept growing throughout the centuries as the city was an "important political and commercial center," which was highly attractive to businesses and new inhabitants.[7]

One of the effects of the history of these expulsions from the city, and specifically from its center, was a predominant settlement of Jews in the Praga district on the right bank of the Vistula River. Praga had been an independent settlement for a long time and was incorporated into the city of Warsaw only by the end of the eighteenth century. As such, the district had been subject to different regulations and had therefore served as an alternative settlement option, particularly in the second half of the eighteenth century when Praga was specifically "exempted from the *de non tolerandis Judaeis* law."[8] On the initiative of Szmul Zbytkower, a Jewish merchant who encouraged Jewish settlement in the district, in the late eighteenth and early nineteenth centuries, the Jewish community built a cemetery and a synagogue in Praga.[9] For a long time, the Praga district was characterized by its rural character, dominated by trade and small-scale manufacturing. It was only in the late nineteenth century, when the entire city experienced a burst of economic growth, that the district became more industrialized.[10] Due to its comparably dense Jewish settlement, in early 1940 the German administration briefly considered Praga as a potential location for the ghetto. By the end of the war, the quarter was not destroyed by the Germans as the remainder of the city was because the Soviet army had held out on the right-hand side of the Vistula during the Warsaw Uprising.[11] Consequently, unlike the rest of the city, architectural reminders of the Jewish past can still be found in Praga. Also, most of Jewish postwar life resorted to this district.[12]

During the Third Partition of Poland, an independent Polish state did not exist. In a gesture to regain independence, Poles supported the Napoleonic War. And, indeed, with the Duchy of Warsaw (1807–1815), Napoleon I partly reinstated Polish sovereignty.[13] The French Revolution had brought the emancipation of

Jews, and Napoleon implemented the same policies in all conquered territories, granting full citizen rights to Warsaw's Jewry as well.[14] Limitations on their settlement, however, were never fully revoked and remained formative for the development of a second center of Jewish residency in the central northern regions of the city. Engelking and Leociak explain, "The key event in the formation of the future Jewish district was a decree by Frederick Augustus, the Saxon king of Poland and grand duke of Warsaw, dated 16 March 1809. He ordered the Jews to leave the city center because their overcrowding in this area was supposed to have brought a danger of fires and was a health hazard. In the decree areas were named (what were termed 'precluded' streets) in which it was forbidden for Jews to live or trade."[15]

Defining Jewish presence *ex negativo*, Frederick Augustus's decree designated certain streets as barred to Jewish settlement, which, conversely, implied that the rest of the city was left open for Jewish appropriation. Limitations on settlement specifically did not apply to Jews who were "sufficiently 'Europeanized,'"[16] making assimilation the precondition for the right to choose one's residency freely. The restrictions issued for the majority of the Jewish community led to the crystallization of a densely populated Jewish area in the northern parts of the city, mainly in the so-called Muranów district and parts of the neighboring areas to the south, including Grzybowski Square and Krochmalna Street.[17] In the course of the nineteenth century, the now predominantly Jewish Muranów developed from a "semi-rural backwater into a lively, populous new district."[18] The quarter, at that time, primarily housed a Jewish community that would be categorized today as lower middle class. It was, however, not an "industrialised, proletarian district" but rather shaped by small-scale factories and manufacturing businesses, with an emphasis on the textile and leather-working trade.[19] To the north, the area was limited by the citadel, which was built and fortified between 1836 and 1854, thus blocking further expansion of Jewish settlement and forcing hundreds of Jewish families to relocate from this particular territory. To the west, the so-called Lubomirskie Ramparts, erected in 1770, marked the limits of possible expansion. Due to these limitations, Jewish settlement generally expanded toward the south and—quite important to note—upward, leading over time to the erection of more and more multistory buildings in the northern district.[20] When the ban on settlement in the "precluded streets" was lifted in June 1862, the patterns of Jewish residency did not change much: "Despite the lack of legal bans on place of residence, the Jewish population chose areas where their coreligionists lived, creating ever more dense concentrations of settlement."[21]

The Jewish population in the northern district was highly "differentiated" and heterogeneous in its makeup.[22] The Jews of Warsaw "comprised not one but

several worlds," with a plethora of different lifestyles, corresponding to varying degrees of "assimilation and acculturation" and differences in "language,
dress, religious practice, and social customs."[23] This diversity also profoundly
shaped the Jewish living environment. Leociak characterizes the densely populated northern district: "[Warsaw's Jews] associate everything that was Jewish in
Warsaw with it. The streets and alleyways, apartment houses and courtyards, the
distinctive atmosphere, the unique local color, and the one-of-a-kind multilingual
hubbub. Jewish Warsaw was a microcosm of its own. It contained an infinite variety of forms and aspects of life, it held enormous contrasts in wealth and customs,
and was a singular example of a city within a city."[24]

These differences, and especially those concerning the economic situation of
an individual, were often reflected in the location and the conditions of people's
respective living quarters, following the logic that social space (i.e., the social,
often hierarchical positions of individuals in relation to one another) is projected
onto physical space.[25] "Various gradations of wealth could be noted," but, for the
most part, the living conditions in the Jewish neighborhood were rather poor,
not least because of high population density.[26] According to Engelking and Leociak's extensive study of the area, Muranów was characterized by a "high housing density," "overcrowding," and "poverty."[27] The works of writers such as Isaak
Bashevis Singer paint a vivid picture of the quarter's busy life.[28] Singer was one
of the many contemporary Yiddish writers who gave expression to Jewish life and
culture, using the very language that also permeated the prewar Jewish streets
of Warsaw.[29]

Although the Jewish population of Warsaw had by no means been free in its
use of space before the German occupation, it is crucial to mark the differences
between the historically developed dense settlement of Jews in the Muranów
(and Praga) area and the Jewish ghetto the Germans established in 1940. With the
establishment of the ghetto, the Nazis, for the first time in the history of Warsaw,
defined spatial restraints such that they specified where Jews could live rather
than where they could not, forcefully establishing not only "Jewish absence" but
a clearly defined and strictly guarded location for "Jewish presence" as well.[30]
Engelking and Leociak underscore that early expulsions from the city, such as the
non tolerandis law or the "precluded streets" principle, in fact contained a latent
exception to the rule "'you can't live there,'" suggesting that Jews "could live anywhere else."[31] This means that there was still room for spatial self-determination.
By contrast, the Nazi ghetto was defined by the principle "'you can live here and
only here.'"[32] This restriction was, by far, more radical and exclusionary in nature.
It is also important to keep in mind that prior exclusions, such as the "precluded
streets" decree, applied only to Jewish settlement; it did not necessarily restrict
freedom of movement within the city.[33] Jews could not locate the centers of their

private life in the "precluded streets," but they still had access to them as part of the shared public space.[34] Contestation of spatial appropriation did not translate into absolute exclusion from the shared urban environment. The ghetto established by the Nazis, however, "excluded [Jewish people] from the urban space" altogether.[35] Generally, the boundaries of the areas in which Jewish settlement was concentrated in prewar Warsaw were still very much permeable: assimilated Jews lived among the Gentile population, and, as evidenced by the extent of resettlement of non-Jewish people during the establishment of the ghetto, many Gentiles lived in the northern district as well. While, in many senses, non-Jewish and Jewish Poles lived in "different geographies" as Konstanty Gebert notes, the two populations were not fully segregated.[36] Instead, as Engelking and Leociak highlight, "exchange and meetings were still taking place" quite naturally.[37] The processes connected with the establishment of the ghetto, however, drastically changed and had a long-lasting impact on the relationships between Jewish and non-Jewish Varsovians.

Even within restrictive settings, in prewar Warsaw the Jewish appropriation of space had never been fully controlled. Most crucially, before the Wannsee Conference of January 1942, when the "Final Solution" was officially ratified by the Nazi leadership, spatial segregation and control had never been coupled with an explicit genocidal agenda. Even when the ways in which the available space was delineated and divided were highly disadvantageous to Jewish inhabitants of the city, and, in many instances, reflected antisemitic attitudes, those spatial arrangements were not linked to a negation of the right to live. As Mazor puts it in his postwar recollections, *The Vanished City*, where he compares the Warsaw ghetto to its historic predecessors, "The medieval ghettos still represented a form of life—one organized, it is true, at a remove from the world. In the twentieth century, especially in Warsaw, the ghetto was no longer anything but an organized form of death—a 'little death chest' (*Todeskästchen*), as it was called by one of the German sentries posted at its gates."[38]

Notes

1. Martyn, "Undefined Town within a Town," 31.

2. For additional information on Jewish Warsaw before the war, see, for example, Dynner and Guesnet, "Introduction," 9–14; Engelking and Leociak, *Warsaw Ghetto*, 13–24; or Löw and Roth, *Das Warschauer Getto*, 9–10.

3. Kazimierz, the city's prominent Jewish quarter, had formerly been a neighboring town to Krakòw. In the late fifteenth century, Kazimierz became a major center of Jewish settlement. Its Jewish community was self-governed, and by the seventeenth century the Jewish settlement was separated from the Gentile population by a wall. The walled-in Jewish quarter was henceforth termed "Oppidum Judaeorum—the

Jewish town" (Jakimyszyn, "Jewish Community in Kraków and Kazimierz," 58). In the late eighteenth century, Kazimierz was incorporated into the city of Kraków (ibid., 58–59, 61; see also Rodov, *Torah Ark in Renaissance Poland*, 5–6, 14–19).

4. Dynner and Guesnet, "Introduction," 4.

5. Węgrzynek, "Illegal Immigrants," 23. In fact, according to Węgrzynek, over the years the *non tolerandis* privilege was confirmed again by several Polish kings: "Stefan Batory in 1580; Zygmunt III in 1609; Władysław IV in 1636 and 1648; Jan Kazimierz in 1667; Jan Sobieski III in 1693; and August II in 1699" (ibid., 22–23). Still, Węgrzynek also shows that even while the "*non tolerandis Judaeis* law was in force," there was "an enormous, underground Jewish community in Warsaw" (ibid., 20).

6. For details on the early expulsions and the *non tolerandis* law see, for example, Dynner and Guesnet, "Introduction," 3–4; Węgrzynek, "Illegal Immigrants," 20–23; Martyn, "Undefined Town within a Town," 26; Bergman et al., *1,000 Years of Jewish Life in Poland*, 4; Engelking and Leociak, *Warsaw Ghetto*, 3–4; or Rubinstein, Dombrowska, and Krakowski, "Warsaw," 666. For details on economic exclusion and anti-Jewish violence, see Węgrzynek, "Illegal Immigrants," 22; Löw and Roth, *Das Warschauer Getto*, 10.

7. Rubinstein, Dombrowska, and Krakowski, "Warsaw," 666; see also Dynner and Guesnet, "Introduction," 4. For information on Jewish settlement in Warsaw during the Third Partition, see, for example, Gutman, *Jews of Warsaw*, xiv; Engelking and Leociak, *Warsaw Ghetto*, 4; Dynner and and Guesnet, "Introduction," 5; and Martyn, "Undefined Town within a Town," 27–28.

8. Bergman et al., *1,000 Years of Jewish Life in Poland*, 6; for more information on Jewish settlement in Praga see, for example, Martyn, "Undefined Town within a Town," 17, 27–28; or Engelking and Leociak, *Warsaw Ghetto*, 5–7. For a detailed history of the Praga district, see Dylewski, *Ruda, Córka Cwiego*. The references in *Violent Space* are to the ebook edition, but the book is also available in print (page numbers might differ).

9. Martyn, "Undefined Town within a Town," 27; Bergman et al., *1,000 Years of Jewish Life in Poland*, 6.

10. Martyn, "Undefined Town within a Town," 21, 27; Dylewski, *Ruda, Córka Cwiego*, 354–356.

11. Bergman et al., *1,000 Years of Jewish Life in Poland*, 6, 20.

12. For a very vivid depiction of Jewish pre- and postwar life in the Praga district, see this documentation prepared for the POLIN museum by Szwarcman-Czarnota, "'Closed Book.' Jewish Warsaw."

13. The duchy was "technically autonomous and constitutional," but Dynner and Guesnet point out that "neither Napoleon, as the ultimate ruler of the Duchy of Warsaw, nor the tsars, as the 'kings' of the Kingdom of Poland [which succeeded the Duchy and lasted from 1815 to 1918], were willing to countenance a truly autonomous Polish state," which is why according to them, "the situation is . . . better described as a kind of 'soft' colonialism" ("Introduction," 6).

14. At least in theory—already by 1808, a restriction on practicing these rights was introduced (Rubinstein, Dombrowska, and Krakowski, "Warsaw," 667).

15. Engelking and Leociak, *Warsaw Ghetto*, 9.

16. Ibid.

17. Martyn, "Undefined Town within a Town," 26. As Martyn points out, this does not mean that Jewish life in Warsaw was limited to its two centers in Praga and Muranów. Martyn emphasizes, "Jews lived to a larger or smaller degree in every part of Warsaw" (ibid., 17). There was, however, a clear concentration of settlement in the Praga and Muranów districts, with Muranów's population being about 90 percent Jewish prior to the German occupation (ibid.). The oftentimes Europeanized upper class commonly evaded the crowded Jewish settlements and preferred setting up their townhouses, palaces, or villas either in the representative Łazienki park region (*Łazienki Królewskie*) or in the city's suburbs (ibid., 29, 30).

18. Ibid., 32.

19. Ibid., 33, see also 21, 34.

20. On these territorial constraints and the respective developments of the quarter, see Martyn, "Undefined Town within a Town," 22, 31–33, 35; Engelking and Leociak, *Warsaw Ghetto*, 9, 11; Dziewulski and Jankowski, "Reconstruction of Warsaw," 210; Leociak "From Żydowska Street to Umschlagplatz," 3.

21. Engelking and Leociak, *Warsaw Ghetto*, 10, 11.

22. Dynner and Guesnet, "Introduction," 2.

23. Boehm, "Introduction," 4.

24. Leociak, "From Żydowska Street to Umschlagplatz," 3.

25. Bourdieu, "Physischer, Sozialer und Angeeigneter Physischer Raum," 26, 28. It is important to keep in mind that the social differentiation within the Jewish community would later also lead to very differentiated experiences, especially in the early days of the ghetto's existence.

26. Engelking and Leociak, *Warsaw Ghetto*, 11.

27. Ibid., 15.

28. See, for example, Singer, *In My Father's Court, Family Moskat*, or *Love and Exile*.

29. Singer's writings were well translated into English and thus gained particular popularity. For a very informative introduction to the history of the Yiddish language, see Winckler, "Language Lost."

30. Cole, *Holocaust City*, 37; see also Cole, "Ghettoization," 80.

31. Engelking and Leociak, *Warsaw Ghetto*, 25.

32. Ibid., 26.

33. This is also one of the main differences between the Nazi ghetto in Warsaw and its historic predecessors. The ghetto established by the Nazis banned Jews from all city space except for the ghetto, whereas in the case of the medieval ghetto in Venice, for example, the Jewish population was still allowed to leave the ghetto area during the day, to "mov[e] out into the city ... and circulat[e] with the ordinary crowd" (Sennett, "Jewish Ghetto in Venice," 13–14).

34.   In "Reading the Palimpsest" (235), Gebert discusses an important exception to this general openness, which marks the ongoing process of claiming and negotiating the prewar city's public space:

> The Saxon Garden was a contested area. Antisemites would complain that Jews spoil the beauty of the spot by their vile looks and jarring voices; young thugs would sometimes attack Jewish passersby, and themselves be attacked by Jewish posses, which stalked the garden; police then, often unsuccessfully, would engage both. This made strolling in Saxon Garden and the Garden by the Old Town a question of principle. Saturday afternoons, after services, were dedicated to the shabbes shpatzieren, Yiddish for a Saturday walk. But Jews would eventually return to their own districts, having again staked the ground but despairing of ever owning it. Sundays in the gardens belonged almost exclusively, by force of custom, to the gentiles.

As Gebert points out, with the start of the occupation, the Nazis quickly officialized the ban on Jews entering public gardens. What had been a question of a sometimes forceful but still open negotiation between two social groups in defining their city's social geography now became exclusionary law.

35.   Engelking and Leociak, *Warsaw Ghetto*, 26.
36.   Gebert, "Reading the Palimpsest," 224.
37.   Engelking and Leociak, *Warsaw Ghetto*, 24.
38.   Mazor, *Vanished City*, 19.

CHAPTER
6

~~~

Creation of the Ghetto

Early Days of the Occupation

It took twenty-eight days from the invasion of Poland on September 1, 1939, for Warsaw to fall. The city had been the target of air raids from the beginning of the war and suffered immense losses and destruction. Eight days after the first attack, the German army was already "at the gates" of Warsaw.[1] The city did not capitulate and was thus turned into both a battlefield and an important symbol of Polish resistance. The defense was organized under the civilian and military leadership of the highly regarded mayor Stefan Starzyński and generals Walerian Czuma and Juliusz Rómmel. The defense relied heavily on the involvement of the city's inhabitants, and, thus, there was a huge number of civilian casualties.[2] During the siege, Varsovians converted many parks, courtyards, and other open spaces into provisional cemeteries to bury the city's dead. Because the Polish population later turned these burial grounds into memorial sites, the German authorities ordered their elimination in November 1939.[3] The narrative of Polish national pride expressed through commemorative practices such as lighting sanctuary lamps on All Souls' Day on the graves of the fallen soldiers and the victims of the German bombardment—spread out all over the city because of the widely dispersed locations of the provisional cemeteries—was a provocation to the occupiers. The German reaction indicates how, early on, the occupation entailed a struggle for the prerogative to interpret the city's space.

During the siege, according to Ofer, about "25% of Warsaw's buildings [were] hit by shells"; about sixty-six thousand apartments were destroyed.[4] The northern quarter of the city, where the Germans would later establish the ghetto, suffered from particularly heavy bombings. On September 28, 1939, the city surrendered, and the German army entered Warsaw a few days later. Helmuth Otto, former mayor of the German city of Düsseldorf, was nominated *Reichskommissar* (Reich commissioner) for Warsaw by the head of civilian administration within the military, Harry von Craushaar. A month later, Otto was appointed *Stadtpräsident* (mayor) by Hans Frank (soon to be appointed governor of the newly founded *Generalgouvernement*,[5] at this point chief administrator of the territory still under military rule). Oskar Dengel became Otto's deputy but quickly superseded his superior and was promoted to the position of *Stadtpräsident* in November 1939.[6] On October 5, the Germans held a parade on the central Aleje Ujazdowskie in honor of Hitler's visit to the city.[7] The parade symbolically marked the German takeover of the city. Varsovians were banned from watching and were to remain indoors under penalty of death.[8] By clearing Poles and Jews from the public space traversed by Hitler and the German triumphal procession, the German occupiers showed early on that their claim to the city was exclusionary in nature. Conversely, as historian and map curator Harrie Teunissen argues on the basis of a map depicting the route of the parade, already at this point the "central Jewish neighbourhood was a no-go-area" for the Germans.[9] The map indeed shows an area that is evocative of the outlines of the future ghetto hachured in dark lines and labeled "*Jüdischer Wohnbezirk. Betreten verboten!*" ("Jewish Residential District. Do not enter!").[10] From the very beginning, the division of the city worked both ways—albeit under very asymmetrical terms. The Germans created spaces "free of Jews" (*judenfrei*) but also Jewish spaces free, at times, of Germans.[11]

A central order concerning the fate of Warsaw's Jewish inhabitants had already been passed even before the Germans set foot in the city. It prompted the eviction and expulsion of Jews all over occupied Poland: in his express letter (*Schnellbrief*) to the commanders of the *Einsatzgruppen* on September 21, 1939, Reinhard Heydrich issued the order to "concentrate Jews in larger urban centers" as a first step toward a "final goal" that was not further specified in this context.[12] The order anticipated the transport of the population of what the Germans classified as smaller Jewish settlements (fewer than five hundred inhabitants) to the city. It applied to the whole of the occupied territories, with the exception of a small region east of Kraków, but did not include a detailed list of the settlements affected.[13] The decision regarding the dissolution of smaller settlements was delegated to the executors in the field. Within the city's limits, the order also suggested a proposed confinement of Jewish residents; in part II of the *Schnellbrief*, Heydrich explains, "For reasons of general police security, the concentration of the Jews in the cities will probably call for regulations in these cities which will forbid their entry to certain quarters completely and that—but with due regard to economic requirements—they may, for instance, not leave the ghetto, nor leave their homes after a certain hour in the evening, etc."[14]

Although, as Dan Michman argues in his study *The Emergence of Jewish Ghettos during the Holocaust*, the use of the term "ghetto" in the *Schnellbrief* does not necessarily indicate a plan for active ghettoization, the order still marks a first step toward the creation of the ghetto.[15] Engelking and Leociak explain, "In ordering the concentration of the Jews in larger cities and near railroad junctions, the Germans were not only preparing the way for future deportation *Aktionen* but also using decrees to establish Jewish living spaces—defining the dimensions of the zone of settlement, separating it from the rest of the city—a harbinger of future ghetto establishment."[16] Both developments—concentration in and within the larger cities—went hand in hand. Heydrich's order was complemented at the end of October by an order signed by Heinrich Himmler that demanded the resettlement of all Jews living in the occupied areas annexed to the Reich and in the Reich itself. They were to be deported to the future *Generalgouvernement* and temporarily resettled there.[17] Heralding a massive act of "dislocative" violence in Reemtsma's sense, this order manifested the ideological assertion that German *Lebensraum* had to be cleared of Jewish presence.[18] Entire territories were from then on defined teleologically as non-Jewish space.

In his foundational work *Die Vernichtung der Europäischen Juden* (*The Destruction of the European Jews*), Raul Hilberg points out that the actual ghettoization process was decentralized, making it highly divergent on a local level and often somewhat disorganized.[19] In the case of the Warsaw ghetto, ghettoization was in fact implemented in a fairly unsystematic manner that included multiple plans and repeated reconsiderations. According to Hilberg, in the beginning, the concentration process was a prestage, a makeshift attempt at the intended mass expulsion of the Jewish population.[20] In the years up until the beginning of 1942, the Nazis were still pursuing a territorial solution of the "Jewish question," and, although plans concerning the destination of the expulsion changed over time, most local German authorities anticipated that they would be able to send the people concentrated in their sphere of influence into other territory—first to a reservation in the Lublin area, then Madagascar, then "further East."[21] The Nazis related to the Jews in their sphere of influence in a "dislocative" sense, as bodies to be "eliminated"—at this point, at least primarily, by means of relocation.[22] In fact, Christopher Browning assumes that, ultimately, the way in which ghettoization played out in Poland was more a result of the failure to go through with the deportation plans than it was the result of Heydrich's initial order to concentrate the Jewish population.[23]

Following part II of Heydrich's express letter, and an ensuing decree by Hans Frank, on October 4 the occupying authorities appointed Adam Czerniaków as chairman of the *Judenrat* (Jewish Council) in Warsaw. Czerniaków presented twenty-four candidates for the *Judenrat*, and the German authorities accepted his list.[24] As stated in Heydrich's order, the members of the *Judenrat* were to be held "fully responsible, in the literal sense of the word, for the exact and punctual execution of all directives issued or yet to be issued."[25] Many—if not most—regulations concerning the Jewish community and its living space were implemented by the Germans through the *Judenrat*. The *Judenrat* became the main intermediary between the Germans and the Jewish community, making it a highly controversial institution for most ghetto inhabitants. From a contemporary perspective, the *Judenräte* fall within the "Grey Zone" as conceptualized by Holocaust survivor Primo Levi. By creating a Jewish self-administration, the Germans not only facilitated their rule over the ghetto; they also "compromised" members of the Jewish community by establishing an "imposed complicity."[26]

Exclusion and Segregation

The German occupiers started to implement anti-Jewish regulations right away.[27] Their measures excluded their victims socially and caused substantial material damage. The Germans went, first, after Jewish possessions: they blocked Jewish bank accounts, imposed a weekly limit on withdrawals, and restricted the amount of cash a Jewish individual could have on hand. From the beginning, Germans also confiscated the private property of Jews.[28] As Yisrael Gutman describes in his study *The Jews of Warsaw 1933–1943: Ghetto, Underground, Revolt*, "Soldiers would turn up at relatively large Jewish apartments, present a signed warrant—or not even bother with such formalities—and make off with furniture, valuables, and cash."[29] Such thefts took place both on an official and a nonsanctioned (private) level: "wholesale looting by soldiers and individual thieves went on alongside the 'official' pillage."[30] Both soldiers, acting on behalf of the German state, as well as private individuals or soldiers without respective orders felt empowered by the Nazi ideology to seize Jewish property solely on the basis of their asserted "racial superiority." In fact, Germans and *Volksdeutsche* were given such a degree of privilege by the authorities as to allow them to take part in lootings and robberies without fear of reprisals.[31] Or rather, the Jewish disenfranchisement deprived the victims of a reliable authority to appeal to even in cases of unsanctioned confiscations.[32] As Samuel Kassow formulates it in *Who Will Write Our History?*, "Even more troubling were the endless raids on private apartments, where German soldiers and civilians had carte blanche to loot to their heart's content."[33] Later, when the ghetto was established, the private seizure of Jewish property declined a little, both because it was forbidden for civilians to enter the ghetto and because Germans tended to shun the area due to the alleged risk of infection.[34] Still, many Gentiles would find ways to cross the boundaries of the ghetto, especially to engage in trade with the Jews.[35]

Acting on a decree signed by Governor General Hans Frank on October 26 and augmented on December 12 with regulations by the head of the SS and police in the *Generalgouvernement*, Friedrich Krüger, the Germans introduced forced labor, and thus began the economic exploitation of the Jewish community.[36] This initiated waves of "raids on Jewish neighborhoods [to] shanghai passersby for day labor."[37] In the hope of ending the random round-ups on the streets, the *Judenrat* started to organize so-called labor battalions (*Batalion Pracy*). The numbers of workers the Germans requisitioned rose ceaselessly.[38]

On October 27, 1939, the Germans arrested Mayor Starzyński and sent him to Pawiak prison; he was later executed, but the details of his death remain unclear.[39] At least symbolically, this marked the end of Polish rule over the city. Three days later, Ludwig Fischer became head of the Warsaw district (the title later changed to governor). Fischer was, from then on, the highest local administrative authority in the district, overseeing the future ghetto and the fate of the Jewish population.[40] Both the commander of the SS and police (Krüger, then Koppe) and the Reich commissioner/*Stadtpräsident* (Otto, Dengel, then Leist) answered to him. At this point, civil administration took over responsibility for Warsaw, which lost its rank as capital to Kraków.[41]

At the end of October, German authorities ordered a first census of the Jewish population and established that 359,827 people whom they classified as Jews lived in Warsaw.[42] At that same time, about ninety thousand more Jews deported from Polish territories incorporated into the Reich arrived in Warsaw. The influx of refugees and deportees from neighboring communities, the annexed territories, other occupied countries, and also from Germany continued over the months and years to come and caused significant housing and provisioning problems for the Jewish community.[43] The fate of these newcomers was diverse, but often the situation of the refugees and deportees was particularly difficult, as they had few resources and lacked the social network of most Warsaw natives.[44] In this context, it can be helpful to follow Engelking and Leociak in differentiating between the two groups: refugees were at least potentially able to influence where they would settle, whereas deportees had no say in choosing their destination. Whether a person had had the chance to bring any belongings with them also made a huge difference. Very often, people arriving in the ghetto were already "worn out by the difficulties of the long journey."[45] The damage done on a material and social level very quickly translated into physical harm: most of the deportees ultimately ended up in refugee centers, so-called *Punkty* (*Punkte* in German), where living conditions were usually very dire and the death rate incredibly high.[46] The continuous arrival of people with different cultural, political, and religious backgrounds, and different nationalities and languages, led to a diversification of the ghetto society.

The Germans did not establish the ghetto in Warsaw right away, nor did they follow a clear-cut plan. Instead, the history of the ghetto's establishment is marked by a series of plans and initiatives discussed by the German authorities but ultimately discarded. Yet, the German ambition to segregate the Jews spatially became evident early on. A first attempt to concentrate the Jewish inhabitants of the city in a certain area was already made in early November 1939.[47] During an extraordinary meeting of the *Judenrat*, SS-Standartenführer Dr. Baatz read out a decree by General Karl von Neumann-Neurode,[48] the military commander of the city at the time. It "ordered that within three days the Jews be concentrated in specified streets of the Jewish district."[49] According to Engelking and Leociak, the maps the Germans provided were imprecise and unclear.[50] This observation suggests that the people who were planning the future ghetto had in fact very little knowledge of the territory. What was to become a question of life or death for the Jews of Warsaw was decided by authorities who were most likely comparatively unacquainted with the city. The order was revoked after a delegation of the *Judenrat* successfully appealed to von Neumann-Neurode.[51] Still, rumors about the establishment of a ghetto spread and unsettled the community.[52]

On November 13, the Gestapo carried out a first act of organized physical (and deadly) violence against a large group of Jewish people. A Polish policeman had been fatally shot and another wounded during the attempted arrest of a Jewish thief, Pinchas Jankiel Zylberger,[53] at his home at 9 Nalewki Street. As a reprisal, fifty-three Jewish men—residents of 9 Nalewki Street or people who were merely visiting—were taken from the building and murdered by the Gestapo, even though the *Judenrat* had paid the demanded ransom ("punishment tax").[54] A similar case of "collective punishment" took place in January 1940. Kazimierz Andrzej Kott, a young Pole from a converted Jewish family and member of the armed wing of the Polish underground movement PLAN, had escaped from German arrest. Although he "had no connection whatsoever with Jews or any Jewish affairs," the Gestapo arrested 225 members of the Jewish intelligentsia in retribution.[55] All of them were presumably killed shortly after. Both incidents are associated with the preemptive terror of the early months of German occupation in the *Generalgouvenement*.[56] These and other ensuing acts of violence elicited fear and agitation in the Jewish community. As Kaplan notes in his ghetto diary on January 24, 1940, as a reaction to the Kott affair, "Every house is filled with sadness and a spirit of depression. . . . Those who have not been arrested live in mortal fear. Every echo of footsteps on the stairs in the dark of night drives mute panic into their hearts. . . . There is no chance of hiding out from the conquerors."[57]

In the meantime, the German occupiers continued their assault on Jewish economic and social participation. In many instances, their anti-Jewish measures were implemented through (or at least entailed) the exclusion of Jews from habitual and communal spaces. In mid-November 1939, German authorities closed all schools, Polish as well as Jewish. The Polish schools were later reopened, but the Jewish ones remained closed until September 5, 1941, when only elementary schools were allowed to open again. By then, an elaborate system of clandestine education had already evolved.[58] The exclusion of Jews from the economy was a process that served two Nazi agendas: a political one and an economic one.[59] While it implemented further segregation and deprived many Jews of their sources of income, it also generated significant gains for both German individuals and the German state. Already in September 1939, the German administration had started to confiscate Jewish businesses, signing them over to compulsory administration under so-called trustees (*Treuhänder*). This procedure was technically designated for businesses whose owners were abroad; in practice, however, it was applied to almost all Jewish-owned businesses.[60] Sometimes, the "trustee" would leave the actual management of a company in the hands of its former owners in order to benefit from their expertise. Most often, though, the management fell into German hands and a Jewish entrepreneur "lost both his property and his source of livelihood at one and the same time."[61] According to Gutman's study, often one "of the 'trustees'' first moves was to fire Jewish employees from the firms under their control."[62] In addition, machinery, equipment, raw materials, and finished products from all over Poland were transferred to Germany.[63]

All this was orchestrated by the so-called *Treuhandstelle* (trustee office) for the *Generalgouvernement*, set up by Hans Frank in November 1939,[64] and led to a fast-growing rate of unemployment among Jews.[65] Generally, as Gutman summarizes, the Jewish population was "consciously deprived of any position in the economy."[66] The consequences of these acts of economic exclusion were serious, given that at the same time, prices for basic food had already tripled or even quadrupled. A few months later, prices would increase again, sometimes up to five or even ten times the prewar prices.[67] These developments not only deprived many Jews of the necessary means to support themselves (or to arrange for possible emigration or relocation); they also quite drastically changed their social status.

In November, the German authorities issued the first orders aimed at isolating what they called the *Seuchensperrgebiet* (an area threatened by epidemics); the first "barbed-wire fences appear[ed] at the entrance to streets in the Jewish district, along with plaques with the inscription 'Infection, entry banned to soldiers.'"[68] The threat of epidemics (i.e., of typhus) was commonly invoked by Nazi German propaganda as a precursor to the spatial segregation of the Jewish community. The justification for segregation was built on a narrative that denounced Jews as "immune carriers of the bacteria of epidemics."[69] In addition, the "separation of the Jews" was meant to undermine "Jewish" influence on the Polish society.[70] The Jewish space was thus conceptualized as a quarantine zone, protecting the

"Aryan" society from contamination both in a sanitary and a sociopolitical sense. At the same time, this narrative "further stigmatize[d] and alienate[d]" the Jews from the non-Jewish population.[71] While most anti-Jewish measures enforced earlier in the occupation had aimed at a continuous exclusion of Jews from public space, the economy, cultural and political life, and so on, the German authorities now began to actively create a continuous, segregated Jewish space, thus shifting their practices toward implementing a "captive" form of violence.[72]

Also in November 1939, Governor General Hans Frank issued an order compelling Jews in the entire *Generalgouvernement* to wear "distinguishing marks" in the form of white armbands with a star of David.[73] The order was implemented in Warsaw by the end of the month with a published decree by the governor of the district of Warsaw, Fischer, "making it compulsory for all Jews over twelve years old to wear armbands."[74] With this, the burden of proof was shifted to the Jews, who had to self-identify in accordance with the Nazi laws. According to Engelking and Leociak, this decree was "an important step on the road to creating a ghetto."[75] It introduced a visible distinction that facilitated the redistribution of spatial rights in relation to a racial matrix. It also made it easier for Germans to identify Jewish individuals as their targets: "any German could recognize a Jew in the street, and this obviously facilitated the daily kidnapping, thefts, and persecutions."[76] It was, as Gutman points out, a measure "designed to isolate the Jews and increase their vulnerability to the Germans and the Polish population."[77] The economic, social, and spatial exclusion initiated a process of gradual (social) ghettoization even before the physical ghetto itself was actually created.

Together with the marking of individuals considered Jewish under the *Nürnberger Gesetze* (Nuremberg Laws),[78] orders were issued that required both that Jewish shops and enterprises be marked with a "poster with a blue Star of Zion on a white background" and that the Jewish population purchase goods only from such shops.[79] In one of his reports from the ghetto, Peretz Opoczynski explains that Jewish shops had to be further marked with Hebrew signboards.[80] It is worth noting that the labeling was to be in Hebrew and not in Yiddish, which was the more common language for the Jews of Warsaw. Opoczynski describes how that order led to the appearance of a flood of "unintentionally comic signs" and to people erratically mixing Yiddish and Hebrew.[81] This order testifies to the degree to which the Nazis' concept of "a Jew" was often performative in nature— socially constructing and implementing an image of Jewishness based on Nazi ideology—and not in alignment with actual Jewish identities.

The marking of Jewish shops is, furthermore, an example of a second widespread practice: the labeling of space. A plethora of signs, posters, announcements, and markers appeared in the streets of Warsaw over time, annotating the city according to Nazi ideology, marking racially organized spaces and regulating access and entitlement. These labels added a new layer of information to the urban space and, at the same time, were an expression of a claim to power exercised by the Germans, who decided on the marking criteria and set the rules of the reorganization of space. Only much later, in the weeks before the Ghetto Uprising would take place, was the German claim on Jewish space increasingly challenged by the Jewish Fighting Organization (ŻOB). This challenge also took place on the level of inscription, with messages of resistance annotating, and posted alongside, the official signage of the occupiers. Such visual manifestations of opposition created a counternarrative of resistance in the public space.[82]

By mid-December 1939, the Germans introduced a system of food rationing. For the time being, there was not yet a distinction between Jewish and non-Jewish Poles regarding the food allowances, but this would change in February, when different ration cards were introduced for Germans, (non-Jewish) Poles, and Jews.[83] Later, the caloric value of the food rations was allotted according to racial principles. With this, the Nazi concept of "race" became the decisive factor for an individual's chances of survival. In 1941, according to Gutman, Germans received 2,613 calories, Poles 699 calories, and Jews 184 calories in official distribution. Referencing Szarota, Engelking and Leociak give somewhat higher numbers for the Jewish rations, ranging from 198 to 503 calories daily for the years 1940 and 1941; a calculation by Jewish scientists from the ghetto specifies a range from 169–219 calories for the months of January–August 1941.[84] The rations were also socially stratified, with higher caloric value allotted to certain groups.[85] At no point were the Jewish rations anywhere close to attaining minimum subsistence levels. Throughout the unusually cold winter of 1939/1940, there was also a considerable shortage of coal and fuel.[86]

During that period, Jewish scope of movement was continuously reduced and increasingly regulated. In the winter of 1939, the Soviet border was closed, and Jews could no longer escape from German- to Soviet-occupied territories without dire risk. According to Opoczynski's report, these escapes to the "Other Side" had been very frequent before, because people assumed they would be treated better in the Soviet-occupied zone and that they would find better living conditions.[87] On January 1, higher SS and police leader in the *Generalgouvernement* Friedrich Krüger issued a decree that strongly restricted the Jewish population's spatial self-determination. In order to change their domicile "beyond the limits of the community of their place of residence," Jews now required special permission by the local German administration.[88] With this order, the Germans exerted control over a decision that usually resided with the individual but that now became a state affair. Even in times when Jewish settlement had been restricted, the general possibility of determining for oneself when or where to move had not been infringed on, even if the options were potentially limited. The new decree was a

drastic interference with personal freedom, expressed in the form of a spatial restriction: Jews were from now on not in a position to determine their whereabouts
autonomously. In addition to that, the order stipulated that Jews needed special
permission to "enter or use pathways, streets and public squares between the
hours of 9:00 P.M. and 5:00 A.M." and were required to register with the German
authorities within twenty-four hours of moving to the *Generalgouvernement*.[89]

In general, the "occupation authorities furthered the restrictions on the Jewish freedom of movement throughout" the *Generalgouvernement*.[90] By the middle
of January, an order of *Stadtpräsident* Oskar Dengel restricted street trading by
Jews. Engelking and Leociak suggest that the Jewish community saw this order as another step toward the establishment of a ghetto, since the streets and
places designated for Jewish trade coincided with the plan for a potential ghetto.[91]
In January 1940, the Germans also closed synagogues and prayer houses and
banned "collective prayers in private houses."[92] Given the particular makeup
of the Jewish community in Warsaw, this last regulation was particularly con-
sequential.[93] Ritual baths were closed as well, and already in 1939 the Germans
had introduced a ban on *shechita* (i.e., slaughter adhering to the Torah).[94] These
interdictions changed social practices drastically by barring access to important
social (religious and cultural) Jewish spaces and shifting the associated practices
to clandestine spheres. With the closing of both schools and synagogues and the
prohibition of private prayer, the German occupiers had targeted particularly
important cultural spaces of Jewish community and identity. In addition to a
continuous process of segregation, there was thus also an evident ambition to
destroy spaces identified with Jewish culture and self-definition.[95]

At the end of January 1940, the *Umsiedlungsstelle* (Department of Resettlement) in Warsaw was opened under the direction of Waldemar Schön.[96] The
Umsiedlungsstelle would become the main Warsaw-based German institution
concerned with the establishment of the ghetto. Another decree issued by Hans
Frank and published in the *Nowy Kurier Warszawski* at the beginning of February forbade the Jewish population of the *Generalgouvernement* from using the
railway, thereby further reducing their scope of movement.[97] While changes to
the situation of Jews in Warsaw were happening very quickly, it is quite obvious
that Nazi Germany did not have a consistent plan regarding the concentration of
Jews. The fact that their plans concerning a potential ghetto changed repeatedly,
and that several different scenarios were entertained at different times, created
great insecurity for the Jewish population. In February 1940, German authorities discussed the idea of opening a ghetto in Praga. According to Engelking and
Leociak, Praga was considered a potential site for the ghetto mainly because its
location on the other side of the Vistula River would have isolated it from the
rest of the city.[98] In a lecture entitled "Steps Leading to the Establishment of the

Warsaw Ghetto," Schön explained that the project elicited strong opposition on the basis of economic considerations and was finally dropped.[99]

In mid-March, Ludwig Leist became *Stadthauptmann* of Warsaw, replacing Oskar Dengel.[100] At the end of March, the situation of the Jewish population deteriorated further. A series of anti-Jewish incidents took place: "shops were broken into and plundered, apartments were looted, passersby wearing an armband were beaten up, and anti-Semitic slogans were shouted."[101] Though Polish hooligans were responsible for the violence, their attacks were instigated by the Germans.[102] The German occupation administration later used the same incidents to justify the establishment of a ghetto as an alleged "safe space."[103] Especially in the early days of the ghetto's establishment, the hope that the ghetto would be a safe space was indeed also expressed by some of its Jewish inhabitants, who hoped that they would "be protected from attacks" inside the walls.[104] As Janina Bauman explains in her postwar memoir, "Besides, no matter how miserable we were, living in a sealed community among people equally vulnerable to outside violence, not being singled out in a crowd, produced a vague, deceptive feeling of relative security."[105]

The same month, Jewish people were banned from entering cafés and restaurants, and notices to this effect started to appear in the city.[106] Access to public space was thus further restricted, both by the experience of violence and by German decree. Again, exclusion was accompanied by a labeling of space that both reinforced the ongoing segregation through regulating access and manifested the segregation visually. Schön states that, at the beginning of March, the idea of establishing a ghetto in Warsaw was "postponed" due to the fact that German authorities were entertaining the project of creating a Jewish reservation in the Lublin area at this time.[107] But this plan, too, was later given up. Still, the Germans continued the fencing off of the *Seuchensperrgebiet*. Later, the *Judenrat* was ordered to build walls that cordoned off the area, and it was also the *Judenrat*—and, in consequence, the Jewish community—who was to pay for their construction.[108] At this point, the German authorities considered creating two smaller ghettos, "both situated on the outskirts of the city—one in the west, including the suburbs of Kolo and Wola, and in the east of the city the suburb of Grochow."[109] The administration considered the idea of building a ghetto outside of the city center the least disadvantageous in terms of the "economy, industry and traffic of the city."[110] Though the authorities had already scheduled the beginning of the resettlement for July 1, it did not, in the end, go through and the project was (temporarily) replaced by the so-called *Madagaskar Plan*—that is, the plan to resettle the European Jews to the island of Madagascar.[111] In the beginning of May 1940, the German army attacked France, Luxembourg, Belgium, and the Netherlands. Since Madagascar was a French colony, the mission to resettle the

Jews there relied on the French capitulation.[112] Ultimately, the Germans abandoned the idea when the attempt to invade Great Britain failed, and the British naval blockade hindered access to the island state.[113] Paris fell on June 14, 1940, sealing the German victory in France. The inhabitants of Warsaw received the news of German successes in the west with growing desperation.[114]

When the erection of walls closing off the *Seuchensperrgebiet* was concluded in June, the German authorities celebrated it as a triumph of their fight against an alleged epidemic crisis, whereas the Jewish inhabitants of the city perceived it as a clear sign of the imminent establishment of a ghetto.[115] According to Tomasz Szarota's historical study *Warschau unter dem Hakenkreuz*, at this point the curfew that had applied to Jews and Poles alike was further specified, and the segregation of the Jewish population thereby increased.[116] Public space was now also segregated along temporal lines. On July 18, an order by *Stadthauptmann* Ludwig Leist again intervened drastically with the right of Jews to public space. The order restricted access to public parks and prohibited sitting on public benches, and several streets and squares were also declared forbidden to the Jewish population.[117] The exclusion of Jews from the public sphere (and thus from social participation) became increasingly drastic and visible. A second decree by Leist, ordering Jewish inhabitants of the quarters projected to become the sole territory of Germans to move out of such areas immediately, marks another step in the ongoing segregation of the Jewish population. Jews living in the projected Polish quarters were allowed to remain there temporarily, but newcomers to Warsaw were obliged to move into the Jewish district at once.[118]

The establishment of a German quarter did not proceed uninterrupted. As Szarota points out, the acquisition of certain buildings for Germans had started immediately after the invasion of the city.[119] Buildings for administrative agencies, for the military, and for private housing were occupied in the most socially and culturally symbolic parts of the city's center (Teatralny Square, Saski Square, Aleja Szucha, Aleje Ujazdowskie, Krakowskie Przedmieście, and Nowy Świat); the requisition of local facilities and utilities followed.[120] Lehnstaedt specifies that administrative buildings were mainly located in the neighborhood of Nowy Świat and Krakowskie Przedmieście, whereas the living quarters were mostly situated in the Mokotów district and in the vicinity of Łazienki Park.[121] The plans to establish three separate quarters were being developed throughout 1940, but the German quarter was not conclusively established until much later. In 1941–1942, the fear of air raids possibly targeting a large concentration of German settlement inhibited its development. In 1942, a series of orders requested the German population to once again move into the German district, but many Germans were seemingly reluctant to comply. In the spring of 1944, the German authorities went a step further and ultimately partitioned a section of the city off, enclosing it with barbed wire and declaring it a quarter *"Nur für Deutsche"* (for Germans only). Only then did the division of the German living quarters from the rest of the city become absolute. Interestingly, this line of action coincided with a growing anxiety on the part of the occupiers who, not least due to the activities of the Polish Underground, did not feel safe in the city anymore.[122] When finally realized, the exclusive German *Lebensraum* within the city was less a manifestation of power than a retreat. Lehnstaedt points out that the creation of the German living quarter was from the beginning linked to the expulsion of Polish residents, who in turn were to be relocated to former Jewish apartments. There also existed a link between the German demand for more living quarters and future reductions to the ghetto space.[123] The entire process corresponded with the Nazis' ideology, in that it prioritized the German need for space over that of Poles and, most notably, Jews, while attempting to create a racially homogeneous German living space. As Szarota points out, the segregation had also been established on a different plane beforehand: there was a huge number of stores, restaurants, theaters, cinemas, parks, stadiums, playgrounds, and schools reserved for Germans, thus establishing a space that was racially exclusive and that limited contact with the local population.[124]

Ghettoization

The month of August 1940 saw the decision to set up a so-called *Jüdischer Wohnbezirk* (Jewish residential district) take full shape. As Schön, head of the Department of Resettlement, explained in his report on the establishment of the ghetto in January 1941, the German Health Department had strongly advocated this course of action, invoking the increased military presence in the district to argue that a ghetto was necessary to protect the soldiers' health, as well as that of the general population.[125] Again, the sanitary narrative served as a pretext for intensifying racial segregation. The German authorities decided to use the area of the *Seuchensperrgebiet*, which due to its centrality also allowed for moderate trade between the Jewish district and the "Aryan" parts of the city.[126] This decision can be seen as "pragmatic" in the sense Cole applies to the case of Budapest, where the location of the ghetto was "motivated by a pragmatic desire to ghettoize 'Jews' where they already lived."[127] Nevertheless, these plans and their implementation initiated a huge wave of expulsion and resettlement. Engelking and Leociak summarize, "A great migration began within the confines of the city."[128]

At the end of August, *Nowy Kurier Warszawski* and *Gazeta Żydowska*, two newspapers licensed by the Germans, announced the establishment of a Jewish district and the orders for the resettlement of the Jewish and Polish population. Both publications listed the streets that were to become the boundaries of the

Jewish district.[129] Over time, however, the district's boundaries were redrawn several times. As Engelking and Leociak observe, this usually meant a reduction of the area designated for Jewish settlement; in fact, the Jewish district in the end only covered two-thirds of the *Seuchensperrgebiet*'s former territory.[130] The continual changes created a high level of uncertainty for many people, as the status of their apartment (inside or outside the ghetto) and, thus, the requirement to move, could change daily.[131] Some people even had to move more than once. As historian Samuel Kassow explains, "For some weeks Jews lived in debilitating uncertainty about the boundaries of the ghetto; some Jews spent all they had on apartments in the new ghetto, only to find out that the apartment was on the wrong street."[132] A desperate fight for particular streets broke out, and the *Judenrat* repeatedly appealed to the German authorities to prevent exclusion of particular buildings or streets. Following Kassow, this process further destabilized Jewish–non-Jewish relationships: "The haggling over boundaries brilliantly exemplified the German policy of 'divide and rule,' as Poles and Jews fought to gain as much space as possible for their own communities."[133] In addition, the Germans extended segregation to public transit. On September 25, another decree by Leist ordered a division regarding the space in trams: the front part of cars was reserved for Germans, the rest was to be used by Poles, while Jews were excluded from these trams altogether.[134] The authorities introduced special Jewish tramways marked as *"Nur für Juden"* (for Jews only) because, as Kaplan sums up the German logic, "two different species must not mingle."[135]

Ultimately, the Warsaw ghetto was officially established on October 2, 1940, with Fischer signing the decree that ordered the establishment of a *Jüdischer Wohnbezirk*.[136] The German authorities avoided, even forbid, the use of the term "ghetto." This was an attempt to mask the nature of the space by creating "the impression that it resembled the German and Polish quarters of the city."[137] Kaplan notes on October 17, 1940, "Instead of a ghetto, which is a medieval concept, they call it a 'Jewish quarter.' And the fact that the same order refers also to a Polish quarter and a German quarter is supposed to be a sign that the enemy treats them alike."[138] But to some degree the term *Jüdischer Wohnbezirk* also reflects how closely the German ideology linked living space and "race." Ghettoization was not an isolated measure but part of an all-encompassing reorganization of living space according to racial criteria (within the city, as well as on the level of entire countries). Fischer's decree was accompanied by a list of its boundary streets and stipulated the "division of Warsaw into three districts, German, Polish and Jewish," further expediting the huge number of forced relocations.[139] The head of the Department of Resettlement, Schön, lists the resettlement of "113,000 Poles and 138,000 Jews." In addition, "700 *Volksdeutsche*" were moved from the territory that was to become the ghetto. According to Schön's report, a "total of 11,567 Aryan apartments were vacated in the Jewish quarter and about 13,000 Jewish apartments taken over outside the Jewish quarter." On the day of the ghetto's sealing in November 1940, another 11,130 Jews were "taken forcibly" to the ghetto and 3,770 Jewish stores outside the ghetto were closed.[140]

Little time was given for the resettlement process: by the end of October everyone was required to have moved to their respective quarters. Władysław Bartoszewski summarizes the order: "'The Poles resident in the Jewish residential area shall move by October 31, 1940 to another part of the city' (but they are prohibited from settling in the German residential area) and 'the Jews resident outside the Jewish residential area shall move thereto by October 31, 1940.'"[141] This deadline was later extended to November 15. The division of the city and the boundaries of the Jewish district were promulgated over street megaphones, adding an aural dimension to the German intrusion into the urban space.[142] In addition to propagandistic posters, decrees, and communiqués plastering the streets, these megaphones were among the most important means of communication used by the occupiers.[143] The German presence thus became both a visible and aural part of the urban environment and propagated both their authority and their ideology. Adler writes in his memoir, "The most fantastic lies and vilifications about Jews were spread through the press, through pamphlets and posters, by loudspeakers in the streets, by any and all means at their disposal."[144] The public space of the city became emphatically anti-Jewish space.

The living space allotted to the Jews continued to shrink: by the time of its establishment, the Germans had reduced the ghetto's area significantly in comparison to the earlier sketches published in the newspapers at the end of August.[145] At that time, most Jewish people still hoped that the ghetto would remain open.[146] Kaplan expresses his anxiety in a diary entry on October 24: "Will there be a closed ghetto? There are signs in both directions, and we hope for a miracle. . . . A closed ghetto means gradual death. An open ghetto is only a halfway catastrophe."[147] During the ongoing resettlements, people often lost most of their furniture and household goods, and Germans confiscated the property that was left behind.[148] Again, political and economic interest went hand in hand: Hilberg suggests that the prospect of confiscating Jewish belongings was often a decisive factor in informing the selection of a location for the ghetto. According to him, the Germans preferred to set up the ghettos in poor neighborhoods so that more valuables would be left behind when people from wealthier quarters were forced to move.[149]

Following a decree issued by Leist in October 1940, Jews and Poles had to "give way to Germans in uniform on the streets and to get off the sidewalks."[150] Kaplan notes in his diary, "Racial segregation is becoming more apparent each day."[151] In mid-October the *Judenrat* published a "communiqué on the boundaries of the

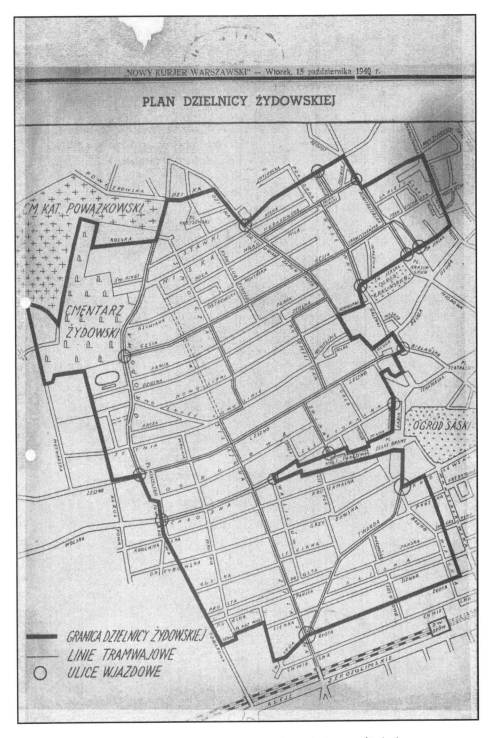

Fig. 6.1. Plan of the projected borders of the so-called Jewish Quarter (*Jüdischer Wohnbezirk/Dzielnica Żydowska*), published on October 15, 1940, in *Nowy Kurier Warszawski*.

Jewish District"; it was followed by two consecutive publications of the projected boundaries in *Nowy Kurier Warszawski* (on October 14 and 15), which differed not only from one another but, yet again, from previous announcements.[152] As Engelking and Leociak observe, the "future boundary of the ghetto would be subject to continual changes, corrections, and adjustments. The printed plans and lists of boundary streets contained discrepancies, were swiftly made out of date, and required correction."[153] The Jewish community remained in an extremely insecure state.

The general layout of the ghetto, as it had taken shape at the end of October, beginning of November 1940, was characterized by its division into two parts: the "small" ghetto in the south and the "large" ghetto in the north. They were divided by Chłodna Street, one of the main east-west connectors in the city. Both parts were initially connected by a narrow passage at the intersection of Chłodna and Żelazna Streets and, after the winter of 1941/1942, by a wooden footbridge.[154] The northwestern border of the ghetto ran along the cemetery on Okopowa Street, which until December 1941 was partly inside the ghetto. The northern border ran mainly along Stawki and Dzika Streets. In the eastern section, the borders were much more dented and irregular, re-formed to exclude Plac Bankowy and Plac Żelaznej Bramy, which had before been part of the *Seuchensperrgebiet*. Until October 1941, Sienna Street designated the southern border of the ghetto. Generally, the small ghetto was considered by the inhabitants to offer somewhat better living conditions than the large ghetto.[155] The Jewish space was internally divided, not only physically but also socially.

Confinement

On November 16, 1940, the ghetto was sealed, and the fate of Jewish Varsovians took another drastic turn. This meant that (officially) all remaining contact with the "Aryan" part of the city was cut and isolation was maximized. The ramifications for the ghetto inhabitants of the decoupling of the two parts of the city were severe, and particularly so in regard to social exclusion. Kaplan describes the sealing in a diary entry on November 17: "Suddenly we see ourselves penned on all sides. We are segregated and separated from the world and the fullness thereof, driven out of the society of the human race."[156] The Jewish community was deprived of almost all direct interaction with the outside world, and the *Judenrat* became its only intermediary. This also meant that internal relations became extremely strained. After the sealing of the ghetto, the Germans ordered the *Judenrat* to create the Jewish Order Service (*Służba Porządkowa/Jüdischer Ordnungsdienst*) to "take over the duties of the Polish police within the ghetto."[157] With this, the internal organization of the ghetto was further decoupled from the rest of the city and the Germans created another Jewish proxy within the community. Although, in the beginning, some inhabitants in fact looked on the Jewish Order Service with a certain pride,[158] for most the members of the Order Service soon came to represent agents of the German order. Ultimately, the Germans implicated the Order Service in their crimes against the ghetto population, thus pitting members of the Jewish community against each other.

In the same month, facing the Germans' ruthless policies, the *Oneg Shabbat* group took up its work on the Underground Archive.[159] The archive's objective was to make sure the life of the Jewish communities under German occupation was documented in all its facets, with as broad a spectrum of perspectives as possible. And, in fact, the archive's members, including Emanuel Ringelblum (its founder), Eliezer Lipe Bloch, Szmuel Bresław, Eliyahu Gutkowski, Rabbi Szymon Huberband, Menakhem Mendel Kon, Shmuel Winter, Abraham Lewin, Józef Kapłan, Szmuel Bresław, Menakhem Linder, Peretz Opoczynski, Izrael Lichtensztajn, Rachel Auerbach, Hersh Wasser, and a number of other members and contributors whose names are not all recorded, would become the most important chroniclers of the ghetto, its life and its people.[160] Their work ensured that knowledge about the ghetto is not solely based on the sources of the perpetrators. As Kassow phrases it in *Who Will Write Our History?*, "Without it, posterity would read the records of the killers but forget the voices of the victims."[161] Along with the memoirs of survivors, it is their studies, reflections, and collected material that the analytical chapters of this book are mostly based on.

The sealing of the ghetto allowed the Germans to control the Jewish space they had created much more extensively. As Cole suggests, a closed ghetto represents an extremely high "degree of territoriality" and "of spatial control."[162] While the social and economic exclusion implemented by the Nazis' anti-Jewish policies had already done a lot of harm, the sealing of the ghetto now made it possible for the German administration to directly manipulate the living conditions inside the ghetto. This concerned first and foremost the question of supplies and trade. With the sealing of the ghetto, the Germans took control over all official movements of goods. The institution that exerted this control was the so-called *Transferstelle* that started its operation at the beginning of December 1940. It was from then on one of the most important points of intersection between the ghetto and the outside world, its function being the regulation of all official trade between the ghetto and the "Aryan" parts of the city.[163] In addition, the *Transferstelle* was responsible for issuing the passes that were necessary for entering or leaving the ghetto.[164]

Spatial segregation and control translated almost directly into physical harm. The gatekeeping function of the *Transferstelle* basically allowed the Germans to decide if the inhabitants of the ghetto would live or die. Consequently, the ideological orientation of its management had the most severe consequences for the ghetto and its inhabitants. This can be illustrated using the example of the two men who consecutively led the *Transferstelle*, first Alexander Palfinger, and from May 1941 onward, Max Bischof. Palfinger pursued a very strict policy toward the ghetto, aiming at its "total isolation" and, ultimately, its population's gradual starvation.[165] Under his aegis, the ghetto became essentially a means of gradual genocide. Bischof's appointment, in contrast, can be seen as the expression of a general shift in the Germans' ghetto policies. A similar shift was evident in the replacement of Schön by Heinz Auerswald, who, after the *Umsiedlungsstelle* (Department of Resettlement) was closed, took over the main responsibilities for the ghetto as commissar of the Jewish district. In both cases, a strongly antisemitic and "attritionist" authority was replaced by a more liberal, economically oriented one; with this, the function of the ghetto changed from being a "means to liquidate the Jews" to being a "productive entity."[166] Both Auerswald and Bischof were put in place with the mission of raising the production of the ghetto and having it achieve "economic self-sufficiency."[167] Their appointment can be seen as an expression of the reorientation of the Germans' ghetto policies toward more efficient economic exploitation.

While the Germans now held significant power over the living conditions in the ghetto, it is—as Goldberg points out—important to remember that until the Germans started the Great Deportation *Aktion* in July 1942, the ghetto as an urban structure was also a living space, operating under "catastrophic conditions" but still operating.[168] Goldberg elaborates, "Its Jewish inhabitants perceived the ghetto not as a prelude to Treblinka which at the time of the ghetto's creation was not even envisioned by the Nazis, but rather as a radically transformed continuation of pre-war Jewish Warsaw and as a part of the German-occupied city."[169] Within the walls, many "urban institutions functioned . . . hundreds of shops and service providers, numerous bakeries, two hospitals, over a hundred coffeehouses, and so forth."[170] Many elements of urban life, such as traffic, for example, were adjusted to the new conditions.

The ghetto walls cut many communication arteries and strongly affected traffic and public transit both inside and outside the ghetto. Before the war, there had been three bus lines and twelve tramlines that traversed the area of the future ghetto,[171] but most of the transportation infrastructure had been destroyed during the war in September 1939. According to Szarota, almost 80 percent of the tram wires had been damaged, and tram tracks had been ripped out.[172] More than half the railcars were not fit for use, and only 55 of the former 136 buses were operational. By the time of the ghetto's sealing, there were six tramlines operating on its terrain.[173] The Germans implemented two separate transportation systems, following the principle of racial segregation: there were Jewish trams operating internally and "Aryan" trams running through the ghetto in transit. The Jewish trams, numbers 15, 28, and 29, were introduced on November 26, 1940, and marked with yellow shields; in February 1941, these lines were closed down and, in their place, one tram line without a number was put into service, its shield "bearing . . . a blue-and-white Star of David."[174] This particular line ran between Muranowski Square and Chłodna Street.[175] The routes of the "Aryan" tram changed throughout the time of their operation, often due to the reduction of the number of the ghetto's entry gateways. The trams stopped running on August 15, 1942, when the deportations intensified.[176]

A very typical phenomenon in the ghetto, mentioned by almost all accounts, was bicycle rickshaws. According to Engelking and Leociak, these rickshaws were "one of the most curious, and at the same time one of the most popular, means of locomotion at the time."[177] These vehicles not only allowed for relatively fast and flexible transportation (for both passengers and goods) but also provided income for many of the ghetto's impoverished inhabitants. Another mode of transport peculiar, in Warsaw, to the ghetto was the system of horse-drawn streetcars operated by "German concessionaires, the Kohn and Heller Omnibus Transportation Company,"[178] which connected "streets that [had] no electric streetcar service."[179] According to ghetto chronicler Emanuel Ringelblum, these streetcars, colloquially called "Uncle Kohn's Cabins," "Lousy Cabins," or simply "Kohn-Hellers," were "a huge success."[180]

The sealing of the ghetto also had an effect on Jewish institutions previously located outside the walls, as they all, once the ghetto was to be sealed, had to move into the ghetto. One example is the Jewish Czyste hospital, the evacuation of which began mid-December 1940.[181] In this case, the move affected the hospital space very drastically. While the institutional space remained coherent, the physical space was dispersed: the hospital's departments were split up and "scattered to various places throughout the ghetto."[182] Two important Jewish orphanages also had to move to the ghetto, one of them being the Janusz Korczak orphans' home.[183] At the same time, the *Judenrat* became responsible for the postal service in the ghetto. The postal service was a crucial institution, since it represented one of the few channels of exchange and contact with the outside world. At first, mail and parcels were forwarded to the ghetto post offices by the German postal service, but, from January 15, 1941, onward, the *Judenrat* took over the entire postal service. The main post office was located in 19 Zamenhof Street in the location of a prewar post office (the building would later house the *Judenrat*), and two substations were located at 20 Ciepła Street and 32 Krochmalna Street (from January 1941 to spring 1942, this building also housed the Jewish Order Service).[184] There were eight letterboxes in the ghetto, and the inhabitants complained that these were not enough and very unevenly distributed.[185] In his report "The Jewish

Letter Carrier," written for the *Oneg Shabbat* archive, Opoczynski gives a very vivid account of the importance that incoming mail and parcels held for the ghetto inhabitants. They often meant that relatives or acquaintances would send provisions from the Soviet-occupied territories or from the countryside or, less frequently, money or food parcels from America.[186]

In terms of spatial access, the situation became more and more constricted for the Jews of Warsaw. In January 1941, following a decree by Leist, the punishment for leaving the ghetto without permission or for providing help to anyone doing so was raised drastically. This transgression was now punishable by penalties ranging from fines to arrest or deportation to a labor camp.[187] Although it was the establishment of the ghetto that had introduced the boundary, the decree issued under Leist further intensified the division. The "free" space that many people envisioned beyond the walls was violently severed from the ghetto, and the possibility of support from the non-Jewish population further ruptured. At the same time, the number of gates to the ghetto was systematically reduced. Gutman notes that of the twenty-two gates that existed in the early days of the ghetto's establishment, only four remained in use by the time the mass deportations to the Treblinka II death camp began in July 1942.[188] At the end of February 1941, a new decree issued by Governor General Hans Frank (and thus applying to the entire General Government) implemented a general ban prohibiting Jews from using railways or public transit without special permission from the *Stadthauptmann* in charge.[189]

Notes

1. Gutman, *Jews of Warsaw*, 5.
2. For information on the German attack on the city see, for example, Löw and Roth, *Das Warschauer Getto*, 14; Gutman, *Jews of Warsaw*, 5; Bartoszewski, "Warsaw under Occupation," 68–69; Kassow, *Who Will Write Our History?*, 105–106; Kaplan, *Scroll of Agony*, 21, 26, 29, 37–39; Berg, *Diary*, 7.
3. Szarota, *Warschau unter dem Hakenkreuz*, 16–17.
4. Ofer, "Gender Issues in Diaries and Testimonies," 146. In his study, Lehnstaedt gives a somewhat lower number. According to him, about 15 percent of the buildings had suffered damages (*Okkupation im Osten*, 77). Szarota speaks of seventy-eight thousand apartments being destroyed—that is 10.3 percent of the prewar housing space (*Warschau unter dem Hakenkreuz*, 154).
5. On October 25, 1939, Hitler's decree concerning the administration of Polish territories came into effect and the *Generalgouvernement* (General Government) was created under the management of Hans Frank as *Generalgouverneur* (governor general) (Gutschow and Klain, *Vernichtung und Utopie*, 24; Musial, *Deutsche Zivilverwaltung und Judenverfolgung*, 20). At this point, the military administration was

replaced by a civil administration. In contrast to the annexed territories (divided into the so-called *Reichsgaue* (Reich districts) Wartheland and Danzig-Westpreußen, or annexed to the provinces Schlesien and Ostpreußen), the *Generalgouvernement* did not officially become a part of the Reich. Legally, its status was not fully clarified, but it was basically treated as a colony, or a so-called *Nebenland* (borderland) (Majer, *"Non-Germans" under the Third Reich*, 262, 264; Gutman, *Jews of Warsaw*, 19). Whereas the annexed territories were subject to a radical policy of *Germanisierung* (Germanization), the *Generalgouvernement* was primarily meant to "serve as a military staging area for the forth-coming war with the Soviet Union (the primary immediate aim) as well as a reservoir of cheap labor for the Reich (the secondary immediate aim)" (Majer, *"Non-Germans" under the Third Reich*, 261; see also Himmler, "Einige Gedanken über die Behandlung der Fremdvölkischen," 198; Wasser, *Himmlers Raumplanung im Osten*, 20). Economically, the *Generalgouvernement* was mainly considered an area of short-term exploitation (Musial, *Deutsche Zivilverwaltung und Judenverfolgung*, 20–21). Corresponding to the different territorial designations, Jews and Poles who were deemed "undesirable elements" by the Nazis were sent from the annexed territories and the Reich to the *Generalgouvernement* in the course of the so-called *"ethnische Flurbereinigung"* (ethnic reallocation of land) (ibid., 20). When, after a short period of military administration, the civil administration took over, the *Generalgouvernement* was organized according to a colonial model, with most of the lower-level local administration left in place, dominated by a strong, centralized German administrative elite (Majer, *"Non-Germans" under the Third Reich*, 276). A similar principle was applied to the juridical system. Polish law, as well as Polish courts, were largely kept in operation (albeit supervised by German authorities); the German legal system was established as a parallel system, only concerned with cases that affected German rule (this in fact meant that in addition to covering all cases involving Germans or the interests of the Reich, as well as all cases concerned with alleged resistance or sabotage and all criminal cases, the German courts and legal authorities retained the right to claim almost every case that seemed of interest to the Germans; their juridical institutions operated with absolute privilege) (ibid., 487–491). Additional "special law" was introduced in matters concerning Jews and Poles, implemented mostly in the form of decrees (ibid., 287–288). In the annexed territories, by comparison, a separate discriminatory law had been established, the so-called *Polenstrafrechtsverordnung* (*"Verordnung über die Strafrechtspflege gegen Polen und Juden in den eingegliederten Ostgebieten"*). Two factors strongly influenced the conditions in the *Generalgouvernement*: first, there was still a Polish majority in the population, which made it impossible for the occupiers to fully control the territory (Broszat, *Nationalsozialistische Polenpolitik*, 177–178); second, the administrative aim was not, as in the case of the annexed territories, an almost complete dissolution of the local population and its replacement by German settlers but rather, due to the prospect of using the local population as workforce, required a certain stabilization of the status quo (Majer, *"Non-Germans" under the Third Reich*, 261).

6. On the German officials in Warsaw, see, for example, Gutschow and Klain, *Vernichtung und Utopie*, 24; Engelking and Leociak, *Warsaw Ghetto*, 30–34.

7. As part of the projected *Germanisierung* (Germanization) of Warsaw, the street was later renamed to Lindenallee and then to Siegesstrasse by the German occupiers (Lehnstaedt, *Okkupation im Osten*, 83).

8. On the parade, see Szarota, *Warschau unter dem Hakenkreuz*, 14–15; Gutschow and Klain, *Vernichtung und Utopie*, 24. Gutschow and Klain date the parade to October 6.

9. Teunissen, "Topography of Terror."

10. Ibid., map 6, "Map of the Route of the Parade on 5 October 1939."

11. Cole, "Geographies of Ghettoization," 272.

12. Engelking and Leociak, *Warsaw Ghetto*, 37; Gutman, *Jews of Warsaw*, 14–15; Hilberg, *Vernichtung der Europäischen Juden*, 201; Browning, "Nazi Ghettoization Policy," 345–346; the *Schnellbrief* is printed in German in Berenstein et al., *Faschismus—Getto—Massenmord*, 37–41; in English in Arad, Gutman, and Margaliot, *Documents on the Holocaust*, 173–178. The German original reads as follows: "*Als erste Vorausnahme für das Endziel gilt zunächst die Konzentrierung der Juden vom Lande in die größeren Städte*" (Berenstein et al., *Faschismus—Getto—Massenmord*, 37). In his article "Why Did Heydrich Write the *Schnellbrief*? A Remark on the Reason and on Its Significance," Dan Michman argues that it is important not to overestimate the role of the *Schnellbrief*. He suggests that the letter had not, as commonly assumed, been the expression of a decision that had been made simultaneously with—or shortly before—the letter's composition, but was, rather, a strategic element in a power struggle between different Nazi authorities. Its purpose was, as Michman phrases it, "*declarative* vis-à-vis the *other* important agencies" and "designed to say: Be aware that *we*—the internal-security system (SS and police)—have already put the wheels into motion, and *we* are implementing the anti-Jewish policy in these areas" ("Why Did Heydrich Write the *Schnellbrief*?," 443). According to Michman, the decision on the establishment of the *Judenräte* as well as the idea to concentrate the Jewish population had, in fact, been developed earlier and had already been partly implemented before the express letter was even written. Therefore, the letter did not initiate the process; it simply is the only written evidence accessible: "By way of summary, therefore, the *Schnellbrief* is indeed a very important document in the history of Nazi anti-Jewish policy as it encapsulates political principles. However, it is not a *point of departure* for the processes that unfolded afterward in Poland and elsewhere. Instead, it is a written phrasing of policies that had been set forth previously and that had *already begun* to be implemented; that is, a very important link in a chain" (ibid., 446; see also Michman, *Emergence of Jewish Ghettos*, 66).

13. Berenstein et al., *Faschismus—Getto—Massenmord*, 38.

14. Arad, Gutman, and Margaliot, *Documents on the Holocaust*, 175; for a slightly different translation, see Friedman, "Jewish Ghettos of the Nazi Era," 63. The German original reads as follows: "*Die Konzentrierung der Juden in Städten wird wahrscheinlich*

aus allgemein sicherheitspolizeilichen Gründen Anordnungen in diesen Städten bedingen, daß den Juden bestimmte Stadtviertel überhaupt verboten werde, daß sie—stets jedoch unter Berücksichtigung der wirtschaftlichen Notwendigkeiten — z.B. das Getto nicht verlassen, zu einer bestimmten Abendstunde nicht mehr ausgehen dürfen usw" (Berenstein et al., *Faschismus—Getto—Massenmord*, 38–39).

15. Michman argues that the reference to the ghetto has to be understood as a reference to the "ghettos" that the Germans believed were already existing—that is, to the Jewish districts in Eastern Europe as perceived through ideological writings such as those of Peter-Heinz Seraphim (Michman, *Emergence of Jewish Ghettos*, 45–60, 66–67; see, for example, Petersen, *Bevölkerungsökonomie—Ostforschung—Politik*, 130). According to Michman, it is therefore wrong to see Heydrich's letter as an indication that at this point the Germans already had a clear concept of the ghettos they were to establish later on (*Emergence of Jewish Ghettos*, 66–67). Browning argues similarly that even though a general idea of ghettos existed, the details "had not yet been clarified" and that at least *"sealed ghettos of prolonged duration* were not part of any policy imposed by Berlin on local German authorities in Poland in September 1939" ("Nazi Ghettoization Policy," 346).

16. Engelking and Leociak, *Warsaw Ghetto*, 53.

17. Berenstein et al., *Faschismus—Getto—Massenmord*, 42–43.

18. Reemtsma, *Trust and Violence*, 57; Piper, "Political and Racist Principles," 11–13.

19. Hilberg, *Vernichtung der Europäischen Juden*, 231.

20. Ibid., 225.

21. Aly, *Endlösung*, 131, 144; Hilberg, *Vernichtung der Europäischen Juden*, 225; Browning, *Entfesselung der "Endlösung,"* 174; Browning, "Nazi Ghettoization Policy," 346–347.

22. Reemtsma, *Trust and Violence*, 60.

23. Browning, *Entfesselung der "Endlösung,"* 174; "Nazi Ghettoization Policy," 364.

24. For detailed information on the appointment and on the members of the council, see Engelking and Leociak, *Warsaw Ghetto*, 138–139; see also Czerniaków, *Tagebuch*, 6–7.

25. Gutman, *Jews of Warsaw*, 14. The German original reads as follows: *"Er ist im Sinne des Wortes vollverantwortlich zu machen für die exakte und termingemäße Durchführung aller ergangenen und noch ergehenden Weisungen"* (Berenstein et al., *Faschismus—Getto—Massenmord*, 38).

26. Levi, "Grey Zone," 54.

27. Since very harsh actions were also taken against the Polish intelligentsia, Polish political and cultural leaders, and every Pole who was considered a potential source of insurgence (Rejak and Frister, *Inferno of Choices*, 16–17), at that time Jewish people did not necessarily feel clearly targeted yet. In his historical study on the German judiciary in the annexed territories (*Mitstreiter im Volkstumskampf. Deutsche Justiz in den eingegliederten Ostgebieten 1939–1945*), Maximilian Becker points out that, in fact, restrictions similar to the early anti-Jewish ones applied to non-Jewish

Poles as well (most drastically in the annexed territories). Poles were, for example, also excluded from many establishments, such as cinemas, parks, restaurants, cafés, theaters, museums, and libraries; they received different rations than did Germans, were drafted for forced labor, expelled from their homes, and suffered from explicit discrimination in many areas of everyday life (ibid., 27). In the annexed territories, Germans implemented the discriminatory penal law of the so-called *Polenstrafrechts-verordnung*, which affected both Poles and Jews alike, and during the *Intelligenzaktion* Germans systematically murdered Polish intellectuals and political and cultural leaders. Similar incidents of organized executions were carried out by the Germans in the *Generalgouvernement* under the cynical title *Allgemeine Befriedungs-Aktion* ("A.B.-Aktion"/pacification action) (Broszat, *Nationalsozialistische Polenpolitik*, 140, 183). However, corresponding to the focus of this book, the parallels will not be elaborated in detail.

28.   On these first economic anti-Jewish measures, see, for example, Gutman, *Jews of Warsaw*, 20, 9; Hilberg, *Vernichtung der Europäischen Juden*, 252; Kassow, *Who Will Write Our History?*, 106; Kazimierski et al., *Ludność Żydowska w Warszawie*, 136–154; Kaplan, *Scroll of Agony*, 48; Adler, *In the Warsaw Ghetto*, 32.

29.   Gutman, *Jews of Warsaw*, 9.

30.   Ibid., 20.

31.   Kaplan, *Scroll of Agony*, 232.

32.   Sznapman, account, 17–18.

33.   Kassow, *Who Will Write Our History?*, 107.

34.   See, for example, Bauman, *Winter in the Morning*, 40; Adler, *In the Warsaw Ghetto*, 32; Mazor, *Vanished City*, 28.

35.   See, for example, Opoczynski, "Goyim in the Ghetto," 54–71.

36.   Berenstein et al., *Faschismus—Getto—Massenmord*, 203, 205–209.

37.   Gutman, *Jews of Warsaw*, 9.

38.   Ibid., 22.

39.   Gutschow and Klain, *Vernichtung und Utopie*, 24. The Pawiak prison was located on the territory of the future ghetto. It was to become a notorious institution under German rule, the site of many executions and for many prisoners the waypoint before deportations to concentration and death camps. The building had already been notorious before the occupation as it had also served as a prison under Czarist rule (Lehnstaedt, *Okkupation im Osten*, 49; Anonymous Man, account, 73).

40.   Gutschow and Klain, *Vernichtung und Utopie*, 24.

41.   Engelking and Leociak, *Warsaw Ghetto*, 33.

42.   Gutman, *Jews of Warsaw*, 18; see also Kaplan, *Scroll of Agony*, 57; Czerniaków, *Tagebuch*, 11–13. Gutman dates the census to September 28, 1939, which is most likely a mistake since the *Judenrat* responsible for the census was not yet established at this point and the city had just capitulated. A second census was ordered by the Germans in November 1940, shortly before the establishment of the ghetto. Officially it was to "provide data on the number of apartments in the Jewish district, their surface area,

and the population density" to help with the allocation of quarters for refugees from outside of Warsaw (Engelking and Leociak, *Warsaw Ghetto*, 72).

43. Engelking and Leociak, *Warsaw Ghetto*, 37, 55, 311–316; see also Berg, *Diary*, 21, 59. Engelking and Leociak give a detailed account of the consecutive waves of new arrivals: in February 1940, a transport of Jewish prisoners of war arrived in Warsaw and was turned over to the responsibility of the *Judenrat* (*Warsaw Ghetto*, 311); in August 1940, there was a large number of refugees from Kraków; from January until March 1941, about fifty thousand people from the western part of the Warsaw district arrived in the then-sealed ghetto; from March until July 1942, people from the eastern part of the district were deported to the ghetto (for a list of places of origin, see ibid. 312–313); in addition, in April 1942, four thousand German Jews arrived at the *Umschlagplatz* (ibid., 313); at the same time a first group of Roma was committed to the Gęsia Street prison (ibid., 43).

44. See, for example, Berg, *Diary*, 60; Adler, *In the Warsaw Ghetto*, 39–40.

45. Engelking and Leociak, *Warsaw Ghetto*, 312; see also Berg, *Diary*, 59; Engelking, *Holocaust and Memory*, 87–89.

46. For descriptions of the conditions in the refugee centers see, for example, 276. RING. II/161; Berg, *Diary*, 60; Kaplan, *Scroll of Agony*, 94; Adler, *In the Warsaw Ghetto*, 79; Engelking and Leociak, *Warsaw Ghetto*, 314–315.

47. Engelking and Leociak, *Warsaw Ghetto*, 53.

48. During the first weeks of the occupation, and before civil administration was established, Warsaw had been under military administration (Lehnstaedt, *Okkupation im Osten*, 38). The military command was first held by Lieutenant-General Conrad von Cochenhausen (October 1–10, 1939), who was present for the military parade of the German army entering the city and for Hitler's visit to Warsaw on October 5, 1939. The next commander was Lieutenant-General Karl-Ulrich Neumann-Neurode. Szarota suggests that Neumann-Neurode was a fanatic follower of the Nazi party and ideology (*Warschau unter dem Hakenkreuz*, 232). After him, Colonel Walter von Unruh took over the military command of the city (fall 1940), then General Fritz von Rossum (spring/summer 1943), General Adolf von Kleist (fall 1943), General Werner Schartow (until July 1944), and from the end of July 1944 onward, General Rainer Stahel. The Jewish population, however, was generally under the executive control of the police forces and the SS, not the military (ibid., 231–232; for detailed information on the organizational structures and personnel of the "German Occupation Authorities" see Engelking and Leociak, *Warsaw Ghetto*, 26–34).

49. Engelking and Leociak, *Warsaw Ghetto*, 53.

50. Ibid.

51. Ibid.

52. Ibid., 54.

53. Gutman refers to him under the name Pinchas Ya'akov Zylberberg (*Jews of Warsaw*, 32); Engelking and Leociak give the names Pinkus Zylberryng (*Warsaw Ghetto*, 37) or Pinchas Jakub Zilberring (ibid., 140), Żbikowski calls him Pinchas

Jankiel Zylberger ("Antisemitism, Extortion," 199), Kaplan Jakub Pinchas Zylbring (*Scroll of Agony*, 80).

54. Gutman, *Jews of Warsaw*, 32–33; see also Edelman, *Das Ghetto Kämpft*, 28; Kaplan, *Scroll of Agony*, 80.

55. Gutman, *Jews of Warsaw*, 33. Gutman writes of 225 (ibid.), Engelking and Leociak of 255 (*Warsaw Ghetto*, 38), Edelman and Lewin of 300 (*Das Ghetto Kämpft*, 29; *Cup of Tears*, 73). For more information on Kott, see Ainsztein, *Revolte gegen die Vernichtung*, 36–37.

56. Broszat, *Nationalsozialistische Polenpolitik*, 183.

57. Kaplan, *Scroll of Agony*, 107.

58. Bethke and Schmidt Holländer, "Lebenswelt Ghetto," 49; Engelking and Leociak, *Warsaw Ghetto*, 344–354; Bauman, *Winter in the Morning*, 32.

59. For specification of these two elements in regard to German policies, see Nałkowska, "Adults and Children of Auschwitz," 46–47.

60. Gutman, *Jews of Warsaw*, 21.

61. Ibid., 20.

62. Ibid., 21.

63. Engelking and Leociak, *Warsaw Ghetto*, 380–381.

64. Ibid., 28. Initially, Hermann Göring asserted a claim on the Jewish property in the *Generalgouvernement* with the establishment of the *Haupttreuhandstelle Ost*. Frank countered this by founding "his own" *Treuhandstelle* for the *Generalgouvernement* two weeks later, limiting the dominion of the *Haupttreuhandstelle* to the territories annexed to the Reich (Hilberg, *Vernichtung der Europäischen Juden*, 251–252).

65. Gutman, *Jews of Warsaw*, 21, 72; see also Kaplan, *Scroll of Agony*, 97; Adler, *In the Warsaw Ghetto*, 7, 244.

66. Gutman, *Jews of Warsaw*, 20. Considering the exploitation of Jewish labor, it should be specified: deprived of any independent position in the economy.

67. Ibid., 25; see also Rejak and Frister, *Inferno of Choices*, 40, Bartoszewski, "Warsaw under Occupation," 77. For a detailed list of prices for various food and household items, both from official channels and the black market, see Engelking and Leociak, *Warsaw Ghetto*, 493–503.

68. Engelking and Leociak, *Warsaw Ghetto*, 37.

69. Arad, Gutman, and Margaliot, *Documents on the Holocaust*, 225.

70. Ibid.

71. Grynberg, *Words to Outlive Us*, 15; see also Lehnstaedt, "Jewish Spaces?," 54; Charlesworth, "Topography of Genocide," 249.

72. Reemtsma, *Trust and Violence*, 57.

73. Engelking and Leociak, *Warsaw Ghetto*, 55; see also Kaplan, *Scroll of Agony*, 78; the order is printed in Berenstein et al., *Faschismus—Getto—Massenmord*, 66.

74. Engelking and Leociak, *Warsaw Ghetto*, 55.

75. Ibid.

76. Gutman, *Jews of Warsaw*, 30.

77. Ibid., 31.

78. According to Hilberg, the regulations by which people were classified as Jewish had, at first, been much broader in the *Generalgouvernement*. They not only included so-called *"Halbjuden"* but also all non-Jewish spouses (*Vernichtung der Europäischen Juden*, 225–226). In May 1940, Hans Frank, who insisted on the application of the Nuremberg Laws, succeeded in establishing them as the guiding principle in the *Generalgouvernement* (ibid., 226).

79. Bartoszewski, "Warsaw under Occupation," 71; see also Kaplan, *Scroll of Agony*, 79; Ernest, account, 21.

80. Opoczynski, "Building No. 21," 8–9.

81. Ibid., 9.

82. Engelking and Leociak, *Warsaw Ghetto*, 101; Gutman, *Jews of Warsaw*, 334; Edelman, *Das Ghetto Kämpft*, 63; Lewin, *Cup of Tears*, 283, 285, 292, 294.

83. Engelking and Leociak, *Warsaw Ghetto*, 37. For an example of a Jewish ration card, see Berenstein et al., *Faschismus—Getto—Massenmord*, 137.

84. Gutman, *Jews of Warsaw*, 66; Engelking and Leociak, *Warsaw Ghetto*, 417; Berenstein et al., *Faschismus—Getto—Massenmord*, 156.

85. Engelking and Leociak, *Warsaw Ghetto*, 417.

86. Gutman, *Jews of Warsaw*, 26.

87. Opoczynski, "Building No. 21," 11–12, 17; see also Michman, *Emergence of Jewish Ghettos*, 63–64; Kaplan, *Scroll of Agony*, 70–71, 77; Markowska, *Ringelblum Archive*, 34–36.

88. Arad, Gutman, and Margaliot, *Documents on the Holocaust*, 179–180.

89. Ibid., 180.

90. Engelking and Leociak, *Warsaw Ghetto*, 56.

91. Ibid.

92. Ibid., 38. While three synagogues inside the ghetto (the Great Synagogue at Tłomackie, Nożyk Synagogue at Twarda Street in the small ghetto, and Moriah Synagogue at Dzielna Street in the large ghetto) were allowed to reopen temporarily in the fall/winter of 1941, they did not operate for long (Jagielski, "Three Synagogues"; Engelking and Leociak, *Warsaw Ghetto*, 650). In March 1942, the Great Synagogue along with the Judaic Library were excluded from the ghetto; the synagogue was henceforth used as a storage facility (Jagielski, "Three Synagogues"; Engelking and Leociak, *Warsaw Ghetto*, 91, 650). Nożyk Synagogue was closed again in July 1942, when the Germans "liquidated" the small ghetto; it was then used by the Germans as "a stable and a depot" (Jagielski, "Three Synagogues"). Moriah Synagogue was destroyed during bombings in September 1942 (ibid.; Gebert, "Reading the Palimpsest," 225–226).

93. In Warsaw, there had been comparably few major synagogues right before the occupation (Martyn, "Undefined Town within a Town," 30). Because Jewish settlement in Warsaw had historically been decentralized—with various separated communities settling in smaller, independent jurisdictions that only by the end of

the eighteenth century were administratively incorporated into the city—a shared religious tradition as in other cities, such as Kraków or Lublin, had not developed. Religious practice was thus highly differentiated, with the different communities following their respective *rebbes* or *tzadiks* and praying in numerous smaller prayer houses, often located in privately owned buildings (Czajka). This also meant that Jewish religious architecture was not as prominent in Warsaw as it was in other Polish cities. Especially the small, private prayer houses bore no clear architectural signature that would have given expression to their religious importance.

94. Engelking and Leociak, *Warsaw Ghetto*, 641.

95. In fact, early on, the Germans, aligning their antisemitism with their general antireligious practices, began with a coordinated attack on Jewish religious institutions and religious practices all over occupied Poland. Synagogues were among the first targets of anti-Jewish violence; countless acts of desecration were committed. Torahs were burned, soiled, and publicly destroyed, and religious objects and sites of religious practice came under attack (ibid., 641).

96. Hilberg, *Vernichtung der Europäischen Juden*, 235.

97. Arad, Gutman, and Margaliot, *Documents on the Holocaust*, 182; see also Opoczynski, "Building No. 21," 9.

98. Engelking and Leociak, *Warsaw Ghetto*, 38, 57; see also Arad, Gutman, and Margaliot, *Documents on the Holocaust*, 222. This approach would have been much closer to the one that was eventually taken in Kraków in March 1941. There, the ghetto was not established in the traditional Jewish district of Kazimierz but in the poor parts of the southern Podgórze district, farther away from the city center. In the *Atlas of the Holocaust*, Martin Gilbert identifies two general patterns: "Starting with the town of Piotrkow on 28 October 1939, the Germans began to confine the Jews in Poland to a particular area of each town in which they lived. Sometimes, this area was the already predominantly Jewish quarter. But often it was a poor or neglected part of the town, away from the center" (51).

99. Arad, Gutman, and Margaliot, *Documents on the Holocaust*, 222.

100. Gutschow and Klain, *Vernichtung und Utopie*, 28.

101. Engelking and Leociak, *Warsaw Ghetto*, 58; see also Kaplan, *Scroll of Agony*, 134–135.

102. Engelking and Leociak, *Warsaw Ghetto*, 58; see also Edelman, *Das Ghetto Kämpft*, 29–30. For the German stance on "local pogroms," see Heydrich, "June 29, 1941, Order No. 1" and "July 1, 1941, Order no. 2" (Rejak and Frister, *Inferno of Choices*, 21–23). In order no. 1, Heydrich states, "No impediments should be made to self-cleansing aspirations occurring in anti-Communist and anti-Jewish circles in the newly seized territories. On the contrary, they should be triggered without leaving a trace, encouraged where necessary, and directed into appropriate channels" (ibid., 21).

103. Engelking and Leociak, *Warsaw Ghetto*, 58.

104. Berg, *Diary*, 27; see also Kaplan, *Scroll of Agony*, 211; Kassow, *Who Will Write Our History?*, 395–396.

105. Bauman, *Winter in the Morning*, 40.

106. Ernest, account, 21; Engelking and Leociak, *Warsaw Ghetto*, 38.

107. Arad, Gutman, and Margaliot, *Documents on the Holocaust*, 223.

108. Hilberg, "Ghetto as a Form of Government," 110; Engelking and Leociak, *Warsaw Ghetto*, 58, 60; see also Kaplan, *Scroll of Agony*, 223.

109. Arad, Gutman, and Margaliot, *Documents on the Holocaust*, 223.

110. Ibid., 224. The village of Wielka Wola was incorporated into Warsaw in 1916. As a traditional workers' quarter and a poorer part of Warsaw, it was more status than location that defined it as "outside of the city center." Koło was a neighborhood within Wola. Grochów was a residential area located on the "other side" of the Vistula; it had been incorporated into Warsaw at the same time as Wola.

111. Ultimately, the Wola-Koło-Grochów plan was discarded in August because of the immense resettlement action it would have required (ibid., 224).

112. Ibid., 216–218.

113. Aly, *Endlösung*, 147; Gutschow and Klain, *Vernichtung und Utopie*, 111.

114. See, for example, Sznapman, account, 20; Stok, account, 22; Blady-Szwajgier, *Erinnerung Verläßt Mich Nie*, 21; Kaplan, *Scroll of Agony*, 163–164; Adler, *In the Warsaw Ghetto*, 5–6. Unbeknownst to Jews in Warsaw, on the same day, a group consisting of 728 political prisoners from the Tarnów prison was transported to the Auschwitz I concentration camp (Czech, *Kalendarium*, 35); this transport ultimately marks the beginning of the camp's operation. The first 30 prisoners transported to Auschwitz on May 20, 1940, were German criminals from Sachsenhausen, deported there to serve as prisoner functionaries in the newly established camp (ibid., 32). Another 40 prisoners were transported to Auschwitz from Dachau on May 29. This transport consisted of a German and 39 young Polish prisoners who were deployed by the Germans as an *Außenkommando* (external work detachment) to put up the fence for the camp (ibid., 34). They left Auschwitz again for Dachau on June 14, 1940. The same day, the 728 political prisoners from Tarnów arrived (ibid., 35). Transports from the Pawiak prison to Auschwitz are repeatedly listed by Władysław Bartoszewski over the years of the ghetto's existence ("Warsaw under Occupation," 77–103).

115. Engelking and Leociak, *Warsaw Ghetto*, 60–61.

116. Szarota, *Warschau unter dem Hakenkreuz*, 24.

117. Engelking and Leociak, *Warsaw Ghetto*, 62; see also Kaplan, *Scroll of Agony*, 173, 193.

118. Engelking and Leociak, *Warsaw Ghetto*, 62. The decree was first made public on August 7, then published in the *Nowy Kurier Warszawski* two days later.

119. The Germans who were in Warsaw during the occupation were not a homogenous group. They had come to Warsaw in different roles and with different ambitions. A large group were Wehrmacht soldiers, who were the first to arrive in the city and remained a large portion of the city's German population during the entire occupation (Lehnstaedt, *Okkupation im Osten*, 35). Lehnstaedt estimates that in 1941 there were up to forty thousand soldiers in town (ibid., 36). Due to its location, Warsaw was

an important waypoint for soldiers on their way to the eastern front and served as a rehabilitation area for those returning; however, there was a great degree of fluctuation, and most soldiers remained in the city for only a short period of time (ibid., 36). Still, the overall military presence in Warsaw was fairly high, constituting about 3 percent of the city's population at almost any point (ibid., 36). Wehrmacht uniforms were a common sight on the streets of the city, visually reiterating the state of occupation and contributing to a gradual "Nazification of public space" (Miron, "'Lately, Almost Constantly, Everything Seems Small to Me,'" 129). The SS and police made up a much smaller number of the Germans in Warsaw, with a maximum mounting to about eight thousand men (Lehnstaedt, *Okkupation im Osten*, 42). About half of them were members of the *Waffen SS* (the armed wing of the SS), and especially in the early years, those were typically ideologically well-versed volunteers who had joined the SS and the Nazi party relatively early (ibid., 42). Due to their predominant involvement in German terror campaigns, the local population feared the members of the SS and police (especially the Gestapo) more than the Wehrmacht. For the population of the occupied city, it thus became extremely important to be able to identify different groups by their uniforms. A third group of Germans in occupied Warsaw were members of the German administration, who were responsible for administering the occupied territories. Many of them were transferred from their previous offices to their new work in occupied Poland, which means they were still formally employed in their old position and anticipated return at some later point (ibid., 53). The highest ranks of administration were usually filled with loyal Nazis (ibid.). The overall number of people employed in administration ranged from five hundred to seven hundred, not including employees of the postal service and the German railroad (ibid., 57–58). Because everyone employed in the German administration wore a uniform, these German civilians were immediately recognizable as belonging to the occupying forces as well (ibid., 63). There were about nine thousand *Reichsdeutsche* or *Volksdeutsche* (Reich's or ethnic Germans) women working for instance as stenotypists and telephonists, often in the social sector (ibid., 65–66). Most of these female employees were young volunteers coming to the occupied east of their own accord (ibid., 65). The women employed with the Wehrmacht or the SS wore uniforms, too, and thus became a visible part of the German occupation society (that was otherwise predominantly visible in the form of men in uniforms) (ibid., 67). A much smaller number of women had come to Warsaw as spouses of men employed in the civilian administration (ibid.). The last major group was that of the *Volksdeutsche*, many of whom had already lived in Warsaw before the occupation. According to Lehnstaedt, in 1943 there were over ten thousand *Volksdeutsche* in Warsaw who had successfully registered in the so-called *Volksliste* (German people's list) and had thus been granted German citizenship (ibid., 67–68). A large number of *Volksdeutsche* were employed on guard duty or became members of the *Selbstschutz* (an ethnic German "self-defense" organization) (ibid., 70).
120. Szarota, *Warschau unter dem Hakenkreuz*, 251.

121. Lehnstaedt, *Okkupation im Osten*, 79–80.

122. Szarota, *Warschau unter dem Hakenkreuz*, 251–253.

123. Lehnstaedt, *Okkupation im Osten*, 82; see also Kaplan, *Scroll of Agony*, 326.

124. Szarota, *Warschau unter dem Hakenkreuz*, 253–254.

125. Arad, Gutman, and Margaliot, *Documents on the Holocaust*, 224–225.

126. Ibid., 224.

127. Cole, "Ghettoization," 81.

128. Engelking and Leociak, *Warsaw Ghetto*, 63.

129. Ibid.

130. Ibid., 64.

131. Bauman, *Winter in the Morning*, 34; Stok, account, 23.

132. Kassow, *Who Will Write Our History?*, 107; see also Kaplan, *Scroll of Agony*, 211, 213.

133. Kassow, *Who Will Write Our History?*, 107; see also Kaplan, *Scroll of Agony*, 211; Engelking, *Holocaust and Memory*, 89–90; Engelking and Leociak, *Warsaw Ghetto*, 64, 68; Browning, *Entfesselung der "Endlösung,"* 190.

134. Engelking and Leociak, *Warsaw Ghetto*, 64.

135. Kaplan, *Scroll of Agony*, 202; Engelking and Leociak, *Warsaw Ghetto*, 64.

136. Arad, Gutman, and Margaliot, *Documents on the Holocaust*, 225; Kazimierski et al., *Ludność Żydowska w Warszawie*, 195.

137. Gutman, *Jews of Warsaw*, 61; see also Mazor, *Vanished City*, 10.

138. Kaplan, *Scroll of Agony*, 210, see also 218, 222.

139. Engelking and Leociak, *Warsaw Ghetto*, 62, see also 65–66, for the decree, see 102. For a map illustrating the specific numbers and origins (in terms of city quarters) of the Jewish population forced to move into the ghetto, see Gilbert's *Atlas of the Holocaust* (52, map 55). Just to indicate some of the most numerically significant movements: according to Gilbert, about 22,456 people moved to the ghetto from Praga (8,758 from Praga-Północ and 13,698 from Praga-Południe), 23,255 from the western district of Towarowy, and about 40,108 from streets located very close to the eastern borders of the ghetto in the city center (ibid., 52, map 55).

140. Arad, Gutman, and Margaliot, *Documents on the Holocaust*, 226. In a conversation in November 2020, Michał Czajka (JHI) noted that usually poorer Poles lived among Jews, whereas more affluent Jews did not live in the area of the projected ghetto but, rather, among the Gentile population in other parts of the city (see also Martyn, "Undefined Town within a Town," 29, 30). Typically, the apartments requisitioned from Jews who had resided outside the ghetto were thus of a higher standard than those vacated by non-Jews in the area that was to become the ghetto.

141. Bartoszewski, "Warsaw under Occupation," 76.

142. Szarota, *Warschau unter dem Hakenkreuz*, 251; Leociak, *Doświadczenia graniczne*, 53.

143. Engelking and Leociak, *Warsaw Ghetto*, 34.

144. Adler, *In the Warsaw Ghetto*, 7.

145. Engelking and Leociak, *Warsaw Ghetto*, 65.

146. Ibid.; see also Adler, *In the Warsaw Ghetto*, 35.

147. Kaplan, *Scroll of Agony*, 213–214.

148. Engelking and Leociak, *Warsaw Ghetto*, 66–67.

149. Hilberg, *Vernichtung der Europäischen Juden*, 253; see also Charlesworth, "Topography of Genocide," 241.

150. Engelking and Leociak, *Warsaw Ghetto*, 66; see also Ringelblum, *Notes from the Warsaw Ghetto*, 69.

151. Kaplan, *Scroll of Agony*, 206.

152. Engelking and Leociak, *Warsaw Ghetto*, 67–68.

153. Ibid. And indeed, on November 14, the *Nowy Kurier Warszawski* published a new "detailed plan of the boundary of the Jewish district" (ibid., 72). On November 16/17, a day after the sealing off of the ghetto, another list of the boundary streets, detailing the house numbers of the buildings located next to the border, was published in the *Nowy Kurier Warszawski* (ibid., 74, 103–104). Another list of the boundary streets would be published on November 22 in *Gazeta Żydowska*; another decree by Leist specifying the boundaries followed on January 14, 1941 (ibid., 104–107).

154. There were other bridges in the ghetto, too, namely at Przebieg Street, at the corner of Sapieżyńska and Mławska Street, and at Żelazna Street north of Leszno. These bridges, however, were not as prominent as the one at Chłodna Street; they connected small exclaves to the ghetto and thus never played a major role in the ghetto's communication network.

155. See, for example, Berg, *Diary*, 62, 76, 80–83, 94, 122; Adler, *In the Warsaw Ghetto*, 52; Ringelblum, *Notes from the Warsaw Ghetto*, 222, 226–227; 504. RING. I/212; see also Engelking and Leociak, *Warsaw Ghetto*, 125–126.

156. Kaplan, *Scroll of Agony*, 225.

157. Engelking and Leociak, *Warsaw Ghetto*, 190. For detailed information on the Jewish Order Service, see Person, *Warsaw Ghetto Police*.

158. See, for example, Berg, *Diary*, 34; Kaplan, *Scroll of Agony*, 234.

159. Engelking and Leociak, *Warsaw Ghetto*, 40.

160. Kassow, *Who Will Write Our History?*, 149, 213, 396; for a more extensive list and detailed portraits of members of the group, see 145–208.

161. Ibid., 333, see also 209–210.

162. Cole, "Ghettoization," 82.

163. Engelking and Leociak, *Warsaw Ghetto*, 40; Gutschow and Klain, *Vernichtung und Utopie*, 126; see also Berg, *Diary*, 105; Adler, *In the Warsaw Ghetto*, 227.

164. Kazimierski et al., *Ludność Żydowska w Warszawie*, 71.

165. Engelking and Leociak, *Warsaw Ghetto*, 394; see also Browning, *Entfesselung der "Endlösung,"* 191, 197.

166. Browning, "Nazi Ghettoization Policy," 352, 355.

167. Ibid., 354–355.

168. Goldberg, "Rumor Culture," 92.

169. Ibid.

170. Ibid. See also Helpland, *Defiant Gardens*, 61–62.

171. Engelking and Leociak, *Warsaw Ghetto*, 108.

172. Szarota, *Warschau unter dem Hakenkreuz*, 163.

173. Ibid., 163, 169.

174. Engelking and Leociak, *Warsaw Ghetto*, 116, see also 110, 112.

175. Szarota, *Warschau unter dem Hakenkreuz*, 169.

176. Engelking and Leociak, *Warsaw Ghetto*, 119, 134; see also Lewin, *Cup of Tears*, footnote on page 269.

177. Engelking and Leociak, *Warsaw Ghetto*, 108. For a more detailed documentation of the appearance of the *Rikschas* and their history, see Szarota's *Warschau unter dem Hakenkreuz*, 164–166.

178. Engelking and Leociak, *Warsaw Ghetto*, 121.

179. Ringelblum, *Notes from the Warsaw Ghetto*, 216.

180. Ibid.

181. Engelking and Leociak, *Warsaw Ghetto*, 76.

182. Ibid.; see also Kaplan, *Scroll of Agony*, 239–241.

183. Despite Korczak's efforts to prevent this, the orphanage actually had to move twice. Once into the ghetto from 92 Krochmalna Street to 33 Chłodna Street, and from there to 16 Sienna Street. The second orphanage, the Central Shelter Home, moved from 127 Leszno Street to 39 Dzielna Street (Engelking and Leociak, *Warsaw Ghetto*, 76, 319–320; Lifton, "Introduction," viii).

184. Engelking and Leociak, *Warsaw Ghetto*, 40, 171, 195; for more information on the postal service see ibid., 367–379; Gordon, "Ghetto Mail Man"; Opoczynski, "Jewish Letter Carrier," 31–53.

185. Gordon, "Ghetto Mail Man"; Engelking and Leociak, *Warsaw Ghetto*, 370.

186. Opoczynski, "Jewish Letter Carrier," 37, 39; Engelking and Leociak, *Warsaw Ghetto*, 374–375.

187. Bartoszewski, "Warsaw under Occupation," 78; Engelking and Leociak, *Warsaw Ghetto*, 76.

188. Gutman, *Jews of Warsaw*, 63; see also Engelking and Leociak, *Warsaw Ghetto*, 76; Browning, *Entfesselung der "Endlösung,"* 237; Adler, *In the Warsaw Ghetto*, 46.

189. Berenstein et al., *Faschismus—Getto—Massenmord*, 116–118.

CHAPTER

7

~~~

Dissolution of the Ghetto

Reduction of the Ghetto

Though the number of inhabitants of the ghetto had reached its maximum of 460,000, March 1941 saw another reduction of the ghetto area.[1] This worsened living conditions inside the walls, further intensifying the immense overcrowding that generally was one of the most critical issues inside the ghetto, greatly affecting living conditions and social space. As Mazor explains in his ghetto recollections, "From the outset, the ghetto was overpopulated; furthermore, its area continually shrank as blocks of apartments and even whole streets were gradually removed from it: the inhabitants of those streets would then swell the ranks, already well beyond capacity, of those in the reduced ghetto."[2] Right from the beginning, the scarcity of space and the forced density of living arrangements had drastically changed social relations in the ghetto. The inhabitants had become an oppressive element in each other's lives.

At the same time, the Germans steered the remaining ghetto further toward economic exploitation. In April, the number of round-ups for labor camps increased drastically and the Germans began the establishment of factories, so-called shops, in the ghetto.[3] By June 1941, when Germany started its Eastern Campaign, these ghetto workshops began to receive large orders from the Wehrmacht.[4] On June 9, 1941, a prison was opened inside the ghetto at 24 Gęsia Street; it was located in the building of a former military jail.[5] At the end of the month, on June 22, 1941, Germany attacked the Soviet Union. The development of the German war efforts in the east would prove particularly significant for the ghetto inhabitants. It shifted the German priorities in regard to resources, but most of all, the eventual failure of their campaign coincided with a radicalization of their anti-Jewish policies. But, at this early stage, the Varsovians took the attack as a beacon of hope: finally, the Soviet Union would join the anti-German coalition.[6] The first Soviet air raids on Warsaw were carried out shortly after.[7]

In September, Heinz Auerswald announced that the ghetto would "be reduced in size and more strictly isolated."[8] The idea of the reduction of the small ghetto had, according to Czerniaków, surfaced for the first time in June of that year.[9] In September, the idea was rekindled, and the Germans proposed changes to the borders so that they would run along streets and not, as previously, between buildings, thus allowing them to be more easily guarded.[10] The new border, which was implemented over the next months, was far more prominent than the old one, which in many places had been basically invisible, "marked by the adjoining 'backs' of rows of tenements which stood between two parallel streets, of which one belonged entirely to the ghetto and the other was entirely on the Aryan side."[11] The change therefore confronted the ghettoized people even more tangibly with the oppressiveness of their environment and significantly impeded smuggling. Allegedly, Auerswald's decision was motivated by a spreading of typhus beyond the ghetto walls that he attributed to smugglers crossing the borders.[12]

The German authorities started the actual reduction in October by cutting off Sienna Street from the ghetto. The reduction continued well into December, with the Germans removing more and more parts mainly of the southern section of the ghetto.[13] New walls and barbed-wire fences were built under the supervision of the *Judenrat*. In fact, there was a separate section of the *Judenrat* responsible for the building of walls and fences, the "Technical and Construction Section."[14] Construction remained ongoing, thus characterizing the space of the ghetto as constitutively unfinished. Bonifraterska, Okopowa, and the rest of Chłodna Street were excluded from the ghetto, and the latter was turned into an uninterrupted "Aryan" traffic corridor between the large ghetto and the small ghetto. The cemetery on Okopowa Street, which had been partly inside the ghetto, was excluded from the ghetto area as well.[15] The cemetery had been an important location for smuggling, but its exclusion also affected funeral rites. From then on, without special permission, the mourning party was not permitted to escort the deceased but had to hand them over to the morticians' staff at the gate.[16] People were thus cut off from their tradition, as well as from the heritage of a familial gravesite. Again, the Germans targeted an important Jewish cultural space.[17] In many regards, the status of the cemetery was unique. Its exclusion meant the disturbance of a central sacred space. Then again, from a cultural standpoint, it remained a Jewish space even when it was outside the ghetto. Fearing typhus, the Germans shunned the area, so it was not repurposed but, rather, remained Jewish.[18]

In the course of the massive reduction of the ghetto area, about seventy-five thousand inhabitants had to move.[19] The constant changes to the boundaries meant that, often, people had to move repeatedly. Many essentially became migrants within the ghetto. The inhabitants could not "own" the ghetto space, and it was repeatedly experienced as alien and new. In October 1941, a new order by Hans Frank declared an illegal crossing of a ghetto border an offense punishable by death anywhere in the *Generalgouvernement*.[20] A few weeks later, the death penalty was extended to those who helped anyone cross such borders.[21] The racial segregation established by the Germans was thus taken to its extreme: the space designated as Jewish became the only space in which Jews had a right to live at all. "Aryan" space, in turn, became the negation of Jewish life. In addition, Frank's order isolated the Jews from their non-Jewish neighbors and undermined potential support even further. Both regulations were implemented in Warsaw by decrees signed by Fischer about a month later on November 10.[22] Soon, these orders led to the first executions: on November 17, six Jewish women and two Jewish men were shot at the Gęsia Street prison for illegally crossing the boundaries. A month later, another fifteen people were shot for the same offense.[23] Many other people, especially smugglers—and among them, many children—were shot as they attempted to cross the borders.[24] The fact that the Germans further enforced the boundaries against smugglers strongly affected the situation inside the ghetto in that it impaired a vital channel that had helped the inhabitants to supplement their provisions. Both directly and indirectly, the Germans' aggressive regulation of space translated into physical harm.

At the end of December 1941, the commissar of the Jewish district, Auerswald, issued a decree demanding Warsaw's Jews to hand over all furs and fur goods to the authorities under threat of the death penalty.[25] The furs were most likely intended for soldiers at the eastern front, but as Engelking and Leociak point out, "the greater part of these valuable outer garments never reached the German soldiers."[26] An underground news bulletin reports that many were destroyed during a fire in a storage facility but also suggests that a large number of the most valuable furs had been stolen. The requisitioned furs were later remade into sleeping bags for the soldiers in one of the ghetto's "shops."[27] Czerniaków reports in his diary that he was able to negotiate with Auerswald the release of 150 prisoners from Pawiak prison in exchange for the furs and an additional fifteen hundred sheepskin coats procured by the *Judenrat*.[28] This is one of many examples illustrating both the Germans' agenda of extorting all valuables from Jews held in the ghetto and the *Judenrat*'s attempts to bargain for lives.

Some testimonies suggest that there might have been a certain ideological dimension to the Germans' exploitation practices as well. In addition to amassing valuables, such as furs, musical instruments, radios, furniture, and so on, they also stripped the Jewish population of outer manifestations of wealth and elegance. Mazor recalls seeing a young man in evening attire, "complete with tails and top hat," being driven through the streets by Germans. He suggests that the Germans must have been enraged when they found the garment during a raid of his home.[29] Especially when the situation of the German occupiers turned for the worse, their racial ideology might have translated into aggression toward any symbol of luxury and distinction in the possession of their Jewish victims.

Mass Murder

Among the inhabitants of the ghetto, the fact that the United States was entering the war,[30] and that it had joined the anti-German coalition, elicited some hope in December 1941. What in fact came next for the inhabitants of the ghetto was a decisive and devastating shift in the Nazis' ghetto politics, a shift ratified at the Wannsee Conference of January 20, 1942. All plans for a "Final Solution" in a territorial sense were abandoned at this point. Before, the ghetto had been a site of "gradual" or "indirect" killing in the sense that while its inhabitants were not "murdered outright," they were subjected to "conditions that clearly accelerated" their deaths.[31] Plans for the next step in the process had remained somewhat unclear, being a matter of changing trajectories. Now, the events escalated quickly, and the German agenda shifted from expulsion to genocide.[32] On February 19, a first group of Jewish prisoners from Gęsia Street was transported to the Treblinka I labor camp, most likely to assist with construction work for the "extermination" camp, Treblinka II.[33] The same month, news about the fate of deported Jews reached the ghetto through an escapee from the Kulmhof "extermination" camp, located close to the village of Chełmno on the Ner, Szlamek Fajner.[34]

On the night of April 17–18, there was a first "organized terror Aktion" in the ghetto: squads of SS men, accompanied by members of the Jewish Police, entered the ghetto and shot fifty-two people in the streets, marking the beginning of an escalating, direct violence that would only grow with time.[35] This incident became known as the "Night of Blood" or "Bartholomew's Night."[36] According to Gutman's study, the shooting was followed by an almost regular series of executions in the ghetto streets, usually taking place on Friday nights.[37] Ghetto fighter Marek Edelman identifies the incident as a turning point in the ghetto: from then on, he states, people were aware that there was no safety for anyone.[38]

At the end of April, when Auerswald asked Czerniaków for a list of the ghetto's inhabitants sorted by streets and individual houses and when one of his employees requisitioned ten maps of the ghetto, Czerniaków took this as a sign that "resettlement" might be imminent.[39] But it would take another two months until his apprehension would prove true. These months were marked by more violence but also by developments that elicited some hope in the Jewish community. On May 30–31, 1942, there was a major air raid by the British in Germany, targeting Cologne. According to Engelking and Leociak, inside the ghetto this was perceived as an "announcement of revenge for the extermination of the Jews."[40] At the beginning of June, several dozen people were murdered by the Gestapo in the streets of the ghetto, and Gutman reports that a little later, "110 Jews incarcerated in the ghetto prison were executed" in an act of retaliation for alleged resistance.[41] A few months later, at the end of June 1942, a radio broadcast by the BBC on the murder of the Polish Jews publicized the Germans' genocidal actions. The broadcast was based on reports by the *Oneg Shabbat* group.[42] In mid-July, the German authorities moved Jewish foreign citizens to Pawiak prison on the pretext of exchanging them for German prisoners of war later on.[43] Only a small number of them would actually make it to their destined countries and survive the war.[44]

The *Grossaktion Warschau* (Great Deportation Action) started on July 22, 1942, following Himmler's order that the "evacuation of the entire Jewish population of the *Generalgouvernement* must be completed by December 31, 1942"; only a certain number of laborers, concentrated in camps in Warsaw, Cracow, Częstochowa, Radom, and Lublin, were to remain in the *Generalgouvernement* by that time.[45] Engelking and Leociak describe the beginning of the Deportation Action in Warsaw as follows: "During the night, the walls of the ghetto were surrounded by guard posts manned by 'blue' (Polish) police as well as Ukrainian, Lithuanian, and Latvian auxiliary formations. In the morning, functionaries of the staff of 'Einsatz Reinhard' headed by SS-Sturmbannführer Hermann Höfle, entered the *Judenrat* headquarters at 26 Grzybowska Street with an order for the so-called resettlement of the Warsaw Jews in eastern territories."[46] Höfle ordered the *Judenrat* to provide a daily quota of six thousand people for deportation. A day after receiving this first deportation order, the chairman of the *Judenrat*, Adam Czerniaków, refusing to act as German deputy in the deportation process, took his own life.[47] Marek Lichtenbaum became his successor. During the deportations, power shifted from Auerswald and his administrative staff to the SS and the "deportation division" (*Umsiedlungsstab*) under Höfle.[48] The fact that the Nazi authorities who were now in power were the same ones that operated the Nazi concentration and death camps clearly reflects how the status of the ghetto had changed.

Posters signed by the *Judenrat* were put up in the streets of the ghetto, informing the inhabitants of what the authorities called "resettlement action." A few days later, they were followed by an announcement that people who voluntarily reported for deportation would get a ration of bread and marmalade.[49] The general population still assumed that people transported "to the east" would be transported there to work.[50] The trains were leaving from the *Umschlagplatz* situated at the northern border of the ghetto at the corner of Dzika and Stawki Streets. Again, the Germans delegated the realization of their crimes to a Jewish agency: during the first week, the Jewish Police was responsible for carrying out the round-ups and supplying the daily quota of deportees. Later, additional SS squads, "German gendarmes and their allied Ukrainian, Lithuanian, and Latvian formations" entered the ghetto to round up the victims.[51]

Various underground publications by different Jewish political organizations warned the inhabitants of the ghetto not to follow the German orders but, rather, to resist deportation.[52] At the same time, Jewish youth organizations began forming the Jewish Fighting Organization, the so-called *Żydowska Organizacja Bojowa* (ŻOB).[53] Documents indicate that the decision to take up armed resistance was voted down within the newly founded ŻOB.[54] More and more aware of the perilous situation, at the beginning of August, the *Oneg Shabbat* group decided to bury parts of their collection in ten tin chests in the cellar of 68 Nowolipki Street.[55] In the beginning, the Jewish Police predominantly targeted people from the refugee centers, hospitals, and ghetto prisons, as well as beggars from the streets, to fill the demanded quota of deportees.[56] According to Jan Mawult's account, this first led people in the ghetto to believe that the Germans were possibly only targeting the weak and the poor. He paraphrases the rumors that expressed the public sentiment: "They're not touching the core; they're only hitting the back streets, driving out the beggars, the paupers, the refugees."[57] It is particularly interesting how Mawult spatializes the social status of those targeted and ties it to a peripheral location, to the "back streets." That hope, however, proved to be misplaced, and in the following days the Nazi forces systematically combed through particular streets and buildings to round up people for deportation (in most accounts, these round-ups are referred to under the German term *Blockaden*).[58] The deportations often tore families apart. With round-ups taking place unannounced and suddenly, people often did not return home, or, upon returning, found their families had been taken away by the German forces.[59] Corresponding to this, Lewin speaks of the "destruction of families" when he describes the deportation of numerous friends and acquaintances in August 1942.[60] Often, the closest of ties were broken in the blink of an eye, with no notice and no time to prepare.[61]

The remains of the small ghetto were then "liquidated," and the *Judenrat* moved its headquarters from 26 Grzybowska Street to 19 Zamenhof Street. Additional streets, between Chłodna and Leszno, were extracted from the ghetto a few weeks later.[62] The Többens factory located on the former territory of the small ghetto was all that remained of this section of the ghetto. Its existence outside the official ghetto was legalized on August 16.[63] In this pivotal time, more news about the fate of the people who had been deported reached the ghetto. David

Nowodorski, an escapee from Treblinka, came to the ghetto with information about the camp.[64] A bit later, Zalman Friedrich,[65] who had followed the "trail of the deportees" on orders of the Bund, returned to Warsaw with another report about Treblinka.[66] At least in underground circles, the true nature of the alleged "resettlement" became known, but among the general population, the Germans' deceptions and illusions "remained steadfast."[67] Between August 19 and 25, the transports from Warsaw came to a brief halt because of deportations of the Jewish population of the Warsaw suburbs Otwock, Falenica, and Miedzeszyn.[68]

While the ŻOB had voted against armed resistance, they nevertheless started a process that would gradually reclaim the ghetto space by challenging the German monopoly on violence: close to the end of August, Yisrael Kanał, member of the Akiva youth movement and the Jewish Fighting Organization, made an attempt on the life of the commander of the Jewish Police, Józef Szeryński.[69] The beginning of September saw a huge setback for the Jewish Fighting Organization's plans due to the arrest and murder of their members Józef Kapłan and Szmuel Bresław and the subsequent discovery of the organization's arms cache.[70] Between September 6 and 12, 1942, the SS and their auxiliaries conducted a massive selection in a cordoned-off section of the ghetto between Smocza, Gęsia, Zamenhof, and Szcęśliwa Streets and Parysowski Square.[71] This selection on Miła Street that ghetto inhabitants called the "cauldron"—*kesl* in Yiddish and *kocioł* in Polish[72]—followed an order for registration signed by the commander of the "Einsatz Reinhard," Hermann Höfle.[73] During these few days, more than fifty thousand people were deported to the Treblinka II death camp, and almost three thousand were shot during the selection. Nine days later, on September 21, the last transport of the Great Deportation *Aktion* left the *Umschlagplatz*.[74] By then, between 275,000 and 300,000 inhabitants of the ghetto had fallen victim to the Nazis' genocidal efforts; about 5,500 more were shot in the streets or at the *Umschlagplatz*.[75] Their remaining belongings were collected and sorted by Jewish workers of the so-called *Werterfassungsstelle*.[76]

Reshaping of the Ghetto

The Great Deportation changed the ghetto drastically, in terms of both topography and demographics. Instead of the layout that had been characterized by the division into the large and small ghetto, the territory of the former ghetto was now divided into three sections, with very different designations. First, a large part of the former ghetto territory was excluded from the ghetto, "annexed to the Aryan side and assigned for residence by Poles."[77] Second, there was an area known as the "wild" area that was officially uninhabited, and third, the so-called rump ghetto, a "few separate, isolated areas designated for residency by the remaining

Warsaw Jews" who were working in the German factories.[78] Overall, the remains of the ghetto were "fragmented": the small enclaves still inhabited by Jewish people were "not contiguous" but "separated by areas that had been completely evacuated."[79] These evacuated areas had become no-go zones, as Gutman points out: "Movement in these deserted areas was officially prohibited without special permission, so that Jews were not allowed to go from one enclave to another even for the purpose of visiting relatives and friends."[80] However, there were still people living illegally in the "wild" sections of the ghetto. In sum, the ghetto had been divided into space designated for the workers of the German shops and space that had been turned into a prohibited zone, in which neither life nor movement was officially permitted.

The population of the ghetto had been "drastically reduced" in numbers but also "fundamentally altered from the standpoint of its composition and age structure."[81] The deportations had hit certain age groups much harder than others. Gutman summarizes, "Children under the age of ten and the elderly over the age of sixty all but totally disappeared from the ghetto."[82] Officially, there were roughly thirty-six thousand Jews remaining in the ghetto by the end of November 1942, the majority of them young men. Gutman estimates that there were about twenty thousand more living in the former ghetto territory clandestinely. He suggests that the proportion of children and elderly people was probably a little higher among the illegal inhabitants of the ghetto but assumes that their numbers must have been fairly low among the "wildcat" population as well.[83] In addition, the living conditions and overall situation had changed. Gutman concludes, "During this last phase of its existence, the ghetto was essentially a mass labor camp."[84] Living in the ghetto was only possible if one was able to obtain work in the factories and show proof of this in the form of a special permit. The life of the remaining inhabitants was mostly reduced to forced labor; social life and exchange had been reduced to an absolute minimum, and living arrangements had become even more transitory.[85]

After the deportations, there was a short respite for the remaining inhabitants of the ghetto.[86] During this time, the Germans intensified their campaign to capture Jews hiding outside the ghetto. They encouraged Jews living on the "Aryan" side to return to the ghetto and promised amnesty for those who did. At the same time, an order by Higher SS and Police Commander Krüger corroborated the punishment for those hiding outside the ghetto.[87] Krüger's order specified a list of Jewish residential quarters for the Warsaw and Lublin region and stated that everyone not yet residing in one would have to move to them by November 30. The consequence of being caught outside of the ghetto after this date was a death sentence. While in reality this order only restated the rules already in existence, it suggested a certain novelty to the arrangements and was aimed at drastically reducing the number of people who had thus far evaded German clutches.[88]

The Great Deportation also changed the situation inside the ghetto for all civil authorities and administrative institutions. Before, the ghetto had been mostly managed by a German administrative apparatus headed by the commissar of the Jewish district and the head of the *Transferstelle*. Now, it remained under the control of the police and Gestapo even after the Great Deportation *Aktion* was concluded. According to Gutman, even the "most basic of administrative procedures" were disregarded from then on.[89] The *Judenrat* lost much of its influence, and so did the Jewish Police.[90] Official Jewish self-administration practically ceased to exist. Inside the factories, things were mostly organized independently by the German factory owners and their assistants. In addition, a *Werkschutz* (factory police), "recruited mainly from among German auxiliary formations— Ukrainian, Latvian, and Lithuanian," was introduced to keep order inside the shops.[91]

Although the German authorities pursued, for the most part, a policy of ostensible "normalization" during the months following the Great Deportation, the Germans and their auxiliaries still committed numerous acts of violence in the ghetto and shot many people on its streets.[92] The German monopoly on violence had, however, been broken: at the end of October, three members of the Jewish Fighting Organization, Elijah Różański, Mordechai Grower and Emilia Landau, executed Jakub Lejkin, a high-ranking officer of the Jewish Police notorious for his brutality during the deportations. The ŻOB would continue to pass and carry out death sentences against various members of the Jewish Police, the *Judenrat*, and known collaborators and informers.[93] Support for the ŻOB had grown significantly as the remaining inhabitants of the ghetto were robbed of any illusions regarding the German occupiers' plans.[94] Another contributing factor was the changed demographic of the ghetto and the fact that most people had lost everyone whom they had previously looked after; the "defenseless" had all been deported—parents, grandparents, younger siblings, children.[95]

The ŻOB received a small number of handguns from the Home Army (*Armia Krajowa*, AK) at the end of October.[96] ŻOB pro-communist sympathies also translated into well-established contacts to the Polish People's Army (the *Armia Ludowa*, AL), an armed communist underground organization that acted independently of the much larger *Armia Krajowa* but was also much smaller and less significant than the AK (which served as an armed force of the Polish government in exile).[97] The AK's emissary, Jan Karski, delivered a report about the ghetto and the fate of the Polish Jews to the Polish government in exile in London and to the Allied governments in November.[98]

Notes

1. Engelking and Leociak, *Warsaw Ghetto*, 41, 77; Browning speaks of 445,000 (*Entfesselung der "Endlösung,"* 190).

2. Mazor, *Vanished City*, 14.

3. Engelking and Leociak, *Warsaw Ghetto*, 40, 145–146.

4. Ibid., 399.

5. Ibid., 41, 202.

6. Szarota, *Warschau unter dem Hakenkreuz*, 275; see also Anonymous Woman, account, 137–138; Adler, *In the Warsaw Ghetto*, 223.

7. Engelking and Leociak, *Warsaw Ghetto*, 41; see also Anonymous Woman, account, 137–138.

8. Engelking and Leociak, *Warsaw Ghetto*, 42; for the respective circular by Auerswald, see Berenstein et al., *Faschismus—Getto—Massenmord*, 127–128.

9. Czerniaków, *Tagebuch*, 158; see also Engelking and Leociak, *Warsaw Ghetto*, 79.

10. Engelking and Leociak, *Warsaw Ghetto*, 80–82.

11. Ibid., 81.

12. Browning, "Nazi Ghettoization Policy," 360–361; Engelking and Leociak, *Warsaw Ghetto*, 81.

13. Engelking and Leociak, *Warsaw Ghetto*, 84–85; see also Auerswald's letter to Czerniaków from September 26, 1941, 213. RING. I/310; 183. RING. I/781/5; 504. RING. I/212; 214. RING. I/299.

14. Engelking and Leociak, *Warsaw Ghetto*, 178.

15. Ibid., 85–86; Hilberg, *Vernichtung der Europäischen Juden*, 237.

16. Mazor, *Vanished City*, 160; Engelking and Leociak, *Warsaw Ghetto*, 86; on the topic of smuggling at the cemetery, see also Mawult, account, 130; Lewin, *Cup of Tears*, 281; Adler, *In the Warsaw Ghetto*, 47, Engelking and Leociak, *Warsaw Ghetto*, 454–455.

17. All over Poland, Jewish cemeteries were destroyed, desecrated, and repurposed; headstones were deliberately broken or used as bricks or for road paving. A similar fate befell the largest of Warsaw's Jewish cemeteries, the Bródno Jewish Cemetery, located on the right bank of the Vistula, near the Praga district.

18. Engelking and Leociak, *Warsaw Ghetto*, 455.

19. Ibid., 42, 86.

20. Ibid., 84; for the decree see Berenstein et al., *Faschismus—Getto—Massenmord*, 128; excerpts in English: Rejak and Frister, *Inferno of Choices*, 30–31.

21. Engelking and Leociak, *Warsaw Ghetto*, 42.

22. Ibid., 86.

23. Engelking and Leociak, *Warsaw Ghetto*, 42, 204; Bartoszewski, "Warsaw under Occupation," 81; Lewin, *Cup of Tears*, 94; for official notice of the November execution see Berenstein et al., *Faschismus—Getto—Massenmord*, 129 or 184. RING. I/781/3. At another point, Engelking and Leociak list twelve people as being shot

in the December incident (*Warsaw Ghetto*, 87). These executions would continue: in February 1942, for example, another seventeen people were shot in Gęsia Street prison for crossing the borders of the ghetto illegally; according to Edelman's testimony, at this point, about seven hundred more were imprisoned for the same offense (*Das Ghetto Kämpft*, 40; see also Lewin, *Cup of Tears*, 94). Lewin specifies in his diary that "women made up the vast majority of those executed" (*Cup of Tears*, 94).

24. Lewin, *Cup of Tears*, 78, 114, 118–119; Stok, account, 51; Bartoszewski, *Warsaw Ghetto*, 15.

25. Czerniaków, *Tagebuch*, 211–235; Hilberg, *Vernichtung der Europäischen Juden*, 259–260; for a collection of entries from Czerniaków's diary that address the *Aktion*, see Webb, "Adam Czerniakow Diary Extracts."

26. Engelking and Leociak, *Warsaw Ghetto*, 211; see also Blady-Szwajgier, *Die Erinnerung Verläßt Mich Nie*, 91.

27. Engelking and Leociak, *Warsaw Ghetto*, 212, 398–399; on the fire, see also Berg, *Diary*, 121.

28. Czerniaków, *Tagebuch*, 211–235.

29. Mazor, *Vanished City*, 25.

30. Engelking and Leociak, *Warsaw Ghetto*, 42.

31. Gutman, *Jews of Warsaw*, 63–64.

32. This is clearly reflected in the rapid construction of death camps in this time period. In October 1941, the Nazis began with the construction of the Auschwitz II-Birkenau camp; the camp started operations in March 1942 (Gutman and Berenbaum, *Anatomy of the Auschwitz Death Camp*, 16–17). Already in December 1941, Kulmhof (Chełmno on the Ner) began its operation (Engelking and Leociak, *Warsaw Ghetto*, 42; Hilberg, *Vernichtung der Europäischen Juden*, 508). In the following months, all *Aktion Reinhard* death camps would become operational in quick succession: in November 1941, construction of the Bełżec death camp was started; in March 1942, the construction of Sobibór began and Bełżec became operational; in April 1942, Sobibór became operational (Engelking and Leociak, *Warsaw Ghetto*, 42–43). The Treblinka II death camp would begin operations in July 1942 with the Great Deportations from the Warsaw ghetto (ibid., 44).

33. Engelking and Leociak, *Warsaw Ghetto*, 43. It is important to note here that the Treblinka I forced labor camp had already been operational before the development of the death camp, Treblinka II. It is possible that this led to further misconceptions on the part of the victims. Since information on the "extermination" process reached the ghetto only slowly, when deportations began, people might have drawn from their previous knowledge and associated Treblinka with the labor camp of earlier times (for an example of the ghetto inhabitants' perception of the Treblinka I labor camp, see Berg, *Diary*, 131–132). Something similar applied to Auschwitz I and Auschwitz II, the names and location of which suggesting that the camps were the same, when, in fact, a fatal differentiation between concentration and death camp existed. Yet, the territorial coherence to some degree masked the difference.

34. Engelking and Leociak, *Warsaw Ghetto*, 43. Gutman refers to Fajner under his pseudonym Ya'akov Grojanowski (*Jews of Warsaw*, 166).

35. Engelking and Leociak, *Warsaw Ghetto*, 43; Gutman, *Jews of Warsaw*, 176; Leociak, *Doświadczenia Graniczne*, 81; see also Edelman, *Das Ghetto Kämpft*, 43; Mazor, *Vanished City*, 34; Berg, *Diary*, 136.

36. Gutman, *Jews of Warsaw*, 176; Lewin, *Cup of Tears*, 90.

37. Gutman, *Jews of Warsaw*, 179; see also Edelman, *Das Ghetto Kämpft*, 43–44.

38. Edelman, *Das Ghetto Kämpft*, 45. Gutman also describes the events as a "turning point," to the effect that from then on, the "political leadership went deeper underground" (*Jews of Warsaw*, 178).

39. Hilberg, *Vernichtung der Europäischen Juden*, 526; Kazimierski et al., *Ludność Żydowska w Warszawie*, 743.

40. Engelking and Leociak, *Warsaw Ghetto*, 44.

41. Gutman, *Jews of Warsaw*, 179. Engelking and Leociak specify that the victims were deported from the Gęsia Street prison and shot at Babice; they do not comment on the reason for the execution (*Warsaw Ghetto*, 44); according to ghetto survivor Edelman, the prisoners were in fact shot for crossing over to the "Aryan" side (*Das Ghetto Kämpft*, 44); Berg gives a similar interpretation in her diary, saying that the executions were meant to intimidate smugglers. According to her, some of the victims were smugglers, but the majority was shot for "crossing over to the Aryan side" (*Diary*, 148). Again, posters with the names of the victims were put up in the streets (ibid.).

42. Engelking and Leociak, *Warsaw Ghetto*, 44.

43. Ibid.; Rejak and Frister, *Inferno of Choices*, 42. Gutman dates this to June (*Jews of Warsaw*, 201).

44. In the last chapters of *The Diary of Mary Berg*, Berg—who was among the very few who survived—describes how her family left the ghetto through Pawiak and ultimately emigrated to the United States.

45. Gutman, *Jews of Warsaw*, 197, see also 198. The German original reads as follows: "*Ich ordne an, daß die Umsiedlung der gesamten jüdischen Bevölkerung des Generalgouvernements bis 31. Dezember durchgeführt und beendet ist*" (Berenstein et al., *Faschismus—Getto—Massenmord*, 303). The Germans now used terms such as "evacuation" or "resettlement" almost exclusively as synonyms for the mass murder they committed; at the same time, these words still helped keep up appearances and mask the German agenda vis-à-vis their victims.

46. Engelking and Leociak, *Warsaw Ghetto*, 93; see also Reich-Ranicki, *Mein Leben*, 234–242; for the detailed order, see Berenstein et al., *Faschismus—Getto—Massenmord*, 305–307.

47. Hilberg, *Vernichtung der Europäischen Juden*, 527–528; Lewiński, "Death of Adam Czerniaków and Janusz Korczak's Last Journey," 224–243; for Höfle's order, see Berenstein et al., *Faschismus—Getto—Massenmord*, 305–307; Arad, Gutman, and Margaliot, *Documents on the Holocaust*, 281–282.

48. Gutman, *Jews of Warsaw*, 206. In the early days of German occupation, the *Judenrat* had answered mostly to the SS and the Gestapo; contact to civil administration was only "sporadic" (ibid., 96). This changed in May 1941 with the appointment of Heinz Auerswald as commissar of the Jewish district of Warsaw and a concurrent strengthening of the role of civil administration. With the beginning of the Great Deportations, the power shifted back to the SS (ibid., 96–97; Birn, *Die Höheren SS- und Polizeiführer*, 203). According to Ber Warm, the SS forces were divided into representatives of the "Szuch Boulevard"—that is, the Gestapo headquarters in Warsaw—and representatives of the *Aktion Reinhard* with their commando base in Lublin (account, 170).

49. Gutman, *Jews of Warsaw*, 203; Hilberg, *Vernichtung der Europäischen Juden*, 528; see also Edelman, *Das Ghetto Kämpft*, 46–51; Mawult, account, 111.

50. Engelking and Leociak, *Warsaw Ghetto*, 705; see also Arad, Gutman, and Margaliot, *Documents on the Holocaust*, 277–278; Mawult, account, 113.

51. Engelking and Leociak, *Warsaw Ghetto*, 214; see also Sznapman, account, 109–110; Mawult, account, 114–115.

52. Gutman, *Jews of Warsaw*, 237; see also Berenstein et al., *Faschismus—Getto—Massenmord*, 485–486; Edelman, *Das Ghetto Kämpft*, 48–49; Krall and Edelman, *Dem Herrgott Zuvorkommen*, 66.

53. Engelking and Leociak, *Warsaw Ghetto*, 44. Gutman emphasizes that there were other fighting organizations, too, such as the Jewish Military Union (*Żydowski Związek Wojskowy*, ŻZW) and smaller, unaffiliated groups (*Jews of Warsaw*, 293–297, 347–350). Their history, however, is much less comprehensively documented. For more details on the different groups and their background, see Ainsztein, *Revolte gegen die Vernichtung*.

54. Hilberg, *Vernichtung der Europäischen Juden*, 528; Edelman, *Das Ghetto Kämpft*, 47.

55. Kassow, *Who Will Write Our History?*, 2, 333; Engelking and Leociak, *Warsaw Ghetto*, 44.

56. Engelking and Leociak, *Warsaw Ghetto*, 707; see also Mawult, account, 112; Berg, *Diary*, 165; Bauman, *Winter in the Morning*, 67; Lewin, *Cup of Tears*, 136.

57. Mawult, account, 113.

58. Hilberg, *Vernichtung der Europäischen Juden*, 530; Kazimierski et al., *Ludność Żydowska w Warszawie*, 677, 760; see also Edelman, *Das Ghetto Kämpft*, 50; Sznapman, account, 110; Bauman, *Winter in the Morning*, 67.

59. Bauman, *Winter in the Morning*, 69.

60. Lewin, *Cup of Tears*, 153. The following day, his own wife, Luba, falls victim to a German blockade and does not return home. Lewin writes, "I will never be consoled as long as I live.... A life together of over 21 years ... has met with such a tragic end" (ibid., 154).

61. See also Anonymous Woman, account, 135

62. Engelking and Leociak, *Warsaw Ghetto*, 44, 95.

63. Ibid., 95; see also Najberg, account, 133.

64. Engelking and Leociak, *Warsaw Ghetto*, 44.

65. In other sources: Zygmunt Frydrych.

66. Gutman, *Jews of Warsaw*, 222–223; see also Edelman, *Das Ghetto Kämpft*, 49; Krall and Edelman, *Dem Herrgott Zuvorkommen*, 15. The information from his report was published in the Bundist *Oyf der vakh* (On Guard) on September 20, 1942.

67. Gutman, *Jews of Warsaw*, 223.

68. Engelking and Leociak, *Warsaw Ghetto*, 44; see also Edelman, *Das Ghetto Kämpft*, 56; Lewin, *Cup of Tears*, 161.

69. Gutman, *Jews of Warsaw*, 238–240, 302; Hilberg, *Vernichtung der Europäischen Juden*, 532–533; see also Birenbaum, *Hope Is the Last to Die*, 71; Lewin, *Cup of Tears*, 167, 282–283.

70. Engelking and Leociak, *Warsaw Ghetto*, 45; Gutman, *Jews of Warsaw*, 243–244; see also Berman, account, 146.

71. Engelking and Leociak, *Warsaw Ghetto*, 45, 96, 727–729; Kazimierski et al., *Ludność Żydowska w Warszawie*, 772; see also Berg, *Diary*, 179–180; Lewin, *Cup of Tears*, 167–177; Edelman, *Das Ghetto Kämpft*, 57–58. Edelman lists the streets as follows: Gęsia, Zamenhofa, Lubecki, and Stawki Streets (57).

72. Gutman, *Jews of Warsaw*, 211; Polonsky, "Introduction," 36.

73. Engelking and Leociak, *Warsaw Ghetto*, 95–96.

74. Ibid., 45, 96, 729.

75. Ibid., 45; Gutman, *Jews of Warsaw*, 197, 211–213; see also Lewin, *Cup of Tears*, 286. Bartoszewski speaks about 310,000 ("Warsaw under Occupation," 84); the exact numbers are difficult to ascertain.

76. Engelking and Leociak, *Warsaw Ghetto*, 99; Adler, *In the Warsaw Ghetto*, 275.

77. Engelking and Leociak, *Warsaw Ghetto*, 96. According to a report by the German housing office in Warsaw, the apartments were often in very poor condition because the situation in the ghetto had forced the Jewish inhabitants to sell parts of the interior or to burn it for heating (Lehnstaedt, *Okkupation im Osten*, 82). A Yiddish account from the Ringelblum Archive describes a short dialogue illustrating these conditions. A woman, noticing children who collect potato peelings from a garbage bin, asks the author how these children could possibly cook their pickings, given that coal and wood were at a price of 2 zloty per kilo. Dryly, the author replies, "There is no shortage of floors and stairways" (496. RING. I/1015).

78. Engelking and Leociak, *Warsaw Ghetto*, 97.

79. Gutman, *Jews of Warsaw*, 269; see also Edelman, *Das Ghetto Kämpft*, 58–59.

80. Gutman, *Jews of Warsaw*, 269.

81. Ibid., 269–270.

82. Ibid., 270; see also Lewin, *Cup of Tears*, 199, 232; Adler, *In the Warsaw Ghetto*, 289.

83. Gutman, *Jews of Warsaw*, 274, see also 270–271; Adler, *In the Warsaw Ghetto*, 289. The monthly report of the *Transferstelle* lists 35,000 workers remaining in the

ghetto (Kazimierski et al., *Ludność Żydowska w Warszawie*, 677); Edelman speaks of 33,400 (*Das Ghetto Kämpft*, 58); Lewin of 34,000 legally remaining and 50,000 counting the ones in hiding (*Cup of Tears*, 180). Zuckerman estimates there were about 50,000 or 55,000 left in the ghetto in total; he adds that there was a real "exodus" from the ghetto after the Great Deportations and that "Jews started leaving in every possible way for the Aryan side of Warsaw" (*Surplus of Memory*, 276).

84. Gutman, *Jews of Warsaw*, 268; see also Berg, *Diary*, 183.

85. See, for example, Lewin, *Cup of Tears*, 178; Berg, *Diary*, 185.

86. Gutman, *Jews of Warsaw*, 268.

87. Engelking and Leociak, *Warsaw Ghetto*, 98–99; Gutman, *Jews of Warsaw*, 272; see also Lewin, *Cup of Tears*, 210; Adler, *In the Warsaw Ghetto*, 275, 291–292; Bauman, *Winter in the Morning*, 110.

88. Gutman, *Jews of Warsaw*, 272; Berenstein et al., *Faschismus—Getto—Massenmord*, 342–344; see also Lewin, *Cup of Tears*, 200–201, 210–211, 214.

89. Gutman, *Jews of Warsaw*, 271.

90. Ibid., 275; see also Birenbaum, *Hope Is the Last to Die*, 70; Adler, *In the Warsaw Ghetto*, 277.

91. Engelking and Leociak, *Warsaw Ghetto*, 396; Gutman, *Jews of Warsaw*, 275, 329.

92. Gutman, *Jews of Warsaw*, 277, 279.

93. Engelking and Leociak, *Warsaw Ghetto*, 45; Gutman, *Jews of Warsaw*, 240, 301–303; Berenstein et al., *Faschismus—Getto—Massenmord*, 487–488; on the execution of Lejkin, see also Edelman, *Das Ghetto Kämpft*, 60; Puterman, account, 162; Berg, *Diary*, 193; Strobl, "Sag nie, du gehst den letzten Weg," 217.

94. Gutman, *Jews of Warsaw*, 283, 293; see also Zuckerman, *Surplus of Memory*, 277, 279; Birenbaum, *Hope Is the Last to Die*, 70–71, 73.

95. Strobl, "Preface," 21.

96. Engelking and Leociak, *Warsaw Ghetto*, 45; Edelman, *Das Ghetto Kämpft*, 61. The *Armia Krajowa* was the army of the Polish government in exile. It represented the vast majority of the Polish underground forces and could rely on a huge number of well-trained military officers and on the support of the Allies (Strobl, "Preface," 14).

97. Krall and Edelman, *Dem Herrgott Zuvorkommen*, 85; Zuckerman, *Surplus of Memory*, 349. For more information on the relations between the ŻOB and the Polish Military Underground, see Gutman, *Jews of Warsaw*, 297–301.

98. Engelking and Leociak, *Warsaw Ghetto*, 46; Gutman, *Jews of Warsaw*, 362–363. Karski also delivered the report to the American government and to Supreme Court judge Felix Frankfurter.

8

Destruction of the Ghetto

Armed Resistance

In early January 1943, Himmler arrived for an inspection of the ghetto and ordered "the deportation of 8,000 Jews and the evacuation of German enterprises to the Lublin area."[1] When the next wave of deportations began, the German forces encountered, for the first time, organized armed resistance.[2] The ŻOB put up posters on the streets, calling on the inhabitants of the ghetto to "resist resettlement" and to join the armed struggle.[3] In addition to being a proclamation of rising Jewish resistance, these posters also manifested a challenge to the German domination of public space. Now, Jewish independent political expression was openly displayed.

The deportations lasted from January 18 to 22, 1943.[4] From then on, many inhabitants of the ghetto went into hiding and thereby evaded the more basic and expected forces of round-ups; arrests became more and more difficult due to a combination of resistance and evasion.[5] In his ghetto memoir, Adler refers to the various hideouts built in the ghetto as "bastions of passive defence."[6] The Germans' course of action became more brutal from January 21 onward. Their forces indiscriminately massacred a large number of people in the streets; yet, they were nonetheless unable to meet the quota of eight thousand deportees that Himmler had demanded by the end of the *Aktion*.[7]

According to Gutman, the "January fighting served to strengthen" the ŻOB and "initiated a new period of organization and readiness";[8] or, as ghetto fighter Yithzak Zuckerman phrases it, "The January Uprising gave us wings, elevated us in the eyes of the Jews, and enhanced our image as fighters, giving us a good name."[9] In view of the situation, the ŻOB's most important objective became to acquire weapons. To that end, the Jewish Fighting Organization started to collect "taxes" from wealthier ghetto inhabitants to finance the acquisition of guns.[10] The ŻOB carried out more and more executions to clear the ghetto of German informers and to establish "authority over the entire ghetto."[11] With their actions, the ŻOB—an independent Jewish organization—reclaimed the ghetto space from the Germans and their representatives and increasingly challenged German rule over the territory.[12] And indeed, according to the accounts of ghetto fighters Marek Edelman and Yithzak Zuckerman, the ŻOB's measures were effective and the Germans felt more and more "uneasy" inside the ghetto.[13]

It seemed clear to most that a new chapter in the history of the ghetto had begun. In light of the overall tenuous state of the ghetto, the *Oneg Shabbat* group hid a second part of their archives in two milk cans, again at 68 Nowolipki Street.[14] Many members of the archive had been killed or deported during the Great Deportation and the January *Aktion*. Fueled by the immense personal losses and seeing that any hope for the survival of the ghetto community had vanished, the remaining *Oneg Shabbat* members centered their efforts on saving lives. But, as Kassow observes, "The Oyneg Shabes had more luck in saving documents than in saving people. Although thousands of pages survived in the tin boxes and in the milk cans (a significant part of the archive was most certainly lost), little more than random traces remain of the men and women who wrote the documents, gathered them, copied them, and hid them."[15]

The defeat of the German army at Stalingrad on February 2 stirred up hope among Varsovians that the war would soon end, but the optimism was short-lived.[16] In mid-February, Himmler ordered the establishment of a concentration camp in the Warsaw ghetto, which was intended to be the first station for the deportation of all remaining Jewish workers to Lublin. Afterward, the ghetto was supposed to be demolished.[17] This course of action indicates that Nazi Germany's perception of, and approach to, the ghetto and its inhabitants had changed drastically, now that it seemed much more difficult to control. This change is reflected in Himmler's order of February 1943 to Higher SS and Police Commander Krüger: "For reasons of security I herewith order that the Warsaw ghetto be pulled down after the concentration camp has been moved. . . . The razing of the ghetto and the relocation of the concentration camp are necessary, as otherwise we would probably never establish quiet in Warsaw, and the prevalence of crime cannot be stamped out as long as the ghetto remains."[18] It is interesting to see how Himmler associates the issue of the ghetto with the city as a whole. This indicates the German fear that resistance would spread. Himmler's order anticipated the full destruction of the ghetto space that would be realized after the suppression of the Ghetto Uprising. Soon, a first transport of Warsaw Jews was sent to the Trawniki camp close to Lublin. Another transport, with a destination of Poniatow camp, followed a week later.[19]

The challenge to German domination persisted. In March, the Home Army issued a warning to blackmailers targeting Jews in hiding that they would be "punished 'with all the severity of the law.'"[20] The ŻOB set fire to the warehouse of the *Werterfassungsstelle* and several other resistance actions were carried out, all of which contested German hegemony on the territory of the ghetto.[21] To give just a few examples: March 13, 1943, a group of ŻOB members successfully intervened against the maltreatment of a group of workers by the *Werkschutz*. When Germans captured a ŻOB fighter, the ŻOB was able to free him and kill two German soldiers in the process.[22] As a reprisal, a large SS unit entered the ghetto the next day, arbitrarily rounded up people from buildings close by, and killed them.[23] Zuckerman reports a similar incident when the ŻOB was able to free sixty people from jail.[24] He also describes occasions when the ŻOB successfully robbed a bank or the treasury of the *Judenrat*.[25] The ŻOB put up more posters calling on the ghetto inhabitants to resist.[26] Jewish resistance increasingly entered the public space of the ghetto and openly challenged Nazi German propaganda. The ŻOB's public appeals were countered by shop owners, most prominently by the industrialist W. C. Többens, who—in a series of counter-publications—tried to convince the Jewish population to resettle voluntarily.[27] Few followed this appeal.

When several SS, police, and Wehrmacht units entered the ghetto on April 19, 1943, they were met with well-organized armed resistance by the men and women fighting for the ŻOB,[28] and the Ghetto Uprising broke out.[29] As one of the ŻOB leaders, Yitzhak Zuckerman, explains in his examination of the "lessons" of the January Uprising, the fighters had learned that they could not withstand their militarily superior opponent in direct confrontation, so they resorted to "guerilla" tactics.[30] Zuckerman recalls in his chronicle of the uprising, *A Surplus of Memory: Chronicles of the Warsaw Ghetto Uprising*, "As long as there are walls, as long as you can find a hiding place, you can set ambushes, and then a small force, even small groups, are worth much more than a larger force in open battle."[31] In this phase, the ghetto space acquired a number of new functions and meanings. While still being an area of confinement and ultimately a deadly trap, it also worked to the fighters' advantage, providing cover and hideouts and making prolonged fighting possible. Zuckerman also points out that the ŻOB had decided to fight in isolated and independent units.[32] The ŻOB had twenty-two of these units, with twelve to twenty members each.[33] They had divided the ghetto into three combat sectors: "(1) the Central Ghetto, under the command of Yisrael Kanał . . .; (2) the 'shop' sector (Többens-Schultz), under the command of Yitzhak Zuckermann (replaced close to the start of the revolt by Eliezer Geller) . . .; (3) the Brushmakers' Area, under the command of Marek Edelman."[34] The overall command resided with Mordechai Anielewicz.

Although they had already encountered resistance during the January *Aktion*, the Germans—first under the command of Ferdinand von Sammern-Frankenegg, then under Jürgen Stroop—clearly underestimated the Jewish Fighting Organization's strength.[35] During the first days of the uprising, the German forces suffered significant losses and were pushed back by the Jewish fighters. This was a remarkable outcome, considering the fact that the ŻOB was vastly outnumbered and outgunned. Information on the number of ŻOB fighters varies, but Edelman speaks of 220 fighters.[36] The Germans, on the other hand, deployed fully equipped and well-trained units of the SS, the police, the Wehrmacht, and Ukrainian auxiliary troops. According to Engelking and Leociak, the German forces deployed during the first three weeks of the Ghetto Uprising consisted of the following: "armored grenadiers and SS cavalry: 821 soldiers, 9 officers; police: 228 gendarmes, 6 officers ... Wehrmacht artillery and sappers: 56 soldiers and 3 officers; Ukrainians: 335 soldiers and 2 officers (Germans)."[37] The ghetto was almost completely isolated in its fight. There was little to no help from outside the walls, with the exception of two incidents involving the Home Army (*Armia Krajowa*) and the Polish People's Army (*Armia Ludowa*): The evening of the second day, a division of the Home Army undertook a planned diversionary attack on the ghetto wall in the section of Bonifraterska Street.[38] A second attack was executed by a combat group of the Polish People's Army the very same night. They attacked a "German artillery crew stationed on Nowiniarska Street."[39] Germans put up posters on the "Aryan" side of the city, announcing that helping the Jews would be met with the death penalty.[40] Some reports indicate that a third part of the Underground Archives of the *Oneg Shabbat* may have been buried at this point, but it has not been discovered and the information is not verified.[41] On the third day, the German forces changed their tactics and entered the ghetto in smaller divisions, thus the fights became less centralized.[42]

During the uprising, most of the remaining ghetto inhabitants, as well as members of the Jewish Fighting Organization, were hiding in bunkers underneath the ghetto buildings. These bunkers, hideouts, and tunnels had been built over the course of the preceding months with the involvement of most of the inhabitants of the ghetto.[43] Adler describes their construction: "A full-scale 'construction' movement began for building hiding places both in the main ghetto area and also in the areas of the 'shops.' Hideouts resembled bunkers and were continuously under construction. Frequently wells were dug out and sometimes tunnels were excavated leading to the Aryan side. These shelters were equipped with indispensable supplies of food and with heating and lighting arrangements."[44] In the end, a huge number of civilians and fighters perished in their hiding places when the

"Germans systematically destroyed the ghetto, burning it house by house, street by street."[45] Ziviah Lubetkin, one of the few ŻOB fighters to survive, recalls that the entire ghetto stood in flames.[46] It was this ruthless German tactic that finally broke "the ghetto front line" and that, in the long run, brought about the defeat of the uprising.[47] Although major fighting nearly ceased after the first days, an ongoing "battle of the bunkers" was still taking place.[48] The bunkers allowed the Jewish fighters to continue their attacks and retreat into hiding immediately after, extending "the life of the revolt" considerably.[49]

From April 23 onward, Stroop sent out his troops to comb through the ghetto in search of bunkers and hideouts. The German forces used poisonous gas and fire to smoke out or kill immediately the people in hiding. They also used explosives to blow up entire buildings.[50] On May 8, 1943, they uncovered the bunker at 18 Miła Street in which a large group of the ŻOB's command was hiding along with a group of civilians. Many of the fighters took their own lives; others were killed by the poisonous gas the Germans used on the bunker.[51] A few days later, Szmuel Mordechai Zygielbojm, a Jewish representative in the Polish government in exile, killed himself in London to protest against the world's passivity in the face of Nazi Germany's brutal murder of the European Jews.[52]

Final Liquidation of the Ghetto

Only about a dozen fighters survived the Ghetto Uprising.[53] On May 16, 1943, when fighting inside the ghetto had almost ceased and most of its inhabitants had been deported or killed, the Germans blew up the Great Synagogue at Tłomackie Street as if to seal the murder of the ghetto's inhabitants with an act of destruction against one of their main cultural landmarks.[54] Still, a very small number of survivors remained in the ruins of the former ghetto; they were commonly called "the Robinson Crusoes of Warsaw."[55]

Already in his order from February 1943, Himmler had coupled the destruction of the city with the suppression of resistance and the deportation of the remaining inhabitants. His order had specified, "In any case, we must achieve the disappearance from sight of the living space for 500,000 sub-humans (*Untermenschen*) that has existed up to now, but could never be suitable for Germans, and reduce the size of this city of millions—Warsaw—which has always been a center of corruption and revolt."[56] But not, Himmler emphasized, before making use of "all parts of houses that can be used, and other material of all kinds."[57] Consequently, in September 1943, "the Germans sent a battalion of Polish laborers into the ghetto and ordered them to demolish the infrastructures and walls that were still standing in the area."[58] As Himmler's order suggested, the German practice of exploiting the Jewish ghetto did not end with the murder of its inhabitants: while the laborers blew up the remaining buildings and leveled the area of the ghetto, they were to dismantle the buildings and to collect all usable building materials from the site of the former ghetto. The SS used Jewish prisoners deported to Warsaw from Auschwitz to carry out most of this work. They were "exclusively foreign Jews, from Greece, France, Germany, Austria, Belgium and Holland" so that the language barrier would keep them from establishing contact with the local population.[59] The forced laborers were housed in the newly established *Konzentrationslager Warschau*, which was also known as *Gęsiówka*, in reference to the location of the camp at the site of the former Gęsia Street ghetto prison. In addition to this group, a number of skilled German and Polish workers were hired.[60] According to Hilberg, it took them more than a year to take down the 2.6 million cubic meters of brickwork and to level what remained of the buildings.[61]

The former ghetto was razed to the ground and the murder of its inhabitants was concluded with the destruction of its physical space—that is, with the Jewish quarter's "physical topocide," to borrow a term from Madeline G. Levine.[62] While this aligns with the general German plan to destroy large parts of the city of Warsaw in order to rebuild and Germanize it,[63] it also indicates how closely the space of the ghetto, in particular, was linked with its inhabitants: ultimately, as Himmler's order reveals, the Germans destroyed the ghetto first and foremost as a Jewish space and as a space of resistance.

Notes

1. Engelking and Leociak, *Warsaw Ghetto*, 46, 100; for the order see Berenstein et al., *Faschismus—Getto—Massenmord*, 349; see also Zuckerman, *Surplus of Memory*, 288.

2. Gutman, *Jews of Warsaw*, 310; see also Edelman, *Das Ghetto Kämpft*, 61; Krall and Edelman, *Dem Herrgott Zuvorkommen*, 84.

3. Engelking and Leociak, *Warsaw Ghetto*, 101; Gutman, *Jews of Warsaw*, 304–306; for some examples of posters and leaflets distributed by the Jewish Fighting Organization, see Berenstein et al., *Faschismus—Getto—Massenmord*, 495–498.

4. Gutman, *Jews of Warsaw*, 307–312. Most people were rounded up the first day, when the *Aktion* was still a surprise (Gutman, *Jews of Warsaw*, 318); Zuckerman, *Surplus of Memory*, 263, 279; Adler, *In the Warsaw Ghetto*, 276.

5. Gutman, *Jews of Warsaw*, 310, 318; see also Blady-Szwajgier, *Die Erinnerung Verläßt Mich Nie*, 76–77; Adler, *In the Warsaw Ghetto*, 297–317.

6. Adler, *In the Warsaw Ghetto*, 282.

7. Gutman, *Jews of Warsaw*, 311; Hilberg, *Vernichtung der Europäischen Juden*, 534.

8. Gutman, *Jews of Warsaw*, 336.

9. Zuckerman, *Surplus of Memory*, 317.

10. Zuckerman, *Surplus of Memory*, 319, 325, 332–335; Gutman, *Jews of Warsaw*, 336–337, 343–345; Mawult, account, 132; Meed, *On Both Sides of the Wall*, 108.

11. Gutman, *Jews of Warsaw*, 341; see also Berenstein et al., *Faschismus—Getto—Massenmord*, 503, 553; Edelman, *Das Ghetto Kämpft*, 65; Zuckerman, *Surplus of Memory*, 319–323, 325, 332, 273; Birenbaum, *Hope Is the Last to Die*, 71; Blady-Szwajgier, *Die Erinnerung Verläßt Mich Nie*, 78.

12. It is important to note here that there had been a huge number of social, cultural, and political initiatives and organizations during the first years of the ghetto's existence, creating Jewish spaces of community, support, resistance, and self-realization within the oppressive environment of the ghetto. These organizations were of the highest importance for the life and the survival of the ghetto's inhabitants. In contrast to the Jewish Fighting Organization, however, none of these organizations used violent means to openly challenge the German dominion on their own territory.

13. "Unbehaglich," Edelman, *Das Ghetto Kämpft*, 64; see also Zuckerman, *Surplus of Memory*, 276; Engelking and Leociak, *Warsaw Ghetto*, 767; Birenbaum, *Hope Is the Last to Die*, 71–72.

14. Kassow, *Who Will Write Our History?*, 5, 357; Engelking and Leociak, *Warsaw Ghetto*, 46.

15. Kassow, *Who Will Write Our History?*, 146, 356–358.

16. Szarota, *Warschau unter dem Hakenkreuz*, 276–277; Engelking and Leociak, *Warsaw Ghetto*, 46.

17. Berenstein et al., *Faschismus—Getto—Massenmord*, 349; see also Zuckerman, *Surplus of Memory*, 287–288.

18. Arad, Gutman, and Margaliot, *Documents on the Holocaust*, 292. The German original reads as follows: "*Aus Sicherheitsgründen ordne ich an, daß das Ghetto Warschau nach der Herausverlagerung des Konzentrationslagers abzureißen ist . . . Die Niederlegung des Ghettos und die Unterbringung des Konzentrationslagers ist notwendig, das wir Warschau sonst wohl niemals zur Ruhe bringen werden und das Verbrecherwesen bei Verbleiben des Ghettos nicht ausgerottet werden kann*" (Berenstein et al., *Faschismus—Getto—Massenmord*, 349).

19. Gutman, *Jews of Warsaw*, 333.

20. Engelking and Leociak, *Warsaw Ghetto*, 47.

21. Gutman, *Jews of Warsaw*, 346; see also Meed, *On Both Sides of the Wall*, 70.

22. Gutman, *Jews of Warsaw*, 346. Edelman dates this (or a similar) incident earlier, to winter 1942/1943; he speaks of three fighters being captured (60–61).

23. Gutman, *Jews of Warsaw*, 346.

24. Zuckerman, *Surplus of Memory*, 315.

25. Ibid., 316–317.

26. Engelking and Leociak, *Warsaw Ghetto*, 101; see also Edelman, *Das Ghetto Kämpft*, 63; Meed, *On Both Sides of the Wall*, 135.

27. Gutman, *Jews of Warsaw*, 334–335; see also Edelman, *Das Ghetto Kämpft*, 63–64; Zuckerman, *Surplus of Memory*, 314–315; Adler, *In the Warsaw Ghetto*, 294.

28. There was a substantial number of female fighters in the ŻOB. See, for example, Strobl, "Preface," 15. Strobl writes in more detail about the role of women in the (armed) resistance in her two monographs *Die Angst kam erst danach* and *"Sag nie, du gehst den letzten Weg."*

29. Engelking and Leociak, *Warsaw Ghetto*, 47.

30. Zuckerman, *Surplus of Memory*, 308.

31. Ibid.

32. Ibid.

33. Gutman, *Jews of Warsaw*, 338.

34. Ibid.

35. Ibid., 369.

36. Krall and Edelman, *Dem Herrgott Zuvorkommen*, 17. Engelking and Leociak give a similarly low number, speaking of "twenty-two groups, each with ten to twelve people" (*Warsaw Ghetto*, 774); Gutman gives the same numbers (*Jews of Warsaw*, 338). In her introduction to Simha (Kazik) Rotem's memoir, Barbara Harshav speaks of 500 fighters ("Introduction," vii).

37. Engelking and Leociak, *Warsaw Ghetto*, 775.

38. Gutman, *Jews of Warsaw*, 379–380; Bartoszewski, *Warsaw Ghetto*, 76; see also Edelman, *Das Ghetto Kämpft*, 95; Berenstein et al., *Faschismus—Getto—Massenmord*, 540. Engelking and Leociak date this incident to the first day of the uprising (*Warsaw Ghetto*, 47, 778).

39. Gutman, *Jews of Warsaw*, 380.

40. Engelking and Leociak, *Warsaw Ghetto*, 47.

41. Kassow, *Who Will Write Our History?*, 5; Epsztein, "Structure and Organization," 9.

42. Gutman, *Jews of Warsaw*, 381.

43. Ibid., 351–353; see also Strobl, "Preface," 17; Zuckerman, *Surplus of Memory*, 277.

44. Adler, *In the Warsaw Ghetto*, 283.

45. Engelking and Leociak, *Warsaw Ghetto*, 101; see also Birenbaum, *Hope Is the Last to Die*, 79.

46. Lubetkin begins her long description of the burning ghetto with the words, *"Das Getto stand in Flammen. Tage- und Nächtelang brannte es, und das Feuer fraß Haus für Haus ganze Straßen auf"* (*Die Letzten Tage*, 5).

47. Engelking and Leociak, *Warsaw Ghetto*, 786.

48. Gutman, *Jews of Warsaw*, 387; see also Strobl, "Preface," 17.

49. Gutman, *Jews of Warsaw*, 389, 390; see also Zuckerman, *Surplus of Memory*, 308.

50. Gutman, *Jews of Warsaw*, 386–387; see also Berenstein et al., *Faschismus—Getto—Massenmord*, 528–532; Birenbaum, *Hope Is the Last to Die*, 79.

51. Engelking and Leociak, *Warsaw Ghetto*, 47, 786–787; Gutman, *Jews of Warsaw*, 395–396; see also Edelman, *Das Ghetto Kämpft*, 75; Krall and Edelman, *Dem Herrgott Zuvorkommen*, 55–56; Lubetkin, *Die Letzten Tage*, 19–20.

52. Strobl, "Preface," 18–19.

53. Engelking and Leociak, *Warsaw Ghetto*, 787.

54. Gutman, *Jews of Warsaw*, 397; see also Bauman, *Winter in the Morning*, 111.

55. Engelking and Leociak, *Warsaw Ghetto*, 804, see also 803–806. The same name was later applied to a similar group that was hiding in the demolished city after the Warsaw Uprising. For a detailed analysis of the term, see Cobel-Tokarska, *Desert Island, Burrow, Grave*, 162–163.

56. Arad, Gutman, and Margaliot, *Documents on the Holocaust*, 292. The German original reads as follows: *"Auf jeden Fall muß erreicht werden, daß der für 500 000 Untermenschen bisher vorhandene Wohnraum, der für Deutsche niemals geeignet ist, von der Bildfläche verschwindet und die Millionenstadt Warschau, die immer ein gefährlicher Herd der Zersetzung und des Aufstandes ist, verkleinert wird"* (Berenstein et al., *Faschismus—Getto—Massenmord*, 349).

57. Arad, Gutman, and Margaliot, *Documents on the Holocaust*, 292; see also Leociak, *Text in the Face of Destruction*, 53. The German original reads as follows: *"wobei alle irgendwie verwertbaren Teile der Häuser und Materialien aller Art vorher zu verwerten sind"* (Berenstein et al., *Faschismus—Getto—Massenmord*, 349). Here, the double meaning of the German word *"liquidieren"* (to liquidate) is quite telling again. It can signify two different things: the winding up of a business, and the execution or murder of a person. In the case of the ghetto, the word meant both—the mass murder of the ghetto's inhabitants (starting with the Great Deportation *Aktion* of July–September 1942 and concluding with the deportation or immediate killing of the remaining ghetto inhabitants in the spring of 1943) as well as the final act of extracting the last economic value from the ghetto's physical remains.

58. Gutman, *Jews of Warsaw*, 400.

59. Engelking and Leociak, *Warsaw Ghetto*, 801, see also 802; Hilberg, *Vernichtung der Europäischen Juden*, 539–540. Yad Vashem prepared an online exhibition titled *Last Months in the Warsaw Ghetto*, which includes oral testimony by survivors describing the work of "clearing the ruins of the ghetto."

60. Engelking and Leociak, *Warsaw Ghetto*, 801–802.

61. Hilberg, *Vernichtung der Europäischen Juden*, 539–540.

62. Levine, "Home Loss in Wartime Literature," 99, 102–103.

63. Gutschow and Klain, *Vernichtung und Utopie*, 13, 16–17, 26.

For further information about these historical photographs, see the "Images" section of the appendix.

Plate 1: Gate at the intersection of Leszno and Żelazna Streets, 1940/41

Plate 2: Outside the ghetto at the intersection of Świętokrzyska and Zielna Streets, fall 1940

Plate 3: Unknown location, summer 1941

Plate 4: Pawia Street at the intersection with Zamenhofa Street, September 1941

Plate 5: Zamenhofa Street near the intersection with Pawia Street, September 1941

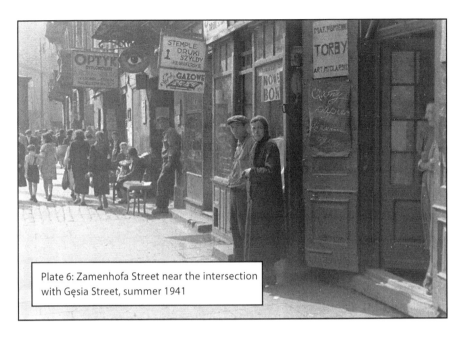

Plate 6: Zamenhofa Street near the intersection with Gęsia Street, summer 1941

Plate 7: Karmelicka Street, most likely spring 1942

138

Plate 8: Smocza Street, May 1941

Plate 9: Koźla Street, summer 1941

Plate 10: Walicόw Street at the intersection with Ceglana Street, before December 1941

Plate 11: Unknown location, spring 1941

Plate 12: Unknown location, spring 1941

Plate 13: Intersection of Chłodna and Żelazna Streets, summer 1941

Plate 14: Bridge over Chłodna Street, after January 1942

Plate 15: Gate at the intersection of Żelazna and Chłodna Streets, most likely early 1942

Plate 16: Gate at the intersection of Żelazna and Chłodna Streets, most likely early 1942

Plate 17: Lubeckiego Street, 1941/42

Plate 18: Lubeckiego Street, summer 1941

Plate 19: Intersection of Żelazna and Grzybowska Streets, June 1942

Plate 20: Bonifraterska Street, early 1942

Plate 21: Miła Street, between July and September 1942

Plate 22: Nowolipie Street near the intersection with Żelazna Street, between April and May 1943

Plate 23: Ghetto Area, spring 1945

PART III

EXPERIENCES OF A VIOLENT SPACE

Introduction

Experiences of a Violent Space

The history of the ghetto elucidates the direct connection that existed between violence and the ghetto's establishment and management at all times: the ghetto was implemented by force, it was governed by violent means, and it served a violent purpose. Direct physical assaults on its inhabitants—that is, "autotelic" violence in Reemtsma's sense[1]—were frequent and ranged from individual harassment and attacks to concerted genocidal campaigns. In addition, as an exemplary culmination of "captive" violence,[2] the ghetto proved to be a very potent form of exercising power and control, effectively facilitating the realization of the Holocaust. Right from the start, ghettoization also entailed assaults on Jewish social and economic resources. Many Jews lost their businesses or their employment because it was located outside of the ghetto. Others lost their income due to the drastic changes to the economic situation and infrastructure brought about by ghettoization and by the Germans' anti-Jewish policies. Most people who were forced to move to the ghetto lost a large portion of their assets in the process. Inside the ghetto, they were subjected to large-scale confiscations and straight-out robbery at the hands of the occupiers and their auxiliaries. All of these practices created severe material and economic damage. At the same time, the aggressive segregation from the remaining Polish population cut important lifelines that were essential for survival. Within the restrictive and undersupplied setting of the ghetto, this social and economic damage translated almost directly into physical harm and, eventually, into the death of many of the victims. The detailed study of the German ghetto politics shows that this effect was not incidental; the occupiers weaponized space and used it against their victims. Step by step, the historical process reveals the many ways in which social and economic exclusion proved fatal for the victims, illustrating how in a Holocaust space, such as the

Warsaw ghetto, all three types of "*Aktionsmacht*" ("power of action") that Popitz conceptualizes—social exclusion, material damage, and violence that affects the human body—converge and collapse into one another.[3]

One characteristic of spatialized violence is that it is not in the same way external to the victims as, for example, a weapon would be. Be it situational or more permanent, space forces people to relate to and interact with it. In the case of the Warsaw ghetto, for the two and a half years of its existence (October 1940 to May 1943), the Nazis wedged people's lives in their entirety into the ghetto. This forced them to profoundly adapt their behaviors and survival strategies to the violent environment the German occupiers created. Jews had to continuously devise new ways to occupy a space that challenged their very existence. In this process, the inhabitants "practiced" the ghetto space, as de Certeau termed it—that is, they appropriated and actualized it by using it.[4] The following part of this book describes and examines these practices and the manifestations of spatialized violence the ghetto inhabitants were exposed to. Building on the information transmitted in testimonies, I explore in detail how the ghetto, as a space, impacted its inhabitants and how they, in turn, tried to cope, struggle, and resist the adverse environment. Following Doreen Massey's observation that "*spatial configurations produce effects*,"[5] I specifically focus on the various ways in which the spatial configuration of the ghetto and the violent practices associated with it affected and effected its inhabitants' sociality, their everyday life, their self-localization, identity, agency, and their relation to the city and their environment. While the chapters of this part of *Violent Space* at times address similar questions as the previous ones, they do so from a different perspective (i.e., from within) and with a different analytical approach. The analysis zooms in to the level of the victims' everyday lives using particular examples, constellations, and recurring situations to further explore how people experienced and navigated the violent environment of the ghetto. The perceptions, interpretations, and behaviors described in personal accounts render visible the intricate imprints that violence left on the ghetto population's lives. A focus on these sources thus complements the analysis with a more nuanced understanding of the subtle, indirect manifestations of spatial violence.

Notes

1. Reemtsma, *Trust and Violence*, 56.
2. Ibid., 57.
3. Popitz, *Phänomene der Macht*, 44.
4. de Certeau, *Practice of Everyday Life*, 99–100.
5. Massey, "On Space and the City," 162 (emphasis in the original).

CHAPTER

9

Destruction

Established in the northern district of the city, the ghetto was located very centrally, close to old town *(Stare Miasto)*, and the most representative and symbolically resonant parts of the city's center, including the Saxon Garden *(Ogród Saski)* and Theatre Square *(Plac Teatralny)*. To understand the space of the ghetto and how it was experienced by its inhabitants, it is important to look more closely at what had happened to the city and to this particular area beforehand.

During the German invasion, the city of Warsaw had been turned into a battlefield, and the four weeks of warfare that preceded the defeat of Poland's capital altered the cityscape drastically. The heavy bombings, but also the inner lines of defense, left their marks on the city. The city had been militarized. Kaplan describes in an entry on September 10, 1939, during the siege of Warsaw, "The streets are sown with trenches and barricades. Machine guns have been placed on the roofs of houses, and there is a barricade in the doorway of my apartment house, just under my balcony."[1] Kaplan's depiction reflects the intrusion of war into civilian space. Warfare became part of the city space with trenches, machine guns, and barricades infiltrating sites of everyday life. With the implementation of military order, the very concrete threat of further death and destruction entered civilians' lives. In the same diary entry on September 10, Kaplan envisages the impending destruction: "If fighting breaks out in the street no stone will remain upon another in the wall within which I live."[2] It is notable that Kaplan reflects on the city of Warsaw as a whole and not only on a "Jewish quarter." His attachment was to the city, without further differentiation, and the experience of initial militarization and destruction was still a shared one for Jewish and non-Jewish Poles. The destruction hit the more-or-less mutually inhabited space of the city. Although, because of the symbolic and practical importance of the city center, some of the most severe damages were sustained by parts of the city that were later to become the Jewish ghetto.[3]

On September 29, following Warsaw's capitulation, Kaplan describes the city's destruction: "Beautiful Warsaw . . . has been destroyed," he writes. He goes on to speak of streets "which have been all but wiped off the face of the earth," while others are "desolate heaps of gravel."[4] While Kaplan differentiates between damage to the urban structure and human casualties, other accounts, at least metaphorically, show a certain merging of the two. In his diary, Sznapman describes the image of the war-stricken city as follows:

> On the morning of Wednesday, 27 September, things quieted down; at noon we heard that Warsaw had surrendered. Those two days of shelling had inflicted terrible damage: The water plant, the gas works, and the radio station all had been hit, among other places. Warsaw was without water, electricity, gas or radio. The streets were covered with rubble and shards of glass. The city was pockmarked with huge craters. The air was thick with dust and soot. When the bombing stopped, everyone sighed with relief and started coming outside to examine the wreckage. Everywhere you turned there were demolished homes, walls torn open or riddled with holes, or else the charred skeletons of apartment houses, their burned-out window frames gaping like empty eye sockets.[5]

Sznapman draws a parallel between the demolished buildings and human corpses ("skeletons of apartment houses," "burned-out window frames gaping like empty eye sockets"). This transfers a sense of more intense brutality, gravity, and suffering from the human body to inanimate objects. His depiction gives the impression that the attack on the city was to some degree perceived along the lines of violence perpetrated against a person.[6] Although he focuses primarily on buildings and infrastructure, Sznapman is, in his depiction, still very telling in regard to the streets. The basic definitions of streets include among the central elements, "roadway" and "pedestrian way," as well as the "flanking buildings."[7] Street and buildings "exist interdependently" and "define each other";[8] or, as urban design scholar Vikas Mehta phrases it, the street "is three-dimensional such that the buildings containing and defining the street space are as important as the two-dimensional surface of the street."[9] The perception of the adjoining buildings is therefore central for the perception of the street, and the damage described by Kaplan and Sznapman would be formative for how the ghetto inhabitants (and other Varsovians) experienced the street. Sznapman's diary also shows the extent of the damage to the city's infrastructure. The cutting off of the most basic supply lines ("water, electricity, gas or radio"), as well as the damage to the buildings and streets, directly affected the city's inhabitants.[10] The damage to residential buildings was highly detrimental to people's living conditions and affected them on the most basic levels. For instance, broken windows alone could be highly problematic during the harsh Polish winters.[11] The dangers to which such damage exposed residents provide a first example of harm done through destructive measures taken against the city—that is, of violence exerted against, as well as through, space.

According to Engelking and Leociak, the Germans forbade the rebuilding of bombed-out houses.[12] Such a policy aligns with the Nazis' general plans for the city. Displaying "totalitarian aspirations" also when it came to urban planning, plans for cities in the eastern occupied territories were based on the destruction of the existing development (the "dismantling of the Polish city") to create a *tabula rasa* that would allow for the all-encompassing creation of a "new German city."[13] In this sense, the destruction wrought in the early days of the war essentially anticipated the "complete destruction of the city" that was at the core of the German urban planning for occupied Poland.[14] Warsaw, specifically, was designated to be reduced in size and in rank to the level of a provincial town.[15] The Germans pursued their project of Germanization by targeting both people and the settings in which they lived, speaking from 1940 onward of the "reorganization of people and things" in the same breath.[16] Violence exerted against people and against their environment went hand in hand.[17] It should be noted that in the history of the German occupation of Warsaw, the destruction of buildings and apartments often also directly entailed human death. As Kaplan writes, on September 29, 1939, "In the midst of the ruins thousands of human beings lie buried. This is the third day that the bodies of people who did not manage to escape are being pulled out from among the ruins."[18] This parallels the situation during the last days of the ghetto, when from April 1943 onward the Germans began blowing up bunkers and setting fire to buildings to crush Jewish resistance and kill those in hiding.

Both Sznapman and Kaplan depict the damage done to "their" Warsaw; they mourn as Varsovians for a city that still belongs to them. In the period directly after the siege, the categories of "us" and "them" still ran primarily along the lines of Poles and Germans. That means that the destruction of the city was similarly experienced by all inhabitants as an act of violence against the space they inhabited. As Till argues, people and groups have "intimate relationships ... with places, and hence the city";[19] this intimacy as well as the importance of the environment for people's everyday life might help explain why cities can be perceived as "wounded"—and not merely as damaged—as Till suggests. Moreover, because buildings were not fully rebuilt and not all damaged streets were restored, the destruction remained a part of the city space, continually reflecting the experience of violence back to its inhabitants.

Notes

1. Kaplan, *Scroll of Agony*, 28; see also Markowska, *Ringelblum Archive*, 7.
2. Kaplan, *Scroll of Agony*, 28.
3. Sloane, "Introduction," xiv.
4. Kaplan, *Scroll of Agony*, 38.
5. Sznapman, account, 16–17; for a similar description see Markowska, *Ringelblum Archive*, 19.
6. Interestingly, the bombardments by the Soviet Air Force in August and September 1942, during the Great Deportation *Aktion*, were perceived very differently. They "gave the ghetto new faith and encouragement," as the account of an unidentified women states (Anonymous Woman, account, 137). She continues, "To my ears, the roar of bombs exploding around Umschlagplatz was a heartening, joyous sound, and others felt the same way. On occasion the bombs also provided an opportunity to escape (I remember that on the night of 1 September some people managed to cross to the Aryan side or to slip away from Umschlagplatz)" (Anonymous Woman, account, 137–138). This emphasizes how identification with the city had changed quite drastically by then. The space under bombardment was hostile space, associated with harm, loss, and violence. The Soviet air raids, in a sense, targeted the city as German—not Jewish or Polish—space.
7. Ellis, "Spatial Structure of Streets," 117; see also Mantho, *Urban Section*, 76.
8. Ellis, "Spatial Structure of Streets," 117.
9. Mehta, *Street*, 12.
10. Szarota, *Warschau unter dem Hakenkreuz*, 16–17, 159–162.
11. Ibid., 159–160. Sznapman's description is replicated by a member of the German administration, Hubert Groß, who describes the situation during the early days of occupation in a conversation in May 1989: "Just imagine: The city substantially destroyed by bombardment and aerial bombers. Entire neighborhoods lying in ruins. There was a lack of water, gas and electricity. The population suffered want of housing and the necessities of life. . . . Plus a persistent Siberian cold" (Gutschow and Klain, *Vernichtung und Utopie*, 26; translation by A. N.). While listing almost the same elements of destruction, the description of the German is evidently lacking identification, but also the parallelization of the city and a human body. The German original reads as follows: "*Man stelle sich vor: Die Stadt durch Beschießung und Fliegerbomben erheblich zerstört. Ganze Viertel lagen in Trümmern. Weithin fehlten Wasser, Gas und Strom. Die Bevölkerung litt Not an Wohnraum und dem Notwendigsten zum Leben. . . . Dazu eine anhaltende sibirische Kälte*" (ibid., 26).
12. Engelking and Leociak, *Warsaw Ghetto*, xiv; see also Gutschow and Klain, *Vernichtung und Utopie*, 24, 55, 129.
13. Gutschow and Klain, *Vernichtung und Utopie*, 13, 16–17, 26.
14. Ibid., 17. While the planned dismantling of the city again referred predominantly to the destruction of buildings, it is important to remember that when we understand the relation of streets and buildings as a relation of "solids" and "voids"

(Ellis, "Spatial Structure of Streets," 115), the disappearance of buildings would also entail the disappearance, or at least the drastic restructuring, of streets. The German original reads as follows: "*ein totalitärer Anspruch*" (Gutschow and Klain, *Vernichtung und Utopie*, 16), "*Abbau der Polenstadt,*" "*die völlige Vernichtung der Stadt*" (17) (English translation by A. N.).

15. Gutschow and Klain, *Vernichtung und Utopie*, 24, 41; Lehnstaedt, *Okkupation im Osten*, 82.

16. Gutschow and Klain, *Vernichtung und Utopie*, 13, 41. The German original reads as follows: "*Neuordnung bei den Menschen wie bei den Sachen*" (Gutschow and Klain, *Vernichtung und Utopie*, 13) (English translation by A. N.).

17. There is a striking parallel between the Nazis' attempts to "decapitate" the Polish society by systematically murdering the Polish intelligentsia and Polish political and cultural leaders, and the dismantling of the country's capital. Hans Frank notes in his diary on September 15, 1939, that he had received the order to turn the "economic, social, cultural, political structure" of the occupied territories into a "field of rubble so to speak" (Geiss and Jacobmeyer, *Deutsche Politik in Polen*, 31; qtd. in Gutschow and Klain, *Vernichtung und Utopie*, 24; English translation by A. N.). Again, many fields of destruction—economic, social, cultural, political, and architectural—are metaphorically brought together. The German original reads as follows: "*es in seiner wirtschaftlichen, sozialen, kulturellen, politischen Struktur sozusagen zu einem Trümmerfeld zu machen.*"

18. Kaplan, *Scroll of Agony*, 38; see also Markowska, *Ringelblum Archive*, 19.

19. Till, "Wounded Cities," 10.

CHAPTER

10

Decreed Space

From the beginning of the occupation of Warsaw, the Germans began to implement a new, segregating order in the streets. They projected their racial convictions onto a spatial matrix and onto the factual layout of the city. This process can be seen as the realization of the spatial aspects of Nazi ideology on a concrete, local level. The city became—as Paolo Giaccaria and Claudio Minca put it—"the field in which Nazi worldview/ideology and its related conceptual apparatus were translated into actual daily decisions and acts."[1] On a geopolitical level, as much as on the level of concrete urban space, these decisions mainly concerned the question "Who should be living and in which space[?]"[2] Quickly, the occupying German forces implemented a very drastic "racialization of space,"[3] which followed the Nazis' principle that "spatial order and racial order were supposed to coincide."[4] The Jewish inhabitants of Warsaw were severely limited in their movements, access to many parts of the city was denied to them, and public space became restricted. In their foundational work *The Warsaw Ghetto: A Guide to the Perished City*, Engelking and Leociak coin the term "decreed space" for this early stage of the Nazis' reorganization of the urban landscape, describing a spatial order that was not yet implemented by means of physical structures but "imposed by force, and ... executed under threat of the gravest penalties."[5]

In his account written in hiding in May 1943, Stefan Ernest recalls the first months of German occupation:

> For quite a while now other signs have been going up on the doors of cafés, restaurants, movie theaters and the like, as well as at a few places of business: JUDEN EINTRITT VERBOTEN—NO JEWS ALLOWED—OR JUDEN NICHT ERWÜNSCHT—NO JEWS WANTED.

This was followed by other restrictions on the use of carriages, automobiles, and streetcars; special trams have been introduced exclusively for Jews, with the number of the line displayed against a yellow background.[6]

These restrictions affected various types of public space, including parks, public benches, certain city squares, and, at some point, even individual streets.[7] In addition, the implementation of a curfew introduced a temporal factor to the restrictions of movement.[8] The streets ceased to be accessible during certain hours of the day. This process of restricting access was accompanied by a practice of labeling public spaces in ways that marked the exclusion visually. Signs, posters, announcements, and visual markers appeared that inscribed the division of Jewish and non-Jewish space into the urban environment.

With the introduction of compulsory armbands for the Jewish population, the division became even more visible, as well as more easily enforced. The anti-Jewish measures implemented by the occupiers, and the visible degradation of the Jewish population, also led to an increase in harassment directed toward Jews. Clearly identifiable by their armbands, Jewish pedestrians regularly became subject to humiliation and sudden acts of violence, originating from the German occupiers but also perpetrated by Polish hooligans.[9] As Sznapman summarizes the situation, "Jews were placed outside the law. A non-Jew could do to a Jew whatever he pleased, take his property or even his life, with complete impunity."[10] Very common were attacks on orthodox Jews, who were humiliated and beaten and whose beards were brutally cut off.[11] Often, Jewish pedestrians were "forced to perform humiliating and exhausting physical exercises in front of watching passers-by."[12] These acts of publicly displayed violence further disrupted the community. The perpetrators of such violence otherized their victims and, at the same time, turned everyone else in the street into a (passive) bystander.

The rising numbers of such incidents turned the street into a place that did not feel safe for a significant proportion of the city's residents. Accounts suggest that many Jews, in fact, avoided going out on the streets at all.[13] All these practices had a drastic effect on—among other aspects of life and well-being—communal life and cohesion. As a space that is by definition accessible to everyone (at least in theory),[14] public space and in particular the streets fulfill important social functions. As Mehta explains, "Streets create opportunities for neighbors and strangers to meet and engage, provide opportunities for a range of social interactions as a part of the daily round, and possibly even reinforce a sense of community."[15] Accordingly, by restricting access to streets and other public spaces, the Germans deprived the Jewish population of this crucial social participation and exchange and, in addition, their right to identify with their city.

Both the spatial restrictions and the labeling of space were means of exercising power and domination. Sznapman describes a practice that illustrates particularly well how domination and humiliation were exerted on a spatial plane: "On the streets, the Germans demanded that Jews step aside and bow to them; anyone who failed to do so was kicked and beaten to a pulp."[16] Similar descriptions can be found in numerous other accounts. They differ slightly in regard to the specifics, from Jewish pedestrians being forced to step aside, as Sznapman describes it, to being required to get off the sidewalk entirely.[17] The latter is particularly noteworthy, because in many Polish cities, such as Gdańsk, Łódź, Lwów, and Radom, sewer systems had been installed only recently,[18] while in smaller towns there often was still no canalization. Stepping off the sidewalk would have therefore meant stepping into the gutter, into excrement and filth. In Warsaw, the sewer system was still relatively new, too, having been constructed by the British engineer William Lindley by the end of the nineteenth century. Before that, "sewage still flowed straight into the Vistula River from open gutters or covered drains."[19] Still in 1939, the canalization did not cover the entire city, so it can be assumed that people were aware of the connotations of being forced off of the sidewalk.

Generally, this spatial practice imposed by the Nazis mirrored their ideology: the right to the street, like the right to the urban space, was racially coded. The submission that the Germans demanded came, moreover, in the form of specific spatial behavior, the enforcement of which was a manifestation of power as much as it was a gesture of degradation and humiliation. Ringelblum recapitulates the consequences of the demanded submission: "This forces the Jews to zigzag across the street in the neighborhoods frequented by Germans."[20] In every direct encounter, Jews' use of the space was dictated by the Germans or, more specifically, by those who were clearly identifiable as Germans—that is, soldiers and other officials in uniform.[21] It is important to keep in mind that everyone in the German civil administration wore a uniform as well, as did women employed in the Wehrmacht or the SS.[22] Their uniforms reinforced the impression of militarization but also visually manifested a claim to the city space.

Something similar can be said about the mounting presence of German posters and swastika flags and the installation of loudspeakers in the streets,[23] a phenomenon that Miron in the context of German cities calls the "Nazification of public space,"[24] with "Nazi symbols conquering both visual and auditory space."[25] The German administration renamed numerous streets and city squares using either a literal translation of the previous (apolitical) Polish name or politicized names paying tribute to high-ranking Nazi officials.[26] During that process, Polish street signs were replaced by German ones.[27] As part of the projected Germanization of Warsaw, the Germans, for instance, renamed the former Piłsudski Square first to *Sachsenplatz* and then to *Adolf Hitler Platz*, and Aleje Ujazdowskie consecutively to *Lindenallee* and only shortly after to *Siegesstrasse*.[28] Jews were banned from both.[29]

German street maps from the time of the occupation suggest something quite remarkable and interesting: most of the streets within the ghetto were, in fact, not renamed.[30] Only those close to a German facility were Germanized—Gęsia Street where the Gęsia prison was located was renamed *Gänsestraße*, and Leszno Street where the court building was, *Gerichtsstraße*. While the Nazis Germanized Polish space (albeit mostly in the city center and in areas that were densely populated by Germans), they let the Jewish space remain alien and, from their perspective, unintelligible. This also indicates that they saw very little need to navigate it.

These German practices and regulations led to a first form of ghettoization before the official ghetto was even established. As Kaplan writes on June 27, 1940,

> There is no formal ghetto in Warsaw for the time being, but in practice a ghetto exists. Such conditions of living have arisen that the Jews themselves have unintentionally created a ghetto. In the broad and beautiful Aryan streets not a Jew is to be found—except for assimilated half-, third-, and quarter-Jews, whose homes are among the Gentiles. A Jew marked with the "badge of shame" simply restrains himself from appearing in those streets. He is afraid of becoming a subject for disgrace and embarrassment.[31]

The Germans had marked and regulated space to such a degree that the Jewish inhabitants felt ghettoized. Kaplan describes the ghetto as existing "in practice," a practice that was, primarily, a spatial one. The "informal" ghetto was to a large degree predicated on the way in which the Nazis translated their ideology into spatial entitlement (or the corresponding lack thereof) and implemented segregation through a series of spatial regulations and labeling. In general, public space and, especially, the city's streets had been turned into an alien and hostile territory for Jews.[32] In addition to the regulation of spatial access, the symbolic occupation instituted through the Germanization of certain parts of the city also created areas that seemed particularly antagonistic to Jewish presence ("the broad and beautiful Aryan streets" on which Jews could not walk safely). In line with the Nazis' *Lebensraum* ideology, the very act of Germanization implied a contestation of Jewish spatial rights.

Notes

1. Giaccaria and Minca, "For a Tentative Spatial Theory," 33.
2. Ibid.
3. Besides several similarities that would be worth exploring in greater depths, this process differs from the "racialization of space" as discussed in the context of segregation in contemporary US American cities (see, for example, Hutchison,

"Racialization"; Lipsitz, "Racialization of Space and the Spatialization of Race"; Calmore, "Racialized Space and the Culture of Segregation"; Sundstrom, "Race and Place"; Massey and Denton, "Hypersegregation in U.S. Metropolitan Areas") in that the Nazis' spatial policies were to a much larger degree explicitly ideologically rooted, actively implemented, and ultimately more ruthless. The US history of racial segregation nevertheless shows many examples that could be interpreted as akin to the Nazi policies. So does the history of Apartheid in South Africa. In the context at hand, the concept of "racialized space" is used to describe the Germans' application of their racial ideology to settlement patterns in the occupied countries and particularly to the urban environment of the city of Warsaw.

4. Giaccaria and Minca, "For a Tentative Spatial Theory," 31.

5. Engelking and Leociak, *Warsaw Ghetto*, 52.

6. Ernest, account, 21.

7. Kaplan, *Scroll of Agony*, 173, 193; Ringelblum, *Notes from the Warsaw Ghetto*, 51; Adler, *In the Warsaw Ghetto*, 7; Lehnstaedt, *Okkupation im Osten*, 270; Engelking and Leociak, *Warsaw Ghetto*, 62, 66; Löw and Roth, *Das Warschauer Getto*, 40.

8. Ringelblum, *Notes from the Warsaw Ghetto*, 11, 65; Kaplan, *Scroll of Agony*, 45; Bauman, *Winter in the Morning*, 30.

9. Löw and Roth, *Das Warschauer Getto*, 30; Lehnstaedt, *Okkupation im Osten*, 270; Gutman, *Jews of Warsaw*, 27–30; Birenbaum, *Hope Is the Last to Die*, 11; Berg, *Diary*, 15; Ringelblum, *Notes from the Warsaw Ghetto*, 17; Markowska, *Ringelblum Archive*, 40–43.

10. Sznapman, account, 20. In his chapter on violence in the ghetto, Lehnstaedt speaks about a complete depravation of rights vis-à-vis the Germans ("*faktische Entrechtung im Umgang mit den Deutschen*") (*Okkupation im Osten*, 255). Berg also points to this when she writes in her diary, "Protests were to no avail: the law does not protect the Jews" (*Diary*, 16).

11. Kaplan, *Scroll of Agony*, 54; see also Gutman, *Jews of Warsaw*, 9. Visibility played an important role here, too. Also, orthodox Jews corresponded most closely to the pejoratively loaded image of the "*Ostjude*" propagated by the Nazi ideology, which further fueled German aggression in the field (see, for example, Michman, *Emergence of Jewish Ghettos*, 72–73).

12. Bauman, *Winter in the Morning*, 30.

13. See, for example, Berg, *Diary*, 15; Bauman, *Winter in the Morning*, 30; Adler, *In the Warsaw Ghetto*, 5; Kaplan, *Scroll of Agony*, 54; Gutman, *Jews of Warsaw*, 9; Warszawa Rada Żydowska 221/4.

14. Mantho, *Urban Section*, 236; Langegger, *Rights to Public Space*, 54; Mehta, *Street*, 9, 20.

15. Mehta, *Street*, 10.

16. Sznapman, account, 17; see also Ringelblum, *Notes from the Warsaw Ghetto*, 69–70; Kaplan, *Scroll of Agony*, 206; Lehnstaedt, *Okkupation im Osten*, 270.

17. Ringelblum, *Notes from the Warsaw Ghetto*, 69; Adler, *In the Warsaw Ghetto*, 32. Other signs of "respect" are mentioned, too, such as lifting one's hat (Ringelblum,

Notes from the Warsaw Ghetto, 86; Berg, *Diary*, 86) or saluting (Ringelblum, *Notes from the Warsaw Ghetto*, 66). In Warsaw, these actions were at first not backed up by an official decree but owed to individual orders and expectations. Kaplan gives an example: "Once there came into the ghetto a certain Nazi from a province where the Jews are required to greet every Nazi soldier they encountered, removing their hats as they do. There is no such practice in Warsaw, but the 'honored guest' wanted to be strict and force the rules of his place of origin on us" (*Scroll of Agony*, 153). Later, as historian Szarota explains, there was, in fact, a regulation by the German occupiers specifically forbidding Jews to greet Germans on the streets (*Warschau unter dem Hakenkreuz*, 35). Szarota also points out that the practice of having Jews step aside and leave the sidewalk when encountering a German in uniform resembles similar regulations implemented in the territories annexed to the Reich and applied to Poles as well (ibid.).

18. Madryas, Szot, and Wysocki, "Upgrading Old Masonry Interceptor Sewers," 1919.

19. de la Motte, "WaterTime Case Study—Warsaw, Poland," 3.

20. Ringelblum, *Notes from the Warsaw Ghetto*, 70.

21. Ibid., 69; Kaplan, *Scroll of Agony*, 206.

22. Lehnstaedt, *Okkupation im Osten*, 63, 67.

23. Ibid., 83; Szarota, *Warschau unter dem Hakenkreuz*, 41.

24. Miron, "'Lately, Almost Constantly, Everything Seems Small to Me,'" 129.

25. Ibid., 123. It is worth noting that this process of Germanizing and claiming public space was countered by offensives of the Polish underground, in which its members vandalized German propaganda and tagged the city with anti-German slogans and symbols (Szarota, *Warschau unter dem Hakenkreuz*, 42–43). One of the most prominent examples was the so-called "*V-Aktion*," carried out all over occupied Europe (ibid., 42). The "V" that was to symbolize the imminent victory of the Allied forces appeared all over the city, mocking the German propaganda efforts (ibid., 42–43).

26. Lehnstaedt, *Okkupation im Osten*, 83; Szarota, *Warschau unter dem Hakenkreuz*, 40–41.

27. Lehnstaedt, *Okkupation im Osten*, 83.

28. Ibid.

29. Engelking and Leociak, *Warsaw Ghetto*, 66.

30. See, for example, Grundmann, "Plan der Stadt Warschau," or Deutsches Militärisches Karteninstitut Warschau, "Plan der Stadt Warschau, 1941."

31. Kaplan, *Scroll of Agony*, 165; see also Engelking and Leociak, *Warsaw Ghetto*, 60. Berg makes a similar observation and writes about the existence of "unofficial boundaries" in occupied Warsaw (*Diary*, 21).

32. For a similar analysis in the context of German cities, see Guy Miron's "'Lately, Almost Constantly, Everything Seems Small to Me'." After describing the continuous exclusion of Jews from public spaces and the increasing climate of hostility toward them, Miron concludes, "The process of Nazi production of space made the German street a hostile territory for Jews" (ibid., 124).

CHAPTER

11

Buildings

Except for war damage, the "landscape of the ghetto"[1] was shaped by an architectural structure that was very familiar to Varsovians and those acquainted with Polish cities of the time. Despite the walls cutting off streets and entrances to "Aryan" buildings being bricked up, the prewar housing structure inside the ghetto had not changed much. Geographer and Holocaust scholar Andrew Charlesworth notes, "What we have are streets and houses that are recognizable to anyone familiar with east European cities in the 1930s. The landscape of the ghetto looks normal."[2] Although Charlesworth speaks here about photographs of the Litzmannstadt ghetto, something similar can be said about the Warsaw ghetto as well. While Warsaw was more heavily bombarded during the German offense in 1939 than the city of Łódź and thus suffered more damage to its building structure, from an architectural point of view, the city's (and thus the ghetto's) houses and facades remained familiar. In his introduction to *Words to Outlive Us: Eyewitness Accounts from the Warsaw Ghetto*, Philip Boehm paints a very concise picture of what this meant in the case of Warsaw. He highlights the particular layout of a typical building in Warsaw's northern quarter, painting a picture that allows conclusions about the architectural structure and the general living conditions but also explicates the relative normalcy of the "landscape of the ghetto" suggested by Charlesworth: "An average of seven residents lived per room, mostly in large buildings of two or four stories constructed around a central courtyard, with shops on the ground level along the street and living spaces above and in the rear wings of the building. An entryway led from the street into the courtyard, where entrances provided access to separate stairwells. While there were also more spacious residences of relative luxury, a typical apartment consisted of a kitchen and one or two rooms."[3]

While the buildings themselves were relatively large, the average apartment was rather small. As Boehm indicates, before ghettoization, the size of the living space had corresponded to the social status of inhabitants. In prewar times, the location of an apartment had also reflected socioeconomic standing: Varsovians had associated a higher social status with the apartments that were facing the street, whereas the further down into the building complex one moved, the less an apartment was considered to be worth. Gebert highlights this when he describes one of the surviving buildings from the ghetto (the elegant tenement house at 20 Chłodna Street, where Adam Czerniaków, the chairman of the *Judenrat*, had lived): "You will see three courtyards, one following another, the connecting passageways gently flowing to ease the eye. Big Warsaw tenements were built like that, the rent getting less the deeper in one went."[4] In a typical building, the so-called "*bel étage*," located in the more representative front building and providing comfortable access to the street, was considered the most desirable living space. However, social differentiation of this kind quickly disintegrated as the immense overcrowding forced people to share their living space in large numbers, and apartments were assigned to those without residence through the *Judenrat*'s Housing Bureau.[5] While the building structure remained more or less the same, the living arrangements did not.

In the prewar northern quarter, the courtyards, around which buildings were constructed, had been important centers of Jewish communal and economic life—a "city" of their own.[6] With the outside world becoming increasingly hostile and dangerous, the relative cover these courtyards provided set them apart from the streets, where people felt particularly exposed.[7] The courtyards represented a form of "Semi-Private" space—that is, a space "related to a private space and accessible by a limited group via Private spaces," but, at the same time, "connected to Public space."[8] As such, they granted inhabitants more security than the streets' public space. Berg describes the special status of the courtyards in her diary on November 22, 1940: "In the homes and in the courtyards, wherever the ears of the Gestapo do not reach, people nervously discuss the Nazis' real aims in isolating the Jewish quarter."[9] To Berg, the homes and the courtyards fall into a similar category as spaces where the inhabitants feel relatively free from intrusion. People could move within the building complex at times when movement outside was potentially dangerous or even prohibited. They were also less visible, which is why the courtyards of border streets were preferred locations for smuggling (at least until the ghetto's boundaries were changed in the fall/winter of 1941 to run along streets and not between buildings).[10]

Especially from 1942 onward, when the German violence in the ghetto further escalated, the building fronts, by contrast, represented a new form of exposure, as "Germans or Ukrainians . . . began taking random shots at windows."[11] During deportations, the fact that all wings of a large building complex were accessible through a "central courtyard" proved fatal for the inhabitants as this layout facilitated the work of the German SS and police forces, "the Ukrainian and Latvian troops," and "the Jewish police" during round-ups and house blockades.[12] With the central entrance blocked, inhabitants of a building complex were gathered in the courtyard, and controlling them became relatively easy for the perpetrators. Bauman recalls in her memoir, "Houses were surrounded by the troops, all gates and exits blocked, residents summoned to the back yards."[13] The courtyards, which had been centers of Jewish life, now became a deadly trap.

Boehm's description also highlights the fact that many buildings in the ghetto were relatively tall. This played a significant role when it came to hiding. When the German forces entered a house to round up its inhabitants, they would go from one floor to the next, starting with the ground level. Many accounts, in fact, report that people hiding on the fourth floor or higher were, by chance, spared from deportation because the perpetrators left before reaching their apartment. Janina Bauman recalls,

> Soon we heard a rumble of heavy boots climbing up the stairs, of smashed locks and doors flung open by force: the hunters were searching through the flats. We could hear them coming up and up, approaching the third floor, then the fourth. We could already hear their voices, make out Polish and Latvian words. The fourth floor was taking them a long time: they were obviously very busy plundering. Now we had only minutes left. We waited.
> Then suddenly, a long sharp whistle and a German command from the courtyard announced the end of the round-up, summoning back the hunters.
> We had survived.[14]

For this reason, hiding places were often located in attics.[15] Yet, as Bauman's depiction also suggests, survival was in the majority of cases a confluence of coincidence. In fact, Adler describes in his memoir a situation where location had the opposite effect and precisely those who lived on the higher floors fell prey to the Germans. An elaborate hiding place he had constructed in the basement of a building "turned out to be useless for those living on the higher stories," because they were not able to get to it in time. When they reached the ground floor, the courtyard had already been "taken over by the S.S."[16] This, according to Adler, "caused the death of dozens of people" in his building.[17] In both instances, a person's location within a building determined their chances of death or survival.[18]

Notes

1. Charlesworth, "Topography of Genocide," 241.
2. Ibid.

3. Boehm, "Introduction," 10.

4. Gebert, "Reading the Palimpsest," 232.

5. Adler, *In the Warsaw Ghetto*, 53.

6. Singer, *In My Father's Court*, 190.

7. Meed, *On Both Sides of the Wall*, 9–10.

8. Mantho, *Urban Section*, 236.

9. Berg, *Diary*, 29.

10. Engelking and Leociak, *Warsaw Ghetto*, 80–82; see also Kostański, *Janek*, 37.

11. Berman, account, 144, 146; see also Lewin, *Cup of Tears*, 141. Lewin describes a particularly extreme example of this practice in a diary entry on May 25, 1942: to block the inhabitants' view on the Pawiak prison,

> all flats overlooking Pawia and Dzielna Streets have for some time been obliged to have their windows completely covered and screened with black paper, just as for the regulation black-out at night, only 24 hours a day. It is extremely dark in these Jewish front rooms, and they can never be aired out. I hardly need describe what it means for the occupants' eyes and lungs, their state of mind, this continual dark existence without fresh air, even ghetto air.... The guard at the Pawiak watches to make sure that the unthinkable doesn't happen and a Jewish window is opened and the black paper or blankets are moved to one side. A few weeks ago a Jew at 30 Pawia Street who shifted the window-covering to one side was shot dead (*Cup of Tears*, 97–98)

12. Bauman, *Winter in the Morning*, 67–68.

13. Ibid.

14. Ibid., 68.

15. Ibid., 82; see also Birenbaum, *Hope Is the Last to Die*, 31; Lewin, *Cup of Tears*, 141.

16. Adler, *In the Warsaw Ghetto*, 298.

17. Ibid.

18. Attics and cellars, the buildings' highest and lowest points, became particularly important again during the Ghetto Uprising. Attacks by the fighters of the ŻOB were often carried out from the buildings' upper floors or rooftops; yet, most fighters and civilians hid in underground bunkers constructed below the building structure.

12

Lost Homes

For those forced by the Germans to move to the area of the future ghetto in October and November 1940, the move meant the loss of their previous apartments or houses. According to the Nazi administration, about 13,000 Jewish apartments "outside the Jewish quarter" were to be vacated by their inhabitants during the resettlement and about 150,000 Jewish Varsovians lost their homes within just a few weeks.[1] The deadline was very tight and left little time to prepare for the move. Because the boundaries of the ghetto were redrawn several times, people living close to the borders often did not know until the very last minute if they were going to have to move or not.[2] Referring to the constant changes that the German plans for the ghetto underwent, Mazor speaks of "torture 'by uncertainty.'"[3] Those who were deported to Warsaw from the surrounding smaller towns and villages were usually forced by the Germans to leave their houses at very short notice. Adler writes about the fate of these people in his memoir *In the Warsaw Ghetto, 1940–1943: An Account of a Witness*, "By the hundreds and the thousands they arrived almost daily. . . . The executioners had forced them to abandon their homes usually without notice, sometimes with fifteen minutes', an hour's, or at best, a day's notice."[4]

In his study on burglary, Chapman argues that people invest in their homes the hope "to create a sphere where they have control over their environment" and that this hope is tied to the "perception that the world 'outside' is unstable, insecure and beyond an individual's control."[5] The home works as a counterbalance, providing stability and controllability that the outside world seems to lack. In a context where the outside world has turned emphatically hostile, this perception can motivate further withdrawal into the private space. And, in fact, when the anti-Jewish measures implemented by the Germans had increasingly excluded Jews from public space, many had retreated to their homes, leaving the house as little as possible.[6] As Kaplan observes in his diary beginning February 1940, "Social visits have ceased. Everyone remains locked in his own unheated room, imprisoned in his own sorrowful thoughts."[7] The violence prevailing in the streets, as well as the curfews implemented by the Germans, shifted social contact to the inside. Because people were confined to their homes for many hours of the day, relationships inside of buildings and apartments intensified. Social relations became more and more defined by proximity.[8] In contrast to the increasing hostility encountered outside, the private sphere seemed to grant a higher degree of safety. But with the resettlement to the ghetto (at the latest), the private space of the home was disrupted as well.

Being expelled from one's house or apartment constitutes a fundamental destabilization, disrupting the feeling of "permanence, safety and privacy" that, according to Chapman, is central to the concept of home.[9] An example of the extent of damage done to the individual can be seen in an entry in Kaplan's diary on October 2, 1939. Kaplan describes the forcible eviction from buildings that were requisitioned by the Germans right after they had invaded the city:

> I was suddenly informed that the newly arrived Germans had already managed to requisition five houses on Nowolipki Street . . . and to expel all their Jewish inhabitants. They did not permit them to take even a shoelace out of their apartments; they did not permit them to don even an overcoat. In a matter of minutes, all the Jews were expelled and all the houses cleared. . . . Within minutes, hundreds of families were left without a roof, without clothes, without food, without an apartment, without money—I among them.[10]

Due to the German policies and the swiftness of the evictions, the loss usually encompassed both living space and tangible assets at once. Because this often meant that people lost their means of subsistence, eviction was for many a threat to the very basis of existence.[11] People lost objects of both monetary and sentimental value, and evictions impaired ties to familial and personal heritage and ruptured people's sense of belonging. In her study "Home Loss in Wartime Literature: A Typology of Images," Madeline G. Levine suggests that the loss of these objects was possibly experienced as even more severe than the loss of the dwelling place itself. Commenting on a poem by Czesław Miłosz, she writes, "Clearly, the exterior structures that encompass a home are not as important as the things contained within them, laden as those possessions are with symbolic value."[12]

Kaplan continues his description of the eviction the following day, describing how he kept returning to the street he used to live on to "gaze at the windows of [his] lovely apartment," which was "now in the hands of strangers."[13] It is not only the loss that troubles him but also the idea of strangers, or more precisely the German occupiers, taking over his most private space. According to Chapman's study on the experience of a burglary, the space of the home can be perceived as "disrupted" or "spoiled" by the presence of the intruder.[14] In the case of confiscated Jewish apartments, private space was not only violated once but in most cases permanently usurped.

The home is also a space that is deeply intertwined with personal history and therefore emotionally charged, as cultural geographer Alison Blunt argues. She calls it a "material and affective space" that is "shaped by everyday practices, lived experiences, social relations, memories and emotions."[15] Some of these qualities become visible when Kaplan writes, "My heart is broken: I sank a whole lifetime's work into that apartment: I lived in it for twenty-four years; I decorated it and beautified it and adorned it; and in one confused hour I lost it."[16] Kaplan's words show how his apartment is endowed with meaning far beyond its practical use. This concerns the history of time lived in it, his personal investment, and the (relative) permanence that he had anticipated. Kaplan specifically mentions the way he "decorated" and "beautified" the apartment, expressing how he personally invested in it and made the apartment his home. This intimate personalization intensified the loss. According to Chapman, the "fabric of a house, its internal space and its contents come to embody the self-identity of the people who live there."[17] Accordingly, people become highly vulnerable to a violation of this personal space.[18] Following philosopher Laura McMahon, one could go even further and argue that a violation of an individual's home or belongings can be "experienced or witnessed as akin to an assault on the physical body."[19] Introducing the concept of "extended bodily vulnerability," McMahon suggests that "it is not only our own bodies that are vulnerable to assault but also the meaningful objects through which we expressively engage with the world as well as the established horizonal context of these embodied engagements."[20] From the perspective of the victim's experience, the violation of an individual's personal space can thus to some extent be likened to a physical assault. Correspondingly, the complete loss of one's home—by force and not by one's own choice—can be experienced as traumatic.[21]

But evictions were also harmful on a practical level. Losing one's home and one's belongings meant a huge loss in resources. Those who, at least in the beginning, had been able to stay in their apartments usually had a lot more furniture, household goods, and other valuables to sell later on.[22] But also the dwelling place itself was a valuable asset. When Kaplan's apartment is returned to him in November 1939, even though he finds everything "broken and destroyed, stolen and plundered," he concludes, "Suddenly we were saved, for an apartment these days, after the fires, the destruction and demolition, and on the eve of the ghetto, is more precious than gold and pearls. If one has an apartment, he has everything; without an apartment, he has nothing."[23] In the area designated for the ghetto, however, it was extremely difficult to find new housing, and usually people who were forced to move had to settle under much poorer conditions.[24] While in theory people were allowed to trade their apartments with Gentiles moving from the area of the projected ghetto, often Jewish apartments were simply confiscated or the exchange took place under very unfavorable terms.[25] In most cases, it took the evicted a long time to find alternative housing. Due to the spatial limitation and the immense number of people forced to resettle, space had been turned into a scarce good inside the walls. Not least because of this, the move itself was for most people a stressful experience. There was immense chaos on the streets because people had to resettle without necessarily knowing where to turn for shelter.[26] Deprived of the stability associated with home, people suddenly found themselves in a situation of utter chaos and insecurity. Toshia Bialer describes the masses of people moving:

> Try to picture one-third of a large city's population moving through the streets
> in an endless stream, pushing, wheeling, dragging all their belongings from
> every part of the city to one small section, crowding one another more and
> more as they converged. . . . In the ghetto, as some of us had begun to call it,
> half-ironically and in jest, there was an appalling chaos. Thousands of people
> were rushing around at the last minute trying to find a place to stay. Everything
> was already filled up, but still they kept on coming and somehow more room
> was found. . . . The narrow, crooked streets of the most dilapidated parts of
> Warsaw were crowded with pushcarts, their owners going from house to house
> asking the inevitable question. Have you room? The sidewalks were covered
> with their belongings. Children wandered, lost and crying, parents ran hither
> and yon seeking them.[27]

Because means of transportation were limited, the relocation meant that people had to drag the few private belongings they could bring outside, cluttering the streets and spilling what was usually a matter of the private sphere outside for everyone to see.[28] The privacy of their home had been violently dissolved, and thus, as Levine explains in her study on wartime literature, home itself was "violated, literally and symbolically."[29] On a practical level, the necessity to take one's belongings out into the streets also heightened the risk for them to be confiscated by the Germans.[30] Quite often, the "transfer to the ghetto meant complete material ruin."[31]

Ultimately, everyone in the ghetto shared the fate of losing their homes. The constant reduction of the ghetto area forced many of those who at first had been able to stay put to eventually move.[32] The history of the ghetto space was one of continuous shrinkage and rearrangement, repeatedly forcing people to resettle internally. The concept of home became increasingly short-lived and unstable. As historian and literary scholar Leociak points out in his study on writers in the ghetto, the "places where the writers stayed changed ever faster, were ever more transitory and unplanned."[33] In fact, in most cases these places were not homes anymore; they were, at best, an "Ersatz home" ("substitute home") as Levine suggests.[34] And again, with every move people also lost more and more of their movable property; things had to be left behind, or they were confiscated, stolen, or damaged during transport.[35]

The Great Deportation *Aktion* marked a particularly drastic and violent wave of evictions. Entire streets were "being emptied of their occupants" in the course of a few weeks in July–September 1942.[36] Leociak summarizes, "The deportations finally broke up the illusion of stability. These tore everyone from their earlier residences."[37] For those who were deported, eviction was permanent and left very little room for individual attempts to cope. Bauman describes the process in her memoir:

> The house at 15 Leszno Street was surrounded and closed off first thing in the morning. From our fifth-floor flat we heard the uproar of troops bursting into the courtyard, the ear-splitting whistle, then the loud cry: "*Alle Juden raus, schnell, schnell, alle Juden herunter*" ("All Jews out, quick, quick, all Jews down here") repeated in Polish. Then the sound of dozens of feet running down, down to disaster. Then shouts, screaming, whistles, lamenting in the court-yard. . . . Two single shots. . . . A turmoil of violence and misery.[38]

During the Great Deportation *Aktion* and the following restructuring of the ghetto, the forced evictions were usually carried out with the utmost brutality.[39] Many people were killed on the spot, the others torn from their homes often without any notice. The trauma of forced eviction was heightened by the violence with which it was enacted but also by the fact that the Germans destroyed almost all remaining agency of the people who were forcibly taken from their homes. People transitioned from a space that had granted them at least a small amount of self-determination and safety to a situation characterized by violence and existential insecurity.

Usually, everything happened very fast, leaving people no time to prepare. This robbed them of the chance to pack their remaining belongings but also of the chance to bid their farewells. As Mawult recalls, "Soon all residents are standing in the courtyard; the selection is over; those who will return to their apartments have been separated from those who will never see their homes again. There's no time for going back, no time for a final look around, no time for any last words."[40] What Mawult describes *ex negativo* is the possibility of taking at least a moment to face the loss that people experienced when they were subjected to the violent German round-ups and ensuing deportations. While these gestures would not have changed what was happening, they would have retained some affective agency for those who were torn from their homes. Instead, people were violently rushed out, without time to process what was happening and what the change meant for them. For those who were not among the deported, the recurrent loss of their living place meant further destabilization. As Abraham Lewin describes in an entry on August 13, 1942, "Our lives have been turned upside down, a total and utter destruction in every sense of the word."[41]

After the Great Deportations, when the remnants of the ghetto were restructured into a work camp, losing one's "place to live" coincided quite literally with losing the right to live.[42] Only those who received "numbers"—that is, proof of their employment at one of the shops—were assigned a flat.[43] Those who didn't lost both their "right to be alive" and their dwelling place at the same time.[44] Again, having to change one's living quarters often also entailed the loss of an individual's few remaining belongings. When houses were cleared by the Germans, people often could not take their possessions. Lewin explains the situation of those who were affected by the "liquidation" of the small ghetto: "There is no possibility for them to take out with them a few of their possessions, clothes and bedding, because there is a danger of being seized while moving."[45] In addition, more and more looting occurred, as a woman whose name could not be established writes in her account:[46] buildings were "plundered for any material goods left behind. This was done by Germans, Ukrainians, and Latvians. On calmer days rabble from the other side would also sneak into the ghetto."[47] Due to the dire living conditions, ghetto inhabitants also stole from each other: "neighbor stole from neighbor."[48]

When Lewin's sisters lose their apartments in the wake of the ghetto's restructuring after the Great Deportations, Lewin is particularly troubled by the prospect of losing his belongings: "If they lose the flats, what little clothing and bedclothes I have will be endangered and I will be naked and destitute. This disturbs me deeply, even though we are in mortal danger and there is no need to get upset at the prospect of having nothing to wear or no pillow for our head, at a time when our very survival is in doubt."[49] The apartment had served as a safekeeper, allowing one to store and protect one's belongings. Lewin is surprised at the attachment he still feels toward his personal effects. But his description suggests that it might not be the value of these possessions themselves but rather their meaning as remainders of the private sphere that explains his attachment. Returning to the importance of the private space as a counterbalance against the perceived instability and insecurity of the "world 'outside,'"[50] it is indeed possible that these personal items, as symbols of private everyday life, might have been meaningful not despite but especially when facing "mortal danger."

Notes

1. Arad, Gutman, and Margaliot, *Documents on the Holocaust*, 226. Non-Jewish Poles also suffered from forced evictions during this time and would continue to do so when apartments were requisitioned by Germans or *Volksdeutsche*. For a description of the situation outside the walls, see Szarota, *Warschau unter dem Hakenkreuz*, 154–157.

2. See, for example, Gutman-Staszewska, account, 25.

3. Mazor, *Vanished City*, 83.

4. Adler, *In the Warsaw Ghetto*, 39; see also Kassow, *Who Will Write Our History?*, 107; Markowska, *Ringelblum Archive*, 59–60.

5. Chapman, "Spoiled Home Identities," 134.

6. Similarly, Miron diagnoses a tendency to "turn to closed Jewish spaces" or withdraw into private space in his case study on the fate of Jews in Nazi Germany ("'Lately, Almost Constantly, Everything Seems Small to Me,'" 122–123, see also 138).

7. Kaplan, *Scroll of Agony*, 114.

8. Bauman explains this phenomenon in a description of the early days of German occupation: "A curfew had been imposed on Warsaw ever since the arrival of the Nazis, we had to stay home from early evening till morning. As a result, unusually close relationships began to flourish between neighbours. People who had very little in common before were now becoming good friends. No evening would pass without a visit from a few neighbours who would call in and stay late to exchange news, discuss the situation and wonder about the future" (*Winter in the Morning*, 30–31).

9. Chapman, "Spoiled Home Identities," 133.

10. Kaplan, *Scroll of Agony*, 42.

11. See, for example, 455. RING. I/428; 504. RING. I/212.

12. Levine, "Home Loss in Wartime Literature," 105.

13. Kaplan, *Scroll of Agony*, 43.

14. Chapman, "Spoiled Home Identities," 141.

15. Blunt, "Cultural Geography," 506.

16. Kaplan, *Scroll of Agony*, 43.

17. Chapman, "Spoiled Home Identities," 145.

18. Ibid., 138, 142, 145.

19. McMahon, "Home Invasions," 362.

20. Ibid., 359.

21. See Colombijn, "Production of Urban Space by Violence," 74.

22. See, for example, Adler, *In the Warsaw Ghetto*, 27; 504. RING. I/212.

23. Kaplan, *Scroll of Agony*, 67.

24. Ibid., 212. In fact, the housing situation in the whole of Warsaw was very difficult. With significant war damage to a large number of apartments and houses, and a huge influx of refugees from the territories annexed to the Reich, accommodation was a critical issue (Szarota, *Warschau unter dem Hakenkreuz*, 154). In the ghetto,

however, the population density was even higher than outside the walls, while at the same time destruction had hit the northern quarter particularly hard.

25. See, for example, Stok, account, 23; Gutman-Staszewska, account, 25–26; Markowska, *Ringelblum Archive*, 50; Adler, *In the Warsaw Ghetto*, 33; Szarota, *Warschau unter dem Hakenkreuz*, 158.

26. Stok, account, 24; Gutman-Staszewska, account, 26.

27. Qtd. in Polonsky, "Introduction," 6.

28. See also Kaplan, *Scroll of Agony*, 213.

29. Levine, "Home Loss in Wartime Literature," 105.

30. Gutman-Staszewska, account, 26.

31. Adler, *In the Warsaw Ghetto*, 33.

32. See, for example, Berg, *Diary*, 96–97; Szarota, *Warschau unter dem Hakenkreuz*, 158; 504. RING. I/212.

33. Leociak, *Text in the Face of Destruction*, 55.

34. Levine, "Home Loss in Wartime Literature," 106.

35. Szarota, *Warschau unter dem Hakenkreuz*, 158.

36. Lewin, *Cup of Tears*, 154.

37. Leociak, *Text in the Face of Destruction*, 56.

38. Bauman, *Winter in the Morning*, 68.

39. See, for example, Markowska, *Ringelblum Archive*, 13–15.

40. Mawult, account, 115.

41. Lewin, *Cup of Tears*, 154.

42. Ibid., 155.

43. Ibid., 182, 185.

44. Ibid., 182.

45. Ibid., 151.

46. The account covers a few days in August and September 1942 and is published in *Words to Outlive Us*, a collection based on diaries and accounts preserved at the Jewish Historical Institute in Warsaw.

47. Anonymous Woman, account, 137; see also Lewin, *Cup of Tears*, 154.

48. Anonymous Woman, account, 137.

49. Lewin, *Cup of Tears*, 182.

50. Chapman, "Spoiled Home Identities," 134.

CHAPTER

13

Violated Homes

The judicial concept of the inviolability of the home—that is, the guarantee of legal protection against anyone entering the private home against the rightful inhabitants' will—formalizes the cultural belief that "the home is a refuge for persons and their intimate relationships against invasion and intrusion, either by government or by others."[1] In everyday life the wish to protect one's private home against intrusion is translated into the sociospatial practice of creating physical boundaries (such as walls, fences, doors).[2] But since most of these boundaries do not withstand attempts at forced entry, they are only effective insofar as they are also recognized and respected as "cultural boundaries."[3] These boundaries depend on mutual recognition and are, as geographer Nicholas Blomley points out, "validated by traditional beliefs, attitudes, and values and sanctioned in custom and law."[4] Chapman elaborates: while most "symbolic markers of personal space are easy enough to traverse physically," as "cultural boundaries" they are nevertheless "expected to deter strangers."[5] They indicate that a certain space is "private" and not "public,"[6] and are thus expected to regulate access rights.[7]

The German occupiers, however, did not adhere to the boundaries of the private sphere, especially not when it came to all those they considered an enemy of the Reich. Already on February 28, 1933, with the *Reichtagsbrandverordnung* (Reichstag Fire Decree), the Nazi party had suspended the respective article of the Weimar Constitution (§115), along with other central civic rights in Germany.[8] In occupied Poland, the Germans unrestrainedly entered private homes for confiscations, searches, raids, round-ups, arrests, and executions.[9] For many, the breach of the boundaries of the private sphere was traumatizing, rupturing the sense of security commonly associated with the home.[10] At the same time, breaking down the boundary of the private home was also a way for the Germans to intimidate, terrorize, and demonstrate power.

In her memoir, Bauman describes three different raids on her family's and her grandparents' apartments that happened in the early days of the German occupation of Poland. Bauman describes all of them in direct succession, as if to mark important changes.[11] During the first raid, the Germans entered the family's home and searched it: "A vehicle full of armed Nazis pulled up at the gate. Soon two of them were banging at the front door of our apartment. We let them in and watched their determined efforts to find something in our wardrobes, drawers and bookshelves. What exactly they were looking for, we never learnt. They were cool and polite. They found nothing and left."[12] The entry to the apartment is enforced by the fact that the intruders are armed representatives of the occupying forces, but it is not yet coupled with direct violence. From what Bauman remembers, the incident seems to take place without any major agitation. The power relations are clear from the outset. The intruders do not inform their victims about their agenda, but there is also no dispute. Bauman's memoir shows that the family had to some degree anticipated the German intrusion. Shortly before the city's capitulation, Bauman's sister-in-law, Jadwiga, had rid the apartment of any books or documents critical of Hitler or Nazi Germany, explaining that there "was little hope that the besieged town would resist the powerful German Army. And when they came we should expect them to interfere in our private lives, search our homes, severely punish us for anything they considered to be against the Nazi regime."[13] While a violation of the family's privacy took place during this first raid, it still seemed in line with their expectations regarding the behavior of the enemy power. This could even indicate that it was within the scope of what the Bauman family perceived as a (more-or-less) "legitimate" violation in the context of occupation. In addition, no one was hurt, nor was anything taken or destroyed. The next time, the Germans came in search of the family's "wireless set."[14] The family had not given up the radio receiver as demanded per German decree (a decree not targeting Jewish households specifically but affecting all Poles, regardless of their ethnicity and/or religion).[15] This "second visit was different,"[16] Bauman notes and explains,

> While we were wondering what to do, three men banged at our door. Two were uniformed Germans, the third, a civilian, was Mr Richter, my grandfather Aleksander's chauffeur, who had driven him for years until Grandfather died. Apart from his German name, Mr Richter had never had anything to do with Germany, nor could he even speak German. Now, seeing him with the two Germans, we thought at first that he had been arrested by them, but soon his behaviour made it clear that he came as an enemy. Always before full of

respect and servility, he now took hardly any notice of us as he entered with his superiors. He led them straight to Stefan's room and pointed to the radio. "*Schöne Radio Apparat*" ("Fine set"). The two Germans laughed briefly, gibbered something amongst themselves, then helped Mr Richter to disconnect the radio. Carrying the huge object in his arms along the corridor, his square face scarlet from effort and excitement, he kept mumbling, "*Present schön, danke schön*" ("Fine present, thank you, fine").[17]

While the raid was formalized by means of a German order, the ensuing process borders between confiscation and robbery. It is mainly the presence of Mr. Richter that delegitimizes the procedure, adding the motive of personal gain to the confiscation. But Mr. Richter's presence indicates something else too: as a *Volksdeutscher* (ethnic German), Mr. Richter is now allied with the German occupiers. It is the Nazi racial ideology that grants him privileges. Power is no longer distributed along the lines of different roles within the war context (i.e., occupiers/occupied), nor, as previously, defined by social status; instead, it is now based on "racial" affiliation. Long-term employee Mr. Richter, who had been "full of respect and servility," now came "as an enemy" and endowed with new power by the Germans. Under their rule, the ethnic German had gained superiority over the family that had employed him for many years. For the Baumans this necessitated a reevaluation of trusted social structures. By entering the family's home and taking their radio, the occupiers demonstrated their power. By allowing Mr. Richter to benefit from the confiscation, they established an order based not only on their status as armed representatives of the occupying forces but also on their ideological notion of racial identity. By doing so, the Germans pitted people who might have had entirely different relationships before the occupation (as employees, colleagues, neighbors, landlords, or the like) against each other. It is also worth noting that Mr. Richter led the Germans to a private room in the apartment, because he knew where the radio would be. This exemplifies how collaborators could often use against their Jewish neighbors intimate knowledge that the Germans did not possess.

The third raid that Bauman describes happened at her grandparents' apartment. Accordingly, Bauman does not describe it as a direct witness but based on a hearsay account. This time, circumstances had changed again: the Germans ostentatiously demonstrated their power and crossed the boundary to direct physical violence, targeting both the bodies of their victims and their apartment:

> Soon after, or perhaps even before this, Grandfather Maks' and Grandma Viera's flat was raided and searched. It happened late at night. They were woken from their sleep and together with Uncle Julian, . . . were forced to stand still facing the wall while the invaders turned the flat upside down. It was not clear

whether they found anything suspicious or not, but they arrested Grandpa Maks and Julian that night. They kept them in prison for several days, beat them, and then let them go. Grandfather and Julian returned home frightened. The injuries from the beatings were not serious and healed quickly, but for Grandpa Maks, who was in his late sixties, the shock was too great. A week or so later, he died suddenly from a stroke.[18]

One evident difference is that the intruders came at night, which means they entered the apartment at a time that was typically not designated for outside contact. In his 1999 study "Spoiled Home Identities: The Experience of Burglary," Chapman argues that the inhabitants of a home usually regulate the way in which they present their living space, and thus themselves, to a visitor. Therefore, according to Chapman, social visits are often "carefully orchestrated performances."[19] This implies that people are used to not only controlling who enters their private space but also how exactly such an entrance takes place and is acted out. At night, when people are sleeping, however, the space of the home is typically closed to the outside and thus reserved for the most intimate relations. Social interaction outside the "small unit" (i.e., commonly, the family[20]) is not foreseen, nor are people prepared for it. In this situation, people are particularly vulnerable. By entering their home during the night, the Germans entered an "intimate space"[21] and demonstrated that they lacked every respect for the Jews whose apartments they raided. Partly because of its unexpectedness, a nighttime house search was an aggressive transgression. The second difference manifested itself in the way the family was treated during the search. Forcing them to stand still while facing the wall was a strong subjecting gesture. While forcing entry to a home, be it by direct violence or by a threat, is in itself a gesture of power, taking over the right to define the practices within the "intimate" space of the home is a particularly strong form of coercion. It means that the rightful inhabitant is overpowered in a space that he or she usually feels in control of.[22] Again, the Germans did not explain the raid or the ensuing arrests to the family. They did not make any attempt to legitimize their intrusion, which, in turn, suggested that anyone could be arrested at any time. Under German rule, Jewish people were as violable as their homes.

Being targeted both in public space and at home, Jews increasingly lost the feeling of security. In October 1939, Kaplan summarizes, "We are not secure either outside or at home. In the house they are afraid, 'Lest they come . . . ,' outside, lest they be seized for forced labor."[23] Similarly, Stanisław Sznapman recalls the early days of the ghetto, writing, "No one felt safe day or night. Unwanted visitors would barge into any home at any moment: uninvited guests answerable to nothing and no one, masters of life and death. They could seize whatever they chose, beat the residents unconscious, take them away or kill them on the spot."[24]

Violence and fear infiltrated the private space. Thus, as historian and philosopher Miron phrases it in the context of the so-called *Judenhäuser* in Germany, "domestic space became a violated and violent space."[25]

Notes

1. McClain, "Inviolability and Privacy," 203.
2. Hughes, "Behavioural Understanding of Privacy," 812.
3. Chapman, "Spoiled Home Identities," 135.
4. Blomley, "Law, Property, and the Geography of Violence," 122.
5. Chapman, "Spoiled Home Identities," 135.
6. Ibid.
7. Mantho, *Urban Section*, 236.
8. Raithel and Strenge, "Die Reichstagsbrandverordnung," 416.
9. See, for example, Kaplan, *Scroll of Agony*, 54, 72, 118; Bauman, *Winter in the Morning*, 32–33; Sznapman, account, 19–20; Berg, *Diary*, 19.
10. Chapman, "Spoiled Home Identities," 138, 140.
11. It is worth noting here that Bauman's memoir was written in 1985, which means that the arrangement was not primarily dictated by the order of events, but it was a conscious choice by the author. Bauman seems to want to depict a certain process or development here.
12. Bauman, *Winter in the Morning*, 32.
13. Ibid., 24.
14. Ibid., 32.
15. Ibid., 33; see also Kaplan, *Scroll of Agony*, 68.
16. Bauman, *Winter in the Morning*, 32.
17. Ibid., 32–33.
18. Ibid.
19. Chapman, "Spoiled Home Identities," 134.
20. Madanipour, *Public and Private Spaces of the City*, 62.
21. Ibid., 67.
22. Chapman, "Spoiled Home Identities," 134.
23. Kaplan, *Scroll of Agony*, 54.
24. Sznapman, account, 19 20.
25. Miron, "'Lately, Almost Constantly, Everything Seems Small to Me,'"140.

14

Overcrowding

After the closing of the ghetto, up to 400,000–460,000 people—about one-third of the city's population—were forced to live in an area covering roughly 2.4 percent of the city.[1] This led to terrible overcrowding, both in apartments and buildings and in the streets. Space was scarce. As Kaplan notes on October 15, 1940, a month before the ghetto's sealing, "This quarter of narrow, crowded streets is full to capacity with refugees from the provincial towns. There is no room in the ghetto—not an empty crack, not an unoccupied hole."[2] The incredible population density inside the walls was a social and psychological issue but also entailed practical questions of housing, provisioning, and hygiene. In addition, it drastically altered the appearance and dynamics of the ghetto streets.

The huge crowd on the streets became a constant hindrance to communication. As Ringelblum observes shortly after the sealing of the ghetto, "Because of the closing of the Ghetto and the feverish buying up of everything, all the Jewish streets are full of people milling about. It's simply impossible to pass through. Pedestrians overflow the sidewalk, spill over on the street."[3] Similarly, he notes on a different day that it is "hard work to walk from Leszno Street to Grzybowska Street. The crowds on Solna and Ciepla Streets making it impossible to get through."[4] When confronted with the new layout of the ghetto and the resulting impediment to traffic flow, what people experienced first and foremost was not necessarily the spatial restriction but the presence of others. The masses of people forced into the ghetto experienced each other as a pressing, heavy crowd that inhibited movement, created jams, and slowed them down significantly. In direct contact in the streets, people often experienced other people as oppressive, and the negative experience shifted from the first-order cause to the other victims. Conversely, the crowd did not allow for much positive interaction. On a street that was overcrowded, all zones of the street—the "transition zone," the "circulation zone," the "amenities zone," the "curbside zone," and even the roadway[5]—were flooded with people. There was no room left to differentiate use, to socialize, or to use the streets for anything but moving forward. In these situations, the streets' important "social role" of supplying "public space for interaction, expression, community and socialisation"[6] was thus limited.

Różycki provides insight into the experience of moving through such a crowded street while describing the passage of pedestrians on Chłodna Street: "I look around in the street. Incredible traffic, noise, density, moaning, crying and quarrels . . . thousands of people flow constantly. Waves of pedestrians slosh incessantly. The sidewalk does not suffice, you have to use the roadway where at the same time heavy traffic prevails. . . . Dirty, dark, stuffy, cold, alien. Brrr!"[7] Różycki's description highlights how the crowd deindividualized its constituent pedestrians. It was experienced as something impersonal, forcing itself on the individual. Różycki describes the movement of the crowd as "waves" flowing and sloshing. Similarly, Vladka Meed speaks of the street becoming "a human sea"[8] and, a few pages later, describes the feeling of being "swept off [her] feet" by a crowd, "carried along in a sea of backs and elbows."[9] Both accounts coincide in describing the masses as a force of nature, overwhelming the individual, impossible to control. At least temporarily, the individual body was overpowered by the crowd, thus creating a sensation of a loss of control, anxiety, and even panic. The overcrowding also created an intense psychological pressure on people, who felt that they could never be alone. Once outdoors, it was nearly impossible to escape the "noisy swarming crowd" on the streets.[10] As Bauman describes in a diary entry from July 21, 1942, "There is nowhere to go, there is no way to be alone. The streets moan and yell with a thousand voices, they reek of rotten fish and dying bodies."[11]

In such conditions, people were constantly transgressing each other's boundaries. Even before the Germans established the ghetto, the situation in the streets of Warsaw had been precarious. At the end of January 1940, Kaplan writes, "One person shoves another on side and shoulder without any malice and without any apology. Both sides concede that no other way is possible. At a time of general trouble, a person has no right to say, 'I'm crowded!'"[12] The number of people on the street changed modes of interaction and the ways in which individuals experienced each other. And while Kaplan's depiction suggests a certain mutual understanding, the forced closeness still turned people into obstacles to each other. To Kaplan, this is owed to circumstances—and not to "malice," as he specifically notes—that require everyone to set aside personal needs and sensitivities. But already at this point, the violation of the individual's personal space seemed worth mentioning. In the ghetto, the spatial layout combined with the extreme population density made basically inevitable both the constant overstepping of the boundaries of one another's personal space and the resulting situation of experiencing others as constant threats to one's own personal space.[13] In his book *Public and Private Spaces of the City*, Madanipour explains the essential role of personal space in providing a feeling of control and safety: "It is this space in which individuals perform their social acts, where they feel safer and in control of their bodies. Social interaction in the public sphere therefore takes place from across personal spaces. Intersubjective relationships depend on the safety and security that the observation of subjective spaces brings about for those involved."[14] The ghetto the Germans had created was a structural violation of that basic need.

Due to the conditions in the ghetto, forced proximity led also to concrete physical dangers. With typhus running rampant, the masses of poor and sick people who inhabited the streets became a threat to those who were not yet infected. When Ringelblum notes down in mid-September 1941 that people were "bound to become infected" when they moved through crowded streets like Karmelicka, or visited public places such as the bazaars or the soup kitchens, he draws a similar connection.[15] In an environment constantly threatened by epidemics, being close to one's neighbors involved a serious risk to one's health.[16] Consequently, as Bauman remembers, "physical contact with strangers was what we tried most to avoid. A lot of people were already destitute, living side by side with those more fortunate. . . . The homeless, tattered, undernourished people we brushed against in the streets were covered with lice and often suffered from infectious diseases."[17]

Running counter to people's most basic needs and to their psychological and physical well-being, and having highly detrimental effects on their living conditions, the overcrowding created in the ghetto is one manifestation of the violence exerted against Jews through the spatial setup of the ghettos in which they were confined. The space that the Germans created turned the sheer presence of others into a burden and a threat. In daily life within the ghetto, fellow inhabitants were experienced as oppressive and encroaching. Positive interaction was made difficult and sociality impaired.

Inside the private space of the home, the overcrowding in the ghetto had the most severe consequences. Scarcity of living space forced people in the ghetto to live together much closer than before the war: those who moved to the ghetto usually had to move in with others; those who had been able to stay in their apartments usually had to accommodate subtenants.[18] Kaplan describes the population increase when he writes in his diary on June 27, 1940, "There is no Jewish courtyard whose population has not multiplied. Those burned out of their homes, refugees, fugitives, and exiles have all been added."[19] In regard to the number of people living in one apartment or room during the ghetto's existence, sources

diverge. According to historian Antony Polonsky—editor of the English translation of Abraham Lewin's diary—the "number of people concentrated in each
room was 9.2."[20] Berg estimates there were "on average . . . six to ten people" in
one room, while Bauman suggests the "average number of persons per room was
13."[21] Personal experiences differed, and the average numbers fluctuated throughout the ghetto's existence. While the ghetto area was continuously reduced, the
number of its inhabitants drastically increased until March 1941, as a result of
people being deported to the ghetto; during the summer and autumn of 1941,
however, mortality rose dramatically, and from July 1942 onward, the number of
inhabitants collapsed due to the Germans' mass deportations.[22]

Generally, occupancy in the ghetto became very dense. In addition, the community within apartments and buildings became more heterogeneous than in
prewar times. The housing shortage limited people's choices for both those who
were looking for a place to stay and for those who were taking people in. Adler,
who was working for the *Judenrat*'s Housing Bureau, reports that "compulsory
lodgers" were very common,[23] and often people with very different backgrounds
were forced into close cohabitation. In her memoir *Winter in the Morning*, Bauman
describes such a group of cohabitants at her uncle's home, where she, her mother,
and her sister found refuge after their house at 15 Leszno Street was raided during
the Great Deportation *Aktion*. Bauman notes, "Since the *Aktion* had begun the
household had tripled in size, including now two young male pianists, students
of Leo's wife, the two nieces' boyfriends, my Aunt Maryla with her mother, and
a young couple with a baby son. Now we had arrived too. We put our bundles on
the floor in one of the four rooms and thus began a new kind of life."[24]

Whenever possible, family, friends, or acquaintances moved in together, but
often apartments were also shared by strangers. Due to this, the status of the
private space of the home changed significantly. As Miron argues in regard to
the overcrowding encountered in German *Judenhäuser*, "This new reality, which
weakened the remnants of domestic Jewish space, yielded the collapse of the
distinction between private and public spaces."[25] Living in forced community
with a large number of people, of whom many were strangers, private space was
barely private anymore. This was a result of both the denseness of occupancy and
the type of relationships present in the house community. While people typically
encounter strangers in the sphere of public space (e.g., on the streets[26]), these less
intimate relationships now regularly also became a part of private space. Also, the
amount of space available to an individual shrunk to a degree that made it impossible to grant privacy to one another. There was always someone else around,
and people rarely had space entirely to themselves. As Bauman summarizes the
conditions on July 21, 1942, in an excerpt of her diary that was incorporated into
her memoir, "There is no way to be alone."[27] This also meant there was no way
not to be seen or heard by others. People lost the ability to define for themselves

how much of their life they wanted to share and with whom. Correspondingly, Adler speaks of a "promiscuous lack of privacy."[28]

Discussing how privacy is experienced, legal scholar Kirsty Hughes suggests that the experience of privacy is based on the individual's ability to establish "barriers." She elaborates, "In his or her social interactions an individual relies upon barriers to preserve the space required for these states of privacy [solitude, intimacy, anonymity, and reserve] to be experienced. Those barriers may be physical, behavioural or normative barriers. . . . Conversely, an invasion of privacy occurs when those barriers are breached and the intruder obtains access to the privacy-seeker."[29]

In the ghetto, the individual's means of both establishing privacy and granting it were severely impaired. Effective barriers could hardly be established. This was to a large degree a spatial issue, as can be seen, for example, in Bauman's description of her ever-changing living arrangements after the Great Deportation. After numerous hasty relocations, Bauman stayed with her mother and sister in a small room that "everyone else had to go through on their way to and from the loo." Next, the family ended up in a room that was "part of the passage," where Bauman hung up a blanket "to cut [them] off from domestic traffic and provide some privacy."[30] Barriers between the family and the other inhabitants of the shared space were insufficient and/or flimsy. Adler explains the consequences in his memoir: "The privacy of family life, even of the bedroom, could not be preserved."[31] Young couples, Bauman remembers, had no place to be alone; intimacy was severely complicated.[32] The forced cohabitation also meant that, often, people of various backgrounds would share the same space. This, in practice, meant different degrees of assimilation, or differences in regard to "dress, religious practice, and social custom," different political orientations, different levels of education, different languages—either Yiddish or Polish for most Varsovians—different social statuses, and different financial means.[33] These differences added to already existing difficulties in negotiating the shared environment, because the cohabitants could not necessarily rely on shared cultural norms and values. Also, the sheer number of people provoked conflicts over access to the basic facilities. Adler summarizes,

> The intimate coexistence of people from different classes, different cultural backgrounds, different dispositions, different ways of life, different conditions of work, and all of them worn out by the experiences of war, left a lot to be desired. . . . It was no wonder that such arrangements were far from ideal. Housewives from the pre-war middle class, fond of their pots and pans, proud of their shining polished floors, had difficulties adapting themselves to conditions in which strangers moved endlessly through their apartments every day and their apartments and toilets were continuously occupied. In the kitchen one had to fight heroically for a free stove. Continual fights took place

for access to the kitchen, the bath, the toilet, and the right to use the gas or get a key to the entrance door.[34]

In addition, as Adler notes, due to the overcrowding, "sanitary conditions deteriorated rapidly." This was aggravated further because the "cost of personal hygiene, laundry, and home sanitation had increased greatly."[35] People became an infection risk to one another. But also their sheer physical presence became more intrusive. As social and legal scholar Alan Westin argues, "What is considered 'too close' a contact and therefore an 'invasion of privacy' in human society will often be an odor, a noise, a visual intrusion, or a touch; the mechanism for defining privacy in these situations is sensory."[36] In the shared living space, the presence of others intruded on an individual on all sensory channels. While Nazi raids, confiscations, and round-ups were an active violation of the victims' private spaces, the ghetto as such produced another interference by forcing people into living arrangements that made them become a violation to each other.

The forced proximity became particularly stressful when people went into hiding. Most hiding places and bunkers were terribly overcrowded, and everyone was tense and in constant fear of discovery. Halina Birenbaum recalls the last days in a bunker in the ghetto in her 1967 memoir *Hope Is the Last to Die* (*Nadzieja umiera ostatnia*):

> Some two hundred people were lying here, packed together on narrow bunks. It was hard to find any room. . . . It was stuffy and crowded. . . . The atmosphere was one of agitation. From the very beginning, more people came than had been bargained for. More and more followed during the succeeding day. . . . The bunker grew increasingly crowded and stuffy. Anyone who went to the watertap or toilet collided with others or stumbled over their neighbors in the darkness. There was no end to the disputes, squabbling, fights over nothing, insults, and name-calling. Exhausted by the want of fresh air and the most elementary facilities, tortured by the incessant fear and uncertainty, people began losing their self-control. The bunker became a real hell.[37]

Under the constant pressure of discovery, the other became not only a nuisance but, in fact, a threat. Every noise could give up the hiding place to the Germans; a crying baby or a frightened lament could mean the demise of a group of several hundred people.[38] The fate of each individual was inescapably tied to a forced community, often consisting of total strangers.

Notes

1. Engelking and Leociak, *Warsaw Ghetto*, 40, 48–49; Browning, *Entfesselung der "Endlösung,"* 190.
2. Kaplan, *Scroll of Agony*, 209.
3. Ringelblum, *Notes from the Warsaw Ghetto*, 87.

4. Ibid., 86.

5. Mantho, *Urban Section*, 57, 75–76.

6. Ibid., 63.

7. "Zamurowany" ("Walled Up") 455. RING. I/428. Translation by Barbara Cze-pek and A. N. The translations are based on the original archival document and on personal transcripts by Jacek Leociak. Excerpts of the text have been published in German in *Faschismus—Getto—Massenmord*, 152–153, and in English in Markowska, *Ringelblum Archive*, 113–115. The text is also quoted extensively in Kassow, *Who Will Write Our History?*, 252–256; in Leociak, *Text in the Face of Destruction*, 48, 51; and in Engelking and Leociak, *Warsaw Ghetto*, 114. For reasons of consistency, I will use my own translation throughout. The Polish original reads as follows: "*Rozglądam się po ulicy. Niesamowity ruch, szum, ścisk, jęki, płacze, kłótnie . . . przewijają się tysiące ludzi, przelewają się nieustannie fale przechodniów. Chodniki nie starczą, trzeba korzystać z jezdni, na której również panuje bardzo silny ruch . . . Brudno, ciemno, duszno, zimno, obco. Brr!*" (455. RING. I/428).

8. Meed, *On Both Sides of the Wall*, 13.

9. Ibid., 18. Szajn-Lewin, as well, uses imagery reminiscent of the sea when she speaks of a stream of people ("*Menschenstrom*") to describe the force of the masses, pulling her away, carrying her off (*Aufzeichnungen aus dem Warschauer Ghetto*, 10).

10. Bauman, *Winter in the Morning*, 62.

11. Ibid., 63. These examples demonstrate the literary qualities inherent to the testimonies—their "poetics" as Leociak calls it (*Text in the Face of Destruction*, 25). For the purpose of analyzing the ghetto's space, these qualities are not peripheral, nor are they a perturbing variable. In fact, they are an essential part of the way the individual writer struggled to express an experience that was highly distressing and traumatic. On the whole, they reflect the process in which the witnesses tried to put into words experiences that oftentimes broke with previous frames of reference (ibid., 20–21, 109; see also Stone, "Introduction," 51). The literary decisions taken by the texts' authors—their choice of specific words or of particular imagery, for example—can be an important key to understanding the environment and the events that they describe.

12. Kaplan, *Scroll of Agony*, 110.

13. For a very insightful analysis of the psychological and social effects of over-crowding in the ghetto, see Barbara Engelking, *Holocaust and Memory*, 91–97. In her book, which is based on a number of extensive interviews with survivors, Engelking, with reference to Edward T. Hall, speaks of the ghetto as a "behavioural swamp," eliciting "behaviour, ties and emotional reactions which prove exceedingly stressful" for people (ibid., 92).

14. Madanipour, *Public and Private Spaces of the City*, 21.

15. Ringelblum, *Notes from the Warsaw Ghetto*, 219; see also Adler, *In the Warsaw Ghetto*, 35, 42, 125. Similarly, the ghetto inhabitants considered the trams to be a site of potential infection. As Kaplan recalls, "There is no filthier place, capable of spreading

contagious diseases, than a Jewish trolley on a single ride, where everything is infected, when sick people sweat and slobber on you" (*Scroll of Agony*, 207).

16. See Engelking and Leociak, *Warsaw Ghetto*, 126; Mazor, *Vanished City*, 120. This is a very obvious example illustrating how the so-called *Seuchenschutzgebiet* was actually turning the pretext for the establishment of the ghetto into a self-fulfilling prophecy (Cole, *Holocaust City*, 31; Neumann, *Die Weltanschauung des Nazismus*, 125; Boehm, "Introduction," 11). The term, to some degree, was thus performative in nature.

17. Bauman, *Winter in the Morning*, 40.

18. Adler, *In the Warsaw Ghetto*, 255.

19. Kaplan, *Scroll of Agony*, 165.

20. Polonsky, "Introduction," 2.

21. Berg, *Diary*, 66; Bauman, *Winter in the Morning*, 37.

22. Engelking and Leociak, *Warsaw Ghetto*, 49–50.

23. Adler, *In the Warsaw Ghetto*, 53; see also 504. RING. I/212.

24. Bauman, *Winter in the Morning*, 69.

25. Miron, "'Lately, Almost Constantly, Everything Seems Small to Me,'" 141.

26. Mantho, *Urban Section*, 45; Jacobs, "Uses of Sidewalks," 152.

27. Bauman, *Winter in the Morning*, 63.

28. Adler, *In the Warsaw Ghetto*, 15.

29. Hughes, "Behavioural Understanding of Privacy," 807.

30. Bauman, *Winter in the Morning*, 73, 82.

31. Adler, *In the Warsaw Ghetto*, 54.

32. Bauman, *Winter in the Morning*, 61–63; see also Berg, *Diary*, 103.

33. Boehm, "Introduction," 4.

34. Adler, *In the Warsaw Ghetto*, 53–54.

35. Ibid., 39.

36. Westin, "Origins of Modern Claims to Privacy," 57; see also Engelking, *Holocaust and Memory*, 96.

37. Birenbaum, *Hope Is the Last to Die*, 77.

38. Ibid., 31, 78, 80; see also Bauman, *Winter in the Morning*, 94; Adler, *In the Warsaw Ghetto*, 306–307.

15

Life and Death

Although the invasion and occupation of Warsaw had gradually pushed Jews out of the public space of the city, the ghetto, at least during the first twenty-one months of its existence,[1] actually allowed for some form of social life to take place. In fact, many areas of life that had traditionally taken place inside were now taken to the streets. With apartments being overcrowded and "no nice places to go to," people spent a lot of their time outside.[2] As Leociak observes, "The street is a public space, where the life of the district was concentrated, a place where goods and information were exchanged, the arena for the events being played out."[3]

One of the important aspects of public life in the ghetto was trade, which served as a source of both income and provisions. In the ghetto, most trading took place outside, on the streets. Describing the street trading in all of Warsaw, Kaplan notes on October 14, 1939, "All the trade has been brought out to the street. Whatever used to be done indoors is now being carried on outside, and the streets have begun to resemble a fair. They are full to capacity. There is no room to pass; everywhere selling and bargaining, trade and barter are going on under the sky.... Never have there been so many vendors among the Jews as in our own days."[4]

Due to the enormous population density, the street markets were busy and crowded. Food and other goods were sold at so-called bazaars, in backyards, and on the streets; everywhere, people were selling their meager belongings, trading whatever they had left to obtain some food or much-needed medicine.[5] People were selling "bread, cigarettes, candies and books," as is noted in an outline for a study on the ghetto's streets that was planned as part of the *Oneg Shabbat* Underground Archive's documentation of everyday life in the ghetto;[6] but household goods, textiles, and other personal belongings could also be bought and sold on the streets. A major location for trading was Gęsia Street, one of the longest ghetto streets running from east to west and also, because of the Gęsia Street prison, a place that was strongly associated with German violence.[7] Street markets also developed at Lubeckiego, Grzybowska, Ciepła, Smocza, and Leszno Streets, as well as at countless other locations.[8] The market at Gęsia is described by Ringelblum in May 1941: "The whole length of Gesia Street has become a gigantic bazaar. Everything from the Jewish part of Warsaw is sold in that street. You can find linens, shirts, handkerchiefs, underwear, suits, shoes—principally linens. There are at least a thousand people standing around trading in it. Christians smuggle themselves past the Wall to get to the Gesia Street bazaar. There never was so great a market in Warsaw, not even in Karcelak Street."[9]

At Leszno there was also a huge market dedicated to books, "where the best works by the modern authors are sold by the basketful."[10] Street hawkers also sold books in Polish, Yiddish, and even in English at Nowolipki and Orla Street.[11] Though street trading required official permission, this rule was rarely observed. According to Engelking and Leociak, the "authorities of the ghetto—on the orders of the Germans and perhaps partly on their own initiative—" tried to limit trade to certain locations and times, to "enclose it within particular geographical limits" and regulate it to certain "trading hours."[12] This was owed not least to concerns regarding the disruption of traffic in these areas.[13] Yet, all attempts to contain the trade proved futile: "Street trade was impossible to restrict, both in space and in time."[14] It was a highly important source of provisioning, supplementing the meager rations assigned to the ghetto population; therefore, it was essential for survival. According to Engelking and Leociak, trade was a major contributing factor as pertains to the "characteristic appearance" of the ghetto streets.[15] This particular appearance is further described in the outline of the study on the streets of the ghetto that was published in English in 1986 in the collection *To Live with Honor and Die with Honor*. Here, the unknown author points in particular to the "oriental character of the street trade" and the ever-present "hawking-calls of the traders."[16]

At the same time as being the "arena" for the most important elements of social life,[17] the street also clearly reflected the poor living conditions of the ghetto and the ever-impending threat of violence and death. Evidence of the immense hardship of life in the ghetto showed on the faces and in the general demeanor of passersby, "their faces black as earth and yellow, drawn with tiredness," as Nehemiah Titelman describes it.[18] Różycki elaborates a bit more on that, explaining how faces had changed, how hardship, malnutrition, the lack of fresh air and free movement, sickness, sorrows, and misfortune had made the ghetto's inhabitants' faces resemble skulls, with their cheekbones protruding, skin like parchment, sunken in, gaunt and sickly looking, a hunted look in their eyes.[19] People's appearances were in large part shaped and marked by the difficult conditions. Titelman continues his description by writing about even more drastic signs of suffering one would encounter on the streets of the ghetto: "There is still a line of all kinds of poor in front of me I must bypass, there is still the parade of lame and crippled. People without hands and legs, entire limbs frozen or rotten. True, some groups stand here and there and converse secretly, having a mystified look, but these are lost in the overall grey appearance of the immense masses marching along."[20] Titelman captures an image of the dejected masses of the hungry, the sick, and the poor, and depicts their presence as dominating the street. In the winter of 1941, Marek Stok similarly takes note of the omnipresence of beggars:

> There are thousands of miserable beggars permanently camped on the street, looking more like phantoms than human beings: ghostly figures in dirty tattered rags, with swollen legs and feverish eyes inside their emaciated faces. They're everywhere: in the courtyards, on the streets and sidewalks, leaning against building walls. They moan and shout and beg for handouts. There's no way to help them and no way to shake them off. . . . If there's a corpse on the street in nothing but rags, people simply walk by and avert their eyes until some merciful soul covers the body with newspaper. Men, women, children— corpses are lying on nearly every street.[21]

Stok's observations reveal to what degree poverty and suffering began to define everyday life in the ghetto and, specifically, on its streets. In his words, poverty and suffering were "everywhere." Huge numbers of people who, due to the German antisemitic policies, were without any income and living far below minimum levels required for subsistence, were pushed onto the streets, either because begging was their only means of acquiring food or because they also lacked a proper place to live. The descriptions of their presence on the streets are myriad in testimonies. Stok, in the description that he offers in his testimony, highlights how these people and their fate became part of the public sphere. They were not hidden inside of buildings, be it institutional or private, but were out in the open for everyone to see. Others who were still living under more fortunate conditions were inevitably confronted with their misery and could only avoid confrontation by deliberately looking away. Inside the ghetto, the social contrast was taken to its extreme.[22] The spatial segregation of poor and rich that is so common for most urban settlement was largely suspended. Although the small ghetto was generally considered the better-off part of the ghetto, and though apartments there were in better condition, in most of the ghetto, the two spheres lay extremely close together. Right outside the cabarets, restaurants, and bars that were the gathering points of the ghetto's elite, people were dying of hunger.[23]

Almost all testimonies attest to the fact that it was difficult to deal with the constant encounter with hunger and death.[24] During the early months of the ghetto's existence, Samuel Puterman states, "Although the ghetto had been in existence for several months, it was still an ordeal just to venture a few steps out of the house, especially for more sensitive people. Not everyone could get used to the magnitude and range of poverty on the ghetto streets."[25] A text by Różycki titled "Morality of the Street" ("*Moralność ulicy*")—written for and deposited in the Ringelblum Archive—gives further insight into how this intrusion of poverty and destitution into the public sphere was perceived. Różycki describes what he understands as a general shamelessness that ran rampant on the streets: people openly attending to their bodily needs, women relieving themselves in public, exposed genitalia, festering wounds publicly displayed.[26] All this became drastically visible under the ghetto conditions, and Różycki's consternation implies that the boundary of shame had been crossed: he perceives these acts as highly inappropriate, and they challenge his understanding of social decency. Poverty and hunger affected people's capacity to adhere to social standards,[27] or more precisely, behavior that was considered private—that is, as belonging to private, inside, spaces—was now displayed openly in the public sphere of the streets. The same observation extends to the topic of death. Not only did the process of dying often take place publicly; it was also very common for dead bodies to remain on the streets for a fairly long time before they were picked up by the ghetto's undertakers. Dying, which, as something sacral, had previously belonged to the private sphere, in the ghetto occurred in public and without the common attendant practices of piety (which were neglected or replaced by residual gestures, such as covering the bodies with newspaper).[28] Testimonies like Różycki's suggest that it was not only the circumstances themselves that felt shocking. Their location—the public character of what was happening—elicited a strong emotional reaction.[29]

Maybe it was precisely the fact that the misery could not be contained spatially that showed how overwhelming it was and proved that the governing agencies and institutions were simply incapable of handling it, that they were not in control anymore. The location of the suffering spoke clearly to the dimensions of the hardship inflicted on the ghetto and on the impossibility of mastering it. It showed that all measures and institutions were failing. And it made it very hard to pretend otherwise. The conditions of Jewish life under German occupation pervaded the entire space of the ghetto. Because they became public spatially, they shaped everyone's experience, even if not everyone was affected by these conditions to a similar degree or at the same point in time. Although there were—for some time—still some relatively calm streets that were home to the privileged, no one could fully evade the hardship that was governing the ghetto. All space, public and private, was influenced and changed by it.

Notes

1. That is, before the Germans in the wake of the Great Deportation *Aktion* drastically restructured both the layout and the basic principles of ghetto life.

2. Bauman, *Winter in the Morning*, 63; see also Adler, *In the Warsaw Ghetto*, 84.

3. Leociak, *Text in the Face of Destruction*, 55; see also Różycki, "Życie ulicy i domu" ("Life of the Street and Home") 455. RING. I/428.

4. Kaplan, *Scroll of Agony*, 50.

5. Engelking and Leociak, *Warsaw Ghetto*, 460.

6. Kermish, *To Live with Honor and Die with Honor!*, 153.

7. Ringelblum, *Notes from the Warsaw Ghetto*, 182; Engelking and Leociak, *Warsaw Ghetto*, 202–203.

8. Lewin, *Cup of Tears*, 100; Ringelblum, *Notes from the Warsaw Ghetto*, 324; see also Engelking and Leociak, *Warsaw Ghetto*, 460–464.

9. Ringelblum, *Notes from the Warsaw Ghetto*, 182. The more common spelling of the name would be "Kercelak," denoting the market, rather than a street.

10. Ibid., 244.

11. Engelking and Leociak, *Warsaw Ghetto*, 462.

12. Ibid., 462–464; see also Ringelblum, *Notes from the Warsaw Ghetto*, 324; Adler, *In the Warsaw Ghetto*, 124–125; 182. RING. I/208.

13. Engelking and Leociak, *Warsaw Ghetto*, 463; Adler, *In the Warsaw Ghetto*, 123.

14. Engelking and Leociak, *Warsaw Ghetto*, 463.

15. Ibid., 460.

16. Kermish, *To Live with Honor and Die with Honor!*, 153.

17. Leociak, *Text in the Face of Destruction*, 55.

18. Kermish, *To Live with Honor and Die with Honor!*, 74.

19. "Zamurowany" ("Walled Up") 455. RING. I/428.

20. Kermish, *To Live with Honor and Die with Honor!*, 77.

21. Stok, account, 38.

22. Mazor, *Vanished City*, 41–42.

23. Kassow, "Introduction," *Those Nightmarish Days*, xvii; Mazor, *Vanished City*, 42.

24. See, for example, Żywulska, *Tanz, Mädchen . . .* , 19–24; 455. RING. I/428.

25. Puterman, account, 28.

26. "Moralność ulicy" 577. RING. I/154; see also "Bezwstyd" ("Shamelessness") 456. RING. I/429. Published in Person, *Warsaw Ghetto*, Vol. I, 48–49 and 28–29.

27. See, for example, Adler, *In the Warsaw Ghetto*, 117–118; "Bezwstyd" 456. RING. I/429.

28. See, for example, Różycki, "Street Pictures" 456. RING. I/429; Edelman, *Das Ghetto Kämpft*, 32–33; Adler, *In the Warsaw Ghetto*, 42; Markowska, *Ringelblum Archive*, 95–96, 100–103; on death in the ghetto see also, Goldberg, "History of the Jews in the Ghetto," 92; Leociak, *Text in the Face of Destruction*, 178–207; Engelking, *Holocaust and Memory*, 119–122.

29.   For a similar argument, see Blomley's paper "Law, Property, and the Geography of Violence," 123. Blomley argues that it is indeed often the location that affects the way particular actions are perceived. He writes, "The location of activities can affect the way in which they are socially policed. Sleeping is fine if it occurs in a private space, while public sleeping, conversely, is often ruled 'out of place'" (ibid.).

16

News

The fact that most communication with the world outside the walls was ruptured did not mean that the need for it declined. In regard to communication in the form of information transmission ("dissemination [of] messages"),[1] quite the opposite held true: the ghetto inhabitants craved news from the outside world. Information on the German war efforts, in particular, was met with both great interest and growing desperation.[2] So, too, were the development of the German anti-Jewish policies and the release of new decrees and regulations. With very little information coming in, the reliability of news was drastically reduced.[3] At the same time, its importance increased significantly, essentially turning it into a question of life or death.

In this respect as well, the streets fulfilled an important function: they became the main space for the exchange of information. First of all, the German officials and the *Judenrat* distributed the majority of information through public notices and decrees posted on the street, or broadcasted them over the loudspeakers that were installed in the ghetto. As Engelking and Leociak explain, "The most popular way for the occupation authorities to communicate with the population of the conquered country was to put up decrees and communiqués on the advertisement posts and to make public communiqués and broadcast information—after confiscating radio sets—through megaphones installed in the streets."[4] There were at least three of these loudspeakers in the ghetto, installed at central intersections, which Ringelblum identifies in an entry in May 1942 as "the corners of Mila and Zamenhofa Streets, Gesia and Zamenhofa Streets, and Nalewki and Nowolipki Streets."[5] According to him, these loudspeakers attracted "large crowd[s]" on a daily basis.[6] The occupiers posted regulations, decrees, and announcements, often on colored paper, on the streets, but the houses were also plastered with lists of people who were shot as a reprisal for smuggling or other clandestine activities. Różycki reports that one could see necrologies on almost every wall,[7] and Edelman points out the yellow notes on doors, warning of typhus.[8] These various publications added a new layer of information to the city streets, keeping people up to date about the continuous flood of regulations affecting their life, but at the same time reflecting the German aggression and the hostile living conditions back to them.[9] In this respect, the announcements were at the same time a symbolic and performative act of imprinting German rule on the streets of the ghetto.

Much of the official German news had to be read "against the grain," because it was heavily infused with German propaganda.[10] Still, with other channels of information severely impaired, any news was of great importance. There were also a number of clandestine publications circulating in the ghetto, including illegally printed pamphlets, posters, and newspapers, as well as the Polish, Russian, and German papers that were smuggled into the ghetto.[11] Engelking and Leociak explain that the main task of the illegally printed newspapers was to "supply information on the external situation (the real situation on the war fronts and in world politics) and the internal situation (underground activities, German policy in the occupied territories), which did not appear in the official papers."[12] Most information was taken from the few radio receivers that remained in the ghetto illegally, and from Polish underground presses.[13] During the Great Deportation *Aktion* in 1942, the publication of clandestine newspapers was discontinued, but underground activists still printed and distributed "leaflets with information about the real aim of the deportations and warnings for the inhabitants of the ghetto."[14] All these publications produced a counternarrative to the German propaganda. By entering public space, no matter in which form, they also represented a certain form of resistance against the German claim on ghetto space and ghetto life.

Most of these channels of information were not bound exclusively to the streets. Since the number of copies of illegal publications was small and they could only be dealt with in secret, the information they contained would usually find further distribution by word of mouth.[15] The publications themselves were seldom read directly on the streets but rather in private spaces to be exchanged again in the public space. Situational (thus unpublished) information and news about round-ups, beatings, blockades, and impending *Aktionen* traveled quickly, and so too did rumors regarding the outside world. In particular, information about the war, the Nazi plans for the fate of the Jews, and the actions of the Allied forces were shared daily on the streets of the ghetto. Due to the scarcity of reliable information, these rumors were often "acts of the interpretive imagination," as Andrew Strathern and Pamela J. Stewart call it.[16] In his paper "Rumor

Culture among Warsaw Jews under Nazi Occupation: A World of Catastrophe Reenchanted," Goldberg gives an excellent analysis of the role of rumors and the "oral transfer of information."[17] He points out that under German occupation the "highly literate prewar Jewish public sphere" had quickly turned into an orally dominated one: "At the same time, oral discourse took over the public sphere, as rumors replaced other modes of public communication such as newspapers and journals, which were almost entirely banned by the Germans."[18] With this development, the roles of written and oral communication were suddenly reversed. While the written word had been dominant in the public sphere before the war, it was now primarily a medium of private communication in the form of diaries or letters.[19] With the outbreak of the war, the spoken word, which used to be predominantly the medium of personal, familial conversations, now prevailed in the public sphere.[20] Spatially, this sphere was almost synonymous with the ghetto's streets. In a text entitled "Life of the Street and Home," Różycki summarizes:

> The street is a sphere of direct contact with friends and acquaintances. Here, the latest news is spread. Gossip, fears and hopes are shared, here you find the exchange, the trade office, the coffeehouse, the club, the editorial department, the information office—here is room for it. . . . That is why people only socialize on the streets, because only here do they have the opportunity to meet, to learn about their common fate. Only here, can we obtain the unreliable and shaky news of what is happening in the world, in the ghetto, on what is happening to one's neighbor, what chances there are for the future, what regulations and decrees were introduced. And only the street gives out the news as to which streets will be emptied, what the final date for the resettlement will be, who will have to report to the labor bureau, who will be sent to the labor camps, who can still be retrieved, if typhus is spreading and which products are getting more expensive, who has been arrested, where and when the ration cards will be distributed et cetera.[21]

According to Różycki, the street created a stage for all kinds of social exchange, taking over the roles of various other prewar institutions and meeting points. But most of all, it was the main channel for information. In his diary entry of March 26, 1942, Lewin gives an account of "the page of 'news' [he] gathered whilst walking about the ghetto for just half an hour."[22] In referring to a "page of news," Lewin almost equates the street with a newspaper that is to be read for information. While this analogy does not consider the specific differences between oral and written transmission, it does suggest that the oral exchange of information on the streets became a substitute for print media.

Only at a very late point in the ghetto's history did Jewish publications enter the public space in a printed and visible form again. Following the Great

Deportation *Aktion* in July to September 1942, the Jewish Fighting Organization (ŻOB) started putting up posters in the ghetto's streets. These posters, containing either warnings or a call to resistance, or announcing death sentences passed and carried out by the ŻOB,[23] were part of a general process of reclaiming the ghetto space. They were both means and manifestations of the increasing challenge the ŻOB posed to the German presence in the ghetto.

Notes

1. Czarnowski, "Street as a Communications Artifact," 207.

2. Sznapman, account, 20; Stok, account, 22; Blady-Szwajgier, *Die Erinnerung Verläßt Mich Nie*, 21; Kaplan, *Scroll of Agony*, 163–164; 491. RING. I/1024.

3. Kaplan, *Scroll of Agony*, 43.

4. Engelking and Leociak, *Warsaw Ghetto*, 34.

5. Ringelblum, *Notes from the Warsaw Ghetto*, 279–280.

6. Ibid. They were called "barkers" by the local population (Engelking and Leociak, *Warsaw Ghetto*, 34).

7. "Zamurowany" ("Walled Up") 455. RING. I/428. *Nekrologi* in the Polish original. In Poland, these *nekrologi* (or rather "*klepsydra*") were the traditional way to announce the death of a family member. Printed obituaries in black and white were hung out at the house of the deceased or even on advertising columns close by. It was therefore most likely less the announcements themselves than their sheer number that caught Różycki's attention. According to Lehnstaedt, this practice had been prohibited by the occupying authorities from 1940 onward (*Okkupation im Osten*, 83–84).

8. Edelman, *Das Ghetto Kämpft*, 33; Bauman, *Winter in the Morning*, 40; Markowska, *Ringelblum Archive*, 87.

9. Similarly, Natan Żelichower writes in his account, "With its relentless reports of dead and dying friends and acquaintances, the street served as a constant memento mori" (account, 46).

10. Adler, *In the Warsaw Ghetto*, 7, 262; Kaplan, *Scroll of Agony*, 68, 72–73.

11. Edelman, *Das Ghetto Kämpft*, 30, 38–40, 45; Krall and Edelman, *Dem Herrgott Zuvorkommen*, 89; Engelking and Leociak, *Warsaw Ghetto*, 685–694; Goldberg, "Rumor Culture," 198.

12. Engelking and Leociak, *Warsaw Ghetto*, 689.

13. Ibid., 689. These papers were in fact also distributed to other ghettos (and vice versa) by "female couriers, who carried them between ghettos," risking their own lives (ibid.).

14. Ibid., 691.

15. Goldberg, "Rumor Culture," 97.

16. Strathern and Stewart, "Introduction," 5; see also Kaplan, *Scroll of Agony*, 70.

17. Goldberg, "Rumor Culture," 96.

18. Ibid., 92.

19. Ibid.

20. Ibid.

21. "Życie ulicy i domu" 455. RING. I/428. Translation by Barbara Czepek and A. N., the Polish original reads as follows:

> *Ulica jest terenem bezpośredniego kontaktu ze znajomymi, tu dzielą się wszyscy ostatnimi wiadomościami, plotkami, obawami, nadziejami. Tu jest giełda, biuro handlowe, kawiarnia, klub, redakcja, biuro informacyjne—oto właściwe ich miejsce. . . . Nikt więc nie ma czasu na wzajemne odwiedzanie się, grzecznościowe wizyty, bo tylko dla załatwienia jakiejś sprawy odwiedza jeden drugiego. Stąd na ulicy ludzie ze sobą nawiązują kontakt, tu tylko mają sposobność stykania się i dowiadywania się o wzajemnym losie. Tu tylko możemy czerpać wiadomości bardzo niepewnych i chwiejnych, co się dzieje na świecie, co w getcie, co u najbliższych, jakie są w najbliższej przyszłości możliwości, jakie nowe zarządzenia, nakazy etc. A więc przede wszystkim tylko ulica dostarcza wiadomości, które ulice mają być opróżnione, jaki jest termin ostateczny wysiedlenia, kto i kiedy ma się zameldować w biurze pracy, kto zostanie wysłany do obozu pracy, a kto będzie reklamowany, jak się rozszerza tyfus, jakie produkty podrożały, kto został uwięziony, kto umarł, kiedy i gdzie przydzielają na bony towary itd. itd (455. RING. I/428)*

22. Lewin, *Cup of Tears*, 61.

23. Ibid., 167, see also footnotes on pages 283, 285, 286, 292, and 294; Engelking and Leociak, *Warsaw Ghetto*, 691–692.

17

Communication

Cultural geographer Doreen Massey describes "spatial openness and intercon-nectedness" as a key characteristic of urban settings. For Massey, "one way of understanding cities, then, might be as particular patterns of . . . connections set within wider patterns of the relations with other cities and with the rest of the world." The assumption that communication is a central element of the city takes as its foundation a similar idea—namely, that city space is generally set up to provide channels for the connection of "people, agencies, institutions, and so forth."[1] Or, as architect Thomas V. Czarnowski phrases it, "the great character-istic of the city . . . is its unique capability to serve as a nodal point for regional communications and, internally, to provide physically for an easily accessible web of contacts and exchanges."[2] The city's street network is an important—if not the most important—physical structure to guarantee that this exchange and contact can take place. The street is seen in this context mostly as a connector, as part of a larger network providing a "link between buildings" and "between people."[3] And while there are many other dimensions to communication—many of which were also ruptured—it is that of movement and "dissemination or exchange"[4] that was impaired most evidently by the building of the ghetto walls. The establishment of the ghetto physically cut communication between the two parts of the city, or, more precisely, it created two distinct parts through the very act of cutting communication.

The walls built on the orders of the German occupiers cut connections to the outside world, but they also fundamentally restructured the space inside the ghetto. The inhabitants experienced the disruption of the communication func-tion of the streets as imprisonment, as a form of "captive" violence in Reemtsma's sense. In the ghetto, everything was "locked and bolted," as Kaplan notes in his diary; there were dead ends at every turn, each cut-off street reinforcing the feeling of being trapped.[5] Summarizing the last entry of a satirical "tourist guide" that reportedly circulated in the ghetto, Mazor pointedly describes the disconcerting character of the ghetto's streets:

> At its conclusion the "Tourist Guide" mentions the ghetto's bustling streets: yes, these streets were much-traveled, but they were also like nothing else found in any other city in the world. For the streets of any other city in the world lead somewhere. They form part of the vast world to which they connect their cities. They open the way to freedom. By walking along them, one can come out at the broad avenues at the center of town or, on the contrary, emerge into the fields, the forests, onto the banks of rivers. . . . The streets of the ghettos led nowhere. They came up against an insurmountable wall, or a German sentry. All the streets of the ghetto were dead ends, and the people thronging them amid the tumult and the stench found themselves facing that impasse: they had nowhere to go, could find no exit.[6]

Mazor's description highlights the fact that the connecting function of the ghetto streets only worked internally, within a closed system, as it were. Regarding their relation to the outside world, all streets were turned into dead ends. Defying much of their basic communication function, the streets were turned essentially into non-streets.

This experience was not a shared one. The erection of fences and the building of walls—first for the so-called *Seuchensperrgebiet* and then for the ghetto—was a measure that did not implicate or affect Jewish and non-Jewish Varsovians alike but, instead, divided them along ethnic and religious lines. The spatial intervention was directed against communal life, and, while the walls changed the environment on both sides, even before they were closed and the formation of the ghetto completed, they implied an inside and an outside to the exclusion they created. Although the full implications could not be foreseen, already at an early stage the enforced social division created through ghettoization was clearly tied to the Nazis' targeted and deliberate policies of social, political, cultural, and economic exclusion. The walls represented the Nazis' will to harm the Jews in the form of segregation and exclusion. Let us note here that the ghetto, just as the camp, displays a remarkable inversion of the exclusion principle. While boundaries traditionally mark the inside as a protected zone and the outside as a threat that is excluded,[7] in both the ghetto and the camp, exterior and interior collapsed into one. What was defined as the inside by the containment function of walls or barbed wire was at the same time the outside of the social community as defined by the Nazis' policies.[8] This can be linked to Agamben's comments on the "space of exception." When Agamben describes the "space of exception" as "a piece of territory that is placed outside the normal juridical order," he immediately afterward specifies that, "for all that, however, it is not simply an external space. According to the etymological meaning of the term *exception* (*ex-capere*), what is being excluded in the camp is *captured outside*, that is included by virtue of its very exclusion."[9] Inclusion and exclusion coincided, in terms of both the community and the territory that its members were forced to inhabit. By the forcible inclusion into a ghetto or camp, the Nazis defined who was part of the "*Volksgemeinschaft*" (the ethnic community) and who was not.[10] In both cases, exclusion from the collective became absolute and was turned into a stable spatial arrangement.[11]

In Warsaw, the erection of such walls seemed all the more aggressive as a result of their location. Established in the center of the city, the ghetto massively severed the street network of the entire city and cut off communication at central arteries. It also forced a relocation of various cultural, social, and religious institutions. Accordingly, shortly before the sealing of the ghetto, Kaplan expresses his disbelief regarding the very idea of a closed ghetto in Warsaw. On November 2, 1940, he writes, "A Jewish Ghetto in Warsaw in the traditional sense is impossible; certainly a closed ghetto is inconceivable. Many churches and government buildings are in the heart of the ghetto. They cannot be eliminated, they fulfill necessary functions. Besides that, it is impossible to cut off the trolley routes going from one end of the city to the other through the ghetto."[12] Kaplan's arguments mostly address functional elements, implicitly referring to streets as connectors, as channels for communication and for accessing buildings.[13] In his book *Streets and Patterns*, Stephen Marshall highlights the importance of connectivity for communication: "It is movement that demands the continuous thread that links one section of street to the next, stitching each part into a single whole."[14] The walls that cut off the streets disabled the functioning of the network. They disabled access to important sites and prevented thoroughfare. As Engelking and Leociak summarize, "The walls erected in the center of the city destroyed its topography, cut through natural communication routes, and caused growing problems in the everyday functioning of the city."[15] Yet, to some degree, the reservations Kaplan expresses in his diary in November 1940 still seem to come from an outside perspective, one that describes the impact on the entire city and the lack of access created for those who would remain outside of the ghetto.[16] But ultimately, on the inside, communication was ruptured even more severely, and the ghetto's boundary determined options more exhaustively.

When walls were built "along a seemingly random zigzag boundary," as Michał Grynberg writes in an introductory paragraph for the collection of firsthand accounts entitled *Words to Outlive Us*, they cut off streets, creating dead ends and impossible spatial entanglements.[17] This led to very practical disruptions in people's everyday movements. On May 18, 1940, before the official establishment of the ghetto, but with the first walls around the so-called *Seuchensperrgebiet* already erected, Kaplan writes in his diary,

> Warsaw, like the Noah's Ark in its day, is full of compartments and partitions that block the roads in the very places where up to now there was the most traffic. Thus for example, on the corner of Nalewki and Nowolipki streets, a dividing wall has been made, and a man whose apartment is at Number 2 Nowolipki Street—a distance of only a few steps—is now forced to go around and around, via Nowolipki-, Zamenhofa-, Gęsia-, and Nalewki Streets—a detour of half an hour. The same is true of the corner of Rymarska-Leszno Streets, and so too in all the other fenced-off streets.[18]

Kaplan's observations tell us a lot about how the ghetto's boundary, manifesting itself in the walling off of individual streets, affected the basic communication function of the streets. While physical proximity still implied closeness, the rupture of the connections between proximate locations led to a radical reorganization of spatial categories. As Leociak points out, the new topography necessitated an adaptation of the categories of near and far: "The old spatial categories and parameters proved useless. Concepts such as 'near and far' or 'here and there' had to be defined again."[19] These changes meant a violation of people's habitual sense of space. They also created very practical complications. What was, in terms of linear and habitual measures, just a few steps away could now require a journey of thirty minutes or more, all while the starting point and the end point were still both located in the same quarter. In many other cases, communication was obstructed entirely. After the ghetto was closed, neighboring buildings that were located on different sides of the wall ceased to have any connection at all, despite their physical proximity.[20] What had formerly been a continuous space was now broken apart.

Under the new circumstances, everything took much longer within the ghetto. As Różycki notes in his study on the ghetto written in December 1941, "Because it is so difficult to get from one street to the next, simply because you have to circumvent the wall, you lose plenty of time to get any business done."[21] On the most basic and fundamental levels, life was made more grueling due to the forced restructuring of urban space. The walls decelerated communication. They also drastically reduced the possible ways in which to go from one place to another inside of the ghetto. This limitation runs counter to the large scope of possible connections characteristic of urban settlement. The vast space of potential accessibility shrank to very limited actual options. Ringelblum notes in his journal in November 1940, "There's no connection between Twarda and Leszno Street. You have to go by way of Zelazna Street."[22] Because in a certain section of the ghetto, all other streets connecting north and south were cut off by the wall, only one way to move from one street to another remained of the many routes available in prewar times. With Twarda Street as part of the so-called small ghetto, and Leszno as part of the large ghetto, the two were separated by the chokepoint that the Germans had created at Chłodna Street in order to satisfy the communication (i.e., traffic) needs of the "Aryan" city. In fact, it was the exclusion of Chłodna Street that led to the division of the ghetto into two sections in the first place.[23]

Chłodna was one of the biggest streets connecting east and west and would have run directly through the ghetto area had it not, instead, been excluded from it. A small, two-hundred-meter-long, section of Chłodna Street, between Wronia and Żelazna Streets, had remained part of the ghetto for the first year of its existence. In December 1941, that section was excluded as well, thus turning Chłodna Street into a continuous "traffic corridor for the Aryan part of the town."[24] The concession made to the communication/traffic needs of the "Aryan" city caused severe complications for people inside the walls. With Wronia Street being outside the ghetto, the only way to get from any street in the small ghetto to any street in the large ghetto was through Żelazna Street. First, this was done through two sets of "swinging iron gates,"[25] then, for pedestrians, over the wooden footbridge that was constructed in the winter of 1941/1942. Even after the building of the footbridge, wheeled Jewish traffic was still crossing Chłodna Street, with the high gateways occasionally opening for them.[26]

Being one of the rare direct intersections of Jewish and "Aryan" space, Chłodna Street was one of the few locations that allowed the ghetto inhabitants to see the other side of the wall (and, conversely, to be seen by the Gentile population). For many ghetto inhabitants, the "Aryan" Chłodna represented the only image of life outside the ghetto. The contrast was stark, also, in regard to communication. The ease with which traffic flowed on the Jewish side and on the "Aryan" side was far from equal. In the "Aryan" part, "Chlodna Street had little commotion on it, the gates stayed open most of the time and the traffic flowed without congestion," the street was "spacious and clean," and "traffic was normal"; whereas, on the Jewish side, "the gates opened only rarely, and very briefly," even though traffic circulation was much heavier.[27] Adler explains the procedure in more detail: "Jewish vehicles were permitted to move along Żelazna and Chłodna only when the Polish policeman on traffic duty there could not detect any Aryan vehicles. Sometimes, a quarter of an hour would pass before a cavalcade of Jewish vehicles could make a move. Then it became a matter of utmost urgency to get through this treacherous passage with the greatest possible speed since traffic could be ordered to stop at any second."[28]

Again, the racial hierarchy of the Nazi ideology was implemented on a spatial plane, entailing different communication rights. "Aryan" communication took

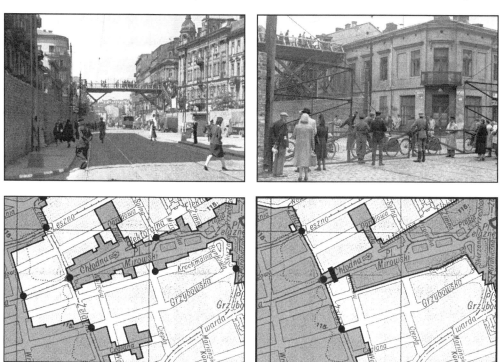

Fig. 17.1(a–d). Bridge and gate at the intersection of Chłodna and Żelazna Streets, 1942; borders of the ghetto in November 1940 and after the reductions in December 1941.

priority and remained basically uninterrupted, while the Jewish communication was complicated significantly, turning it into a physical and emotional exertion. At the same time, the arrangement of spatial rights and different spatial orders conveyed the Nazis' notions of superiority and inferiority and a clear imbalance of power back to the ghetto inhabitants (as well as to the "Aryans" on the other side of the spectrum). In his 1941 study on the ghetto, *To jest getto!* (*This Is the Ghetto!*), Różycki comments on the imbalance of spatial rights and the disregard for Jewish communication needs with bitterness:

> While no one cares for the general concerns of the population. It doesn't matter if at a whim, a crazy idea is realized and half a million people now have to give a wide berth to a street, where up until now normal communication was happening. And this communication takes twenty minutes up to an hour these days, even though the streets are adjacent to each other. Just like this, the ghetto is divided in two parts, the so called small ghetto on the southern side and the actual ghetto on the northern side, to exclude one single street.[29]

The communication of vehicular traffic was similarly disrupted, both in its movement within the ghetto and to the "Aryan" city. With the establishment of the ghetto, wheeled traffic was limited in the same ways as was pedestrian traffic. But again, the communication needs of the "Aryan" side of the city were granted exceptions from such restrictions. The exceptions came in the form of transit trams that traversed the ghetto. The Germans, in fact, implemented two separate transportation systems, adhering to the principle of racial segregation and the corresponding spatial rights. There was a system of Jewish trams, "whose route did not cross the walls and which was designated exclusively for inhabitants of the ghetto," and three "Aryan" trams that "ran in transit through the ghetto, designated exclusively for Aryan passengers."[30] These trams maintained west-east and north-south connections for the "Aryan" part of the city that had otherwise been ruptured by the establishment of the ghetto. At the same time, the "Aryan" trams, as Engelking and Leociak point out, "constituted a breach of the principle of complete isolation."[31] But even though they were passing through the ghetto, these trams were still meant to remain separate from it, thereby minimizing the breach: "'Aryan' trams in transit through the now sealed ghetto had a blue police escort, traveled at maximum speed, and did not halt at the stops."[32] They constituted a very particular space that was at the same time inside and outside the ghetto. Moreover, taking a transit tram was one of the few occasions when non-Jewish Poles and German civilians would actually see the inside of the ghetto. In fact, Lehnstaedt reports that these trams were often used by German soldiers to illegally visit the ghetto during their oftentimes short stays in Warsaw.[33] According to Lehnstaedt, there was a veritable "ghetto tourism" ("*regelrechter Ghetto-Tourismus*") taking place among the German soldiery.[34]

Internally, the establishment of the ghetto drastically altered public transportation and traffic in general. With the use and possession of motorized vehicles forbidden to Jews, there were no automobiles in the ghetto, except for those that belonged to Germans.[35] The most common means of transportation were rickshaws and horse-drawn streetcars. While trams were still in operation until August 15, 1942, they were quite expensive and therefore not accessible to most ghetto inhabitants. All in all, as Mazor observes, "the vast majority of the population went about on foot."[36] For most people, getting from one place to another therefore involved much more physical strain than it had previously. Although the space accessible to them had shrunk significantly in size, its relative size in proportion to their mobility still made it difficult to master.

Another significant change concerned the utilization of streets and, in particular, the distribution of traffic load to individual streets. The establishment of the ghetto had created a general traffic overflow inside the walls. Due to the particular layout of the streets, there were only limited channels of communication available, and the disproportionate traffic volume aggravated conditions on the streets. According to principles of urban planning, there is usually a certain hierarchy between streets based on their size, their design, and their use. This hierarchy is to ensure "the functional efficiency of traffic flow" but also concerns issues like "safety [or] amenity."[37] While physical variables by no means determine the "conforming use" of a street, they do mark certain "constraints," and the physical environment can "sugges[t], suppor[t], or . . . tolerat[e]" specific forms of use to different degrees.[38] In regard to the sidewalk, for example, there is usually a certain "relationship of width to the pedestrian load."[39] Simply put, a narrow residential street will show different architectural qualities (overall width, ratio of sidewalk and road, road surface, separation) and encourage different uses than will a major traffic artery. In the ghetto, these distinctions carried no weight anymore. The overcrowding and the drastic changes to the layout put enormous pressure on the street network and imposed a use that often ran counter to the habitual and practical uses of particular streets. In his *Kronika getta warszawskiego* (*Chronicle of the Warsaw Ghetto*), Ringelblum describes one prominent example when he explains, "The walling up of Przejazd and Nowolipie Streets created an impossible situation in Karmelicka Street. It's terribly crowded there, enormously heavy traffic. In Karmelicka Street the traffic is incredible. The pavements and the roadway as well are [flowing with] a dense wave of people; it's almost impossible to drive that way and it takes a terribly long time."[40]

Because of the walling up of all other north-south connectors, the "narrow Karmelicka Street was until the autumn of 1941 the only link between the northern and southern parts of the large ghetto."[41] Although not at all suited for this function, Karmelicka became a central "nerve of the ghetto," as Mazor phrases it in his 1955 recollections *The Vanished City*, simply because the layout of the ghetto had eliminated all alternative routes.[42] The new topography, combined with the immense population density within the ghetto, translated into serious problems regarding traffic. As Mazor states, "Certain main thoroughfares in the ghetto were always congested; this was a city with a lack of space not only in housing, but in the streets as well."[43] Ringelblum's description paints a vivid picture of the effects of the overcrowding and overloading of infrastructure created by the German intervention: the street was crowded, traffic was heavy, and the sidewalk could not hold the huge number of people. This again slowed down communication significantly, but, furthermore, it also created a stressful and dangerous situation in which pedestrians could be pushed onto the road and into the vehicular traffic.[44] Indeed, accidents were frequent inside the ghetto and posed a serious risk for everyone on the streets.[45] It can therefore only be seen as cynical when, on April 30, 1942, the director of police (*Polizeidirektor*), Otto Bethke, complained in an official announcement about the "poor traffic discipline" of pedestrians, motorists, droshky drivers, and coachmen.[46]

Fig. 17.2. Karmelicka Street before July 1942.

Going back to Czarnowski's definition of communication as "every kind of dissemination or exchange, whether it be of persons, goods, messages or energy, and whether it be transcribed, transported, or transmitted,"[47] helps explain further how severely the ghetto was affected by the fact that its streets no longer connected to the outside world. The rupture in communication also entailed an interruption of trade and supply. The few remaining intersections between the "Aryan" parts of the city and the ghetto were tightly guarded by the Germans and their auxiliaries, thus putting them in control of all exchange.[48] Being cut off from the rest of the city usually involved a high degree of "material harm" and, for many ghetto inhabitants, resulted in an almost complete "loss of means of subsistence."[49] Alternative channels to compensate for this—in the form of smuggling—were only found under utmost difficulties and great personal risks. Moreover, the rupture in communication entailed a deep social disruption, thus severing lines of potential support and assistance to the inhabitants of the ghetto and "diminishing [their] social participation (social integrity)."[50] The lack of communication furthered the social divide between Jewish and non-Jewish Poles. While some contacts persisted, most social interaction was cut off. The sealing of the ghetto ruptured communication on all levels.

Considering these manifold disruptions, the general deceleration that turned every daily errand into an act of exertion, and the stress and heightened risk of accidents, it can be concluded that the building of the walls cordoning off the ghetto acted as a form of indirect violence. Similarly, Leociak interprets the new frontiers as "yet another form of persecution to trouble the Jewish community of Warsaw."[51] Still, the violence exerted here has to be distinguished from other, more direct forms of violence that include, for example, physical assault. An important difference in this context is that between intention and effect. Although the German spatial policies can be interpreted as a form of violence in regard to their effects on the city structure and on its inhabitants, and although testimonies indicate that they were experienced as such,[52] it is highly problematic to conclude that exerting violence through these spatial measures was necessarily the intention of the German administration.[53] It is likely that, from the Nazis' perspective, the ghetto was considered a means to exert violence only in the sense of actual physical aggression (such as beatings, executions, or random shootings), deliberate killing through undersupplying and neglecting the inhabitants of the ghetto, and through deportations to death camps. In light of the dehumanization of the victims called for within Nazi ideology, it may even be questionable whether these acts were considered violent at all by the perpetrators, insofar as violence is perceived as something exerted against one's own kind.[54] Especially at first, the establishment of the ghetto was probably mostly thought of as a practical and discriminatory measure. However, even if clear telic "intention" cannot be established for every effect, intent can be broadly assumed for the German authorities and local administration. In any case, the explicit will to harm or, at least, to participate in willful neglect, are sufficient preconditions to read the effect of the spatial measures as a form of violence.

Notes

1. Massey, "On Space and the City," 159, 161.
2. Czarnowski, "Street as a Communications Artifact," 207.
3. Mehta, *Street*, 12.
4. Czarnowski, "Street as a Communications Artifact," 207.
5. Kaplan, *Scroll of Agony*, 210; see also Berg, *Diary*, 117. For a detailed analysis of the experience of being imprisoned and of the metaphor of the prison in the context of the ghetto, see Leociak, *Doświadczenia graniczne*, 62–65, 68; see also Neumann, *Die Weltanschauung des Nazismus*, 127.
6. Mazor, *Vanished City*, 118.
7. Razac, *Barbed Wire*, 73.
8. Ibid., 83; see also Buggeln and Wildt, "Lager im Nationalsozialismus," 186.
9. Agamben, "What Is a Camp?" 40.
10. Buggeln and Wildt, "Lager im Nationalsozialismus," 186.
11. Agamben, "What Is a Camp?" 38.
12. Kaplan, *Scroll of Agony*, 218.
13. See, for example, Anderson, "People in the Physical Environment," 1; Czarnowski, "Street as a Communications Artifact," 207; Marshall, *Streets and Patterns*, 48; Mehta, *Street*, 12.

14. Marshall, *Streets and Patterns*, 191.

15. Engelking and Leociak, *Warsaw Ghetto*, 60.

16. The map of the ghetto boundaries at the time of its closing (November 15, 1940) shows how the Germans tackled the issue of accessibility from the outside. They created many small "Aryan enclaves" in the ghetto, the most well-known of them probably being the "evangelical enclave" at Leszno, Mylna, and Karmelicka Street. The authorities created this particular enclave to exclude the "Działyński Palace, the Evangelical hospital at 10 Karmelicka Street, the house at 20 Leszno Street and the Reformed Evangelical church at 16 Leszno Street" from the ghetto area (Engelking and Leociak, *Warsaw Ghetto*, 74). The buildings could be reached through a "narrow corridor from 5 and 7 Przejazd Street" outside the ghetto (ibid.). Similar, smaller dents in the boundary were located at Biała and Ogrodowa Street (according to Stanisław Adler to "provide a passage to the courthouse" [*In the Warsaw Ghetto*, 34]), and at the corner of Waliców and Ceglana Street in the small ghetto (according to Adler to accommodate the needs of the "companies of Haberbusch, Schiele, and Ulrich" [ibid.]).

17. Grynberg, *Words to Outlive Us*, 16.

18. Kaplan, *Scroll of Agony*, 154–155. Leociak adds to the text: "and a man whose apartment is at Number 2 Nowolipki Street [in order to get to the house at number 5 Nalewki Street]—a distance of only a few steps—is now forced to go around and around, via Nowolipki-, Zamenhofa-, Gęsia-, and Nalewki Streets—a detour of half an hour" (*Text in the Face of Destruction*, 50–51). Similar examples can be found at the "Aryan" enclave at Biała and Ogrodowa Street, where again, residents of buildings who before simply had to cross a street to see each other now had to go around a full block (Ogrodowa—Solna—Leszno—Żelazna—Ogrodowa Street); or at the corner of Waliców and Ceglana Street, where the zigzagging boundary cut out some buildings of Ceglana Street (which in December 1941 were included into the ghetto area again), along with the corner where the two streets met.

19. Leociak, *Text in the Face of Destruction*, 45.

20. Ibid., 44.

21. "Życie ulicy i domu" ("Life of the Street and Home") 455. RING. I/428; see also Kermish, *To Live with Honor and Die with Honor!*, 155; Mazor, *Vanished City*, 119. Translation by Barbara Czepek and A. N. The Polish original reads as follows: "*Ponieważ dostać się z jednej ulicy na drugą jest rzeczą bardzo trudną z powodu konieczności okrążania murów, więc załatwienie każdego interesu wymaga straty bardzo dużo czasu[s].*"

22. Ringelblum, *Notes from the Warsaw Ghetto*, 86.

23. Marking the boundary between these two parts of the ghetto, the passage at Chłodna also meant the crossing between better and worse living conditions, with the large ghetto generally housing the poorer population under very crowded conditions and the small ghetto encompassing "better" streets—such as Sienna—a little more space and a little less destitution (Berg, *Diary*, 62, 76, 80–83, 94, 122; Adler, *In the Warsaw Ghetto*, 52; Engelking and Leociak, *Warsaw Ghetto*, 125–126; Szarota, *Warschau unter dem Hakenkreuz*, 36, 157–158; Ringelblum, *Notes from the Warsaw*

Ghetto, 222, 226–227; for an example of the conditions in one of the "worse" streets [Wołyńska], see "Warsaw, an excursion to Jews who nourish themselves on dogs, cats, and rats . . . !!!" [499. RING. I/1005]).

24. Berg, *Diary*, 115.

25. Leociak, *Text in the Face of Destruction*, 50.

26. Engelking and Leociak, *Warsaw Ghetto*, 131.

27. Mazor, *Vanished City*, 115–116.

28. Adler, *In the Warsaw Ghetto*, 115.

29. "Mury, mury, mury" ("Walls, walls, walls") 455. RING. I/428. Translation by Barbara Czepek and A. N., the Polish original reads as follows: "*Przy tym nikt tu się nie liczy z najżywotniejszymi interesami ludności. Nic to, że dla spełnienia jakiegoś kaprysu czy niewczesnego pomysłu pół miliona ludności musi okrążać całe ulice, między którymi komunikacja dotychczas zupełnie normalna trwa obecnie 20 minut do jednej godziny, choć są to ulice bezpośrednio ze sobą sąsiadujące. Nic to, że dla wyłączenia jednej ulicy podzielone jest getto na dwie części, tzw. małe getto po południowej stronie i właściwe północne getto, a te dwie części połączone są jedną ulicą154, zresztą również do połowy tylko przechodzącą przez getto, wąskim kory- tem, przez które przetacza się równocześnie kilkanaście tysięcy ludzi*" (455. RING. I/428).

30. Engelking and Leociak, *Warsaw Ghetto*, 110.

31. Ibid., 112.

32. Ibid.; see also Leociak, *Doświadczenia graniczne*, 74.

33. Lehnstaedt, *Okkupation im Osten*, 88.

34. Ibid., 89.

35. Those had a very different status than did the Jewish means of transportation and usually posed a much higher risk to Jewish traffic participants (see, for example, Bauman, *Winter in the Morning*, 45–47). The only exceptions applied to the head of the *Judenrat*, Adam Czerniaków, and the head of the Jewish Order Service, Józef Szeryński, who, according to contemporary accounts, were driven to certain appointments in a car (Adler, *In the Warsaw Ghetto*, 108).

36. Mazor, *Vanished City*, 120; see also Engelking and Leociak, *Warsaw Ghetto*, 125.

37. Marshall, *Streets and Patterns*, 47.

38. Anderson, "People in the Physical Environment," 1–2.

39. Mantho, *Urban Section*, 77.

40. English translation in Leociak, *Text in the Face of Destruction*, 49 (insertion in the original); for a similar passage, see also Ringelblum, *Notes from the Warsaw Ghetto*, 42.

41. Leociak, *Text in the Face of Destruction*, 49; see also Engelking and Leociak, *Warsaw Ghetto*, 114, 121.

42. Mazor, *Vanished City*, 116; see also Adler, *In the Warsaw Ghetto*, 114.

43. Mazor, *Vanished City*, 121.

44. See also Kaplan, *Scroll of Agony*, 166.

45. Engelking and Leociak, *Warsaw Ghetto*, 120–121.

46. 21 . RING. II/397.

47. Czarnowski, "Street as a Communications Artifact," 207.

48. Cole, "Geographies of Ghettoization," 276.

49. Popitz, *Phenomena or Power*, 27; see also Adler, *In the Warsaw Ghetto*, 33.

50. Popitz, *Phenomena of Power*, 26.

51. Engelking and Leociak, *Warsaw Ghetto*, 113; for a similar passage, see also Leociak, *Text in the Face of Destruction*, 50.

52. See, for example, 455. RING. I/428; Adler, *In the Warsaw Ghetto*, 34, 38, 255.

53. Some accounts even express the belief that the specific spatial layout of the ghetto was explicitly designed to terrorize and hurt the Jewish community. Adler, for example, writes, "This population was not a subject for regulation but an object for destruction, all the more pleasing to the invader's eyes when it was accompanied by pain and suffering. The wooded areas, therefore, were purposely and maliciously excluded from the Quarter" (*In the Warsaw Ghetto*, 34), or "The boundaries of the ghetto had been purposely and maliciously defined to force hundreds of thousands of people to use the single communication artery along Ciepla, Grzybowska, Waliców, Krochmalna, Żelazna, Leszno and Karmelicka Streets" (ibid., 114, see also 38, 255; 455. RING. I/428). While these statements tell a lot about the experience of the ghetto, the interpretation of the victims is, however, not necessarily consistent with the perpetrators' actual intentions.

Cole discusses a similar matter in the context of concentration camps (*Holocaust City*, 13–14), questioning van Pelt's assumption of "architectural intentionality" in regard to the "manipulation and creation of space" in German concentration and death camps (ibid., 13). Cole criticizes the fact that van Pelt builds his analysis on the postwar memoir of a survivor without applying the appropriate analytical caution. Cole argues that while the account "certainly suggests that the space was both perceived and experienced by the victim as intentional," it is problematic to conclude that this perception and experience "matched the original intentions of the perpetrators" (ibid., 13–14). Instead, Cole suggests seeing "intentionality and functionality" as "intertwined" (ibid., 14).

54. For a similar line of reasoning, see Popitz, *Phänomene der Macht*, 68–69.

18

Orientation

Kevin Lynch's foundational 1960 work on urban planning *The Image of the City* emphasizes the correlation between personal well-being and the ability to orient oneself. Lynch argues for the importance of what he calls "legibility" of a city and stresses the "need to recognize and pattern our surrounding."[1] According to Lynch, the "generalized mental picture" of the environment is based on both "immediate sensation and the memory of past experience" and is of "wide practical and emotional importance to the individual."[2] The ghetto, however, undermined people's ability to rely on their past experiences, and, even more than that, it significantly reduced "legibility" of the cityscape by breaking up the habitual patterns of orientation and creating a seemingly arbitrary layout. The result was a strong feeling of disorientation and of being lost—a word that according to Lynch "carries an overtone of utter disaster."[3] And indeed, accounts from the ghetto suggest that the new topography created by the Germans was experienced as deeply disruptive and unsettling. In his 1997 study on firsthand accounts (*Tekst wobec zagłady/Text in the Face of Destruction*), Leociak concludes, "Space was now experienced differently from before—oppressively and traumatically."[4] Mazor's remarks on the ghetto streets might help explain this effect. His description of streets failing to connect and leading nowhere suggests that it was not captivity alone that people experienced as painful.[5] It was the sharp contrast between the new spatial order and people's habits and expectations that heightened the traumatic effect. While the ghetto was connected to people's previous experience, it was at the same time fundamentally alien, and the ghetto inhabitants were no longer able to rely on their "memory of past experience" to structure their environment.[6] The fact that there was such a thing as the ghetto tourist guide that Mazor mentions suggests how alien and outlandish the ghetto space appeared to its inhabitants. Although Jewish Varsovians were technically still in their native city, the walls erected on German orders had created a space that they could not reconcile with their knowledge of the Warsaw they had inhabited previously. The ghetto was alien territory, also—or maybe especially—for those who were familiar with the prewar northern district. It was not their city anymore, but a very different place that required explanation. As Leociak argues, the "picture of the city that was fixed in people's minds by earlier experience was dismantled, and people lost what was known, safe and familiar. The area of the ghetto became an area of disinheritance."[7]

Różycki describes a similar alienating effect in the study on the ghetto that he wrote for the Ringelblum Archive in December 1941 (To jest getto!/This Is the Ghetto!). Różycki had just returned from Lwów (Lviv/Lemberg) in October. He, like many others, had fled to the east from the advancing invasion of the German armed forces in 1939,[8] but he decided to return home because he assumed his fate would be more bearable if he were "among [his] own, surrounded by family, friends, among people who mean each other well, fellow believers and companions of misery."[9] It is that conjuncture of personal circumstances that gives his report particular meaning. Having been absent during the phase of the ghetto's establishment, Różycki did not become accustomed to the new conditions gradually. Instead, he was confronted abruptly with the changes to his home city made over the first two years of the occupation. Moreover, Różycki returns to Warsaw in the hope that a familiar environment will help him to cope. After two years of wandering, of being on the run and suffering from loneliness in foreign territories, he expects to return to a place he identifies as home. And indeed, passing through the "Aryan" parts of the city, Różycki is still somewhat optimistic. After all, what he sees reminds him of the Warsaw of the past: "The city slowly removes the traces of the bombing, lives more or less a normal life. People stroll calmly in the streets, the shops are full of goods. It's expensive, because it's expensive, there is no work, but," he writes, "life goes on."[10] His first impressions help reassure him of his familiarity with the city. Despite the damage wrought by war, despite the occupation, Różycki can still relate to Warsaw. Shortly before entering the ghetto, Różycki calms himself, thinking that "a few meters of boundaries won't be able to change the appearance of the streets,"[11] he assures himself that he knows the city very well. But the moment he turns onto smaller side streets, he is suddenly hit by the realization that his internal "street map" has failed him.[12] It seems like, all of a sudden, the environment had become unfamiliar. He notes, "In a sophisticated and incomprehensible way, the streets have been fragmented, cut out and disfigured. Here, the walls run right through the middle of a street, there an apartment house is cut out of the Jewish Quarter. One street is cut into two parts, the middle part belonging to one quarter, the two ends to another."[13]

What is noticeable again is how Różycki's words indicate a violation of the city. The streets are "fragmented" ("*posiatkowane*"), "cut out" ("*wycięte*"), "disfigured" ("*pokiereszowane*"). Buildings are extracted from the quarter, streets ruptured. These actions seem arbitrary to him, following no apparent logic. Instead of highlighting aspects such as exclusion, segregation, or forced relocation, Różycki describes the German interventions in the city space in terms of their relation to the city as such. The seemingly arbitrary spatial measures defeat the inner logic of the built environment, defeat common sense. This has a strong impact on his own sentiments. He feels anxious and is severely disoriented by the new spatial order. The "barred streets" disrupt his sense of place and his ability to locate himself properly.[14] His environment does not seem to make much sense anymore. Describing how he felt when he had finally entered the ghetto, Różycki writes, "What has happened to me? After all, I know every street here, almost every house, every other person. And yet I don't recognize these streets, I don't recognize the people. I don't know which street I'm in. I'm not able to find the way to my house. It's supposed to be only five minutes from here, but I go around in circles and don't know how to find my house."[15]

Again, Różycki contrasts the fact that he knows the city well, that he is familiar with its streets, its houses, its inhabitants, with the devastating experience of not finding his way home. In an environment that he used to know most intimately, all previous markers of orientation seem to fail him. The spatial changes elicit strong feelings of dislocation and destabilization. And not only does Różycki cease to recognize his surroundings; he is also unable to master them. This experience creates a profound feeling of anxiety, he writes: "I cannot cast off the eerie anxiety and fear that suddenly seizes me."[16]

Różycki's account shows the strong impact the spatial changes had on him. His reactions seem to confirm Till's assumption that place has "a central function in an individual's emotional and social ecosystem." Referring to clinical psychiatrist Mindy Thompson Fullilove (*Root Shock: How Tearing up City Neighborhoods Hurts America, and What We Can Do about It*) and her concept of "root shock," Till argues that "our patterns of movement are a kind of 'mazeway' that ... provides us with security."[17] When this "mazeway" is ruptured, it can be experienced as a trauma. In the case of the ghetto, the concept of "root shock" can be applied to different scenarios. For most people who were forcibly moved to the ghetto, the traumatic rupture happened through an initial act of "dislocative" violence.[18] For those who had already lived on the territory of the future ghetto, "root shock" most likely happened when familiar structures of the environment were severed, connections cut off, and the layout forcibly reorganized. Often, this experience was repeated with recurring moves within the ghetto itself or with general changes to its layout. In the case of Różycki, it was the discovery that the once-familiar environment had "suddenly" become alien and incomprehensible that disrupted his safety, "familiarity, routine," and his "sense of belonging and security."[19] The fact that Różycki interprets the changes to the city as an act of violence adds to that sense. The new spatial order is experienced not only as "alien" but also as "hostile," as Leociak suggests in his study on the ghetto space.[20] This impression of hostility was tied to the fact that the ghetto's inhabitants interpreted the spatial changes as an act of aggression directed at them, as the expression of a will to harm and to neglect.[21] The new spatial order was therefore experienced in a way similar to a physical assault, as a shock.

In addition to the disruption of the personal environment—of what Till calls "social ecologies of place" and describes as the sum of "everyday routines, social institutions, material landscapes (the fabric, taste, sounds, and scents of places), symbolic systems of meaning and identity, and shared memories"[22]—there was also a rupture with regard to identification and belonging in a broader sense. The establishment of the ghetto further compromised its inhabitants' feelings of both belonging to the city and belonging to the Polish community.[23] While Kaplan's early depictions of the war damage still show his affiliation with Warsaw as a whole, and Różycki takes the seeming normality of the "Aryan" city as a sign of reassurance, the connection between the ghetto inhabitants and the remaining city was, in fact, continually challenged and ruptured. From October 1940 onward, those deemed Jewish by the Nazis were forcibly identified with and confined to a marked-out territory that henceforth defined them as Jewish and Jewish only. At the same time, Jews were excluded from all other previous affiliations, be it spatial or communal, and deprived of previous identities formed in any way other than by the German Nazi laws.

Philosopher Ronald Sundstrom highlights the nexus of space and the production of racial categories and identities—with "race" understood as a socially constructed "category of human organization and experience"—in his 2010 study "Race and Place: Social Space in the Production of Human Kinds." Referring to racial segregation in the United States, Sundstrom argues that there is a general link between sorting "people by categories" and sorting them spatially.[24] And while the process of segregation was implemented even more radically and explicitly in the context of the Nazi ghetto, Sundstrom's arguments concerning mechanisms of identity formation still hold explanatory value. He concludes, "When we divide spatially we cannot help but to inscribe and produce categories associated with our spatial divisions. With racialized spaces come race." What is separated spatially acquires different meaning. Accordingly, racial identity is produced through space, because "place is a component of the self-conception of individuals" and a "component of inter-individual conceptions. Likewise, place is a component of the way communities view themselves and how others view them.

In our inhabitation of places there is a looping effect between our identification of places and our identities."[25] Similarly, in the context at hand, ghettoization was explicitly coupled with racial conceptualization. As a practice of segregation, the "Jewish" space created by the Nazis was set up to reduce the multifaceted, often inconsistent individual identities to an imposed, simplified, and devaluing one. It both reflected and produced an image of "Jewishness."

Różycki's report gives an example of the deep-acting effect of this spatial attribution when he recounts his first moments in the ghetto: "I have been here only for a few moments, but something inside of me already broke. . . . Maybe I am wrong again, but that much is clear: it took only a few moments to lose my spirit, faith, hope and balance, it was enough to turn me into one of the prisoners of the ghetto in one fell swoop."[26] The ghetto absorbs and transforms Różycki's identity. The identifying power of the space seems to be enormous, and it implies how much the two—space and identity—coincided when at a later point Różycki calls the inhabitants of the ghetto *"gettowcy"*—ghettoites.[27] Concurrently, it became less and less clear what people referred to when they spoke of their city. Without access to it, most of what people knew about "Aryan" Warsaw was based on hearsay, on speculation and previous knowledge. The "other" city became part of the realm of the imaginary. Another description by Mazor emphasizes the deep rupture between the two parts of the city. Talking about the continuous reduction of the area of the ghetto, Mazor writes, "Some connecting artery which, just the evening before had been in its rightful place, suddenly ceased to exist."[28] The fact that Mazor describes the exclusion of a street as it "ceasing to exist" implies how far removed the "Aryan" city felt from his inside perspective. It was as if it didn't even exist.[29]

Notes

1. Lynch, *Image of the City*, 2, 4.
2. Ibid., 4.
3. Ibid.
4. Leociak, *Text in the Face of Destruction*, 43.
5. Mazor, *Vanished City*, 118.
6. Lynch, *Image of the City*, 4.
7. Leociak, *Text in the Face of Destruction*, 51.
8. Löw and Roth, *Das Warschauer Getto*, 86; Kassow, *Who Will Write Our History?*, 229; Adler, *In the Warsaw Ghetto*, 4.
9. "Powrót do gniazda rodzinnego" ("Return to the Familial Nest") 455. RING. I/428. Translation by Barbara Czepek and A. N., the Polish original reads as follows: *"Będęmiędzy swoimi, otoczony rodzinąodprzyjaciółmi, ludźmi wzajemnie sobie dobrze życzącymi, współwyznawcami i współtowarzyszami niedoli"* (455. RING. I/428).

10. "Powrót do gniazda rodzinnego" 455. RING. I/428. Translation by Barbara Czepek and A. N., the Polish original reads as follows: *Miasto powoli usuwa ślady bombardowania, żyje jako tako normalnym życiem. Ludzie kręcą się po ulicach spokojnie, sklepy zawalone towarami. Drogo, bo drogo, pracy nie ma, ale jakoś się żyje* (455. RING. I/428).

11. "Powrót do gniazda rodzinnego" 455. RING. I/428. Translation by Barbara Czepek and A. N., the Polish original reads as follows: *Przecieżrpółnocna dzielnica nie leży tak daleko, przeciеżrkilka metrów granicy nie potrafiąozmienić oblicza ulicy* (455. RING. I/428).

12. "Powrót do gniazda rodzinnego" 455. RING. I/428.

13. "Mury, mury, mury" ("Walls, walls, walls") 455. RING. I/428. Translation by Barbara Czepek and A. N., the Polish original reads as follows: *W jakiś wyrafinowany i niezrozumiały sposób zostały ulice posiatkowane, wycięte i pokiereszowane. To mury przechodząrprzez środek ulicy, to znów kamienica zostaje wyłączona z dzielnicy żydowskiej. Jedna ulica jest pocięta na dwie części, środkowa część należy do jednej dzielnicy, a dwa końcowe odcinki ulicy należąalezinnej dzielnicy. Opowiadająpowiznajomi, jak to zostało wszystko misternie i cudacznie urządzone* (455. RING. I/428).

14. "Powrót do gniazda rodzinnego" 455. RING. I/428. Translation by Barbara Czepek and A. N., the Polish original reads: *zamknięte ulice* (455. RING. I/428).

15. "Zamurowany" ("Walled Up") 455. RING. I/428. Translation by Barbara Czepek and A. N., the Polish original reads as follows: *Co się stało ze mną? Przecież znam tu każdą ulicę, niemal każdy dom, co drugiego człowieka. A mimo to nie poznaję ulic, nie poznaję ludzi. Nie wiem, na jakiej ulicy się znajduję, nie umiem znaleźć drogi do swego domu. Przecież stąd jest podobno do mojego domu pięć minut, a ja krążę i chodzę, i nie wiem, jak trafić do domu* (455. RING. I/428).

16. "Zamurowany" 455. RING. I/428. Translation by Barbara Czepek and A. N., the Polish original reads as follows: *Nie mogę ochłonąć z niesamowitego niepokoju i strachu, jaki mnie nagle ogarnia* (455. RING. I/428). For another in depth analysis of Różycki's study, see Kassow, *Who Will Write Our History?* 254–256.

17. Till, "Wounded Cities," 9.

18. Reemtsma, *Trust and Violence*, 57.

19. Till, "Wounded Cities," 10.

20. Leociak, *Text in the Face of Destruction*, 43.

21. See, for example, Różycki's text "Mury, mury, mury" ("Walls, walls, walls") (455. RING. I/428), or Adler, *In the Warsaw Ghetto*, 38, 114, 255. To some degree, the impression of hostility might also have been tied to the highly detrimental living conditions in the ghetto and suggest that the ghetto was a space that was generally hostile to life.

22. Till, "Wounded Cities," 10.

23. See also Levine, "Home Loss in Wartime Literature," 101.

24. Sundstrom, "Race and Place," 88, 92.

25. Ibid., 90, 92–93.

26. "Inferno" 455. RING. I/428. Translation by Barbara Czepek and A. N., the Polish original reads as follows: "*Jestem tu dopiero od kilku chwil, a już nagle załamało się coś we mnie, . . . Nie wiem, może i teraz mylę się znowu, ale jedno jest pewne: wystarczyło tych kilka chwil, aby stracić nawet resztki pogody ducha, wiary, nadziei, równowagi, wystarczyło, aby za jednym zamachem upodobnić się do wszyst-kich więźniów gettowych*" (455. RING. I/428).

27. "Inferno" 455. RING. I/428.

28. Mazor, *Vanished City*, 118–119.

29. Something similar can be seen in the case of the concentration and death camps, where prisoners describe the feeling of the entire outside world disappearing (Semprún, *Die Große Reise*, 21–23; Levi, "If This Is a Man," 122–123; Szmaglewska, *Smoke over Birkenau*, 229).

19

Topography of Violence

In the early days of German occupation, direct violence had been a factor that intensified segregation. It had forced Jews off the streets and, along with spatial regulations, had made the city less and less accessible to them. For this reason, some of the Jewish inhabitants of the city had at first actually hoped that the establishment of the ghetto would grant them a little more safety and protection, since living in a "Jewish environment," so they assumed, would lessen the number of aggressive encounters with Germans and Poles on the streets.[1] But this hope proved to be in vain. In fact, the violence became all the more intense once Jews were confined to the ghetto, with regular, indiscriminate round-ups, robberies, severe beatings, random shootings, and executions taking place in the streets, culminating in the great waves of deportations and, finally, the "liquidation" of the ghetto.[2] In the confined setting of the ghetto, this direct violence further exacerbated the inhabitants' situation. It intensified the pressure and added a crucial factor to an environment that was, for many reasons, already difficult to navigate. Violence added a necessary additional layer to people's "mental picture"[3] of their environment and, thus, made significantly more difficult the process of their spatial orientation and appropriation. Not only was it necessary to understand the physical topography of the ghetto; it was also essential to be constantly aware of the ever-changing patterns of the danger and violence that pervaded its streets.

The ability to read the increasingly dangerous environment and to react to it became more and more pressing. As Boehm explains in his introduction to *Words to Outlive Us*, "Jews especially—whether inside the ghetto or out—needed to know which neighborhoods were 'quiet,' where a roundup was being conducted, or how to navigate the sewer system to reach the Aryan side."[4] The inhabitants of the ghetto had to become "topographers," as Boehm phrases it. They had to learn to navigate the new "topography of violence" that was created through the conjunction of the specific layout of the ghetto and the violence exerted by the Germans and their auxiliary forces. In so doing, they formed both new patterns of movement and new perceptions of the meanings of particular streets and landmarks. The importance of this new spatial knowledge might also be one of the reasons why those who were not native to the city—such as deportees from rural areas, other towns, or foreign countries—fell victim to violence even more often. Being foreign to the city's layout and often precluded from essential channels of information, they were less likely to come to a sufficient understanding of their environment. Deeply disorienting and psychologically damaging though it was for locals to find their city disfigured by the imposition of the ghetto, on a practical level, they did still have some contextual knowledge of the layout of the streets and the buildings as compared to those who had never lived in the city. Moreover, those who had not experienced the dual dislocation of forced relocation from an area outside of Warsaw and, then, forced confinement within the ghetto typically had social networks that were not as much ruptured. For the same reasons, those who had already lived on the premises of the future ghetto before the war were at a certain advantage over those who were forced to relocate from other parts of the city.[5]

Before the great wave of deportations started in July 1942, there were two major categories of more-or-less unsystematic (i.e., sudden and spontaneous) violence in the streets: space-bound and mobile violence. Often, violence was tied to specific locations, such as certain intersections, the footbridges, watchtowers, or gates, as well as to streets close to places that were marked by the presence of Germans, for example, the streets leading toward the Pawiak prison. In the case of "mobile violence," the violence originated with Germans "roaming" the streets, individually or in groups, or driving by in a car or truck.[6] While there was still a chance to foresee the former—though not necessarily a chance to evade it—Germans moving through the ghetto posed a threat beyond all control, a danger that could "swoop down like a hawk" at any time.[7]

This unpredictable form of violence elicited widespread fear among the ghetto's inhabitants. Moving about in the ghetto was experienced as terrifying and "nerve-racking."[8] As Kaplan notes on October 10, 1940, "You go out trembling, full of panic lest you meet a Nazi."[9] Thus, the inhabitants of the ghetto constantly monitored their environment. In his memoir written right after his liberation from Buchenwald, Natan Żelichower recalls the conditions in the ghetto: "Everyone stayed alert. No one left home without first asking, 'What's it like out today?' Once outside, people focused trained eyes on their surroundings, searching for danger."[10] Ghetto inhabitants tried to avoid Germans at any cost. When they spotted a German or one of their cars, people did their best to flee or at least to avoid contact. Kaplan's diary is full of descriptions of such encounters. Already in May 1940, he writes, "Jewish passersby are aware of every appearance of a car whose occupants are the servants of the Führer. When they first notice it from a distance, a flight begins, an escape into the doorways of the houses. In every place they go, there is silence, and you won't find a living soul on the street. Thousands flee, but many are caught."[11] As the attacks became harsher and more frequent and the risk of severe physical harm rose, people's reactions became more and more immediate and drastic. According to Kaplan, people reacted to the appearance of a German in uniform as they would have reacted to the presence of a wild beast: "everyone crosses over to the opposite sidewalk, just as one keeps one's distance from a beast of prey."[12] These random encounters on the street reiterated again and again that even within the "Jewish" space of the ghetto, a Jewish right to space ultimately didn't exist. Jews still navigated hostile territory.

Since it became crucial to avoid the Germans, the inhabitants of the ghetto passed on crucial information and warnings to each other. Information on dangers traveled quickly in the streets. As Żelichower writes, "Pedestrians traded words of warning that could suddenly shift the direction of traffic. Mere mention of a threat, the slightest gesture, could send a crowd of several thousand back inside, leaving the street empty and bare."[13] Also, when it came to round-ups and blockades, it was of the utmost importance to locate, or better yet, to foresee, their exact locations. Accordingly, such information was the topic of many conversations. As Mawult recalls in his account, written in hiding in 1944, "You hear the same question over and over: 'Where's the roundup today?' 'Where's the Aktion?' 'How did the selection go on Gęsia?'"[14] Lewin gives a similar account, citing the "never-ending question: 'Meken do durkhgen?' ['Can one get through there?']," which, in a footnote to his posthumously published diary, _A Cup of Tears_, is explained as, "That is, is there no danger of being ambushed here? Is the street blockaded?"[15] The importance of locating danger precisely is also reflected in a particular characteristic most accounts from the ghetto share: they "abound with names of streets and districts," as Boehm observes.[16] And indeed, most testimonies are correspondingly thorough in their naming of locations.

With the addition of violence to the equation, orientation processes were rendered fundamentally and precariously dynamic. Streets and entire neighborhoods could change their status—from safe to unsafe, from passable to impassable—at any moment. In her 1985 memoir, Bauman describes how during the deportations, people adjusted their lives to the "timetable" of the _Aktionen_, leaving the house only when the daily round-ups for deportations were completed.[17] Often, the threat of violence entailed long periods in which people were unable to change location at all. When a danger was detected, but there was no way of bypassing the afflicted area, people were temporarily immobilized. As Ringelblum noted in

November 1940, "It has been taking an hour and more to get to the office lately. You have to wait at the courtyard gate a long time before the danger of seizure is past. When people are seized for forced work on Leszno Street, it is known immediately at Muranowska Street."[18] Berman reports a similar situation when, in late August 1942, due to an "*Aktion*" and the violence carried out in the streets, he was unable to cross a distance of a few meters: "Terrible things happened on the streets that evening. At seven I went next door to confer with Herman, one of the social activists; on my way back I had to wait a whole hour to cross the few steps to our building, so frightful were the scenes taking place. When I finally managed to dash across and inside our building, I could still hear the horrible cries of the murdered right outside our window."[19]

In addition to all the difficulties caused by the confusing layout of the ghetto, the factor of violence created variable blockages, necessitated additional detours, and caused long periods of waiting and hiding. The fear of violence changed the way the environment was perceived and navigated. Over the course of the ghetto's existence, it became the main factor informing people's movements in the streets. The question was now less how to get from one place to another in the sense of connectivity and mobility and more how to get anywhere safely. Fear dominated spatial appropriation.

Another structural element added to people's internal street map was the certain locations where people were particularly at risk of becoming victims of abuse. In these cases, it was the meaning associated with a place that changed due to the violence that was exerted there. Sentries positioned at the ghetto exits or at the footbridges were one such hazard. The sentries' presence and propensity for violence led to a general shift in the meaning of these locations: while their communicative function—letting people pass through—was drastically reduced, their relevance as locations of physical danger increased.[20] For most people, they became danger zones and landmarks of fear. As Berg describes in her diary on February 27, 1942, "Shootings have now become very frequent at the ghetto exits. Usually, they are perpetrated by some guard who wants to amuse himself. Every day, morning and afternoon, when I go to school, I am not sure whether I will return alive. I have to go past two of the most dangerous German sentry posts: at the corner of Zelazna and Chlodna Streets near the bridge and at the corner of Krochmalna and Grzybowska Street."[21]

It was, however, not the presence of sentry posts alone that rendered certain locations particularly dangerous. Often, the particular spatial layout created by the walls also significantly increased people's vulnerability. This was the case at the passage at Żelazna/Chłodna Street, connecting the small and the large ghetto. Due to the narrowness of the passage and the heavy traffic passing through, avoiding contact with the Germans was almost impossible at this chokepoint, and herded as they were in a dense crowd, people had not much room to evade abuse. They were directly exposed while in the passage.[22] But since it was the only point of crossing between the two parts of the ghetto, people often still had to risk using it.[23] Mazor describes the experience of crossing:

> On approaching this intersection, the Jews could not help but feel feverish agitation. The crowd would pack in, and everyone would try to squeeze inside in order not to be exposed to the blows of the Germans. For this reason, movement slowed, and the riding crops came down all the more furiously on the hapless outsiders. What is more, it was routine for these defenseless people to be humiliated. The policemen would pick some poor wretch from the crowd at random, and force him to do calisthenics while beating him mercilessly, or in winter make him kneel in the puddles of melting snow.[24]

The fact that, knowing very well what to expect, people still had to somehow pass through, is paradigmatic for the general dilemma the inhabitants of the ghetto faced. Even at a point where the streets had become extremely dangerous and violence had reached a peak, people had many different reasons that forced them to take their chances outside—be it to see close friends or family, to acquire food, or to work. Lewin discusses this dilemma in a diary entry on August 25, 1942, at the height of the Great Deportation *Aktion*. Even though it was extremely dangerous for him to go from his place of work at 30 Gęsia Street to where he could see his daughter at 14 Pawia Street—again a distance of only one block—he simply felt unable to stay put. He expresses his despair, asking himself, "And how can I not go and see Ora? Especially when I am tortured with worry over her fate and that of the remainder of my family. I will certainly go and take the risk."[25]

Karmelicka Street is another example that demonstrates how the layout of the ghetto could essentially force people to expose themselves to violence. Because the "streets parallel to it on both sides were Aryan,"[26] Karmelicka itself became the only north-south connector in a certain section of the ghetto. Thus, one inevitably passed along it when crossing from the southern to the northern part. But Karmelicka also "offered a very convenient path toward the historic Pawiak prison," as Mazor notes, thus becoming a very common route for German trucks on their way to the prison.[27] According to Kaplan, the street was "always ripe for acts of savagery."[28] The layout created by the ghetto boundary, in connection with the street's proximity to a location frequented by Germans, created a similar dilemma as in the case of Chłodna Street, in that people were forced to use the street despite the increased risk. Mazor highlights another aspect that turned Karmelicka into a particularly perilous street—its narrowness: "The street was very narrow, and the Germans, armed with wooden or iron sticks whose length reached both sidewalks, would amuse themselves, from atop their trucks, by

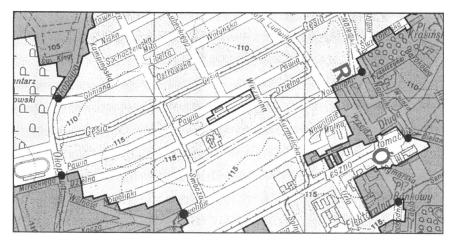

Fig. 19.1. Pawiak Prison and its vicinity, including Karmelicka, Dzielna, and Więzienna Streets.

hitting passersby over the head. Many received skull fractures. On hearing the trucks approach, people would flee on all sides and hide under the carriage entrances, but the narrowness of the street forced them to huddle together, creating an excellent target for the Germans."[29] Karmelicka's highly disadvantageous setup, in combination with the overcrowding and the new topography, rendered the street, essentially, a trap.

Generally, the ghetto inhabitants considered the vicinity of the Pawiak prison particularly dangerous. In addition to Karmelicka, this also included Dzielna Street, as well as Więzienna, a small alleyway next to the prison. Both were frequently used by German vehicles going to and coming from the prison. As Kaplan writes about Dzielna Street in May 1942, "The traffic of the Nazi hangmen in that street never stops, and every time a Nazi car goes by, its passengers beat the Jew they encounter with the whips they carry in their hands."[30] Similarly, the ghetto's inhabitants regarded the little north-south alley, Więzienna, that ran along the side of the prison as dangerous. According to Lewin, the guards randomly arrested people on this street, taking them straight to Pawiak, from where many never returned.[31] Others were killed on the spot or severely beaten.[32] Lewin calls Więzienna a "deadly" and "infamous" alleyway,[33] indicating precisely the new meaning that had been added to the city streets by the use of violence.

The space of the ghetto was not only pervaded by violence but also enabled it. Ghettoization forced the Jewish community into spatial configurations that made it very difficult to evade abuse and violence. People were no longer able to navigate space freely. Thus, their capacity to cope with the already highly disadvantageous environment was further reduced. Violence increasingly defined the space of the ghetto so that, in the end, it was basically uninhabitable. Although designated as "Jewish" space by the Germans, Jews ultimately could not own it.

Notes

1. Adler, *In the Warsaw Ghetto*, 33, 53, 220–221; see also Gutman, *Jews of Warsaw*, 66.

2. For a more detailed description of such acts of violence, see, for example, Lewin, *Cup of Tears*, 70, 71, 73, 77, 79, 90, 96, 114, 118, 119, 123, 126, 131, 146, 150; Kaplan, *Scroll of Agony*, 144, 241–242, 246–247, 331–332, 339–340, 343–345, 360–361, 363; Ringelblum, *Notes from the Warsaw Ghetto*, 86, 88, 248, 266; Berg, *Diary of Mary Berg*, 86, 129–130, 151; Stok, account, 51; or Berman, account, 146.

3. Lynch, *Image of the City*, 4.

4. Boehm, "Introduction," 3.

5. Mazor, *Vanished City*, 47–48. Those who had lived outside of the ghetto area beforehand, however, potentially had closer contacts to the "Aryan" side.

6. Lewin, *Cup of Tears*, 150, 168; see also Bauman, *Winter in the Morning*, 45; Żelichower, account, 47; Stok, account, 51; Berman, account, 146; Ringelblum, *Notes from the Warsaw Ghetto*, 53.

7. Żelichower, account, 47.

8. Hasenfus, account, 35.

9. Kaplan, *Scroll of Agony*, 206.

10. Żelichower, account, 46.

11. Kaplan, *Scroll of Agony*, 145.

12. Ibid., 334.

13. Żelichower, account, 46–47; see also Berg, *Diary*, 17–18.

14. Mawult, account, 113.

15. Lewin, *Cup of Tears*, 137.

16. Boehm, "Introduction," 3–4.

17. Bauman, *Winter in the Morning*, 67.

18. Ringelblum, *Notes from the Warsaw Ghetto*, 83–84.

19. Berman, account, 146; for the description of a similar incident, see also Berg, *Diary*, 89.

20. See also Leociak, *Text in the Face of Destruction*, 46–47.

21. Berg, *Diary*, 129–130.

22. On November 19, 1940, this leads Kaplan to the following assessment: "In reality we have not one ghetto, but two, and there is almost no connection between them. For the sake of accuracy, I must point out that actually there is one connection but I consider it nonexistent because it is too difficult to use" (*Scroll of Agony*, 225).

23. Adler, *In the Warsaw Ghetto*, 115.

24. Mazor, *Vanished City*, 116; see also Adler, *In the Warsaw Ghetto*, 115.

25. Lewin, *Cup of Tears*, 167.

26. Mazor, *Vanished City*, 116.

27. Ibid. Because Pawiak also served as a place of imprisonment for people interrogated by the Gestapo on Aleja Szucha, prisoners were transported every day between Pawiak and Szucha.

28. Kaplan, *Scroll of Agony*, 241.

29. Mazor, *Vanished City*, 116–117.

30. Kaplan, *Scroll of Agony*, 331.

31. Lewin, *Cup of Tears*, 69–70.

32. Kaplan, *Scroll of Agony*, 90.

33. Lewin, *Cup of Tears*, 90, 97.

Public Violence

Violence destabilized the living situation in the ghetto by making the environment increasingly unpredictable. It therefore disrupted attempts to claim ownership of the space the Jewish population was forced to inhabit. By publicly displaying their violence, the Germans furthered this process. Beatings and acts of humiliation, but also shootings and an ever-increasing number of executions, were performed openly in the streets. Social and cultural anthropologist Freek Colombijn emphasizes the "performative element" inherent to such public violence. Since, as Colombijn notes with reference to Goran Aijmer, "violence is an idiom . . . through which messages are conveyed," it always also communicates something to the "audience," the third party in Strathern and Stewart's "triangle of violence."[1] And indeed, the killings had an immense impact on the inhabitants of the ghetto, who became helpless bystanders while at the same time being concerned parties to every act of violence. Everyone was always also a potential victim.

People communicated incidents widely, noting down names of the victims and locations of the incidents most carefully in diaries and memoirs. There were numerous authors who, when documenting some of the countless acts of violence, put great effort into accurately listing the victims' names as well as the exact circumstances of the events. In addition to chronicling the atrocities committed by the Nazis, these detailed lists seem also often to work as some form of memento for all those who fell victim to their aggression. Violence was overtly present and clearly left a mark on people's perception of the streets around them, both psychologically and quite literally. In June 1942, Kaplan recounts several incidents of people being executed "in broad daylight in the sight of hundreds of passersby" and, again, "in broad daylight, while hundreds of ghetto dwellers are witnesses."[2] As did many others who chronicled such events, he also reports that the Germans left lying in the streets the people whom they had executed at night: "Last night, fourteen people were shot to death in the streets of the ghetto. In the morning, their naked corpses were found near the gates of the houses."[3] The killings were not hidden. On the contrary, the Germans used the public space of the streets to display their violence. Both Ringelblum and Stok assume that this was intended to serve the specific purpose of terrorizing the inhabitants of the ghetto. In this context, Ringelblum reports an incident that took place in May 1942: "At night they [four Jewish men, "Slar, Feist, Zaks . . . and Tenenbaum"] were taken out of the Pawia Street prison and shot outdoors, each in a different street. This shooting of people in the streets has become a deliberate tactic since April. The aim: to terrify the populace, to terrorize them."[4] The fact that each of the four people was shot in a different street is, for Ringelblum, not a random occurrence but, rather, a strategic choice.[5] In that context, the shootings are deciphered as a message, a threat. The fact that the victims' bodies were found dispersed among different locations implies that the message, too, was meant to be spread out. The two-step process—first, to take the victims from the closed environment of the prison to the public space of the streets, and second, to spread their bodies out over the terrain of the ghetto—corroborates this conclusion. The spatial element thus becomes crucial for the scope of the Nazi terror. It is the spatial component that turned a "simple" act of violence into an act of communication, amplifying its potential to instill terror. Applying Popitz's concept of "binding power of action," the implicit threat of the gesture can, furthermore, be seen as a demonstration of power to assert German rule.[6]

The Germans occasionally also used the ghetto streets for the execution of non-Jewish victims. "Polish youths" were brought to the ghetto and shot there.[7] Kaplan, who did not know that, in fact, many non-Jewish Poles were also executed on the "Aryan" side, concludes that the Germans did not want to provoke the Poles. In the context of one of these shootings, he reflects, "Why was this man brought to the ghetto to be killed? In order not to irritate the Aryans. . . . His relatives know only that he has been arrested, not that he has been killed, and his body is taken to the Jewish cemetery."[8] Kaplan assumes that for people outside the walls, the ghetto was opaque and that, as a result, what happened inside the walls had very little effect on the outside. In fact, it is precisely Kaplan's own lack of knowledge about the executions taking place on the other side of the wall that shows the degree to which the two worlds were decoupled (although, of course, the sheer proximity, as well as the few remaining channels of communication and exchange, ruled out a complete separation). Kaplan's interpretation also shows how, in the absence of information about the outside world, the actual Warsaw under occupation was replaced by an imaginary. Yet although Kaplan's interpretation is flawed as a result of missing information, it is still true that the level of violence and suffering inflicted on both sides of the walls differed. The standards of what was possible and what was not varied between the two spheres. Like the camp, the ghetto also became a "space of exception" in Agamben's sense.[9]

The fact that people in the ghetto were often unable to detect a pattern to the violence made it particularly threatening. According to Kaplan, people were constantly puzzling over the system behind the nightly arrests and subsequent shootings. On May 26, 1942—before the Germans started the Great Deportation *Aktion* and violence swept through the ghetto much more broadly and indiscriminately—Kaplan writes in his diary about a list with the names of those who were going to be killed on a certain night, but he remains uncertain about the reasons why anyone would end up on the list:

> There are lists of "suspects," and for everyone on the list the sentence is death. The condemned is not arrested beforehand, nor interrogated and examined, nor brought to judgement. Following their list, the killers enter his home and order him to go—they don't say where or why. When they get outside, the one marked for death is ordered to walk ahead, and the executioners remain behind him. Not many moments pass before a shot is heard. The sentence has been carried out wordlessly. The killers disappear. The corpse of the victim lies in the dust of the streets until the morning light.[10]

A few days later, Kaplan elaborates on the fact that the inhabitants of the ghetto were particularly distraught because they could not identify the system behind the killings.[11] People were desperate to find the common motive, because "[if] there is a motive, there is a possibility of estimating the proximity of individual danger."[12] The fact that it was impossible to locate the precise danger, to assess its "proximity," created a feeling of helplessness. Just as with all attempts to foresee violence or to react to it in the streets, the search for a pattern of violence was ultimately an attempt to regain control. The fact that this proved to be impossible intensified the effects of the German terror. The dead bodies left behind on the street were a constant reminder of a fate that could befall anyone at any time. Ultimately, most people failed in their attempts to protect themselves by reading the new topography. The violence they faced remained too unpredictable and overwhelming.

Notes

1. Colombijn, "Production of Urban Space by Violence," 70.
2. Kaplan, *Scroll of Agony*, 360, see also 376.
3. Ibid., 363, see also 339; Bauman, *Winter in the Morning*, 50; Berman, account, 144.
4. Ringelblum, *Notes from the Warsaw Ghetto*, 266.
5. Stok comes to a similar conclusion when describing a wave of killings during the first days of the Great Deportation in July 1942: "People turned pale with fright,

which is what the Germans wanted: to terrorize and disorient us completely" (account, 103).

6. Popitz, *Phenomena of Power*, 28.

7. Kaplan, *Scroll of Agony*, 376.

8. Ibid.

9. Agamben, "What Is a Camp?" 40.

10. Kaplan, *Scroll of Agony*, 339.

11. In his study on the ghetto *The Jews of Warsaw 1939–1943*, Gutman also addresses the puzzlement of the ghetto inhabitants in regard to the German motives and the pattern of the killings. Referring specifically to the "Night of Blood" (April 18, 1942), he summarizes, "After the operation, the ghetto was haunted by questions. What did the Nazis hope to achieve by murdering dozens of ghetto residents? And what was the common denominator that established the victims of such calculated murder?" (*Jews of Warsaw*, 176). The broad spectrum of social background made it difficult to explain the events. Most commonly, to Gutman, the killings were interpreted as an act targeting the political underground or, more specifically, the underground press. According to Gutman, some underground organizations believed that the Germans' actions were part of a "broader strategy," a "more pervasive Nazi plan" (ibid., 179). Noticing that similar killings took place in other ghettos as well (even when the activities of political groups and clandestine press were not worth mentioning), it was assumed that the "Night of Blood" was the prelude to a bigger *Aktion*, meant to "heighten the sense of psychological stress, instigate internal conflict, and thus further weaken the ghetto from within" (ibid.). The killings were also interpreted as a preventive action, undermining potential resistance.

12. Kaplan, *Scroll of Agony*, 349.

Sound of the Ghetto

In her work *Nazi Soundscapes*, media studies scholar Carolyn Birdsall refers to R. Murray Schafer's 1977 study *The Soundscape: Our Sonic Environment and the Tuning of the World* to argue for the historical value of "earwitnessing within site-specific contexts."[1] According to Birdsall, the concept of the "earwitness" is based on "the premise that the sounds heard in a given place are as distinctive and as important as the things to be seen there. In other words, the soundscape can be studied to gain insights into social organisation, power relations and interactions with urban space."[2] And indeed, life in the ghetto also had a distinct aural dimension, and many accounts from the ghetto capture that along with visual impressions. As Kaplan notes, "The streets of the Jewish quarters are full of noise."[3] There were, for example, the insistent calls of the street hawkers,[4] the voices of "wailing children who . . . beg[ged] for alms,"[5] the "monotonous, unrelenting, continuous lament of the beggars,"[6] the "hum of conversations and quarrels,"[7] the turmoil created by acts of thievery, as well as musicians who were "giving . . . concerts in the street" to earn a living.[8]

Very often, the specific sound of the ghetto streets is described by the ghetto inhabitants as one intrinsically bound to violence. Round-ups, arrests, shootings, and beatings elicited expressions of fear, pain, and distress. When, in February 1941, Kaplan describes how an act of violence set a crowd in the street in motion, he also notices the acoustic dimension of this event. He writes about the "terrible sound of a mass of people moving, like the roaring of the sea."[9] Here, the sound of the masses in movement is indistinct, almost nonhuman. Bauman dehumanizes the sound of the street even further, attributing it to the street itself: "The streets moan and yell with a thousand voices."[10] Both descriptions suggest that there was a certain background noise created by a population under constant threat. This noise was not that of an individual and not necessarily that of a specific, clearly identifiable sequence of events. Rather, it was a result of the immense density and misery of a large number of people forced into the ghetto and exposed to severe acts of violence.

In other cases, the descriptions are much more specific. In her 1967 memoir, Birenbaum recalls a round-up that she had watched from her window: "The coarse abuse and curses of the Nazi soldiery mingled with the shrieks and cries of the wounded, and the panic-stricken clatter of feet running away."[11] The utterances of agitation again highlight the fact that violence and panic often have an acoustic dimension. At the same time, the sounds that Birenbaum remembers give a clear outline of the events, presenting different actors and their condition. They encapsulate a sequence of violence that can be identified even without any visual context. A similar description can be found in Szajn-Lewin's account. She concludes the description of her experiences during one of the *Blockaden* with a list of condensed acoustic impressions: "on the street—screams, whistles, weeping."[12] Although the list is very short, it still permits identification of different actors (those responsible for the whistles, conversely, for the weeping) and indicates violence, both performed and endured (screams/weeping). In both cases, the observing party is removed from the scene of violence, sharing with the reader not what they see of the events but what they hear. And although the picture might thereby become a little less precise, anxiety and fear are conveyed to no lesser degree.

Both the background noise of the crowded streets and the specific sounds of an individual incident have in common that they intensified the general atmosphere of terror and anxiety. The humming of the crowd was a constant reminder of the densely packed conditions of the ghetto, and the myriad utterances of misery and distress a reiteration of the dire fate of those confined to the ghetto. The sounds of round-ups, beatings, shootings, and arrests were also, in and of themselves, experienced as a threat. And this is what makes these sounds especially significant from a spatial perspective: often, the sounds of violence had a much farther reach than the acts themselves, penetrating into spaces that were removed from the actual scene of events. Their reach was not limited to what the individual could see, and it affected people even when they were in hiding or fleeing from the site of the disaster. Adolf (Abram) Berman describes how, after he managed to get away from a dangerous and brutal nightly round-up, he could "still hear the horrible cries of the murdered right outside our window."[13] Even after he escaped, the threatening sound persisted, reiterating the proximity of danger. This experience was especially drastic for those in hiding. Often, people could hear the sound of the German search parties going through streets and apartment houses for hours on end, knowing that discovery would mean certain death.[14]

Birenbaum recalls in her memoir, "I knew that every sound that reached us from the street, every slightest rustle, could decide my life or death. When the noise of a 'campaign' drew near, I silently prayed that the Nazis would not find us."[15] Similarly, for most people, the Ghetto Uprising was, in fact, mainly the sound of fighting heard from a bunker.[16]

Often, the acoustic element was described as haunting, as pressing in on people even when they were trying to evade the harsh realities of their environment. In his study *Text in the Face of Destruction*, Leociak gives a very vivid description of this: "The untamed hubble of the street came in through the window of Henryka Łazowert's flat. 'The street. And now, while I'm writing to you, it's here with me in the room,' she noted in a letter to Roman Kołoniecki, sketching for him a whole gallery of singing, importunate, starving beggars. In the picture she paints, the almost aggressive presence of the yelling streets in the writer's room is striking, as is her feeling of being cornered, of being sucked in."[17]

Sounds made the physical boundaries more permeable, rendering the lines between inside and outside porous and, thereby, removing protection. In Łazowert's description, the street is intruding into the home, and the outside world is pressing in on the author, leaving almost no room to evade it. In the context of the ghetto and the analysis of its spaces, the accounts of "earwitnessing" found in diaries and memoirs not only can provide a more nuanced depiction of the individual experience but also highlight to what degree the space of the ghetto was pervaded by the misery and violence the Germans inflicted on the Jews. Through the acoustic dimension, the conditions on the ghetto street infiltrated the private space and became basically omnipresent.

Notes

1. Birdsall, *Nazi Soundscapes*, 12.
2. Ibid.
3. Kaplan, *Scroll of Agony*, 166.
4. Kermish, *To Live with Honor and Die with Honor!*, 153.
5. Ringelblum, *Notes from the Warsaw Ghetto*, 241.
6. Adler, *In the Warsaw Ghetto*, 41.
7. Kermish, *To Live with Honor and Die with Honor!*, 153.
8. Ringelblum, *Notes from the Warsaw Ghetto*, 283.
9. Kaplan, *Scroll of Agony*, 241.
10. Bauman, *Winter in the Morning*, 63.
11. Birenbaum, *Hope Is the Last to Die*, 12.
12. Szajn-Lewin, *Aufzeichnungen aus dem Warschauer Ghetto*, 12. There is no English version of Szajn-Lewin's memoirs. Translation by A. N., the German's original reads as follows: "*auf der Straße—Schreie, Pfiffe, Weinen.*"
13. Berman, account, 146.

14. Bauman, *Winter in the Morning*, 68–69, 94; Birenbaum, *Hope Is the Last to Die*, 31–32; Adler, *In the Warsaw Ghetto*, 314–315.

15. Birenbaum, *Hope Is the Last to Die*, 32.

16. For descriptions of the events of the January 18–22, 1943, deportations and the ensuing fighting as witnessed from hiding, see, for example, Bauman, *Winter in the Morning*, 94, 96; or Adler, *In the Warsaw Ghetto*, 314–315.

17. Leociak, *Text in the Face of Destruction*, 54. For a similar description, see Ringelblum, *Notes from the Warsaw Ghetto*, 158; Leociak, *Text in the Face of Destruction*, 148.

22

Deserted Apartments

In his article "The Topography of Fear," architectural scholar Donald Kunze quotes from Aldo Rossi's work *The Architecture of the City* to begin his analysis of the uncanny sight of bombed-out houses: "Anyone who remembers European cities after the bombings of the last war retains an image of disemboweled houses where, amid the rubble, fragments of familiar places remain standing, with their colors of faded wallpaper, laundry hanging suspended in the air, barking dogs—the untidy intimacy of places."[1] What Kunze describes in the following is how the "half-room, with doors opening onto canyons and interiors exposed to the unforgiving elements, as well as an equally callous public view" basically resembles a movie set, or a theatrical stage. But in the case of the war-damaged house, the "audience is a scandal." Kunze explains, "The fourth wall is an 'inside frame,' which converts the inside to the outside. The eye's invasion of the private interior inverts visibility, space, time, and causality."[2] What Kunze highlights in Rossi's quote is the "untidy intimacy" that becomes visible to an outsider who is not entitled to this sight. Both authors imply that the very act of seeing is in this case a violation of said intimacy. The eye enters a space that is not meant for an outsider; it "invades," as Kunze phrases it, the privacy of the home, a home that is already violated by destruction and that might actually demand not only cover but also piety.[3]

While there is a parallel to the destruction done by the German bombardment during the siege of Warsaw, in the case of the ghetto it is especially the sight of the apartments of those evicted and/or deported that accounts from within the walls refer to. As an unidentified woman explains in her testimony, most "of the abandoned apartments had been left open," and if they were locked "the doors were taken off their hinges or broken down."[4] Apartments were looted by the

German SS and police forces or their auxiliaries but also by people coming from the "Aryan" side.[5] Courtyards and streets were cluttered with the belongings of people who had been deported, household items scattered everywhere.[6] Berg describes such a street scene in her diary on January 17, 1943:

> At ten in the morning, we left the Pawiak in trucks. The streets of the ghetto were empty and dead. In many houses the windows were wide open despite the cold, and the curtains fluttered in the wind. Inside one could see the overturned furniture, broken cupboard doors, clothes, and linen lying on the floor. The looters and murderers had left their mark.
>
> The doors of many stores were ajar, and merchandise chaotically littered the counters. Some streets were strewn with furniture and broken china.[7]

Passing an evicted building, one of the "empty houses with the air of a grave-yard" as Lewin calls them,[8] people were confronted with the remains of the households of those who had been violently torn from their homes. They could see what was once carefully preserved, now trampled, shattered, and scattered on the ground. These apartments were the epitome of their inhabitants' fate, reflecting the violence that had been exerted against them. As Bauman observes in the case of a friend's apartment, "The flat he shared with strangers stood open, deserted. The usual signs of violence and plundering told me my friend's tragic story."[9] In addition, the deserted apartments were also a constant reminder of the lives that had been destroyed, and they exposed both the privacy and the violation of the "people who once lived and worked there" to every passerby.[10]

Notes

1. Rossi, *Architecture of the City*, 22; see also Kunze, "Topography of Fear," 176.
2. Kunze, "Topography of Fear," 176.
3. See also Levine, "Home Loss in Wartime Literature," 103.
4. Anonymous Woman, account, 137.
5. Ibid.; Lewin, *Cup of Tears*, 151–153.
6. Lewin, *Cup of Tears*, 160; see also Leociak, *Text in the Face of Destruction*, 52.
7. Berg, *Diary*, 209.
8. Lewin, *Cup of Tears*, 194.
9. Bauman, *Winter in the Morning*, 95.
10. Lewin, *Cup of Tears*, 201.

Death Space

Although the Germans sometimes specifically targeted individual people for arrests, hostage-taking, or executions, German violence was more often indiscriminate, targeting people randomly. And while there were many cases of chance encounters that ended fatally for the Jewish victims, the most common pattern by which the Germans selected their victims was, in fact, spatial. In the case of the Nalewki 9 massacre, for example, the fifty-three men who were shot by the Germans in retaliation for the escape of Pinchas Jankiel Zylberger were taken from the building he had lived in. The Germans "went from apartment to apartment arresting all the men they found."[1] These victims had no particular relationship to Zylberger; some of them had not even lived in the building but merely visited.[2] On November 30, 1939, when Kaplan discusses the incident in his diary, he notes that the victims were largely "frightened merchants and landlords; some were learned in Torah and others just plain Jews whose eyes and hearts were turned only toward their dwindling businesses"; neither of the individuals was in any way involved in acts of rebellion as the Germans had claimed. In fact, according to Kaplan, the victims didn't even know Zylberberg, had "perhaps never seen [him] before . . . and if they knew him they had no dealings with him."[3] Kaplan elaborates,

> In every courtyard in Warsaw there live various elements, and two neighbors who are separated by only a thin wall might not know each other even after many years of living side by side. What does a merchant who is mainly occupied with his business have to do with a ne'er-do-well who lives in the same courtyard and whose occupation is theft and robbery? But there is no place for legal logic when there is an excuse to bring catastrophe upon fifty-three Jewish families. All those who lived in the courtyard were imprisoned and taken to an unknown place. After two weeks, they were all shot.[4]

By pointing out the lack of connection between the accused Zylberberg and the fifty-three victims, Kaplan focuses on the individual case, on personal relations and on the legitimacy—or rather lack of legitimacy—of the German actions. He calls the logic he summons "legal" and stresses that there are no grounds for associating the victims with the thief sought by the Germans. Thus, he implies, there are no grounds for holding them accountable for Zylberberg's deeds. But Kaplan himself notes that the Germans do not adhere to such logic. In fact, what the incident shows is that the Germans did not relate to Jewish people as individuals in the first place. To them, as David B. Clarke, Markus A. Doehl, and Francis X. McDonough point out, "millions of heterogeneous human bodies came to be categorized as one of 'the jews'";[5] thus, distinction did not matter. Correspondingly, all arguments pertaining to personal relations, to actual behavior, or even to potential guilt were of no concern to the Nazis. While Zylberger was indeed wanted for a particular offense, the ensuing victims were picked haphazardly. The Nazis chose them by proximity and practicability. While in some cases collective punishment indeed targeted the family of an accused person,[6] mostly the victims were chosen randomly from among those living in the same apartment, building, or street. The Nazis' passed their sentence on them based merely on their location.[7]

Following a similar logic, people were rounded up by apartment or street during the Great Deportation *Aktion*. When Lewin writes on August 1, 1942, "Germans are in the process of emptying whole buildings and sides of streets," it is the sheer number of people implicated by the German strategy that shocks Lewin. He continues, "They took about 5,000 people out of 20–2 and other buildings on Nowolipie Street."[8] But his note also indicates the main principle by which the victims were targeted. During the deportations, accounts abound with the names of streets and entire blocks that were cleared by the Germans.[9] Bauman describes how a round-up would typically play out: "Now the Nazis, keenly helped by the Ukrainian and Latvian troops as well as by the Jewish police, launched a systematic house-to-house hunt. Houses were surrounded by the troops, all gates and exits blocked, residents summoned to the back yards. Their documents were checked. . . . Meanwhile, the flats were searched; anybody found hiding was, as a rule, killed on the spot."[10]

During the round-ups, the Nazis and their Ukrainian and Latvian auxiliary troops were again not concerned with the individual; they categorized the victims by their papers, which at this point became equivalent to the decision of whether they should live or die.[11] This categorization was paralleled by the creation of two different types of space: first, spaces that were "cleared" and thus became spaces antithetic to life, and second, spaces assigned to the people who were allowed to remain in the ghetto, spaces of work and production. The former, emptied of their inhabitants, became a prohibited zone; as the unidentified woman whose account is preserved at the Jewish Historical Institute phrases it, "No one was permitted back inside the houses of death."[12] Those who were found in them after the round-up were killed.[13] During the deportations, some people consciously chose this fate, as Berg describes in her diary: "A large number of people barricaded themselves in their apartments, choosing to die at home rather than in the camp."[14] After the deportations, the Nazis turned whole areas of the ghetto into a no-man's land (commonly called "wild"[15] territory by the inhabitants). This territory housed only those who, by Nazi definition, had lost their right to live. Mawult explains,

> The buildings inside the district that are not assigned to any workshops are now beyond jurisdiction. They do not exist. No one can live there or even visit them; they are "wild" houses. But it would be a mistake to assume they're empty. The wild houses are occupied by wild people—people with no official living space, no papers, no workshop—old people, and women with children. They live in secret. They spend their days hiding in some secret place with a hidden entrance, a cubbyhole or a garret, and only emerge in the early morning and in the evening.[16]

The paradox of a space that "does not exist," where no one "can live," but that is still very much alive and inhabited by people is emblematic of the ghetto's last months. It is the space of people who, according to the Nazi logic, did not exist anymore either. It thus, to some extent, resembles the space of the death camps, in that everyone who was in it was already "ontologically" dead, as historian Boaz Neumann phrases it. Neumann suggests that the Jews, in fact, did not "lose" their right to live at some point but, according to the Nazi *Weltanschauung*, were not part of what was considered life in the first place.[17] In this sense, Neumann argues, for the Nazis the Jews were essentially already dead, even if they "happened" to still be alive physically.[18] In the case of the "wild" territory, the space people lived in was quite literally a "*Todesraum*" (death space)[19] in the sense that the territory coincided with a pending death sentence that applied to every Jew the Germans caught in it, no matter their "official" status. Death occurred as "*future antérieur*," as Neumann puts it, as an accomplished future ("*vollendete Zukunft*").[20]

The few people officially allowed to remain in the ghetto were concentrated in the working areas of the factories and shops. The spaces of work and production were strictly limited and confined; within them, freedom of movement was strongly restricted. Lewin writes in his diary on October 5, 1942,

> We spend the whole day at the "shop." We are not allowed on the street during the day at all. The street casts a pall over the chance passer-by or over those

who march in groups. Not a living soul to be seen. The streets are deserted, streets that were once humming with bustling crowds of Jews, like a bee-hive.

The head of the Jewish community has issued an order that no one at all is permitted south of Leszno Street and during working hours no one is permitted into the small ghetto. Anyone found in the street without a special permit will be deported from Warsaw, to their death.[21]

In October 1942, the Germans issued an order that forbade workers to "walk alone in the streets, irrespective of the hours."[22] As a result, Jewish life took place almost exclusively in the workshops and the workers' apartments; movement outside was strictly regulated. The workers, as Lewin notes, were "shut up all day in the workshop" only to march in groups to their "blocks" after their shift had ended.[23] Summing up the new conditions, Berg concludes that the "ghetto is now nothing but a huge labor camp."[24] Also, people were very much "exposed," as Bauman notes.[25] Everyone moving about in the ghetto streets became clearly visible. In addition, the Germans and their auxiliary forces had easy access to the workshops and their housing, which substantially facilitated seizure. Therefore, some people decided to move to the "wild" areas, even though they had found employment in a shop. Bauman explains, "They [Jadwiga and Stefan] survived the registration but left the factory soon after and settled in a deserted attic in the police block, staying there as 'wilds.' They thought it was better to go into hiding than stay exposed and defenseless in the factory."[26] While the factories initially promised some security, their status was, in fact, very unstable, and people were eventually rounded up right from their workspace. Papers that had guaranteed exemption from deportations could turn worthless in a fraction of a second.[27] The space that was officially "living space," both literally and figuratively, was ultimately a holding area for deportations. People sensed that space created by the Germans was not to be trusted. Therefore, as Mawult recalls, more and more people decided to hide, "following the advice a certain German gave a Jew who was proudly showing his papers with all the proper seals and signatures: '*Du dummer Kerl! Das ist alles Quatsch! Der beste Ausweis ist und bleibt der Keller-Ausweis!*'—You dummy! That is all just a lot of rubbish. The best document around is and always will be the cellar."[28]

Ultimately, every space the Germans had access to became hostile to Jewish life. Only spaces specifically designed to evade the German clutches offered a chance of survival. Adler observes, "Thus it was that the only course of action that gave a fair promise of survival was hiding in a shelter and this method of passive defence became universally sought out."[29] Burrowed into the structures of their previous habitation, these bunkers and hideouts were the last self-created living space most of the ghetto inhabitants would ever inhabit. At this point, living space had, however, long ceased to be anything resembling a home.

Notes

1. Gutman, *Jews of Warsaw*, 32.
2. Ibid.
3. Kaplan, *Scroll of Agony*, 80.
4. Ibid.
5. Clarke, Doel, and McDonough, "Holocaust Topologies," 459.
6. Kaplan, *Scroll of Agony*, 107.
7. This was a common pattern all over occupied Poland and applied both to those non-Jewish Poles who were helping Jews and to those who were accused of sabotage or resistance. The principle of collective punishment instrumentalized the fear and the instinct of self-preservation of neighbors to turn them against those who were defying German orders.
8. Lewin, *Cup of Tears*, 144–145.
9. Lewin, for example, lists during the course of a few days: July 23, 1942: "Buildings are being blockaded. 23 Twarda Street. Terrible scenes" (*Cup of Tears*, 136); July 24, 1942: "Buildings on Karmelicka and Nowolipie Streets are being surrounded" (ibid.); July 26, 1942: "The buildings at 10–12 Nowolipie Street are surrounded" (ibid., 138); August 7, 1942: "In the evening they drove out the people from the flats in the square bounded by Dzielna, Zamenhof, Nowolipki and Karmelicka Streets" (ibid., 148–149).
10. Bauman, *Winter in the Morning*, 68.
11. Of all those participating in the round-ups, only the members of the Jewish police force had a personal relationship to the individuals they rounded up for deportation.
12. Anonymous Woman, account, 140.
13. Bauman, *Winter in the Morning*, 69; Lewin, *Cup of Tears*, 145.
14. Berg, *Diary*, 180; see also Bauman, *Winter in the Morning*, 68.
15. The Polish word "*dziki*" can also be translated as "unlisted" or "unauthorized."
16. Mawult, account, 127; see also Lewin, *Cup of Tears*, 157–158.
17. Neumann, *Die Weltanschauung des Nazismus*, 34–35.
18. Ibid., 14. For a similar argument, see Clarke, Doel, and McDonough, "Holocaust Topologies," 458–459, 475.
19. Aldor, qtd. in Cole, *Holocaust City*, 7.
20. Neumann, *Die Weltanschauung des Nazismus*, 40.
21. Lewin, *Cup of Tears*, 187. The footnote to this passage explains: "This order was dated 28 Sept. and bears the signature of the head of the *Judenrat*. It forbade the presence of Jews south of a line from Franciszkańska to Gęsia Streets unless they were on their way to work and accompanied by police. North of this line, in the now-diminished ghetto, Jews were forbidden to be in the streets during work hours. Peddling, gathering and aimless wandering were also prohibited" (ibid., 291; see also Engelking and Leociak, *Warsaw Ghetto*, 96). Gutman summarizes a similar order by von Sammern-Frankenegg (at this point SS and police commander of Warsaw),

dating a bit earlier (September 14). The order specifies that factories and housing in the ghetto should "constitute a single, closed unit . . . surrounded by walls or appropriate barriers." The Jewish workers were forbidden to leave this area, and in case housing and factories were not adjacent to one another, they were to be escorted from their place to sleep to their place of work. The order closes with the regulation, "Jews found outside the factory or housing-block area without the express personal permission of the commander of the SS will be shot" (*Jews of Warsaw*, 276).

22. Lewin, *Cup of Tears*, 189.
23. Ibid.
24. Berg, *Diary*, 184.
25. Bauman, *Winter in the Morning*, 82.
26. Ibid.
27. Mawult, account, 127.
28. Ibid.; see also Adler, *In the Warsaw Ghetto*, 283.
29. Adler, *In the Warsaw Ghetto*, 273.

Spaces of Resistance

Confronted with a spatial setup that was highly detrimental and practices that were increasingly hostile to their lives, the inhabitants of the ghetto desperately tried to find ways to cope with their situation. Especially during the first two years of the ghetto's existence, those attempts took various forms, including, for example, the activities of the Jewish Self-Help; the dedicated work of medical professionals; the realization of clandestine education (both secular and religious) and the continuation of religious practice in clandestine prayer houses (all in defiance of significant threats and penalties by the Germans); the establishment of soup kitchens, various cultural initiatives, and house committees; the work of political groups and activists, including the work of the *Oneg Shabbat* group and numerous other attempts to chronicle the events in the ghetto; the work of smugglers, as well as the extensive underground work, including organized escapes; the organization and upkeep of hiding places on the "Aryan" side; the clandestine press; the forming of armed resistance; and many more.

The entire time, people were also trying to find ways to endure by creating alternative spaces to evade the oppressive conditions of the ghetto. There were clandestine libraries, covert venues for cultural events, secret houses of prayer, and secret meeting places for study groups and political organizations.[1] Young people created small temporary spaces of escape, meeting for parties and dances in private homes.[2] There were cafés opened on the sites of bombed-out houses, as Berg notes in her diary: "In the Little Ghetto on Ogrodowa Street, a garden café called 'Bajka' [Fairy Tale] has been opened. The tables are outside and there is a little grass and two trees. This café covers the site of a completely bombed-out house." There was even a so-called beach that Berg writes about: "a piece of ground on which a few deck chairs have been placed. For two zlotys one can bask in the sun there for an entire day."[3] Similarly, at 20 Chłodna Street, there was a "charge for entering the terrace-like roof," which was equipped with "folding chairs" and offered "cool drinks, and a bird's-eye-view of Warsaw."[4] At the same time, the TOPOROL Society for the Support of Agriculture made use of "every inch of free land, every courtyard and every balcony" to plant crops, creating veritable gardens on the territory of bombed-out buildings and even that of the Jewish cemetery.[5] Greenery was an exceptional sight in the ghetto because the Germans had excluded from it almost all public parks and gardens and because "whatever greenery there was soon became firewood or was eaten by cold and starving ghetto dwellers."[6] In addition to providing a little more sustenance for the ghetto population, the creation and maintenance of gardens was, as Kenneth Helpland puts it in his remarkable study *Defiant Gardens*, a "mechanis[m] of resistance to the horrific conditions under which people lived."[7] The gardens also potentially provided a momentary respite: sites such as the "little park" on the grounds of a "bombed house, where Toporol gardeners have planted grass and flowers" and "Jewish workmen have constructed swings, benches, etc." were experienced as "little refuge[s] of freedom for the little prisoners of the ghetto," as Berg phrases it.[8]

These spaces of escape and resistance can be described—some more than others—as "tactics" in the sense expressed by de Certeau in his *Practice of Everyday Life*. De Certeau describes a tactic as a "calculus which cannot count on a 'proper' (a spatial or institutional localization) nor thus on a borderline distinguishing the other as a visible totality." He elaborates, "The place of the tactic belongs to the other. A tactic insinuates itself into the other's place, fragmentarily, without taking it over in its entirety, without being able to keep it at a distance."[9] In the context of the ghetto, all actual Jewish space was continuously contested. The ghetto itself never truly belonged to those who inhabited it but was dominated by the Germans, their policies, practices, and auxiliaries. When the ghetto inhabitants created alternative spaces within it, these remained unstable and temporary.

The concept of a "tactic" can also be applied to the way the ghetto inhabitants moved through streets that were ultimately not theirs. With the Jewish right to space increasingly challenged and movement restricted most rigorously, people created new paths through the city to evade the pressure of the overtly present violence. Due to the immensely restricted setting of the ghetto, however, finding bypasses and "round-about routes" was very difficult.[10] Often, these new routes were at some point discovered by the Germans (or Jewish and Polish police) and rendered useless. As Ringelblum writes in November 1940, "To avoid the Zelazna-Chlodna corner you have to go way down Chlodna, then through 29 Chlodna Street into Krochmalna Street. But they found out about this bypass and walled up the passageway through the 29 Chlodna courtyard."[11] Still, people used all kinds of alternative itineraries to try to evade the terror on the streets. Mazor describes another case of such an attempted evasion at Karmelicka: "To bypass this street, an inner passage was devised by connecting adjacent courtyards, so that one could pass from Nowolipki Street into Leszno Street. Street vendors set up their stalls in this passageway. The bottleneck and the crush that resulted were impossible to describe."[12]

After the deportations, when the streets were, for the most part, forbidden territory and the danger outside was at a maximum, people became both even more inventive and more willing to take ever-larger risks. Sometimes the war damage created new opportunities to move, defying the official limitations. Szajn-Lewin describes how her husband, Arthur, who worried greatly about his parents, found his way through the remaining parts of the ghetto to see them. The two elderly people lived as "wild" people—that is, as people without permission to be in the ghetto—at 37 Zamenhof Street in the central ghetto. To get to them, Szajn-Lewin's husband had to first crawl through a hole in the wall of a bombed-out building to arrive at 35 Zamenhof Street. There he had to cross a field of rubble and a bomb crater, balance a wooden plank between two walls, then enter the stairway of the house at no. 35. From there, he could go to the building next door. But, as Szajn-Lewin states, "if there is a guard posted in the empty, closed off street, he will most certainly catch a bullet."[13] De Certeau's theory can again help classify these kinds of practices. Writing about the *"appropriation* of [a] topographical system" by a pedestrian, de Certeau argues that every act of walking is, in fact, an "actualization" of the "possibilities" of the existing spatial order.[14] With the "possibilities" of the streets challenged and ruptured by numerous "interdictions,"[15] the inhabitants of the ghetto resorted to other "tactics," actualizing the space around them in ways that were highly unconventional and subversive.

With the Germans maximally restricting and regulating movement in the ghetto, the creation of alternative routes was the only possible way to reclaim any freedom of communication, even if extremely limited. In addition to using "natural" opportunities formed by war damage or a beneficial spatial layout, people also began to alter their environment in order to create their own alternative routes; they built tunnels and broke through walls in cellars and attics to allow for passage outside of German control. Szajn-Lewin, for example, describes how workers in the central ghetto would move from one shop to another by using new openings in the attics, where they had removed the walls between adjacent houses. According to her memoir, a hidden passage in the cellars of buildings on Nalewki Street also allowed passage from cordoned-off ghetto exclaves into the central ghetto.[16] In sum, such alterations created a new multidimensional space of movement in the ghetto. Leociak explains, "The urban material of the ghetto resembled a sponge with passages, corridors and communications routes burrowed at various levels from the rooftops to the sewers." All vertical layers of urban space were integrated to form a "clandestine network of below-ground and above-ground routes."[17] The main function of this network was to be concealed from and inaccessible to the Germans.

Over the course of the Great Deportation *Aktion*, the construction of hiding places had become more and more important for the ghetto inhabitants as well. Except for employment in one of the shops, hiding from the Germans and their auxiliaries was essentially the only way to stay alive—at least temporarily.[18] Taken by surprise by the round-ups, many people hid in makeshift and improvised hiding places at first. These hideouts, as Marta Cobel-Tokarska notes in her book *Desert Island, Burrow, Grave. Wartime Hiding Places of Jews in Occupied Poland*, were "temporary" in the sense that they were "used to hide in until an imminent threat passed"; they were typically "not searched for in particular" but rather "chosen in the heat of the moment."[19] After the experiences of the July–September deportations, however, the remaining ghetto inhabitants resorted to the construction of much more elaborate and complex shelters. People worked on them with the utmost ingenuity and dedication, creating hiding places in attics, cellars, and apartments, behind heavy cupboards or fake walls, digging shelters in the ground, or walling themselves in.[20] Often, these spaces were extremely well equipped, with water pumps, ventilation systems, electricity, lighting, sound isolation, supplies, waste disposal, bunk beds, et cetera.[21]

Natalia Romik points out that people most commonly created their hiding places by repurposing existing structures. In her paper "Hiding Places. The Architecture of Survival," Romik explains, "A hiding place was normally an overlay on an existing space, which, as a rule, could not change in form, while at the same time drastically changing its functions: a wardrobe ceased to be a place reserved 'solely' for hanging articles of clothing in, and became an entryway to a living space." People's primary objective was for these spaces to "disappear," or, rather, to remain undetected.[22] To this end, people in the ghetto worked with much dedication and craftiness to conceal their hiding places. In his memoir, Adler describes two shelters in the same building, highlighting in particular the effort to camouflage their entrances. The first—a "temporary" shelter—was constructed above ground in the quarters of "several families" who "lived in 'one-room' dwellings situated along a single passageway": "One of the larger rooms had been narrowed, by about sixty-five centimeters, by means of a partition which had been whitewashed. Afterwards, the whole room was so well painted that nobody, other than a partner in the secret, could suspect the alteration. Between the walls, benches had been fixed for the inhabitants of all the rooms of the corridor to be used for a few hours of rest when necessary."[23] The second shelter was located in the basement of the building. Here, the inhabitants had put in place a highly complex mechanism to hide the entrance:

> Imagine now a dark empty cellar near the domestic water meter. Someone initiated to the secret first removes the soil in a certain place, finds the button and presses it. Part of the cellar floor comes down. We put soil back into the exact place where the button is located. We go down by a ladder through the opening, then we replace the cover and put in action an ingenious automatic device that covers the trap door with earth, thus obliterating all traces of a cover. Through an underground passage, about five to six meters long, we reach the entrance, mount a ladder and are in the shelter. The one meter thick walls completely muffle the sound of our voices.[24]

The basement shelter was equipped with a water pump, electricity, heating, "comfortable bunks," and "shelves for food." Both shelters were connected by an "air shaft" through which people in the upstairs shelter could drop letters to communicate with the "principal" shelter below.[25] In addition to giving a very vivid impression of the thought-out construction of such hiding places, Adler's description also highlights how important it was for those in hiding not to be heard. For a hiding place to fulfill its purpose, people not only needed to disappear from sight but also required "acoustic protection."[26] Hideouts and bunkers had to be decoupled, physically, visually, and acoustically, from the "official" space of the ghetto—a space that, over time, had become an emphatic negation of Jewish life.

When the Ghetto Uprising broke out on April 19, 1943, the inhabitants of the ghetto had created an underground structure of tunnels and bunkers that was so extensive that the entire remaining ghetto population could disappear in it.[27] With no actual "living space" remaining above ground, the space intended for survival had to be, quite literally, "clawed away" from the space under German control.[28] In his memoir, *A Surplus of Memory: Chronicles of the Warsaw Ghetto Uprising*, Zuckerman recalls, "The Jews built themselves an underground city to hide in."[29] Together with the many clandestine passages and routes created above ground, the hiding places and bunkers formed a space of evasion that infiltrated and subverted "Jewish space" as designed by the Germans—creating an "anti-ghetto," so to say.

Notes

1. See Weszpiński, "Social Life"; see also Helpland, *Defiant Gardens*, 73–74, 98–100.
2. Bauman, *Winter in the Morning*, 61.
3. Berg, *Diary*, 52.

4. Ibid., 142.

5. Mazor, *Vanished City*, 53; see also Berg, *Diary*, 52, 140–141; Bauman, *Winter in the Morning*, 48, 57; Engelking and Leociak, *Warsaw Ghetto*, 440. For a more detailed description of the work of TOPOROL and the various sites used for gardening and agriculture, see Helpland, *Defiant Gardens*, 75–85.

6. Gebert, "Reading the Palimpsest," 236; see also Różycki, "Zamurowany" 455. RING. I/428; Helpland, *Defiant Gardens*, 69, 76.

7. Helpland, *Defiant Gardens*, 61.

8. Berg, *Diary*, 141–142.

9. de Certeau, *Practice of Everyday Life*, xix.

10. Lewin, *Cup of Tears*, 158; see also Engelking and Leociak, *Warsaw Ghetto*, 114.

11. Ringelblum, *Notes from the Warsaw Ghetto*, 91.

12. Mazor, *Vanished City*, 117.

13. Szajn-Lewin, *Aufzeichnungen aus dem Warschauer Ghetto*, 60. There is no English version of Szajn-Lewin's memoirs. Translation by A. N., from the German: "*Wenn in der leeren, abgeriegelten Straße eine Wache steht, ist ihm eine Kugel sicher.*"

14. de Certeau, *Practice of Everyday Life*, 97–98.

15. Ibid., 98.

16. Szajn-Lewin, *Aufzeichnungen aus dem Warschauer Ghetto*, 66. Very early on, smugglers had been similarly invested in devising new pathways that avoided the Germans and defied their regulation of space. Some of the structures created and used for smuggling were now incorporated into the hidden communication network of the ghetto.

17. Leociak, *Text in the Face of Destruction*, 52.

18. Highlighting the way in which such evasion defied the Germans' genocidal campaign, Gutman classifies hiding as a "passive approach to resistance" (*Jews of Warsaw*, 353). In a similar sense, Adler refers to the hideouts as "bastions of passive defence" (*In the Warsaw Ghetto*, 282).

19. Cobel-Tokarska, *Desert Island, Burrow, Grave*, 55.

20. Bauman, *Winter in the Morning*, 94; Lewin, *Cup of Tears*, 141; Berg, *Diary*, 80; Adler, *In the Warsaw Ghetto*, 275, 283–284, 297–298.

21. Birenbaum, *Hope Is the Last to Die*, 75; Adler, *In the Warsaw Ghetto*, 283; Gutman, *Jews of Warsaw*, 352.

22. Romik, "Hiding Places. The Architecture of Survival" (without pagination).

23. Adler, *In the Warsaw Ghetto*, 283–284.

24. Ibid., 284.

25. Ibid.

26. Ibid., 310. Nikita Hock highlights two opposing ways in which sound was of concern for those in hiding: first, "the need to control one's own sound production so as not to be discovered," and second, "the almost constant emotional and mental engagement with the sounds outside" (Hock, "Making Home, Making Sense," 7).

27. Paulsson, "Evading the Holocaust," 309.

28. Cobel-Tokarska, *Desert Island, Burrow, Grave*, 53.

29. Zuckerman, *Surplus of Memory*, 336. Already during the Great Deportation *Aktion*, Berg noted there was "now a real underground ghetto" in which the inhabitants hid (*Diary*, 180); Gutman phrases it similarly: "It is no exaggeration to state that the network of cells and tunnels resembled a subterranean Jewish city" (*Jews of Warsaw*, 354; see also Lubetkin, *Die Letzten Tage*, 10).

PART IV

CONCLUSION

CHAPTER

25

Violent Space

The concept of spatial violence, as I use it in this book, suggests a very specific way of looking at spaces such as the ghetto but, in fact, lends itself to possible application to any space in general. Creating a heightened sensitivity for the violent potentials that space holds, the concept and associated terminology help detect mechanisms and manifestations of violence that might go unnoticed otherwise. An analysis that focuses on spatial violence also sheds light on dimensions of experience that have not yet been sufficiently accounted for in the field of Holocaust studies.

Space as an analytical category unlocks numerous different perspectives and thus fans out analysis rather than limiting it. Therefore, defining the exact scope of each segment of inquiry was important, as decisions on the material and theoretical framework conditioned which space exactly my work would make visible. Relative to their material basis and analytical focus, the two main parts of *Violent Space* indeed yield very different insight into the ghetto space. The sociospatial history of the ghetto I outlined in part II showed in detail how the Germans instrumentalized space to facilitate and implement their antisemitic agenda. The case study of the Warsaw ghetto made visible the potential for space to be used to identify, define, segregate, isolate, marginalize, and control people. To these ends, the Germans had clearly recognized space as a very potent sociopolitical tool and used it as such. In its function as a site of "captive violence,"[1] the ghetto was also a means to facilitate the exploitation and murder of the Jews. Coupling disenfranchisement with spatial confinement, ghettoization significantly facilitated the extortion of even the last possessions and resources from the Jews and left them vulnerable and exposed to raids and round-ups for forced labor, executions, or deportations. Through ghettoization, the Germans induced social exclusion, effectively otherizing the Jews and undermining their chances of finding support outside the walls. The inhabitants of the ghetto suffered significant material damage, with the Germans and their auxiliaries systematically robbing them of their belongings and resources and cutting them off from opportunities to support themselves. The high level of control instituted by ghettoization provided the Germans with the means to tightly regulate and almost directly determine the living conditions inside the ghetto. As a spatial measure, ghettoization significantly increased the Jews' vulnerability to the German assaults on their livelihood, which very quickly translated into actual physical harm—into sickness, hunger, and death. The decision to include in the definition of violence I use herein such acts of "causing material harm" and "diminishing social participation"[2] thus prove very appropriate for the example of the Warsaw ghetto.

The spatial violence documented in the chapters devoted to the history of the Warsaw ghetto was oftentimes "instrumental"—to use Reemtsma's term[3]—in that it was aimed at objectives other than the physical destruction of the victims. The study of the sources indicates that space was not always intentionally instrumentalized to hurt the victims. Rather, the Germans used it as a means to solve "problems" they encountered in the process of implementing their anti-Jewish campaign. Sometimes, these problems were of an administrative nature, sometimes logistical; sometimes the German measures were guided by economic interests or served to reinforce control. In all these instances, however, space was organized with an inhuman (and eventually genocidal) disregard for the Jews and, almost always, had highly detrimental consequences for the inhabitants of the ghetto. Here, the analysis of the ghetto as a site of indirect spatial violence made very clear the damage that could also be done through measures that did not directly aim at hurting the victims. Decisions that were, for the most part, pragmatic from the perspective of the Germans (e.g., the exclusion from the ghetto of a building or street) usually caused much distress for the ghetto inhabitants, affecting them in multiple ways—for example, robbing people or institutions of their abode and of essential resources, intensifying the already existing overcrowding, cutting channels of communication, making the ghetto environment even more strenuous and difficult to navigate, further exposing people to violence, disrupting interpersonal relationships, tearing families apart, closing possible routes for smuggling or escape, and the like. Overall, this detailed study of the history of the Warsaw ghetto shows that, no matter the immediate objective or intention of a measure, spatialized violence continually caused severe damage and, taken as a whole, cost many people their lives.

This suggests something quite crucial: spatial violence cannot be described accurately by focusing exclusively on what it was meant to do or how it was used. The German occupiers were formative for the creation of the space of the Warsaw ghetto, but it is not their perspective that shows the full extent of its violent nature. For this reason, the focus on the reality of the victim that von Trotha advocates is very important in the context of Holocaust studies.[4] It is the victims who can tell us the most about the intricate ways in which spatial violence shaped and affected their world. In the end, the central maxim of this book is therefore to locate violence where it hurt. To understand in what sense and in which way the ghetto was a violent space, it is imperative to listen to those who suffered from it. And, indeed, working closely with personal accounts from the ghetto in part III of this book clearly confirms that, in the ghetto, there was not always a direct link between the objective for which the Germans implemented a spatial measure and the results that it yielded for the people inside. In fact, the analysis of testimonies leads to the conclusion that, in the case of indirect violence, there can be an enormous gap between intent and effect.

Spatial violence does not exhaust itself in being instrumental; it has a broader impact on the spaces and the people it affects. Although it is possible to identify the perpetrator as the one who establishes the space and the victim as the one subjected to it, such a binary model oversimplifies matters. Because spatial violence is not instantaneous but has a certain duration (be it short-lasting or more permanent), it warrants a response. Everyone who is in a violent space's range, in one way or another, has to relate to it and, in turn, is affected by it. This means that there is potential for a violent space to be shaped or even, to some degree, be appropriated by its victims (as was the case in the Warsaw ghetto). It also means that neither the perpetrator nor the bystander (or upstander, for that matter) is left unaffected. Violence reverberates; it changes space, impacts relationships, and affects and effects perceptions, actions, potentials, and possibilities.

To capture the wide spectrum of the effects of spatial violence, in the third part of *Violent Space*, I explore occurrences and patterns of spatial violence as recorded in firsthand accounts of the victims. The first aim in this part of the analysis was to detect any indication for space being the cause of or intensifying the victims' suffering. And, indeed, testimonies abound with depictions of the ghetto's space and space-related experiences of violence and trauma, confirming the hypothesis that space was a central category of the victims' experience. A close reading of wartime diaries and accounts reveals that, early on, many Jews were painfully aware of the processes through which the German occupiers were creating a space that was adverse to life, as well as to Jewish culture and identity. Their observations and reflections suggest that the authors were, in fact, highly attuned to the ways in which the Nazi German antisemitic ideology translated into spatial practice. Repeatedly, the victims themselves interpreted the German spatial policies as harassment, torture, or an act of violence. This tells us a lot, both about the Germans' overt will to harm the Jews and the drastic effects of their spatial practices.

Identifying central motifs, situations, locations, and dynamics and bringing their various depictions into a meaningful constellation, I carved out in the
analyses how the violent space of the ghetto affected and shaped the lives of Jews
inside the walls. The study of the firsthand sources shows that, from the victims'
perspective, spatial violence manifested itself on a wide spectrum—one that
could not be pinned down in a preformulated systematic order, and, as such, requires, above all, an unbiased and careful reading of their narratives. Alongside
experiences of a brute-force nature, such as round-ups, executions, or deportations, which all had a distinct spatial dimension to them, there were a myriad of
other instances where the organization or German practice of space unsettled,
alienated, or hurt people in more intricate ways. In fact, different manifestations
of spatial violence often ran concurrently and potentiated one another. Spatial
violence seeped into every corner of people's existence, affecting their range (and
means) of motion, their ability to orient themselves, their self-perception and
-localization, their emotional state, their sociality, their interactions, their agency,
their possibilities for action, their access to supplies and support, their exposure
to physical violence, and, as a result, their chances for survival.

The framework of spatial violence, but also the use of theoretical tools and
terminology from various space-related fields of study, proves very helpful for
identifying and further examining characteristics of the ghetto space. The aspects explored in the individual chapters illustrate the many ways in which the
space of the ghetto was harmful to its inhabitants and give testimony to the way
in which people experienced space itself as violent. The negative impact of space
was, in many senses, a direct inversion of the importance it had previously held
in people's lives. All the ways in which space had helped constitute community,
an intact sense of one's self, a sense of belonging, the ways in which it had catered
to everyday life, made communication possible, allowed for orientation, cultural
representation, and appropriation, and sheltered the individual, often without
even being noticed, were ruptured and distorted by ghettoization. Given the
affective value of space and the strong bond between people and their environment, people reacted quite strongly to its violation. In testimonies, prominent
examples of this were the militarization of the city during the siege of Warsaw,
the war damage to its buildings and infrastructure, the walling off of streets and
buildings as part of the establishment of the ghetto, the stunting of its street network, but also the many ways in which the boundaries of people's private spaces
were dissolved and transgressed by the Germans and their auxiliaries. Jewish
Varsovians experienced and decidedly described all of these occurrences as hurtful and their experiences as violent in nature. Similarly, the fact that, within the
ghetto, the urban environment ceased to work the way people expected it to work
had a very destabilizing effect on the ghetto inhabitants. The space of the ghetto

was dysfunctional to a degree that it physically and mentally exhausted people. The continuous changes that the Germans made to the ghetto added to this an immense insecurity and instability, making it basically impossible to adjust to the new environment more permanently. The German spatial politics established within the confines of the ghetto a sense of structural homelessness. Moreover, due to the extreme conditions the Germans created, space inside the ghetto became highly socially disruptive. People were forced into a situation where they were a constant nuisance to each other, inadvertently overstepping each other's boundaries, posing a health risk, pressing in on each other, hindering movement, or, potentially, embodying the risk of one's hiding place being discovered during a raid. Pervaded by ever-escalating violence, over time, the space of the ghetto became so hostile that it was basically uninhabitable.

Such phenomena and mechanisms corroborate the hypothesis that a strong nexus between space and violence existed and help explain in which way this nexus was formative for the experience of people in the Warsaw ghetto. The actual virtue of *Violent Space*, however, lies not in such findings but in the textual work itself. The book's most important results are difficult to subsume because they come in the form of a narrative weaved from the firsthand accounts, creating an evocation of spaces and experiences for which there is simply no shortcut. The words and imagery that people in the ghetto chose to express the existential threats they were facing are not incidental to the understanding of their experiences. The very detail and tone of their accounts, their "poetics" as Leociak calls it,[5] are needed to evoke the world they experienced. Also, the analysis of spatial violence in this book is site-specific. It is bound to the very particular and defining setup of the ghetto in the city of Warsaw, which means that specifics and details cannot necessarily be generalized. In light of the immeasurable pain the ghetto caused for every single one of the victims, respect for the uniqueness of their concrete reality and the world that surrounded them remains the *sine qua non* of my analysis. Attempting to do justice to the "minutiae of individual experience,"[6] the book itself, as far as practicable, seeks to avoid subsumption. Accordingly, I also refrain from the attempt to formulate any overarching theory of spatial violence. Instead, I give precedence to the material, to the firsthand accounts and the experiences articulated in them. The function of the theoretical approaches and concepts I borrow from various disciplines is to frame, explore, and showcase what people in the ghetto shared of their world.

In history, but also in our present-day world, there are countless instances where racism (be it latent or explicit), genocidal politics, perilous power imbalances, and the potential to harm manifest themselves in and through space. Some examples are related and, to some degree, similar to the Warsaw ghetto, for example, the other Jewish ghettos and segregated spaces that the Germans established in occupied Poland and all over Europe.[7] Others differ from the case of Warsaw in many regards, such as the Nazi concentration camps and prisons, but also current-day internment and penal camps, such as the ones existing in the Chinese province of Xinjiang,[8] or the various camps and makeshift spaces housing internally displaced persons, refugees, or asylum seekers worldwide (not least of all, those at both the North American and European borders). *Violent Space* can provide a heightened awareness for the violent potential of such spaces and, to some degree, serve as a blueprint for analyzing them. The terminology and concepts introduced in the first chapters, as well as the theoretical tools used in the analyses, will hopefully prove helpful for such a task, because, all differences aside, all of these spaces warrant a critical examination that is sensitive to their violent potential and respectful of the individual experience.

In the context of the Holocaust, the situation is such that many of the violent spaces that existed under German rule can never be accounted for in such a way. Of many of the violent spaces that were so formative for the victims' experiences, only a few narrative traces remain. Many experiences can only be commemorated symbolically, never to be told in the words of people who lived through them. At the Treblinka Museum, for example, seventeen thousand stones distributed across the site of the former "extermination" camp symbolize the over nine hundred thousand victims who were killed there at the hands of the Nazis. Of these stones, 216 carry the names of the various cities and towns from where the victims were deported to the camp.[9] Before their murder in Treblinka II, the majority of these victims had passed through one or, in fact, several of the numerous smaller and larger ghettos the Germans had established all over occupied Poland. Each of these cases was unique; each of these violent spaces would have to be read anew—and, yet, more often than not, the voices of their inhabitants have never reached posterity. Therefore, even though the narratives of the Warsaw ghetto cannot stand for them, in a way, they might have to.

Notes

1. Reemtsma, *Trust and Violence*, 57.
2. Popitz, *Phenomena of Power*, 26.
3. Reemtsma, *Trust and Violence*, 62.
4. Von Trotha, "Zur Soziologie der Gewalt," 20–21.
5. Leociak, *Text in the Face of Destruction*, 25.
6. Waxman, "Transcending History?" 148.
7. Even when looking at other ghettos in German-occupied Poland, however, differences concerning, for example, the location of the ghetto (the size of the respective city or town, as well as the ghetto's location in the settlement's periphery or center), the ghetto's size, the duration and exact time of its existence, its type (open

or closed), its setup (walled in or fenced off), the type of buildings included, the street network affected, the social makeup of the inhabitants and surrounding society, the Jewish-Gentile relations, the stance and actions of the Jewish self-administration, the mindset and local policies of the German actors on-site, and many more, will have to be considered.

8. "Amnesty International Report 2020/2021," 38.

9. Muzeum Treblinka, "Treblinka II – Commemoration." For images of the monument and more information on the memorial itself, see the Treblinka Museum's homepage "The Nazi German Extermination and Forced Labour Camp (1941–1944)."

APPENDIX

Maps

The history of the ghetto was characterized by constant revisions and reductions at the hands of the Germans. For the people who were directly or indirectly affected by these changes, because, for example, the street or building they had lived in was excluded from the ghetto or yet another vital thoroughfare was blocked, each alteration to the ghetto's layout was felt very strongly. And yet, from an analytical standpoint, it can be useful to examine snapshots in time of distinctive configurations the ghetto took, as some of them are particularly well suited to describe different stages of the ghetto's history.

The first of these configurations *Violent Space* presents in the form of a map is the *Seuchensperrgebiet*. After a series of incisive yet somewhat disjointed anti-Jewish measures, the (gradual) establishment of the *Seuchensperrgebiet* marked the first continuous urban intervention that targeted the Jewish community and spatialized the Germans' exclusionary politics. Both ideologically and spatially, it laid the ground for the ghettoization that was to follow. The second configuration shown in this book is the ghetto as it was set up at the time of its closing on November 15, 1940. After a period of painful uncertainty, marked by ever-changing announcements of boundary streets (August–November 1940), this was the first somewhat definitive shape the ghetto took. Although soon affected by new changes, it remained formative for the ghetto inhabitants' experiences until December 1941, when the ghetto layout and the principles of its border regulation had changed again substantially. This spatial setup of the ghetto is the third configuration to be shown in the book. The last map of the ghetto shows its boundaries after the Great Deportations of July–September 1942. The organization of the new fragmented ghetto followed very different principles than the earlier configurations, linking (at least temporarily) the right to live to economic productivity. Especially internally, the ghetto segments that were still officially inhabited were regulated much more strictly than ever before; at the same time, there were also those who tried to survive in hiding in the so-called wild areas.

Mapping

The maps were created specifically for this book. The graphic design and digital implementation of the boundaries was done by Nick Antonich and Corina Fuchs from *zmog* (Weinheim) in consultation with Tilo Schwarz (Mannheim). The borders of the ghetto are layered on a Polish map of the city of Warsaw from the year 1939 that comes from the collections of the Urban Media Archive of the Center for Urban History, Lviv, courtesy of the Scientific Library of the Ivan Franko National University of Lviv. The original title of the map is *Plan miasta stołecznego Warszawy*; it was prepared and published by a "private cartographical publishing company" (Ksiaznica-Atlas), founded by Prof. Eugeniusz Rome.[1] The scale of the map is 1:25,000. However, it contains a note indicating that "the scale does not pertain to street widths."[2]

The source for the information on the course of the borders are the extraordinarily detailed and well-researched maps by Paweł Weszpiński, published in Engelking and Leociak's *The Warsaw Ghetto: A Guide to the Perished City*. Weszpiński's maps were cross-referenced with historical photos of the walls, gates, streets, and buildings of the ghetto and with aerial photos of the area. When in doubt, the more current version of the maps, made available online, was consulted.[3] In addition, the detailed information on the inclusion and exclusion of streets and buildings, as well as the lists of border streets published in *The Warsaw Ghetto*, was taken into account.

Maps are not only representations of physical givens; they create a reality of their own. Every decision made in the process shapes what we see and how we interpret the space that is presented. The decision to draft the borders of the ghetto on a historical map meant that we had to embrace all the decisions the makers of the historical plan had made. On the one hand, as a map made for civilian use, our base layer brought with it a certain sense of concreteness and vividness. It presented a living city to which a contemporary reader of the map could potentially have gained access. In addition, it carried the same time stamp as the events discussed in this book, which matched it more effectively with the depictions of those who write about the ghetto. On the other hand, the map could not always be aligned one to one with the maps that served as the source of information for the boundaries. In some instances, streets were mapped differently, and where Weszpiński's maps provide details up to the level of individual buildings,[4] many of these elements could not be discerned in our historical plan of the city. Also, as noted above, the streets' width was not scaled consistently, which in some instances led to a certain contortion of proportions.

The mapping of a historical reality—particularly one whose physical manifestations have come as close to being obliterated as the ghetto has—is a process that is fallible by definition. With the small number of documents available, uncertainties and gaps in our knowledge cannot be avoided. And while the graphic representation might give a very factual, evident impression, the maps in this book, just as any map, can only be approximations. And yet, they tell a story of their own, providing a different perspective on the environment and the phenomena analyzed in this book.

List of Maps

Map base layer: From the collections of the Lviv Media Archive, courtesy of the Scientific Library of the Ivan Franko National University of Lviv, archival title: "Plan of the Capital City of Warsaw," 1939; archival signature: ID 769950; source: 769950.

Map 1: City of Warsaw, 1939; before the German occupation.
This map was cropped from the original plan and shows the most central parts of the city in prewar times. It allows us to put into a wider context the area the Germans ultimately chose for the ghetto but also shows the second center of Jewish settlement, Praga, and the other locations the Germans had considered for ghettoization (Kolo and Wola to the west, Grochow, only partly visible on the map, to the east).

Map 2: Northern Quarter, 1939.
This map zooms in on the northern quarter, providing a frame of reference for the way the quarter had been organically connected to the rest of the city before the German occupiers forcefully restructured the urban environment.

Map 3: Seuchensperrgebiet, 1940.
The Germans had begun to put up signs with the inscription "Infection, entry forbidden to soldiers" and fenced off individual streets already by the end of 1939.[5] It was only in the months of March, April, and June 1940, though, that the *Seuchensperrgebiet* (area threatened by epidemics) took full shape.[6] The border of the *Seuchensperrgebiet* as shown on this map has to be seen as a conceptual line rather than a representation of the border's actual physical manifestation, which, over the months of the *Seuchensperrgebiet*'s establishment, consisted of an ever-changing mix of signs, banners, blocked roads, fences, and newly built walls.

Map 4: Ghetto, November 15, 1940, at the time of its closing.
The map shows the borders of the ghetto at the moment when the deadline for resettlement—namely, November 15, 1940—had passed. By the next morning, the ghetto was officially sealed. After a long period that had been characterized for Warsaw's Jewish population by the looming threat of ghettoization and by a painfully long process of drawing and redrawing the boundaries, the ghetto was now a fact. When looking at the map, it is important to remember that the physical manifestation of the border was not continuous. The Germans had ordered to wall off thoroughfares but also made use of the existing urban structures: quite frequently, the border ran along building blocks or incorporated walls that separated adjoining plots; doorways and windows were simply bricked up.

Because the map shows only the state of the ghetto at this particular moment, certain elements are not visible: the exclaves in the north, for example, were connected with the main ghetto area by small footbridges, built in February 1941 (Mławska Street) and June 1941 (Przebieg Street), respectively.

Map 5: Ghetto, December 1941, after reductions.
In December 1941, the Germans concluded the restructuring of the ghetto with a series of very drastic changes. Borders that had run along buildings or through back-yards were now moved to the middle of streets, making it easier for the Germans to guard them and to tighten control over the ghetto inhabitants. At this point, the shape of the ghetto was straightened and streamlined, removing many of the characteristic irregularities of the earlier ghetto boundary. As a result, the wall—as the physical embodiment of ghettoization—became much more visible. In the process, the ghetto area was also significantly reduced.

Again, because the map shows only a moment in time, some structures are not represented. Some of the gates shown on the map would be closed just a few weeks later: the one at Grzybowska and Żelazna Streets, for example, or the one at Chłodna and Żelazna Streets, which were both closed in February 1942. Others that were opened shortly after December 1941 are not shown on the map either: the one at Grzybowska and Rynkowa Streets, for example, or at Dzika and Stawki Streets, which were opened January 1942. Because of its particular significance for the topography and function-ing of the ghetto, we added the bridge over Chłodna Street to the map, even though it was not opened before end of January 1942. Construction of the bridge, however, had already begun in December 1941.

Map 6: Ghetto, September 1942, after the Great Deportations.
The Great Deportation *Aktion* of July–September 1942, which cost nearly three hun-dred thousand people their lives, went hand in hand with a drastic reduction of the ghetto. Afterward, the Germans divided the area of the former ghetto into three dif-ferent sections: the workshops and living quarters for workers, fenced off or walled in and controlled tightly; the so-called wild areas, which were officially uninhabited but, in reality, still housed roughly twenty thousand people hiding from the Germans; and the areas that were annexed to the "Aryan" city and "assigned for residence by Poles."[7] The walls of the former ghetto remained standing; the workshops and work-ers' quarters were enclosed with wooden fences, barbed wire, and newly built walls.[8] There were a number of external gates remaining in operation and several "internal gateways" added.[9]

Map 7: Warsaw ghetto area, December 1944.
The aerial photo of the ghetto area comes from the collections of the US National Archives and Records Administration. Archival signature: GX 12293-SD (2) N52E20 Nr. 015. It was retrieved with the help of professional NARA researcher Dirk Burgdorf.

The photo was taken in December 1944 by the German military. This means that the thorough destruction of the ghetto area that the Germans had ordered after the

Ghetto Uprising had already been carried out. However, because the Warsaw Uprising (August–October 1944) had also been suppressed at this point, the concerted destruction of the rest of the city had already begun as well. Even so, the contrast between the two parts of the city is still clearly visible and very telling.

Notes

1. Krupski and Janusiewicz, "Commercial Cartography in Poland," 1.
2. Ksiaznica-Atlas/Urban Media Archive, "Plan of the Capital City of Warsaw."
3. Available at Polish Center for Holocaust Research, "Warsaw Ghetto Database."
4. Many of the more evident differences concerned the question whether or not a "street" was actually a street or maybe only a passage between buildings, whether or not a pathway in a park or cemetery should be included or not. In some cases, streets that were included in Weszpiński's maps simply did not exist in ours (the extension of Bonifraterska, south of Franciszkańska Street, for example, or a segment of Marszałkowska Street, right next to the Saxon Garden [Ogród Saski]); in other cases, it was just the opposite (the extension of Smocza Street north of Stawki Street, for example, but also Smętna Street, Wawrzyszewska Street, Mireckiego Street, and parts of Młynarska and Spokojna Streets, all in the vicinity of the cemetery on Okopowa Street). Some streets were shifted slightly so that their alignment with other streets looked different than in Weszpiński's maps.
5. Engelking and Leociak, *Warsaw Ghetto*, 55–56.
6. Ibid., 55–58.
7. Ibid., 96; Gutman, *Jews of Warsaw*, 274.
8. Engelking and Leociak, *Warsaw Ghetto*, 95–99.
9. Ibid., 97.

Images

The photos included in this book are not meant to provide an exhaustive overview of the ghetto or life within it. Instead, the images are meant to create a panoramic view of the architecture and the urban structures of the ghetto, its buildings and its streets, as well as the spatial interventions implemented by the German occupiers. Some of the images will show particular locations mentioned in the written testimonies, but mostly the photos are meant to create a backdrop for these accounts, providing a more general impression of the ghetto environment. It was a conscious decision to refrain almost entirely from showing people who are begging or dying in the streets.

As all sources, the photos will have to be contextualized and assessed with a critical eye. To counteract the seeming evidentness of visual testimony, it is of the utmost importance to ask whose perspective it is that we take, whose reality it is that we see. Ideally, this begins with establishing authorship. Photos in ghettos were taken by a number of different actors, with very different purposes and intentions. While for some ghettos, such as, for example, Litzmannstadt (Łódź) or Kaunas (Kovno), an extensive photographic record from within the ghetto exists,[1] a large part of the photos that survived from the Warsaw ghetto were taken by Germans. Many of these photos were taken on official order and clearly reflect the National Socialists' ideology and propagandistic objectives.[2] The photos taken by members of the *Propagandakompanie* (propaganda troops) fall in this category (examples in this book would be the photos by Ludwig Knobloch and Amthor).[3] Others were taken privately (and often illegally) by German soldiers stationed in Warsaw (examples in this book would be the photos by Heinrich Jöst and Willy Georg but also those by the unidentified Luftwaffe soldier, who took them for an album entitled "The Warsaw Ghetto: A Cultural Document for Adolf Hitler"). These private photos are taken with varying degrees of empathy toward the ghetto inhabitants. Some clearly reflect ideological bias; others seem more compassionate in their stance toward their subjects. In all cases, however, it is important to remember that the people who were photographed faced a uniformed member of the occupying forces, which, no matter the mindset of the photographer, implied a significant power imbalance and a potential threat.[4] Although "severe restrictions were put in place curtailing unofficial photography and the ownership of cameras and photographic equipment,"[5] people inside the ghetto also continued to create photographic documentation. For these photos taken by members of the Jewish community, there are different contexts to consider as well. Some of the photos were commissioned by the *Judenrat* for official purposes. In these cases, photographers were instructed to document "the apparent efficiency of ghetto institutions and its workforce."[6] There were also a number of photo studios operating inside the ghetto, which, at least for some time, continued to take portraits of people in the ghetto. Photographers, both professionals and amateurs, also took photos clandestinely to document the Nazis' crimes. These and other photographs were, at least partly, collected by the *Oneg Shabbat* group and reached posterity together with the other documents buried in the ghetto's grounds. Often, the authors of these photos cannot be identified. There is, however, one exception, as many of the photos that survived can be attributed to Foto-Forbert, a "fashionable portrait studio" located inside the ghetto.[7] The studio, which was operated during the German occupation by coproprietor Henryk Bojm, continued to take portraits but also fulfilled commissions by the *Judenrat* and the Joint Distribution Committee and provided a number of photographs for the clandestine collections of the Ringelblum Archive.[8]

The surviving photos of the Ringelblum Archive were published in 2019 in *Dispersed Contact: Photographs from the Ringelblum Archive Reinterpreted*, edited by Anna Duńczyk-Szulc.

List of Figures

The graphic design and technical implementation were done by Nick Antonich and Corina Fuchs from *zmog* (Weinheim) in consultation with Tilo Schwarz (Mannheim). The images were kindly provided by the E. Ringelblum Jewish Historical Institute, the Ghetto Fighters' House Archives, Yad Vashem, the United States Holocaust Memorial Museum, the Bundesarchiv, and the Muzeum Powstania Warszawskiego (Warsaw Rising Museum).

Fig. 4.1a: Borders of the ghetto at Plac Mirowski and Krochmalna Street in November 1940 and after the reductions in December 1941. Cropped from the original maps.

Fig. 6.1: From the collections of the E. Ringelblum Jewish Historical Institute. Archival title: "Map of the Jewish District." Archival signature: ARG I 1283_3.

The map was published by *Nowy Kurier Warszawski* on October 15, 1940, together with a list of streets in which Jews were not allowed to live and a list of streets to which they were supposed to move.

GALLERY

Plate 1: From the collections of the E. Ringelblum Jewish Historical Institute. Archival title: "Ghetto Gate at the Intersection of Leszno Street and Żelazna Street." Archival signature: DZIH F 2949.

The photographer could not be ascertained. According to the information provided by the Jewish Historical Institute, it was taken between 1940 and 1941.[9] It shows a group of people carrying bundles with their belongings and queuing up in front of the gate at Leszno and Żelazna Streets to enter the ghetto. The authors of *Extermination of Polish Jews* further specify that the group consisted of Jews who were forcefully resettled to Warsaw from "the surrounding Towns."[10] The first building to the right is that of 79 Leszno Street (outside the ghetto); the building behind the gate is 77 Leszno Street (inside the ghetto). The sign above the wooden fence says, first in German and then in Polish, "*Seuchensperrgebiet. Nur Durchfahrt gestattet / Obszar zagrozony tyfusem. Dozwolony tylko przejazd*" ("Area threatened by typhus. Only transit allowed"). As the researchers at the JHI note, two street signs can be identified. The one on top shows the Germanized name of the street

(*Gerichtsstrasse*), and the one below its Polish name (*Leszno*). The researchers also point out a "pharmacy with a broken sign above the door" located in the building at 77 Leszno Street, just behind the gate.[11] To the left, not visible in the picture, is the former Collegium Grammar School at 84 Leszno Street, which was included into the ghetto in April 1941.[12] From September 1941 onward, the small exclave could be reached over a wooden footbridge.

Plate 2: From the Yad Vashem Photo Collections. Archival title: "Warsaw, Poland, 1940, A street scene in the ghetto." Archival signature: 27CO4.

The photo shows one of the walls built on German order to close off the ghetto. In Władysław Bartoszewski's *Warszawski pierścień śmierci 1939–1944*, the photo is dated to fall 1940, which means it most likely precedes the closing of the ghetto. According to Bartoszewski's book, the wall blocks Świętokrzyska Street, just behind its intersection with Zielna Street. This means that the wall was photographed from outside the ghetto. The white building that is visible right behind the wall is the one at 1 Bagno Street in the so-called small ghetto; to its left is the building at 2 Bagno Street. The sign on the left-hand side of Świętokrzyska Street advertises a bar, which goes by the name *"pod murem"* ("by the wall").

The photographer could not be ascertained.

Plate 3: From the collections of the United States Holocaust Memorial Museum, courtesy of Rafael Scharf. Archival title: "A Jewish woman carries a pail along a street in the Warsaw ghetto." Photograph number: 20669.

The photo was taken inside the ghetto in the summer of 1941 by a German soldier, Willy Georg. The location could not be ascertained.

Plate 4: From the collections of the E. Ringelblum Jewish Historical Institute. Archival title: "Warsaw Ghetto. Trade in Pawia Street." Archival signature: DZIH F 4702.

The photo shows Pawia Street in the so-called large ghetto. It was taken by a German soldier, Heinrich Jöst, in September 1941. Some more information can be deduced with the aid of another of Jöst's photos, which shows the same street corner from a slightly different angle. For this photo (DZIH F 4701), the location can be identified as the intersection of Pawia and Zamenhofa Streets.[13] Consequently, in the photo at hand the buildings that are visible on the right-hand side of the street are those at 2–8 Pawia Street, and the building on the left-hand side is that at 1 Pawia Street.

Plate 5: From the collections of the E. Ringelblum Jewish Historical Institute. Archival title: "Warsaw Ghetto. In Front of M. Pinkiert's Funeral Home." Archival signature: DZIH F 4671.

The photo was taken in September 1941 by a German soldier, Heinrich Jöst. According to the information provided by the JHI, it shows pedestrians "in front of M. Pinkiert's funeral home at 11 Zamenhofa Street," which lies at the corner of Pawia Street.[14] The house number can be seen at the left side of the large gateway. Engelking and Leociak note that Model Pinkiert's "Eternity funeral parlor," mentioned in numerous diaries and memoirs, was the "best-known undertakers' firm in the ghetto."[15] Pinkiert's firm had its headquarters in "24 Grzybowska Street" and several branches in different parts of the ghetto, including offices in "11, 38, 42 Zamenhof Street," as well as "27 and 31 Smocza Street, . . . 1 Dzielna Street, and . . . 5a Karmelicka Street."[16] In their description of the image, the researchers at the JHI further observe that there is a "sign in the storefront [that] reads: 'Grocery store,'" and a "poster behind the streetlight [with] a pricelist of cobbling services."[17]

Plate 6: From the collections of the United States Holocaust Memorial Museum, courtesy of Rafael Scharf. Archival title: "View of a commercial street in the Warsaw ghetto." Photograph number: 16010.

The photo was taken in the summer of 1941 by a German soldier, Willy Georg. The JHI, who also hold a copy of this photo in their collections (DZIH F 3308), identify the location as 17 Zamenhofa Street close to the intersection with Gęsia Street. They translate the signs at the storefronts as follows: "Stationery, bags, soap"; "Black paper for darkening windows"; "We register new coupons"; "Stamps, prints, store signs, engravings"; "Gas products"; "Qualified optician A. Honigsberg, manager B. Grabina, 101 Marszałkowska Street."[18]

Plate 7: From the collections of the E. Ringelblum Jewish Historical Institute. Archival title: "Necrologies." Archival signature: ARG I 683–29.

The photo was part of the materials that were buried by the members of the *Oneg Shabbat* group. According to the information compiled by Duńczyk-Szulc in *Dispersed Contact*, it was most likely taken by Henryk Bojm.[19] Jan Jagielski suggests that the photograph was taken on Karmelicka Street.[20] In a second photo of the same location, the names of the deceased can be deciphered: "Szlama Fagot," who "died 16 March 1942" at the age of seventy-three and was "buried at the cemetery on Okopowa Street," the "musician Bela Berlandsztejn (Berland)," as well as "Helena Trilling, Władysław Teszner—a chemical engineer from Łódź," and "Cyna Oberrotman," who "died 10 March 1942."[21]

Plate 8: From the collections of the Bundesarchiv. Archival title: "Polen. Warschauer Ghetto, Marktszene." Archival signature: 101I-134-0782-24.

According to the archival information, the photo was taken in May 1941 by a member of the German *Propagandakompanie 689*, Ludwig Knobloch. The location shown in the picture is Smocza Street. Leociak specifies further, pointing out that the photographer is looking north and that the next intersection is that with Gęsia Street. Way back, the T-junction with Stawki Street is visible.[22]

Plate 9: From the collections of the United States Holocaust Memorial Museum, courtesy of Rafael Scharf. Archival title: "Jews mill around on a side street in the Warsaw ghetto." Photograph number: 20634.

The photo was taken in the summer of 1941 by a German soldier, Willy Georg. The JHI, who also hold a copy of this photo in their collections, identify the location as Koźla Street. The street was located in the so-called large ghetto and "mostly inhabited by poor people (the proletariat, displaced persons, etc.)."[23] It was a part of the ghetto only until December 1941, when all streets east of Bonifraterska Street were excluded from its territory. As the JHI points out, the first building to the right (12 Koźla Street) is one of the few buildings to have survived the war.[24]

Plate 10: From the Yad Vashem Photo Collections. Archival title: "Warsaw, Poland, 1943, A ghetto street." Archival signature: 1105/7.

The photo shows Walic\ów Street at the intersection with Ceglana Street. While Walic\ów and a small part of Ceglana were part of the so-called small ghetto, the houses at 4, 6, 8, 11, and 13 Ceglana Street were excluded from it. The walls and the fences shown in the photo create a corridor that connects the "Aryan" city with these buildings. The photo is probably taken from the corner building at 8 Walic\ów Street. Right in front of the building, a fence with barbed wire (visible in the foreground of the photo) cuts off the southern side of Walic\ów Street from Ceglana Street. On the other side of the intersection, another fence and a wall cut off another section of Walic\ów Street, running along the building with the house number 11, blocking access to Ceglana from the north as well. The people who are visible next to the wall are thus inside the ghetto, whereas the depopulated section of the street lies outside. In December 1941, this part of Ceglana Street was included into the ghetto, which changed the topography of this particular section of the ghetto again.

The photographer could not be ascertained.

Plate 11: From the Yad Vashem Photo Collections. Archival title: "Warsaw, Poland, Entrance to a ruined building in the ghetto." Archival signature: FA109_41.

The photo was taken in spring 1941 by an unidentified German Luftwaffe soldier. It was part of a personal album, entitled "Das Warschauer Ghetto: Ein Kulturdokument für Adolf Hitler" ("The Warsaw Ghetto: A Cultural Document for Adolf Hitler").[25]

Plate 12: From the Yad Vashem Photo Collections. Archival title: "Warsaw, Poland, Children sitting on the sidewalk under the ghetto theater placards." Archival signature: FA109_21.

The photo was taken in spring 1941 by an unidentified German Luftwaffe soldier. It was part of a personal album, entitled "Das Warschauer Ghetto: Ein Kulturdokument für Adolf Hitler" ("The Warsaw Ghetto: A Cultural Document for

Adolf Hitler").[26] One of the posters in the background possibly advertises a revue entitled "Ałe Glach" (all alike)—reminiscent of the well-known exclamation of Abraham Rubinsztajn, a refugee from Łódź, who was often seen begging on the streets.[27] Rubinsztajn, who had a very remarkable appearance, is mentioned in many testimonies from the ghetto.[28]

Plate 13: From the collections of the E. Ringelblum Jewish Historical Institute. Archival title: "Warsaw Ghetto, Chłodna Street. Crowd of Ghetto Residents at a Crossing in Chłodna Street." Archival signature: DZIH F 5467.

The photo was taken by a German soldier, Willy Georg, in the summer of 1941. It shows a group of pedestrians crossing the street at the intersection of Chłodna and Żelazna Streets. The photo was taken before the wooden bridge over Chłodna Street was built. As the researchers at the JHI observe in their description, the people in the photo "are headed south, towards the so-called Small Ghetto."[29] Leociak observes that the men in the foreground took off their hats as was required in the presence of uniformed Germans.[30] The corner building is that of 26 Chłodna Street/72 Żelazna Street. A neon sign advertises a bar called *Bar Dla Wszystkich* (bar for everyone).[31] It can be seen in many of the photos taken of this street corner.

Plate 14: From the collections of the E. Ringelblum Jewish Historical Institute. Archival title: "Bridge on Chłodna Street." Archival signature: ARG I 683–34.

The photo shows the bridge from within the ghetto walls, drawing attention to the huge crowds of people passing over it. To the left, the ghetto wall is visible, along with a small wooden shed, probably a guardhouse. The white building that is visible behind the bridge is that at 25 Chłodna Street. It housed a German police post, the so-called Nordwache (northern checkpoint).[32] The photo was part of the materials that were buried by the members of the *Oneg Shabbat* group. According to the information compiled by Duńczyk-Szulc in *Dispersed Contact*, it was most likely taken by Henryk Bojm. Duńczyk-Szulc notes that "at the time the photo was taken, the Foto-Forbert studio was located at 20 Chłodna Street, very close to where the photographer was standing."[33] Incidentally, 20 Chłodna Street is also where Mary Berg located the "terrace-like roof" that offered "a bird's-eye-view of Warsaw"[34] and where Adam Czerniaków was living after the reductions of the ghetto in December 1941.[35] It is one of the very few ghetto buildings that survived the war.

Plate 15: From the collections of the E. Ringelblum Jewish Historical Institute. Archival title: "Cycle rickshaws waiting in line at the gate on Żelazna Street." Archival signature: ARG I 683–51.

The photo shows a line of rickshaws waiting at the gate at the intersection of Żelazna and Chłodna Streets.[36] Duńczyk-Szulc notes that it was probably taken in "winter or early spring of 1942, when wheeled traffic between the large and small ghetto went through gates at the intersection, through a narrow strip of Żelazna Street."[37] The white building that is visible behind the wall is that at 25 Chłodna Street. It housed a German police post, the so-called Nordwache (northern checkpoint), whose personnel, as Duńczyk-Szulc explains, "guarded the gates, terrifying the populace."[38]

The photo was part of the materials that were buried by the members of the *Oneg Shabbat* group. According to the information compiled in *Dispersed Contact*, it was most likely taken by Henryk Bojm.[39]

Plate 16: From the collections of the E. Ringelblum Jewish Historical Institute. Archival title: "Metal gate on Chłodna Street." Archival signature: ARG I 683–45.

The photo was taken at the same time and in the same location as ARG I 683–51 (Plate 15). It shows the gate at the intersection of Żelazna and Chłodna Streets up close, capturing the rickshaws with their passengers, the "Aryan" pedestrians who are walking along Chłodna Street, and also the policemen who open and close the gates, regulating Jewish traffic. From this perspective, the entrance to the police post at 25 Chłodna Street can also be seen.

The photo was part of the materials that were buried by the members of the *Oneg Shabbat* group. According to the information compiled by Duńczyk-Szulc in *Dispersed Contact*, it was most likely taken by Henryk Bojm.[40]

Plate 17: From the collections of the Muzeum Powstania Warszawskiego/Warsaw Rising Museum. Archival signature: MPW-IP/1294.

According to the archival description, the photo shows the market on Lubeckiego Street, seen from the first floor of 20 Lubeckiego Street. The photographer faces south and, in the background, "closing the perspective," several buildings along Gęsia Street can be seen.[41] Behind the wall to the right, barely visible in the photo, there are the ruins of the large building at 15 Lubeckiego Street, which can be seen more clearly in another photo of the same location, held in the collections of the Bundesarchiv (Bild 101I-134-0783-38, Knobloch).

The photograph was most likely taken by Mieczysław Bil-Bilażewski in 1941 or 1942.

Plate 18: From the collections of the United States Holocaust Memorial Museum, courtesy of Rafael Scharf. Archival title: "Vendors and buyers in an open-air market in the Warsaw Ghetto." Photograph number: 15990.

The photo was taken by a German soldier, Willy Georg, in the summer of 1941. The JHI, who also hold a copy of this photo in their collections, identify the location as Lubeckiego Street.[42] As can be seen in the other photo on this page (Plate 17, MPW-IP/1294), the market extended into Gęsia Street, which was well known for its lively trade. Just around the corner, at 24 Gęsia Street, the infamous Gęsia Street prison (or *Gęsiówka*) was located.

Plate 19: From the collections of the Bundesarchiv. Archival title: "Polen, Warschauer Ghetto.- Mauer, Stacheldrahtzaun, Passanten auf Gehweg; PK 697." Archival signature: Bild 101I-270-0298-07.

The photo was taken in June 1942 by a member of the German *Propagandakompanie 697*, Amthor. It shows the intersection of Żelazna and Grzybowska Streets in the so-called small ghetto. At this point, the gate that used to be at this very corner had already been closed. On the right-hand side, behind the wall, there is the corner house at 56 Żelazna Street. The white building that is visible to the right, a bit farther down the street, marks the corner of Grzybowska Street and Walicόw Street. To the left, there is the corner house at 58 Żelazna Street/48 Grzybowska Street.

Plate 20: From the collections of the E. Ringelblum Jewish Historical Institute. Archival title: "The wall on Bonifraterska Street." Archival signature: ARG I 683–50.

The photo was part of the materials that were buried by the members of the *Oneg Shabbat* group. The photographer could not be ascertained. The photo shows Bonifraterska Street and was taken in early 1942. Duńczyk-Szulc notes in *Dispersed Contact* that the photo was part of a series that showed locations that were impacted by the revisions of the ghetto boundaries in December 1941.[43] At this point, all buildings east of Bonifraterska Street (namely, Sapieżyńska Street, Mławska Street, parts of Franciszkańska Street, Koźla Street, Nowiniarska Street, and a small section of Świętojerska Street) were excluded from the ghetto. The border, which had been rather irregular before, now ran straight along Bonifraterska Street.

Plate 21: From the Yad Vashem Photo Collections. Archival title: "Warsaw, Poland, A Jew standing beside Jewish property on a ghetto street." Archival signature: 28AO3.

The JHI, who also hold a copy of this photo in their collections (DZIH F 2984), identify the location as Miła Street. The photo was taken during the Great Deportation *Aktion* between July and September 1942. In *The Extermination of Polish Jews*, the image is grouped with three others and captioned "Plundering of Jewish Goods left after an Expulsion."[44]

The photographer could not be ascertained.

Plate 22: From the collections of the United States Holocaust Memorial Museum, courtesy of Howard Kaplan. Archival title: "Jews captured by the SS during the suppression of the Warsaw ghetto uprising march past the St. Zofia hospital down Nowolipie Street towards the Umschlagplatz for deportation." Photograph Number: 80095.

According to the archival description, the photo was taken between April 19 and May 16, 1943, that is, during the Ghetto Uprising. It shows a column of Jews,

most likely civilians, being led to the *Umschlagplatz* by armed Germans. The photo
is taken from inside a building, looking down onto what the archive identifies as
Nowolopie Street.

The photo was taken by Leszek Grzywaczewski, a Polish firefighter sent to the
ghetto on German order. It is part of a series of photographs Grzywaczewski took
illegally during his work in the ghetto. These photos constitute probably the only
surviving documentation of the suppression of the Uprising not created by the
Germans themselves.[45]

Plate 23: From the collections of the Ghetto Fighters' House Archives, courtesy
of the Korczak Association in Warsaw. Archival title: "The ruins of the Warsaw
ghetto." Registry No.: 31783P; Catalog No.: 1043.

According to the archival records, the photo was taken by Julian Dankowski
in spring 1945.

Fig. 17.1a: From the collections of the *Muzeum Powstania Warszawskiego/*Warsaw
Rising Museum. Archival signature: MPW-IP/1277.

The photo in the top left corner was taken in 1942. It shows the bridge over Chłodna
Street coming from the east. According to the information from the museum, the
building to the right with a "dome on [the] corner house" is the one at 26 Chłodna
Street. The white building on the left side is the one at 25 Chłodna Street, which
housed a "station of the German gendarmerie," the so-called Nordwache.[46] This
building is one of the few to have survived the war.

The photographer is most likely Mieczysław Bil-Bilażewski.

Fig. 17.1b: From the collections of the Bundesarchiv. Archival title: "Polen,
Warschauer Ghetto.- Drahtzaun, Passanten auf Straße; PK 697." Archival Signature:
101I-270-0298-10.

The photo in the top right corner shows one of the iron gates opening and closing
Żelazna Street for Jewish traffic crossing the "Aryan" Chłodna Street. In the background, the wooden footbridge is visible. At the corner building (23 Chłodna/70
Żelazna), four street signs can be seen. The ones on top show the Germanized names
of the two streets (*Eisgrubenstraße/Eisenstraße*), and the ones below their Polish
names. The photo is taken from the western side of Chłodna Street, and the wheeled
traffic that is passing crosses from the so-called large to the small ghetto. Except for
the relatively small corner building, none of the buildings of the "aristocratic" and
broad Chłodna Street is visible in the photo. This creates a very particular perspective
on this busy intersection.

The photo was taken in June 1942 by a member of the German *Propagandakompanie 697*, Amthor.

Fig. 17.1c and 17.1d: Borders of the ghetto at the intersection of Chłodna and Żelazna
Streets in November 1940 and after the reductions in December 1941. Cropped from
the original maps.

Fig. 17.2: From the collections of the E. Ringelblum Jewish Historical Institute. Archival title: "Karmelicka Street." Archival signature: ARG I 683–57. Cropped for publication in *Violent Space*.

The photo was part of the materials that were buried by the members of the *Oneg Shabbat* group. According to the information compiled by Duńczyk-Szulc in *Dispersed Contact*, it was most likely taken by Henryk Bojm.[47] An exact date could not be established, but it must have been taken before July 1942, when the Great Deportation *Aktion* began. The original, uncropped image shows a longer stretch of the street's surface in the front.

Fig. 19.1: Pawiak Prison and its vicinity, including Karmelicka, Dzielna, and Więzienna Streets. Cropped from the original maps. The map shows the main prison building at the eastern corner of Pawia and Więzienna Streets but also includes the Serbia women's prison, which was located a bit farther down the street.

Notes

1. In the case of the Litzmannstadt ghetto, there are, for example, the collections of photographs taken by Henryk Rozencwaijg-Ross and Mendel Grossman (published in *With a Camera in the Ghetto*); in Kovno, George Kaddish photographed various aspects of ghetto life from the inside perspective of a member of the Jewish community (published, for example, in Gong, *George's Kaddish. For Kovno and the Six Million*, or Reich, *Hidden History of the Kovno Ghetto*).

2. There are also several rolls of propagandistic film material prepared by a German film crew in the summer of 1942, which can be seen in Yael Hersonski's excellent 2010 documentary *A Film Unfinished*.

3. Arani, "Fotografien der Propagandakompanien," 5. Biographical information on the photographers can be found in the "Biographies" section of the appendix.

4. Some of the most well-known images of the ghetto originate from the so-called *Stroop Bericht* (Stroop report), a report prepared by and named after the commander of the German forces suppressing the Ghetto Uprising. The images from the report were taken by the perpetrators during the commitment of their crimes and document the brutal "liquidation" of the ghetto and the murder of its remaining inhabitants. They were accompanied by a series of inhuman captions, reflective of their author's dehumanizing perspective on their victims. It was a conscious decision to not include any of them in this book.

5. Struk, *Photographing the Holocaust*, 35.

6. Ibid., 84.

7. Ibid.; see also Duńczyk-Szulc, *Dispersed Contact*, 51.

8. Struk, *Photographing the Holocaust*, 84–86; Rypson, "What Do Those Images Want from Us?" 155; Mémorial de la Shoah, "Les Photographes."

9. Information on the photos can be found online through the "DELET" portal, which is run by the Association of the Jewish Historical Institute (AJHI) and the Jewish Historical Institute (JHI).

10. Friedman and Taffet, *Zagłada Żydostwa Polskiego/Extermination of Polish Jews*, 18.

11. Jewish Historical Institute and Association of the Jewish Historical Institute, "Warsaw Ghetto Photography."

12. Engelking and Leociak, *Warsaw Ghetto*, 78.

13. Jewish Historical Institute and Association of the Jewish Historical Institute, "Warsaw Ghetto Photography."

14. Ibid.

15. Engelking and Leociak, *Warsaw Ghetto*, 474.

16. Ibid., 474.

17. Jewish Historical Institute and Association of the Jewish Historical Institute, "Warsaw Ghetto Photography."

18. Ibid.

19. Duńczyk-Szulc, *Dispersed Contact*, 89; see also Epsztein, "Photographs in the Ringelblum Archive," footnote 3, 42–43.

20. Shapiro and Epsztein, *Warsaw Ghetto: Oyneg Shabes–Ringelblum Archive*, 152.

21. Duńczyk-Szulc, *Dispersed Contact*, 88.

22. Leociak, *Biografie Ulic*, 461.

23. Jewish Historical Institute and Association of the Jewish Historical Institute, "Warsaw Ghetto Photography."

24. Ibid.

25. Struk, *Photographing the Holocaust*, 76–77.

26. Ibid., 76–77.

27. Engelking and Leociak, *Warsaw Ghetto*, 573.

28. Ibid., 592–593, 830.

29. Jewish Historical Institute and Association of the Jewish Historical Institute, "Warsaw Ghetto Photography."

30. Leociak, *Biografie Ulic*, 138.

31. Jewish Historical Institute and Association of the Jewish Historical Institute, "Warsaw Ghetto Photography."

32. Duńczyk-Szulc, *Dispersed Contact*, 92.

33. Ibid., 90.

34. Berg, *Diary*, 142.

35. Duńczyk-Szulc, "Reinterpreted," 54.

36. Shapiro and Epsztein, *Warsaw Ghetto: Oyneg Shabes–Ringelblum Archive*, 153; Duńczyk-Szulc, *Dispersed Contact*, 92.

37. Duńczyk-Szulc, *Dispersed Contact*, 92.

38. Ibid.

39. Ibid.

40. Ibid., 93.

41. Information on the photos can be found online through the Muzeum Powstania Warszawskiego/Warsaw Rising Museum, "Photo Library."

42. Jewish Historical Institute and Association of the Jewish Historical Institute, "Warsaw Ghetto Photography."

43. Duńczyk-Szulc, *Dispersed Contact*, 69.

44. Friedman and Taffet, *Zagłada Żydostwa Polskiego/Extermination of Polish Jews*, 68.

45. POLIN Museum of the History of Polish Jews, "A Unique Discovery."

46. Muzeum Powstania Warszawskiego/Warsaw Rising Museum, "Photo Library."

47. Duńczyk-Szulc, *Dispersed Contact*, 78.

Archival Material

While ultimately not all documents I collected and studied at the Jewish Historical Institute in Warsaw became a part of this book, the work on the original texts helped greatly in informing my understanding of the ghetto environment and reinforced my deep admiration for the work of the individual authors and their efforts to document life in the ghetto. Our translations included, but were not limited to, the announcement of the new borders of the ghetto in October 1941 (183. RING. I/781/5); the transcript of a letter to the *Judenrat* by the commissioner for the Jewish Residential District in Warsaw concerning the reduction of the ghetto in September 1941 (213. RING. I/310); a circular to the apartment house administrators concerning relocation in October 1941 (214. RING. I/299); a personal account on the reduction (504. RING. I/212); an account entitled "Eve of Passover in Warsaw Ghetto, 2nd Year of War 1941" in Yiddish (491. RING. I/1024); an account on life in the ghetto in Yiddish (496. RING. I/1015); an account entitled "Warsaw, an excursion to Jews who nourish themselves on dogs, cats, and rats . . . !!!" in Yiddish (499. RING. I/1005); and an account on the sanitary conditions and the high mortality at a refugee center in Leszno Street (276. RING. II/161).

In addition, we translated three studies by Stanisław Różycki, whose writings became particularly important for this book as a result of his specific focus on the ghetto's streets and the important and often very personal insight into life and experiences on the ghetto streets they provide. We translated Różycki's study *To jest getto! (Reportaż z inferna XX wieku)* (*This Is the Ghetto!* [*Reporting from the Inferno of the 20th Century*]) (455. RING. I/428), most likely written in December 1941 and preserved as both a handwritten manuscript and a typed transcript, his collection of reports *Obrazki uliczne getta. Sceny z życia getta warszawskiego* (*Street Pictures of the Ghetto. Scenes from the Life of the Warsaw Ghetto*) (456. RING. I/429), written most likely in March 1942 and preserved as a handwritten manuscript with some damages to the text, and parts of a handwritten fragment most likely written by Różycki in July 1942, entitled *Ulica* (*Street*) (577. RING. I/154). The last of the three (*Ulica/Street*) unfortunately proved difficult to transcribe because the manuscript had suffered some damage that made deciphering the handwriting very difficult. Already during editorial work on the new critical edition of Walter Benjamin's radio works (*Rundfunkarbeiten*) and the *Berliner Chronik* and *Berliner Kindheit um Neunzehnhundert*, I had learned how demanding a task the deciphering of manuscripts can be. Here, knowledge of the text's origin and evolution, but most of all well-trained linguistic sensitivity, experience, and an academically informed understanding of the text's subject matter are indispensable. It was therefore incredibly helpful to have been able to rely for our own translations on a number of personal transcripts by Professor Jacek Leociak (Warsaw).

In 2017, the first volume of the English edition of the *Ringelblum Archive* ("Warsaw Ghetto. Everyday Life") provided translations for two of Różycki's text, "Street Pictures from the Ghetto" (translated a bit differently as "Street Scenes from the

Ghetto," 22–44) and "Street" (44–63). For reasons of consistency, quotes from Różycki are, wherever possible, taken from my own translations. These translations reflect the work that we have done on the text with the particular research focus of this book in mind. They embody an inquiry into particular idiosyncrasies, ambiguities, and linguistical details that was an important step in my research. The excellent translations in *Ringelblum Archive* Volume I were still incredibly helpful for my work and were used as a cross-reference when needed; page numbers of the volume are provided for each quote along with a transcription of the Polish original. For "Street" (577. RING. I/154), I use the *Ringelblum Archive* translation entirely.

Sources Cited

Translations from Polish by Barbara Czepek and Anja Nowak. Translations of 491. RING. I/1024, 496. RING. I/1015, 499. RING. I/1005 and 276. RING. II/161 from Yiddish by Magdalena Siek; translations of 455. RING. I/428 and 456. RING. I/429 based on a transcription by Jacek Leociak.

182. RING. I/208. "Strassen- und Markthandel im jüdischen Wohnbezirk in Warschau." *Mitteilungsblatt für den jüdischen Wohnbezirk in Warschau* [*News Gazette for the Jewish Residential District in Warsaw*], no. 1, February 1, 1942, Warsaw. (German.)

183. RING. I/781/5. Heinz Auerswald, Commissioner for the Jewish Residential District in Warsaw, "Announcement of 23.10.1941 on new boundaries of the ghetto," October 1941, Warsaw. (Polish.)

184. RING. I/781/3. Heinz Auerswald, Commissioner for the Jewish Residential District in Warsaw, "Announcement about the shooting of 8 Jews on 17.11.1941 for illegal departure from the ghetto, on the basis of the verdict of the Special Court of 12.11.1941," November 1941, Warsaw. (German and Polish.)

213. RING. I/310. Heinz Auerswald, Commissioner for the Jewish Residential District in Warsaw, "Letter of 26.09.1941 to Jewish Council in Warsaw Order for the Jewish population to vacate by 5.10.1941 the buildings located on the south side of ul. Sienna and to the south of ul. Sienna from the streets: Twarda, Sosnowa, and Wielka," after September 26, 1941, Warsaw Ghetto. (Polish transcript.)

214. RING. I/299. *Pismo okólne z 21.10.1942 r. do administratorów domów* [*Circular of 21.10.1941 to Apartment House Administrators*], October 21, 1941, Warsaw Ghetto. (Polish.)

455. RING. I/428. Różycki, Stanisław. *To jest getto! (Reportaż z inferna XX wieku).* [*This Is the Ghetto! (Reporting from the Inferno of the 20th Century)*]. Including: (1)

"Pierwsze wrażenia" ("Powrót do gniazda rodzinnego," "Mury, mury, mury . . .,"
"Zamurowany," "Inferno"); (2) "Rządy Żydów" ("Marzenie i realizacja," "Gmina
i jej organy," "Policja," "Życie gospodarcze: 'Szafa gra . . .,'" "Wszystko wolno! Nic
nie wolno!"); (3) "Życie społeczne" ("Instytucje społeczne," "Lecznictwo," "Życie
kulturalne i towarzyskie," "Życie ulicy i domu"); (4) "Prawo do życia" ("Prawo sil-
niejszego"; "A sprawa słabszych . . ."; "Budżet szarego człowieka," "Perspektywy");
(5) "Średniowiecze." [(1) "First Impressions" ("Return to the Familial Nest"; "Walls,
Walls, Walls . . .," "Walled Up," "Inferno"); (2) "Jewish Administration" ("Dreams
and Accomplishments," "The Community and Its Organs," "Police," "Economic
Life: 'Everything's OK,'" "Everything's Allowed! Nothing Is Prohibited!"); (3)
"Social Life" ("Social Institutions," "Medical Treatment," "Cultural and Social
Life," "Life of the Street and Home"); (4) "Right to Life" ("The Right of the More
Powerful," "And the Rights of the Weaker . . .," "Life of the Ghetto Man," "Perspec-
tives"); (5) "The Middle Ages."], December 7, 1941. (Polish manuscript and typed
transcript.)

456. RING. I/429. Różycki, Stanisław. *Obrazki uliczne getta.* [*Street Pictures of the
Ghetto*]. Including: "Nagi trup i nagie fakty"; "Wróg społeczeństwa Nr 1"; "Bezwstyd"; "O namiastkach, falsyfikatach i niefachowości"; "Orientalna egzotyka"; "Ofic-
jalna granda"; "Samosąd" ["Naked Corpse and Naked Facts"; "Public Enemy no.
1"; "Shamelessness"; "About Substitutes, Forgeries and Incompetence"; "Oriental
Exoticism"; "An Official Racket"; "Mob Rule."], March 1942 [?]. (Polish manuscript.)

491. RING. I/1024. NN. *Erev Peysekh in varshever geto, 2-ter yor fun milkhome 1941*
[*Eve of Passover in Warsaw Ghetto, 2nd Year of War 1941*], after April 11, 1941, Warsaw
Ghetto. (Yiddish manuscript.) Translated from Yiddish by Magdalena Siek.

496. RING. I/1015. N.N. *Account of Life in the Warsaw Ghetto*, after May 26, 1941,
Warsaw Ghetto. (Yiddish manuscript.) Translated from Yiddish by Magdalena Siek.

499. RING. I/1005. N.N. *Varshe, an ekskursie tsu yidn velkhe dernern zikh mit hint, kets
un shtshures . . . !!!* [*Warsaw, an excursion to Jews who nourish themselves on dogs, cats,
and rats . . . !!!*], after July 4, 1941, Warsaw Ghetto. (Yiddish manuscript.) Translated
from Yiddish by Magdalena Siek.

504. RING. I/212. N.N. *Zmniejszanie getta warszawskiego na początku października
1941 r.* [*Reduction of the Warsaw Ghetto at the Beginning of October 1941*], after November 11, 1941, Warsaw Ghetto. (Polish.)

577. RING. I/154. Różycki, Stanisław [?]. *Ulica* [*Street*]. Including: "Moralność
ulicy"; "Wygląd zewnętrzny" ["Morality of the Street"; "External Appearance"], July
1942. (Polish manuscript.)

21. RING. II/397. Director of Police Dr. [Otto] Bethke, Proclamation dated April 30, 1942. (German.)

276. RING. II/161. N.N. "Punkt Leshno 2" ["Punkt Leszno 2"], date unknown, Warsaw. (Yiddish manuscript.) Translated from Yiddish by Magdalena Siek.

Warszawa Rada Żydowska 221/4. "Die neuen Aufgaben der Jüdischen Gemeinde in Warschau und die Lage der jüdischen Bevölkerung," March 26, 1940. (German.)

Biographies

The people for whom biographies will be provided include survivors of the ghetto and contemporary witnesses who perished during the Holocaust but also the main German agents who were responsible for the Warsaw ghetto. The information on the latter is meant to help assess their role in the events and explain the inner workings of the German administration. The biographies also, if possible, provide information on the ideological mindset of the respective perpetrator. The assumption is that knowledge of the network of responsibilities and motives is essential for an informed understanding of the events; since the dimensions of the perpetrators' ideological orientation played a role in their interaction with the Jewish population and sometimes also had a slight influence on the decision-making (although only gradually, no authority mentioned here ever officially questioned the Nazi genocidal agenda or sided with the victims to a degree that made a real difference).

In the case of sources from within the ghetto, the biographies fulfill three different functions. They are meant to provide a frame of reference with regard to the perspective of the author. Social and professional background, occupation before and during the war, involvement in the administration, Jewish self-help or resistance, contact with the "Aryan" side, social relations, religious affiliation, but also the specific period spent in the ghetto will individually define the particular space a person inhabited and make an immense difference with regard to the experience of the ghetto that he or she lived and recorded. Often, information will be regrettably incomplete, especially when an author has perished. The biographies will also, if possible, identify the type of source at hand: Is it a diary written during the war? Is it a study, a letter, or a postwar memoir? When was the text written, and what was its initial purpose?

Last but not least, these biographies are also meant to pay tribute to the individuals who left these accounts for future readers. Many of them perished, and those who did not saw the world they knew fall to pieces, witnessed their loved ones die under the most brutal and inconceivable circumstances, suffered violence and loss on a massive scale. The few sentences provided here can by no means do justice to their full and unique lives, but they at least give a small nod of acknowledgment to their existence as individuals and to the reality of their experiences.

Stanisław Adler (1903?–1946) was a lawyer by profession. After having fled from the German occupation to the Soviet-occupied territories, he returned to Warsaw in March 1940 to be with his elderly parents. Adler became a member of the Jewish Order Service, but his tasks were limited to office work. Adler left the Order Service shortly before the Great Deportations. He then became director of the ghetto's housing office. As a member of the administration and because he was still in possession of his Order Service insignia, Adler was able to move relatively freely through the ghetto. His account gives much insight into the workings of the Order Service and the *Judenrat*. He was also personally involved in the creation of hiding places and bunkers. After surviving a German blockade during the Deportation Action of January

1943 in one of the bunkers that he had helped to build, Adler escaped to the "Aryan" side. Adler wrote many notes and several versions of his memoir, which got lost during the tumultuous war years. His published memoir is based on the fourth and last version the author had buried on the "Aryan" side. After the war, Adler was involved in the formation of the provisional government of Poland. Upon hearing about the Kielce pogrom, Adler died by suicide on July 11, 1946.[1]

Mordechai Anielewicz (1919–1943) was born in the small town of Wyszków close to Warsaw. Coming from a lower-middle-class family, Anielewicz had attended a Hebrew secondary school. He had been politically active early on. In 1940, he became a member of the leftist, Zionist *Ha-Shomer Ha-Tza'ir* movement. Anielewicz was a cofounder of the ŻOB and during the Ghetto Uprising became its commander in chief. He died by suicide together with other members of the ŻOB when their bunker in 18 Miła Street was discovered by the Germans on May 8, 1943.[2]

Władysław Bartoszewski (1922–2015) was born to a Catholic Polish family in Warsaw. In 1940, he was incarcerated in Auschwitz for about seven months. Bartoszewski was very active in the Polish underground and became a member of the Home Army in 1942; he was also a cofounder of the *Żegota* (Polish Council to Aid Jews) and, as such, actively supported Jewish resistance and escapes from the ghetto. Bartoszewski took part in the Warsaw Uprising. He remained politically active after the war. Yad Vashem recognized Bartoszewski as one of the Righteous among the Nations in December 1965.[3]

Janina Bauman, neé Lewinson (1926–2009), was a Warsaw native, born into a large Jewish family. Her father, who was a Polish officer, was murdered in the Katyn massacre in 1940. Bauman escaped from the ghetto with her mother and sister and survived the war in hiding. Bauman and her family had to leave Poland in 1968; after a short time in Israel, they settled in Leeds, Great Britain. Bauman wrote *Winter in the Morning* in 1985, based on her wartime diaries.[4]

Mary Berg, neé Wattenberg (1924–2013), was born in Łódź to a fairly well-to-do Jewish family. During the early days of the German invasion, the family fled to Warsaw. Berg was fifteen at the time. Her family lived in the ghetto until July 1942, when, shortly before the Great Deportations began, due to her mother's US citizenship, the family was taken to Pawiak prison to be exchanged with German prisoners in the US. They were sent to the Vittel internment camp in January 1943 and emigrated to New York in March 1944. Her diary was published early in 1945, before the war had even ended.[5]

Adolf (Abram) Berman (1906–1978) was "a social activist and a member of the Po'alei Tzion-Left" before the war.[6] In the ghetto, he became the director of the Central Association for the Care of Orphans. In September 1942, Berman left the ghetto to go into hiding on the "Aryan" side but continued his political and social activism. After the war, Berman initially remained in Poland and became president of the Central Jewish Committee. In 1950, he emigrated to Israel, were he remained politically active, eventually serving as a member of the Knesset. His account is listed in the Archives of the Jewish Historical Institute as "anonymous," but Grynberg suggests that it is clear the manuscript was written by Berman.[7]

Biographical information on **Toshia Bialer** could not be established.

Mieczysław Bil-Bilażewski (1912?–1965) was a Polish photographer from Poznań. In the early 1930s, he moved to Warsaw, where he opened a photo studio ("M. Bill"). During the German occupation, Bil-Bilażewski worked for the Germans, taking photos of official events but also of life in the ghetto. Many of the motifs in his photos bear a certain resemblance to photos taken by members of the *Propagandakompanie* (propaganda troops; for example, those by Ludwig Knobloch). It is possible, but not confirmed, that Bil-Bilażewski handed copies of his photos over to the Home Army.[8]

Halina Birenbaum was born in 1929 in Warsaw. Because their house was burned down during the siege of Warsaw, Birenbaum's family moved to an apartment on Muranowska Street in the first days of occupation. When the ghetto was established, this proved beneficial, because the street was part of the ghetto area and the family was spared the rushed resettlement inflicted on many others. In 1943, Birenbaum and her family hid in a bunker during the Ghetto Uprising. When their hiding place was discovered by the Germans, Birenbaum, along with her mother, her sister-in-law, and one of her brothers, was deported to Majdanek, then sent to Auschwitz-Birkenau, later to Ravensbrück and Neustad-Glewe. Birenbaum survived the war and, in 1947, emigrated to Israel, where she worked as a writer and a translator. According to her account, it was the Eichmann trial of 1962 that encouraged her to write of her experiences. Her text, *Nadzieja umiera ostatnia* (*Hope Is the Last to Die*), was published in 1967.[9]

Henryk (Jechiel) Bojm (1898?–1943) was probably born in the Polish town of Sochaczew. He was a very successful and widely published photojournalist. Together with Leo Forbert, Bojm founded the Warsaw-based photo studio Foto-Forbert (also known as "Foto-Bojm-Forbert").[10] The two also operated a successful film company. After Forbert's death in 1938, Bojm continued to run Foto-Forbert.[11] Many of the photographs buried by the *Oneg Shabbat* group can be attributed to him.[12] Bojm was married to Ruchla Gliksman, who also worked with him. The couple had one son. The entire family perished during the Ghetto Uprising.[13]

During the siege of Warsaw, the Jewish engineer **Adam Czerniaków** (1880–1942), a native Varsovian who had studied in Warsaw and Dresden, had been appointed "president of the Jewish commune" at the behest of Mayor Starzyński, as many of the prewar community leaders had fled the city.[14] Due to the time he spent in Dresden, Czerniaków was proficient in German; his knowledge of Yiddish and his affiliation with Yiddish culture, on the other hand, was reportedly only nominal.[15] Although Czerniaków had been politically active before the war, he was not particularly well known in the Jewish community. Czerniaków's role as head of the *Judenrat* made him a very controversial figure in the ghetto.[16] His diary, preserved by his wife, Felicja, is an important source for the study of the ghetto's history and the history of its administration.[17]

Biographical information on **Julian Dankowski** could not be established.

Marek Edelman (1921?–2009) was one of the very few fighters of the Ghetto Uprising to survive the war. During the ghetto's existence, Edelman worked in the Berson-Bauman hospital as a messenger. He had been a member of the socialist *Bund* and joined the ŻOB leadership as their representative. Together with a small group of other fighters (such as, for example, Ziviah Lubetkin), Edelman was able to leave the ghetto through the sewers after the uprising was defeated. In 1944, he joined the Warsaw Uprising. After the war, Edelman remained politically active, joining the *Solidarność* labor union. Unlike many other survivors, Edelman remained in Poland, living in Łódź and working as a cardiologist. Edelman wrote down his experiences during the uprising right after the war, and they were published in Polish under the title *Getto walczy* (*The Ghetto Fights/Das Ghetto Kämpft*). Edelman came back to his experiences again thirty years after the war for the book *Zdazyc Przed Panem Bogiem* (*Dem Herrgott Zuvorkommen/To Outwit God*), which was based on interviews that journalist and author Hanna Krall conducted with Edelman and was published in 1977. Both texts differ greatly in composition but also in terms of Edelman's assessment and description of the events. While *The Ghetto Fights* is largely concerned with reporting the events of the Ghetto Uprising in a relatively factual manner that follows the order of events, *To Outwit God* blends the events in the ghetto with scenes from Edelman's postwar life as a cardiologist, takes on questions of representation, and challenges the heroic postwar narrative of the uprising.[18]

Not much is known about **Stefan Ernest**. He was born in Warsaw and worked in the Employment Office of the Jewish Council. He lost this position in late 1942 and escaped to the "Aryan" side a few months later. His "report from the ghetto" covers the time between 1940 and January 1943. He most likely perished shortly afterward.[19]

Zbigniew Leszek Grzywaczewski (1920–1993) was born in Warsaw to a Catholic Polish family. After graduating from high-school, he started working for the Warsaw Fire Brigade. During the Ghetto Uprising, the Germans sent Grzywaczewski together with a group of other Polish fire fighters to the ghetto to "to ensure the fire did not spread to the houses on the 'Aryan' side."[20] During this time, Grzywaczewski took about thirty-three photos of the ghetto, depicting the burning buildings, the work of the fire fighters, but also groups of captured Jews who were led by the Germans to the *Umschlagplatz*. Grzywaczewski was a member of the Home Army and fought in the Warsaw Uprising. He passed away in August 1993 in Gdańsk. Some of his photos were donated to the United States Holocaust Memorial Museum, others were found more recently by his son Maciej Grzywaczewski.[21]

Chaim Aron Kaplan (1880–1942 or 1943) was born in Horodyszcze in Belorussia. He received a Talmudical education and later studied at the Pedagogical Institute in Vilnius (Wilno). He settled in Warsaw in 1902, where he founded a progressive elementary Hebrew school and worked as its headmaster. He was the author of several pedagogical works and textbooks. Kaplan's diary covers the period from September 1, 1939, until August 4, 1942, but some parts of it are missing. It was smuggled out of the ghetto by the end of 1942. Most likely, Kaplan and his wife were deported to Treblinka in December 1942 or January 1943.[22]

Janusz Korczak (1878 or 1879–1942), born under the name **Henryk Goldzmit** (Goldszmit) to an assimilated Jewish family, was a renowned writer, pediatrician, and educator who advocated strongly for children's rights. He was the author of well-known children's books, plays, and pedagogical writings (such as *Jak kochać dziecko/How to Love a Child*, *Prawo dziecka do szacunku/The Child's Right to Respect*, and *Pedagogika żartobliwa/Playful Pedagogy*). Korczak was the head of a very progressive orphanage in which children held their own court and were strongly involved in the self-governance of their community. Korczak devoted himself with all his might to the well-being of the children in his care, trying to provide for them under the difficult conditions in the ghetto. His diary is an expressive testimony to the personal turmoil of that uphill battle. When his orphanage was evicted on August 6, 1942, Korczak, his close colleague **Stefania Wilczyńska**, and their staff joined the children on their way to the *Umschlagplatz* in a calm and orderly procession that is depicted in many ghetto testimonies; as Lewiński describes, "without having to be driven by the Nazi killers, they marched in columns of four."[23] Korczak and Wilczyńska supposedly rejected the offer to stay behind and boarded the train to Treblinka together with the children. They were, in fact, not the only wardens of orphanages to do so. On August 8, 1942, Lewin mentions, for example, the fate of the orphanage in 67 Dzielna Street in his diary.[24] The headmistress, Sarah Janowska, along with her entire staff also joined the children for deportation.[25]

Jan Kostański (1925–2010), his mother, Wladislava, and his two younger sisters, Jadzia and Danuta, were close friends of the Jewish Wierzbicki family. When the Germans established the ghetto, the Kostańskis helped the Wierzbickis by smuggling food into the ghetto. Later, they hid members of the Wierzbicki family to save them from deportation. After the war, Kostański's mother married the father of the Wierzbicki family, Ajzyk, and Kostański himself married Ajzyk's daughter, Nacha. In 1958, Kostański, Nacha, and their two sons emigrated to Melbourne, Australia. Both

Kostański and his mother were recognized by Yad Vashem as Righteous Among the Nations. Kostański published his memoirs, *Janek. A Gentile in the Warsaw Ghetto*, in Melbourne in 1998.[26]

Henryka Łazowert (Łazowertówna) (1909–1942) was a poet who wrote numerous essays and reports for the *Oneg Shabbat* archive. Łazowert also continued to write poetry in the ghetto. According to Kassow, one of her most popular poems was entitled "To the Child Smuggler" (*Mały szmugler*). Łazowert reportedly followed her mother to the *Umschlagplatz* and was killed in Treblinka.[27]

Abraham Lewin (1893–1943) was born in Warsaw to a strictly orthodox Hasidic family. Before the war, he had worked as a secondary school teacher at the Yehudia high school for girls. Lewin was a member of the *Oneg Shabbat* group and head of the youth division of the Jewish Self-Help (*Aleynhilf*); he was also a close friend of Emanuel Ringelblum. In August 1942, Lewin's wife, Luba, was deported to Treblinka. Lewin himself most likely perished in Treblinka shortly after writing the last entry to his diary on January 16, 1943. His daughter, Ora, did not survive the ghetto either. Lewin's diary was found as part of the buried *Oneg Shabbat* archives after the war.[28]

Ziviah (Cywia) Lubetkin (1914–1976), born in the small *shtetl* Byteń, was a member of the Zionist *Dror* movement and became one of the leaders of the ŻOB. In the ghetto, Lubetkin (together with Yitzhak Zuckerman) had lived in the "Dror kibbutz at no. 34, Dzielna Street."[29] She was one of the few fighters to survive the war, leaving the ghetto through the sewers after the uprising was defeated. Like Edelman and Zuckerman, she later joined the Warsaw Uprising. After the war, she married Yitzhak Zuckerman, a fellow ghetto fighter, and in 1947 the couple immigrated to Israel. There they founded the Ghetto Fighters' Kibbutz *Lohamei HaGeta'ot* together with other surviving fighters. Lubetkin's memoirs were published in Hebrew in 1953 (*Bi-yemei kilayon va-mered*) and in an English translation in 1981 (*In the Days of Destruction and Revolt*).[30]

A lawyer by profession, **Jan Mawult** (Stanisław Gombiński) (birth and death dates could not be ascertained) "directed a department of the Jewish police force" in the ghetto.[31] Mawult wrote his account in 1944, while in hiding. It is assumed that he emigrated to Paris after the war.[32]

Michel Mazor was born in Kiev (birth and death dates could not be ascertained). At the outbreak of the civil war, Mazor left Russia and moved to Warsaw. A lawyer by profession, Mazor became an active member of several Jewish social organizations. He continued his involvement in social activities in the ghetto, becoming especially involved in the work of the tenement committees. Mazor was forced onto a train to Treblinka in September 1942 but managed to escape on the way. He survived the war and emigrated to Paris. Mazor's recollections, *La cité engloutie (Souvenirs du ghetto* *de Varsovie)*, were published in French in 1955; an English translation, *The Vanished City*, was published in 1993. The book is not a classic memoir in that it is not centered on its author's experiences (which still inform it), but, rather, in large parts attempts a study of the ghetto's structures and its history.[33]

Vladka Meed (Feigele Peltel) (1922–2012) was a Warsaw native who had been politically active from a very young age. During her time in the ghetto, Meed was an active member of the Jewish underground and resistance. Meed's father, Shlomo, died of pneumonia in the ghetto; during the Great Deportation *Aktion*, her mother, Hanna, and her two siblings, Henia and Chaim, were deported to Treblinka, where they perished. Shortly after this, Meed crossed over to the "Aryan" side, where she continued her clandestine work, smuggling weapons to the ghetto and assisting Jews in hiding. Vladka Meed and her husband, Benjamin Meed (Czeslaw Benjamin Miedzyrzecka), emigrated to the United States in 1946. Her memoir *On Both Sides of the Wall* first appeared in Yiddish in 1948 and was translated into English in 1971.[34]

Peretz (Perec) Opoczynski (1895–1943) was born in Lutomiersk, a small town close to Łódź, as son to a very religious family. Opoczynski grew up in poverty, spending most of his childhood away from home, studying in different *yeshivas*. When he returned to Lutomiersk, he was cast out of the community because he was considered a "heretic" for having studied with a progressive rabbi. Abandoning the career path his family had intended for him (that of becoming a rabbi), Opoczynski became a shoemaker and moved to Kalisz, where he joined a culturally and politically progressive "commune." In 1914, Opoczynski was drafted to join the Russian army. He spent most of the war as a prisoner in a POW camp in Hungary. Afterward, Opoczynski and his wife spent a few years in Łódź, where he worked as coeditor of a successful weekly publication. After their first two children died, he and his wife, Miriam, moved to Warsaw. There Opoczynski worked as an editor for a newspaper affiliated with the (right) *Poalei Tsiyon* (Poale Zion). In 1935, Opoczynski's son, Danchik, was born. In the ghetto, Opoczynski, who had lost his position as a reporter, worked as a letter carrier. He also remained politically active, especially in the context of his house committee. Opoczynski became an important member of the *Oneg Shabbat* group, contributing several reports and studies for the archive in Hebrew and Yiddish. According to Kassow, Opoczynski's last diary entry is dated January 5, 1943; there is no information about his fate or that of his family. Kassow assumes they were probably deported to Treblinka during the round-ups in mid-January.[35]

Samuel Puterman (?–1955) was a member of the Jewish Order Service. He survived the war and emigrated to France.[36]

Emanuel Ringelblum (1900–1944) was born in the small—and predominantly Jewish—town of Buczacz (Buchach) in eastern Galicia. At an early age, Ringelblum became a member of the Marxist-Zionist (left) *Poalei Tsiyon* (Poale Zion) movement.

After being rejected by the medical faculty in Warsaw due to the anti-Jewish *numerus clausus*, Ringelblum enrolled at the faculty of history. From the very beginning, his work as a historian was strongly influenced by his interest in Judaism and his love for the Yiddish language and culture. Warsaw, being the "political and cultural center of Polish Jewry" in the interwar period,[37] offered a vibrant and inspiring environment for the young historian and political activist. Before the German offensive, Ringelblum worked as a teacher and translator; he published numerous essays on historical and political topics. With the beginning of the war, Ringelbum's involvement as a "relief worker and community organizer" intensified;[38] Ringelblum, who had already worked for the Joint Distribution Committee before the war, became an important figure in the Jewish Self-Help (*Aleynhilf*). Ringelblum was the founder of the *Oneg Shabbat* group, responsible for the creation of the largest—albeit not the only—"secret archive in Nazi-occupied Poland,"[39] collecting a plethora of documents, artifacts, testimonies, and studies on life in the ghetto and the fate of Jews in the provinces. In March 1944, Ringelblum, together with his wife, Yehudis, and his son, Uri, was arrested from their hiding place on the "Aryan" side and executed in Pawiak prison. The documents of the *Oneg Shabbat* archive (also known as *Ringelblum Archive*), as far as they have been recovered after the war, are preserved at the Jewish Historical Institute in Warsaw.[40]

There is not much information on **Stanisław Różycki** other than what can be deduced from his writings for the *Oneg Shabbat* Underground Archive. Różycki was probably a high school teacher and fled to Soviet-occupied Lwów in 1939; he returned to Warsaw in the fall of 1941.[41]

Stefan Bronisław Starzyński (1893–?) had been appointed mayor of Warsaw in 1934; he was democratically reelected in 1938. During his term of office, Starzyński invested substantially in infrastructure projects. At the outbreak of the war, Starzyński refused to leave the city with the other officials and, instead, became a major agent in the city's defense efforts. His regular radio broadcast during the siege of Warsaw reportedly played an important role in boosting the city's morale. Starzyński was arrested by the Germans in October 1939 and held prisoner in the Pawiak prison; he was later killed by the Germans, but the exact circumstances of his death are still debated.[42]

Marek Stok (birth and death dates could not be ascertained) was a lawyer by profession. In September 1939, Stok fled Warsaw with his family; he returned in April 1940 and found work in a "garment workshop."[43] Later, he earned some money sporadically by giving legal advice. Stok left the ghetto in April 1943 to go into hiding on the "Aryan" side. He started to write his account in early 1944. Stok survived the war and emigrated to Brazil.[44]

Eugenia Szajn-Lewin (1909–1944), neé Szajn, was born in Łódź. She studied Polish and journalism in Warsaw, working as a journalist after her graduation. She published a novel, *Życie na nowo*. Before the German occupation, Szajn-Lewin lived in Łódź with her husband and daughter. She relocated to Warsaw with her entire family. Szajn-Lewin was able to bring her daughter over to the "Aryan" side, while she herself stayed in the ghetto. She perished in September 1944 during the Warsaw Uprising. Her account covers the time between July 1942 and April 1943. Her sister saved the manuscript from a hiding spot after the war.[45]

Not much is known about **Stanisław Sznapman** other than that he escaped to the "Aryan" side in July 1943, where he wrote his account in hiding. He presumably perished before the end of the war, but the circumstances of his death are unclear. His journal, *A Diary of the Ghetto/Dziennik z getta* (despite its title written in retrospection from outside the walls), was handed over to the Jewish Historical Institute in Warsaw by Helena Boguszewska and Henryk Kornacki.[46]

Nehemiah Titelman (Tytelman) (?–1943) was a member of the *Oneg Shabbat* group and contributed greatly to their archive, writing numerous essays and sketches, conducting interviews, and collecting songs and jokes from the streets of the ghetto. Titelman was a member of the left *Poalei Tsiyon* (Poale Zion) and was therefore well acquainted with Emanuel Ringelblum. Titelman, who had been the leader of the party's sports organization before the war, remained politically active in the ghetto. According to Kassow, Titelman was killed in 1943.[47] The notes referred to here were written on May 14 and 16, 1941.[48]

Ber Warm (birth and death dates could not be ascertained) was a member of the Jewish Order Service. He was first assigned to the "SS command post for the deportation" and later worked at the so-called *Werterfassungsstelle*.[49] In April 1943, Warm went into hiding on the "Aryan" side, where he wrote down his account. It was delivered to the Jewish Historical Institute by Adolf Berman, who also reported that Warm had perished.[50]

Natan Żelichower (Jan Kurczab) was born in Warsaw. Before the German occupation, he worked as a dental technician. Żelichower lost both his wife and his daughter during the deportations of 1942. He was deported to Majdanek in April 1943, then sent to several other camps until he was liberated at Buchenwald in 1945. His account was written right after his return to Poland.[51]

Yitzhak Zuckerman "Antek" (Icchak Cukierman) (1915–1981) was born in Vilnius (Wilno) in today's Lithuania. He was a member of the *Dror* movement and one of the organizers and leaders of the ŻOB. Zuckerman survived the war. Being on the "Aryan" side when the uprising broke out, Zuckerman was not able to join the other fighters. Together with Simcha "Kazik" Rotem, he organized the escape of a small group of fighters through the sewers after the uprising (including, among others, Marek Edelman and Ziviah Lubetkin). Zuckerman later joined the Warsaw Uprising.

After the war, he remained in Poland and helped Jewish survivors who were returning from the camps, hiding, or exile. Zuckerman was also in charge of evacuating
the remaining Jews from Kielce after the 1946 massacre and helped organize illegal
Jewish immigration to Palestine (as part of the *Brikha/Bricha* organization). In 1947,
he left Poland for Palestine, together with his wife, ghetto fighter Ziviah Lubetkin.
Together with other surviving fighters from the ghetto, they founded the Ghetto
Fighters' Kibbutz *Lohamei HaGeta'ot*. Zuckerman's memoir, which was based on extensive interviews with him, was published posthumously in Hebrew in 1990 (*Sheva
ha-Shanim ha-Hen: 1939–1946*), then in English in 1993 (*A Surplus of Memory*).[52]

German Agents

Biographical information on **Amthor** could not be established. As a member of the
Propagandakompanie 697, Amthor took photos with the clear objective of furthering
the Nazi German propaganda efforts.

Heinz Auerswald (1908–1970) was born in Berlin. He joined the SS in 1933; in 1939,
he also became a member of the NSDAP. Auerswald came to Poland as a member of
the Wehrmacht; he was then called to serve for the *Schutzpolizei* (uniformed police)
before he became part of the civil administration on the order of Governor Fischer.
According to Browning, Auerswald was not a "fanatic anti-Semit[e],"[53] and in his
dealings with the *Judenrat* he was not predominantly driven by his ideological mindset. Browning refers to Czerniaków, who in his diary from May 12, 1941, notes that
at his first meeting with Auerswald, the commissar of the Jewish district of Warsaw
"announced that his attitude to the [Jewish] Council was objective and matter of
fact, without animosity."[54] Yet, when it came to the strict isolation of the ghetto, the
suppression of smuggling, or when the Great Deportations began, Auerswald showed
no lenience.[55] After the war, Auerswald worked as a lawyer in Düsseldorf. He did not
face prosecution.[56]

Max Bischof (1898–1985), a banker by profession, was responsible for the coordination of Polish banks in the *Generalgouvernement*. From May 1941 to 1943, he was head
of the *Transferstelle*. Bischof was less of a hardliner than his predecessor Palfinger, his
policies in regard to the ghetto more "liberal" and pragmatic.[57] Browning points out
that this change in ghetto policies is clearly reflected in Czerniaków's diary for this
period.[58] After the war, Bischof went back to Vienna, where he resumed his career in
the financial sector.[59]

Oskar Rudolf Dengel (1899–1964) was born in the small town of Waldbüttelbrunn
close to Würzburg. A lawyer by profession, Dengel worked as an assessor for the
local municipality. Due to his early loyalties to the NSDAP (he became a member
in 1931), Dengel's career developed rapidly; after Hitler's rise to power, Dengel became more politically active, taking over several posts on a city as well as district
(*Gau*) level. When his political reliability was reviewed by the party in 1939, he passed

with flying colors; his ideological convictions and his loyalty to the NSDAP seem to have been beyond doubt. Roth points out that Dengel had also been a member of a Freikorps in Würzburg and was therefore habituated to a milieu with a high affinity for violence.[60] Dengel was appointed deputy for *Reichskommissar* (Reich commissioner)/*Stadtpräsident* (mayor) Helmuth Otto, the head of the civil administration in Warsaw; however, he quickly superseded his superior and took over his post as *Stadtpräsident*. Dengel was heavily involved in the urban development and planning for the city of Warsaw. He staffed the respective sections of the administration with trusted colleagues from Würzburg, and his team worked on plans for the architectural Germanization of the city, developing several blueprints for "Warschau, the new German city" (*"Warschau, die neue Deutsche Stadt"*), which were presented to Governor General Hans Frank in February 1940. These blueprints are commonly referred to as "Pabst-Plan," although Friedrich Pabst, in fact, did not work on them.[61] According to the testimony of Julian Kulski (mayor of Warsaw under German occupation), Dengel displayed strong anti-Polish sentiments and a brutal character.[62] At some point Dengel's ambitions backfired, and in March 1940 he was stripped of all his offices and sent back to Würzburg. After holding several other posts in the German civil and military administration, Dengel was arrested by the Americans in 1947; the following year, he was sentenced in Warsaw to fifteen years in prison.[63]

Ludwig Fischer (1905–1947) was born in Kaiserslautern; he was a lawyer by profession and joined the NSDAP in 1926. Fischer was well acquainted with Governor General Hans Frank, a fact that, according to Lehnstaedt, furthered his career and led to his appointment as governor of the district of Warsaw in October 1939.[64] Fischer was responsible for many fatal orders concerning the fate of the Jewish population. According to Szarota, Fischer was an ardent antisemite who held strong anti-Polish sentiments.[65] He held his post to the very end of the German occupation, overseeing the establishment of the ghetto as well as its "liquidation." After the war, Fischer was sentenced to death by Polish authorities and hanged in March 1947 in Warsaw.[66]

Hans Michael Frank (1900–1946) had joined the DAP in 1919 and became a member of the NSDAP in 1923. Frank was the leading jurist of the Nazi party and mainly responsible for the *Gleichschaltung* (forcible coordination) of the German judiciary. In October 1939, Frank was appointed *Generalgouverneur* (governor general) for the occupied Polish territories not annexed to the Reich (i.e., for the *Generalgouvernement*) by Hitler. In this capacity, he was the highest local administrative authority for the Warsaw district; he also had "exclusive legislative competence in the territory under his command."[67] Frank was enmeshed in a continuous power struggle with the local police and SS authorities regarding the authority over the Jewish population and their property. On a local level, his main opponent was Friedrich Krüger (higher SS and police commander for the *Generalgouverment*); at a higher authority level, it was Krüger's superior Himmler. In the summer of 1942, the power shifted in favor of Krüger and Himmler, and the police and SS temporarily "assumed power" over the Jewish population; this coincided with the beginning of the Great Deportation *Aktion*.[68] During his time in office, Frank resided in the Wawel Castle in Kraków; he was known for his excessive and luxurious lifestyle, and for the corruption and nepotism running rampant in his sphere of influence.[69] He was an outspoken antisemite and a fervent advocate of the Nazi "extermination" plans.[70] Frank was sentenced to death during the Nuremberg trials and was hanged in October 1946. His *Diensttagebuch* (official diary) served as important evidence during the trial and was published posthumously (Geiss and Jacobmeyer, *Deutsche Politik in Polen 1939–1945. Aus dem Diensttagebuch von Hans Frank, Generalgouverneur in Polen 1939–1945*).[71]

Willy Georg (1911–?) was a radio operator for the Wehrmacht who was stationed in the Mokotów district in Warsaw in the summer of 1941. Georg, a professional photographer, went to the ghetto on an order by his commanding officer. When he was controlled by a German police detachment, his camera was confiscated. Georg, however, had kept four film rolls in his pockets, which he developed in Warsaw. It was almost fifty years later that Georg made his photos public, handing them to Rafael F. Scharf, who, in 1993, published a selection in the book *In the Warsaw Ghetto: Summer 1941*.[72]

Reinhard Tristan Eugen Heydrich (1904–1942) was born in Halle an der Saale. Early on, Heydrich showed a strong affinity to nationalistic ideology. In April 1931, he was dishonorably discharged from the navy. Most likely influenced by his wife, Lina, who was an early follower of the National Socialists, he became a member of the NSDAP in 1931. In his role as general of police and chief of the Reich Main Security Office (*Reichssicherheitshauptamt*/RHSA), Heydrich, together with his superior and patron Heinrich Himmler, held control over the *Sicherheitsdienst* (SD/SS intelligence service) and the *Sicherheitspolizei* (SiPo/Security Police; consisting of the *Geheime Staatspolizei* [Gestapo/Secret State Police] and the *Kriminalpolizei* [Kripo/Criminal Police]). These agencies combined all German police and security forces, making Heydrich one of the most influential actors in Nazi Germany. Until his death in 1942, Heydrich was involved in most decisions and actions concerning the "Final Solution": he established and supervised the *Einsatzgruppen* and organized and presided over the Wannsee Conference in January 1942; Göring conferred on him the title *Beauftragter für die Vorbereitung der Endlösung der europäischen Judenfrage* (commissioner of the Final Solution of the Jewish Question). His role as acting Reich protector of Bohemia and Moravia brought Heydrich to Prague, where he was wounded during an assassination attempt at the end of May 1942; he died eight days later.[73]

Heinrich Luitpold Himmler (1900–1945) was the second-most powerful man in the German Nazi state. He was a very early Nazi sympathizer, joining the NSDAP as early as 1923. As head of the SS (1929–1945), chief of German police (1936–1945), and minister of the interior (1943–1945), he answered directly to Hitler. Himmler was also appointed *Reichskommissar für die Festigung des Deutschen Volkstums* (Reich commissioner for the strengthening of German nationhood), making him responsible for the resettlement and Germanization of the eastern occupied territories. In April 1945, Hitler removed him from office due to secret armistice negotiations. Himmler died by suicide in May 1945 while in British custody.[74]

Hermann Julius Höfle (Hoefle) (1911–1962) was an Austrian SS-Sturmbannführer who had joined the SS and the NSDAP in 1933. He played a crucial role in the deportation and "extermination" process as coordinator of the *Aktion Reinhard* and deputy to Odilo Globocnik, the SS and police leader in the district of Lublin. According to Reich-Ranicki, Höfle died by suicide right before his trial in Vienna in 1962.[75]

Heinrich Jöst (1898–1983) was a Wehrmacht sergeant stationed in the Praga district. On his birthday on September 19, 1941, the amateur photographer Jöst took his camera to the ghetto and shot about 140 photos. He had them developed in Warsaw but did not make them public until forty years later, when he gave them to Günther Schwarberg, who worked for the German magazine *Stern*.[76] His photographs were published repeatedly in books as well—for example, in 2001, in *Im Ghetto von Warschau. Heinrich Jösts Fotografien.*

Ludwig Knobloch (birth and death dates could not be ascertained) was a member of the German *Propagandakompanie 689*. His photos show life in the ghetto, as well as ghetto institutions, such as the Jewish Police, and clearly reflect strong antisemitic bias.[77] As many other German propaganda photographers, Knobloch put special emphasis on creating a contrast between the allegedly well-off ghetto "elite" and people starving and dying on the street—reiterating a very common Nazi propaganda trope vis-à-vis the ghetto's population.[78]

Friedrich-Wilhelm Krüger (1894–1945) was born in Strasbourg to an officer's family. He served during World War I but could not further his military career afterward. In the following years, Krüger passed through a series of different, unsuccessful occupations and a period of unemployment. Before joining the NSDAP in 1929, he had been a member of two paramilitary groups. In his biography, Larry von Thompson characterizes Krüger as an opportunist who only turned to the Nazi ideology when it served him.[79] He was appointed *Höherer SS- und Polizeiführer* (Higher SS and police commander) in the *Generalgouvernement* by Himmler in October 1939, thereby holding one of the most powerful executive positions in occupied Polish territories. In this capacity, he oversaw most of the anti-Jewish measures and "extermination" efforts in the *Generalgouvernement*; Krüger's responsibilities concerned particularly questions of forced labor and resettlement; he was also directly responsible for the so-called *Aktion Erntefest* in Majdanek, Trawniki, and Poniatowa. As Jürgen Stroop's superior, Krüger also oversaw the suppression of the Ghetto Uprising and the final "liquidation" of the ghetto. In November 1943, the continuous power struggles with Governor General Hans Frank cost him his rank, and he was superseded by Wilhelm Koppe. Krüger died by suicide in 1945.[80]

Ludwig Leist (1891–1967) had followed Oskar Dengel from Würzburg to Warsaw and took over his post after Dengel was removed from office. According to Lehnstaedt, Leist owed this career leap mainly to his connections to the governor of the district of Warsaw, Ludwig Fischer, who, like Leist, was originally from Kaiserslauten.[81] Accounts indicate that Leist was not necessarily a fanatic antisemite and, in contrast to other Germans, showed no strong anti-Polish resentments.[82] According to the testimony of Julian Kulski (mayor of Warsaw under German occupation), Leist even showed small signs of sympathy and generally treated the Polish and Jewish administration fairly respectfully.[83] Leist was tried together with Fischer but received a much lower sentence (eight years in prison). He willingly testified during the trial, and according to the account of Tadeusz Walichnowski, who had conducted several lengthy conversations with Leist, he himself characterized the trial as fair.[84] Leist claimed that his role in the establishment of the ghetto and the maltreatment of the Jewish population had been negligible; he insisted that the ghetto had mainly been Fischer's project, whereas he himself had not been part of the most "drastic" measures but had only issued minor orders.[85]

Alexander Palfinger (birth and death dates could not be ascertained), a German businessman, had worked as deputy to Hans Biebow in the Litzmannstadt ghetto before coming to Warsaw, where he was appointed head of the *Transferstelle* by the head of the Department of Resettlement, Waldemar Schön. To illustrate Palfinger's attitude toward the Jewish population and the conditions during his time in office, Browning refers to Emanuel Ringelblum, who states in an entry from April 26, 1941, "The director of the Transfer Station makes it a practice not to talk to Jews. There are dignitaries like that, who won't see a Jew to talk with as a matter of principle. They order the windows of the Transfer Station kept open because of the stench the Jews make."[86]

Karl Alexander Waldemar Schön (1904–?) was born in Merseburg in Saxony-Anhalt. He joined the NSDAP in 1930. A lawyer by profession, Schön became the head of the Department of Resettlement in the Warsaw district on January 23, 1940. In this capacity, Schön was at that point effectively the main authority responsible for matters concerning the ghetto on the local administrative level. He was thus responsible for the planning and establishment of the ghetto as well as for its management. According to Löw and Roth, he was an ardent antisemite,[87] a member of the "attritionist" wing who advocated a very drastic course of action against the Jewish population, focused on exploitation and gradual starvation.[88] Due to a general change in the German ghetto policies, he was replaced by Heinz Auerswald in May 1941, who took over the role as main authority over the ghetto under the title of commissar of the Jewish district of Warsaw. Schön did not face trial after the war.[89]

Jürgen Stroop (1895–1952) had joined the SS and the NSDAP in 1932. During the National Socialists' reign, Stroop had risen from the position of a land registry official to the higher ranks of the SS. Before being sent to Warsaw as a replacement for

Sammern-Frankenegg by Himmler, Stroop had worked as SS and police leader in Lwów (Lviv/Lemberg). Stroop documented the suppression of the Ghetto Uprising and the "liquidation" of the ghetto in a report entitled *Es gibt keinen Jüdischen Wohnbezirk in Warschau mehr* (*The Jewish Quarter of Warsaw Is No More*) that was handed over to Himmler and Krüger. The Stroop report was later used as evidence during the Nuremberg trials; it was published along with the many accompanying photographs. Stroop was tried twice, once in Dachau and once in Warsaw, where he was hanged in March 1952. His conversations with Kazimierz Moczarski during his imprisonment in the Mokotów prison in Warsaw were later published by Moczarski under the title *Rozmowy z katem* (*Conversations with an Executioner*). Stroop's self-portrayal in these conversations and in postwar times in general differs greatly from the convictions displayed in his report on the "liquidation" of the ghetto.[90]

Notes

1. Zeldowicz, "Personal Notes on Stanislaw Adler," xi–xviii; Leociak, *Text in the Face of Destruction*, 40, 73; Engelking and Leociak, *Warsaw Ghetto*, 815.

2. Roszkowski and Kofman, *Biographical Dictionary of Central and Eastern Europe*, 25–26; Krall and Edelman, *Dem Herrgott Zuvorkommen*, 8–11.

3. Roszkowski and Kofman, *Biographical Dictionary of Central and Eastern Europe*, 65.

4. Bauman, *Winter in the Morning*, "About the Author."

5. Pentlin, "Introduction," xv–xx; Leociak, *Text in the Face of Destruction*, 33–34.

6. Grynberg, *Words to Outlive Us*, 455.

7. Ibid., 455; Engelking and Leociak, *Warsaw Ghetto*, 816–817.

8. Muzeum Powstania Warszawskiego/Warsaw Rising Museum, "Mieczysław Bil-Bilażewski."

9. Birenbaum, *Hope Is the Last to Die*, 5, 10–13, 75–83, 99–100, 119–120, 224, 228.

10. Duńczyk-Szulc, *Dispersed Contact*, 52.

11. Struk, *Photographing the Holocaust*, 84.

12. Duńczyk-Szulc, *Dispersed Contact*, 54–55.

13. Ibid., 51.

14. Engelking and Leociak, *Warsaw Ghetto*, 138; Leociak, *Text in the Face of Destruction*, 29; Kassow, *Who Will Write Our History?*, 108.

15. Gutman, "Introduction," xi.

16. Ibid., xii–xiii; Engelking and Leociak, *Warsaw Ghetto*, 160.

17. For an examination of the specific character of Czerniaków's diary and problems concerning its use as a historic source, see Leociak, *Text in the Face of Destruction*, 132–140; for a more detailed portrait, see Gutman, "Introduction"; Engelking and Leociak, *Warsaw Ghetto*, 159–165, Lewiński, "Death of Adam Czerniaków and Janusz Korczak's Last Journey," 224–243; Reich-Ranicki, *Mein Leben*, 243–248.

18. Strobl, "Preface," 9–10; Blady-Szwajgier, *Die Erinnerung Verläßt Mich Nie*, 205; Lubetkin, *Die Letzten Tage*, 9–10, 13–18, 21–32; Edelman, *Das Ghetto Kämpft*, 75–76; Krall and Edelman, *Dem Herrgott Zuvorkommen*, 13, 99.

19. Grynberg, *Words to Outlive Us*, 458; Leociak, *Text in the Face of Destruction*, 35.

20. POLIN Museum of the History of Polish Jews, "A Unique Discovery."

21. Ibid.

22. Katsh, "Introduction," 12–16; Leociak, *Text in the Face of Destruction*, 38, 72; Engelking and Leociak, *Warsaw Ghetto*, 824.

23. Lewiński, "Death of Adam Czerniaków and Janusz Korczak's Last Journey," 245.

24. Lewin, *Cup of Tears*, 150, 280.

25. Lifton, "Introduction," vii–xxx; Rudnicki, "My Recollections of the Deportation of Janusz Korczak," 219–223; Lewiński, "Death of Adam Czerniaków and Janusz Korczak's Last Journey," 243–250; Veerman, "In the Shadow of Janusz Korczak," 8–15; Leociak, *Text in the Face of Destruction*, 176; Berenstein et al., *Faschismus—Getto—Massenmord*, 313–314.

26. Rosenkranz, "Memoir of Janek Kostanski," 9–10; Josem, "Obituaries," 10.

27. Kassow, *Who Will Write Our History?*, 181–182; Leociak, *Text in the Face of Destruction*, 32.

28. Kassow, *Who Will Write Our History?*, 170–173; Polonsky, "Introduction," 1–57.

29. Ubertowska, "'Masculine'/'Feminine' in Autobiographical Accounts of the Warsaw Ghetto," 167.

30. Engelking and Leociak, *Warsaw Ghetto*, 677; Lubetkin, *Die Letzten Tage*, 9–10, 13–18, 21–32; Zuckerman, *Surplus of Memory*, viii; Gutterman, *Fighting for Her People*, 11, 25; Ubertowska, "'Masculine'/'Feminine' in Autobiographical Accounts of the Warsaw Ghetto," 166–168.

31. Grynberg, *Words to Outlive Us*, 464.

32. Ibid.

33. Schneersohn, "Foreword," 4–5; Kassow, *Who Will Write Our History?*, 152–153.

34. Wiesel, "Introduction," 6; Meed, *On Both Sides of the Wall*, 39–42, 46; Engelking and Leociak, *Warsaw Ghetto*, 827; Saidel, "Vladka Meed 1921–2012."

35. Kassow, "Introduction," *Those Nightmarish Days*, xiii–xxv; Leociak, *Text in the Face of Destruction*, 31.

36. Leociak, *Text in the Face of Destruction*, 128; Grynberg, *Words to Outlive Us*, 466.

37. Kassow, *Who Will Write Our History?*, 25.

38. Ibid., 91.

39. Ibid., 210.

40. Ibid., 17–128; Kassow, "Introduction," *Warsaw Ghetto*, xvi–xxiv.

41. Kassow, *Who Will Write Our History?*, 146, 229, 253–256.

42. For a description of Starzyński's role in the defense of the city and his radio speeches, see Szpilman, *Der Pianist*, 26; some of the radio broadcasts can be accessed through the online archives of Polskie Radio; for information about Starzyński's life and the investigations into his death, see the respective articles on the Polskie Radio homepage (b.s., "Stefan Starzyński—prezydent, który poświęcił życie dla stolicy" or "Zagadka śmierci prezydenta Starzyńskiego"); for a detailed biography, see Piątek, *Sanator*.

43. Grynberg, *Words to Outlive Us*, 470.

44. Ibid., 470–471.

45. Line, "Introduction," 7–8; Siemens, "Die Menschenerniedrigungsmaschine"; Leociak, *Text in the Face of Destruction*, 32, 71.

46. Grynberg, *Words to Outlive Us*, 471; Leociak, *Text in the Face of Destruction*, 39–40, 127.

47. Kassow, *Who Will Write Our History?*, 180.

48. Ibid., 179–180, 257; Kermish, *To Live with Honor and Die with Honor!*, 73.

49. Grynberg, *Words to Outlive Us*, 169.

50. Ibid., 472.

51. Grynberg, *Words to Outlive Us*, 474.

52. Zuckerman, *Surplus of Memory*, vii, xi, 350–351, 367–369, 378–387; Ubertowska, "'Masculine'/'Feminine' in Autobiographical Accounts of the Warsaw Ghetto," 166–168.

53. Browning, "Nazi Ghettoization Policy," 354, 367.

54. Ibid., 354; see also Czerniaków, *Tagebuch*, 147.

55. Browning, "Nazi Ghettoization Policy," 367–368; Gutman, *Jews of Warsaw*, 97, 99–101.

56. Lehnstaedt, *Okkupation im Osten*, 60; Wulf, *Das Dritte Reich und seine Vollstrecker*, 313–322; Browning, "Nazi Ghettoization Policy," 354, 367–368; Gutman, *Jews of Warsaw*, 97, 99–101.

57. Engelking and Leociak, *Warsaw Ghetto*, 394; Löw and Roth, *Das Warschauer Getto*, 46; Gutman, *Jews of Warsaw*, 101.

58. Browning, "Nazi Ghetto Policy," 354–355.

59. Ibid., 353–354, 362–363; Gutman, *Jews of Warsaw*, 101; Löw and Roth, *Das Warschauer Getto*, 46; Engelking and Leociak, *Warsaw Ghetto*, 394.

60. Roth, *Herrenmenschen*, 30.

61. Gutschow and Klain, *Vernichtung und Utopie*, 28, 41.

62. Qtd. in Roth, *Herrenmenschen*, 333.

63. Ibid., 154–156; Roth, *Herrenmenschen*, 30, 108, 111, 333–334; Szarota, *Warschau unter dem Hakenkreuz*, 232.

64. Lehnstaedt, *Okkupation im Osten*, 56; see also Roth, *Herrenmenschen*, 82.

65. Szarota, *Warschau unter dem Hakenkreuz*, 233–234; see also Roth, *Herrenmenschen*, 341.

66. Klee, *Das Personenlexikon zum Dritten Reich*, 154; Lehnstaedt, *Okkupation im Osten*, 56; Engelking and Leociak, *Warsaw Ghetto*, 33; Szarota, *Warschau unter dem Hakenkreuz*, 233; Wulf, *Das Dritte Reich und seine Vollstrecker*, 311–312.

67. Engelking and Leociak, *Warsaw Ghetto*, 27.

68. Ibid., 32; Roth, *Herrenmenschen*, 58.

69. Roth, *Herrenmenschen*, 57.

70. Gutman, *Jews of Warsaw*, 98.

71. Klee, *Das Personenlexikon zum Dritten Reich*, 160; Engelking and Leociak, *Warsaw Ghetto*, 26–32; Roth, *Herrenmenschen*, 57–60, 80–83; Wulf, *Das Dritte*

Reich und seine Vollstrecker, 340–373; Birn, *Die Höheren SS- und Polizeiführer*, 198–206.

72. Struk, *Photographing the Holocaust*, 77; Rypson, "What Do Those Images Want from Us?," 156; Mémorial de la Shoah, "Les Photographes."

73. Kogon, *Der SS-Staat*, 45–56; Sydnor, "Reinhard Heydrich—Der 'Ideale Nationalsozialist,'" 208–219; Albury and Weisz, "Attempt on the Life of Reinhard Heydrich," 212; Klee, *Das Personenlexikon zum Dritten Reich*, 253.

74. Klee, *Das Personenlexikon zum Dritten Reich*, 256.

75. Ibid., 260–261; Wulf, *Das Dritte Reich und seine Vollstrecker*, 275–287; Reich-Ranicki, *Mein Leben*, 242.

76. Struk, *Photographing the Holocaust*, 77–78; Rypson, "What Do Those Images Want from Us?," 156–157; Mémorial de la Shoah, "Les Photographes."

77. Mémorial de la Shoah, "Les Photographes."

78. Weinhold, "Zum Umgang mit Fotografien aus der Zeit des Holocaust im Geschichtsunterricht."

79. von Thompson, "Friedrich-Wilhelm Krüger—Höherer SS- und Polizeiführer Ost," 324, 329.

80. von Thompson, "Friedrich-Wilhelm Krüger—Höherer SS- Und Polizeiführer Ost," 320–331; Engelking and Leociak, *Warsaw Ghetto*, 27–32; Klee, *Das Personenlexikon zum Dritten Reich*, 343; Wulf, *Das Dritte Reich und seine Vollstrecker*, 225–238; Birn, *Die Höheren SS- und Polizeiführer*, 204–205.

81. Lehnstaedt, *Okkupation im Osten*, 56.

82. Szarota, *Warschau unter dem Hakenkreuz*, 232–233; Roth, *Herrenmenschen*, 332–333.

83. qtd. in Roth, *Herrenmenschen*, 333.

84. qtd. in Ibid., 340.

85. Ibid., 330–333, 340–343; Lehnstaedt, *Okkupation im Osten*, 56; Szarota, *Warschau unter dem Hakenkreuz*, 232–233.

86. Ringelblum, *Notes from the Warsaw Ghetto*, 158; see also Browning, "Nazi Ghettoization Policy," 354.

87. Löw and Roth, *Das Warschauer Getto*, 46.

88. Browning, "Nazi Ghettoization Policy," 351–352, 360.

89. Engelking and Leociak, *Warsaw Ghetto*, 30, 38; Lehnstaedt, *Okkupation im Osten*, 60; Wulf, *Das Dritte Reich und seine Vollstrecker*, 327–330; Browning, "Nazi Ghettoization Policy," 352–354.

90. Wulf, *Das Dritte Reich und seine Vollstrecker*, 16–38, 40–43; Klee, *Das Personenlexikon zum Dritten Reich*, 609–610.

WORKS CITED

Primary Sources

Adler, Stanisław. *In the Warsaw Ghetto, 1940–1943: An Account of a Witness*. Jerusalem: Yad Vashem, 1982.

Anonymous Man. "Account." In *Words to Outlive Us: Eyewitness Accounts from the Warsaw Ghetto*, edited by Michał Grynberg, translated by Philip Boehm, 73–78. New York: Metropolitan Books, 2002.

Anonymous Woman. "Account." In *Words to Outlive Us: Eyewitness Accounts from the Warsaw Ghetto*, edited by Michał Grynberg, translated by Philip Boehm, 73–78. New York: Metropolitan Books, 2002.

Arad, Yitzhak, Israel Gutman, and Abraham Margaliot, eds. *Documents on the Holocaust: Selected Sources on the Destruction of the Jews of Germany and Austria, Poland, and the Soviet Union*. Jerusalem: Yad Vashem, 1981.

Bańkowska, Aleksandra, and Tadeusz Epsztein, eds. *Oyneg Shabes. People and Works*. The Ringelblum Archive 3. Warsaw: Jewish Historical Institute, 2020.

Bartoszewski, Władysław. *The Warsaw Ghetto. A Christian's Testimony*. Translated by Stephen G. Cappellari. London: Lamp Press, 1989.

Bartoszewski, Władysław. "Warsaw under Occupation: A Timeline." In *Inferno of Choices. Poles and the Holocaust*, edited by Sebastian Rejak and Elzbieta Frister, 66–114. Warsaw: Oficyna Wydawnicza RYTM, 2011.

Bartoszewski, Władysław. *Warszawski pierścień śmierci 1939–1944*. Warsaw: Wydawnictwo Interpress, 1970.

Bauman, Janina. *Winter in the Morning: A Young Girl's Life in the Warsaw Ghetto and Beyond 1939–1945*. London: Virago, 1991.

Berenstein, Tatiana, Artur Eisenbach, Bernard Mark, and Adam Rutkowski, eds. *Faschismus—Getto—Massenmord*. Berlin: Rütten & Loening, 1960.

Berg, Mary. *The Diary of Mary Berg: Growing Up in the Warsaw Ghetto*. Edited by S. L. Shneiderman. Oxford: Oneworld, 2006.

Berman, Adolf (Abram). "Account." In *Words to Outlive Us: Eyewitness Accounts from the Warsaw Ghetto*, edited by Michał Grynberg, translated by Philip Boehm, 140–146. New York: Metropolitan Books, 2002.

Birenbaum, Halina. *Hope Is the Last to Die*. Translated by David Welsh. Oświęcim: Auschwitz-Birkenau State Museum, 1994.

Blady-Szwajgier, Adina. *Die Erinnerung Verläßt Mich Nie: Das Kinderkrankenhaus im Warschauer Ghetto und der Jüdische Widerstand*. Translated by Joachim Rehork. München: List Verlag, 1993.

Borowski, Tadeusz. *This Way for the Gas, Ladies and Gentlemen*. Translated by Michael Kandel. London: Penguin Books, 1976.

Czerniaków, Adam. *Das Tagebuch des Adam Czerniaków: Im Warschauer Getto 1939–1942*. München: Beck'sche Reihe, 2013.

Czerniaków, Adam. *The Warsaw Diary of Adam Czerniakow: Prelude to Doom*. Edited by Raul Hilberg, Stanislaw Staron, and Josef Kermisz. Chicago: Elephant Paperbacks, 1999.

Duńczyk-Szulc, Anna. *Dispersed Contact: Photographs from the Ringelblum Archive Reinterpreted*. Warsaw: Jewish Historical Institute, 2019.

Edelman, Marek. *Das Ghetto Kämpft: Warschau 1941–1943*. Translated by Ewa Czerwiakowski and Jerzy Czerwiakowski. Berlin: Harald Kater Verlag, 1999.

Edelman, Marek. *The Ghetto Fights: Warsaw 1941–1943*. London: Bookmarks, 1990.

Edelman, Marek, and Paula Sawicka. *Die Liebe im Ghetto*. Edited by Paula Sawicka. Frankfurt: Schöffling, 2013.

Engelking, Barbara, Alina Skibińska, and Ewa Wiatr, eds. *The Last Stage of Resettlement is Death. Pomiechówek, Chełmno on the Ner, Treblinka*. The Ringelblum Archive 5. Warsaw: Jewish Historical Institute, 2021.

Ernest, Stefan. "Account." In *Words to Outlive Us: Eyewitness Accounts from the Warsaw Ghetto*, edited by Michał Grynberg, translated by Philip Boehm, 105–107. New York: Metropolitan Books, 2002.

Georg, Willy. *In the Warsaw Ghetto: Summer 1941*. Edited by Rafael F. Scharf. New York: Aperture, 1993.

Grossman, Mendel. *With a Camera in the Ghetto*. New York: Schocken Books, 1977.

Grynberg, Michał, ed. *Words to Outlive Us: Eyewitness Accounts from the Warsaw Ghetto*. Translated by Philip Boehm. New York: Metropolitan Books, 2002.

Gutman-Staszewska, Helena. "Account." In *Words to Outlive Us: Eyewitness Accounts from the Warsaw Ghetto*, edited by Michał Grynberg, translated by Philip Boehm, 24–28. New York: Metropolitan Books, 2002.

Hasenfus, Chaim. "Account." In *Words to Outlive Us: Eyewitness Accounts from the Warsaw Ghetto*, edited by Michał Grynberg, translated by Philip Boehm, 31–37. New York: Metropolitan Books, 2002.

Himmler, Heinrich. "Einige Gedanken Über Die Behandlung der Fremdvölkischen im Osten." Edited by Hans Rothfels and Theodor Eschenburg. *Vierteljahrsheft Für Zeitgeschichte* 5, no. 2 (1957): 195–198.

Jöst, Heinrich. *Im Ghetto von Warschau. Heinrich Jösts Fotografien.* Edited by Günther Schwarberg. Göttingen: Steidl, 2001.

Kaplan, Chaim Aron. *Scroll of Agony: The Warsaw Diary of Chaim A. Kaplan.* Edited and translated by Abraham Isaac Katsh. Bloomington: Indiana University Press, 1999.

Kazimierski, Józef, Jan Grabowski, Marta Jaszczyńska, and Danuta Skorwider, eds. *Ludność Żydowska w Warszawie w Latach 1939–1943: Życie—Walka—Zagłada.* Warsaw: Wydawnictwo DiG, 2012.

Kermish, Joseph, ed. *To Live with Honor and Die with Honor! . . . Selected Documents from the Warsaw Ghetto Archives 'O.S.' ['Oneg Shabbat'].* Jerusalem: Yad Vashem, 1986.

Klüger, Ruth. *Still Alive. A Holocaust Girlhood Remembered.* New York: The Feminist Press, 2001.

Klüger, Ruth. *Weiter Leben: Eine Jugend.* München: Deutscher Taschenbuch Verlag, 1995.

Korczak, Janusz. *Ghetto Diary.* New Haven: Yale University Press, 2003.

Kostański, Jan. *Janek. A Gentile in the Warsaw Ghetto.* Melbourne: Puma Press, 1998.

Krall, Hanna, and Marek Edelman. *Dem Herrgott Zuvorkommen.* Translated by Hubert Schumann. München: BTB, 1998.

Levi, Primo. *If This Is a Man; The Truce.* Translated by Stuart Woolf. London: Abacus, 1987.

Lewin, Abraham. *A Cup of Tears: A Diary of the Warsaw Ghetto.* Edited by Antony Polonsky. Translated by Christopher Hutton. London: Fontana, 1988.

Lubetkin, Ziviah. *Die Letzten Tage des Warschauer Ghettos.* Berlin: VVN-Verlag, 1949.

Lubetkin, Ziviah. *In the Days of Destruction and Revolt.* Translated by Ishai Tubbin. Tel Aviv: Hakibbutz Hameuchad and Am Oved Publishing House, 1981.

Markowska, Marta, ed. *The Ringelblum Archive: Annihilation—Day by Day.* Warsaw: KARTA Centre, History Meeting House, Jewish Historical Institute, 2008.

Mawult, Jan. "Account." In *Words to Outlive Us: Eyewitness Accounts from the Warsaw Ghetto,* edited by Michał Grynberg, translated by Philip Boehm, 111–117. New York: Metropolitan Books, 2002.

Mazor, Michel. *The Vanished City: Everyday Life in the Warsaw Ghetto.* Translated by David Jacobson. New York: Marsilo, 1993.

Meed, Vladka. *On Both Sides of the Wall.* Translated by Steven Meed. New York: Holocaust Library, 1999.

Moczarski, Kasimierz. *Gespräche Mit dem Henker: Das Leben des SS-Gruppenführers und Generalleutnants der Polizei Jürgen Stroop, Aufgezeichnet im Mokotow-Gefängnis Zu Warschau.* Translated by Margitta Weber. Frankfurt: Fischer Taschenbuch, 1982.

Nagiel, Henryk. *Tajemnice Nalewek: Kryminał Żydowski.* Warsaw: Ciekawe Miejsca, 2013.

Najberg, Leon (Arie). "Account." In *Words to Outlive Us: Eyewitness Accounts from the Warsaw Ghetto,* edited by Michał Grynberg, translated by Philip Boehm, 133–135. New York: Metropolitan Books, 2002.

Opoczynski, Peretz. "Building No. 21." In *Those Nightmarish Days: The Ghetto Reportage of Peretz Opoczynski and Josef Zelkowicz*, edited by Samuel D. Kassow, translated by David Suchoff, 3–30. New Haven: Yale University Press, 2015.

Opoczynski, Peretz. "Goyim in the Ghetto." In *Those Nightmarish Days: The Ghetto Reportage of Peretz Opoczynski and Josef Zelkowicz*, edited by Samuel D. Kassow, translated by David Suchoff, 54–71. New Haven: Yale University Press, 2015.

Opoczynski, Peretz. "The Jewish Letter Carrier." In *Those Nightmarish Days: The Ghetto Reportage of Peretz Opoczynski and Josef Zelkowicz*, edited by Samuel D. Kassow, translated by David Suchoff, 31–53. New Haven: Yale University Press, 2015.

Opoczynski, Peretz. "Smuggling in the Warsaw Ghetto." In *Those Nightmarish Days: The Ghetto Reportage of Peretz Opoczynski and Josef Zelkowicz*, edited by Samuel D. Kassow, translated by David Suchoff, 72–84. New Haven: Yale University Press, 2015.

Person, Katarzyna, ed. *Warsaw Ghetto. Everyday Life*. The Ringelblum Archive 1. Warsaw: Jewish Historical Institute, 2017.

Puterman, Samuel. "Account." In *Words to Outlive Us: Eyewitness Accounts from the Warsaw Ghetto*, edited by Michał Grynberg, translated by Philip Boehm, 28–31. New York: Metropolitan Books, 2002.

Reich-Ranicki, Marcel. *Mein Leben*. Stuttgart: Deutsche Verlagsanstalt, 1999.

Rejak, Sebastian, and Elzbieta Frister, eds. *Inferno of Choices. Poles and the Holocaust*. Warsaw: Oficyna Wydawnicza RYTM, 2011.

Ringelblum, Emanuel. *Kronika getta warszawskiego: wrzesień 1939–styczeń 1943*. Edited by Artur Eisenbach, translated by Adam Rutkowski. Warsaw: Czytelnik, 1983.

Ringelblum, Emanuel. *Notes from the Warsaw Ghetto: The Journal of Emmanuel Ringelblum*. Edited and translated by Jacob Sloane. New York: Schocken Books, 1974.

Różycki, Stanisław. "The Street. July 1942." In *Warsaw Ghetto. Everyday Life*, edited by Katarzyna Person, 44–63. The Ringelblum Archive 1. Warsaw: Jewish Historical Institute, 2017.

Różycki, Stanisław. "Street Scenes from the Ghetto." In *Warsaw Ghetto. Everyday Life*, edited by Katarzyna Person, 22–44. The Ringelblum Archive 1. Warsaw: Jewish Historical Institute, 2017.

Rudnicki, Marek. "My Recollections of the Deportation of Janusz Korczak." In *Jewish Life in Nazi-Occupied Warsaw*, edited by Antony Polonsky, 219–223. Oxford: Littman Library of Jewish Civilization, 2008.

Sakowska, Ruta, ed. *Children: Clandestine Education in the Warsaw Ghetto*. The Ringelblum Archive 4. Warsaw: Jewish Historical Institute, 2021.

Semprún, Jorge. *Die Große Reise*. Frankfurt: Suhrkamp Verlag, 1981.

Singer, Bernard. *Moje Nalewki*. Warsaw: Czytelnik, 1959.

Singer, Isaac Bashevis. *The Family Moskat*. New York: Random House Vintage Classics, 2000.

Singer, Isaac Bashevis. *In My Father's Court*. London: Penguin Books, 1966.

Singer, Isaac Bashevis. *Love and Exile*. Garden City: Doubleday, 1984.

Stok, Marek. "Account." In *Words to Outlive Us: Eyewitness Accounts from the Warsaw Ghetto*, edited by Michał Grynberg, translated by Philip Boehm, 21–24, 37–38, 49–51, 102–105. New York: Metropolitan Books, 2002.

Stroop, Jürgen. *Es gibt keinen Jüdischen Wohnbezirk in Warschau mehr: Stroop-Bericht*. Darmstadt: Luchterhand, 1976.

Szajn-Lewin, Eugenia. *Aufzeichnungen aus dem Warschauer Ghetto: Juli 1942 Bis April 1943*. Translated by Roswitha Matwin-Buschmann. Leipzig: Reclam Verlag, 1994.

Szmaglewska, Seweryna. *Smoke over Birkenau*. Translated by Jadwiga Rynas. Oświęcim: Auschwitz-Birkenau State Museum, 2008.

Sznapman, Stanisław. "Account." In *Words to Outlive Us: Eyewitness Accounts from the Warsaw Ghetto*, edited by Michał Grynberg, translated by Philip Boehm, 16–20. New York: Metropolitan Books, 2002.

Szpilman, Władysław. *Der Pianist: Mein Wunderbares Überleben*. Translated by Karin Wolff. Braunschweig: Schroedel, 2006.

Teitelbaum, Abraham. *Warschauer Innenhöfe. Jüdisches Leben um 1900 — Erinnerungen*. Göttingen: Wallstein Verlag, 2017.

Warm, Ber. "Account." In *Words to Outlive Us: Eyewitness Accounts from the Warsaw Ghetto*, edited by Michał Grynberg, translated by Philip Boehm, 169–181. New York: Metropolitan Books, 2002.

Żbikowski, Andrzej, ed. *Accounts from the Borderlands, 1939–1941*. The Ringelblum Archive 2. Warsaw: Jewish Historical Institute, 2018.

Żelichower, Natan. "Account." In *Words to Outlive Us: Eyewitness Accounts from the Warsaw Ghetto*, edited by Michał Grynberg, translated by Philip Boehm, 46–48. New York: Metropolitan Books, 2002.

Zuckerman, Yitzhak. *A Surplus of Memory: Chronicles of the Warsaw Ghetto Uprising*. Edited and translated by Barbara Harshav. Berkeley: University of California Press, 1993.

Żywulska, Krystyna. *Tanz, Mädchen . . .: Vom Warschauer Getto nach Auschwitz; Ein Überlebensbericht*. München: Dt. Taschenbuch-Verlag, 1989.

Secondary Sources

Agamben, Giorgio. "What Is a Camp?" In *Means without End: Notes on Politics*, translated by Vincenzo Binetti and Cesare Casarino, 37–45. Minneapolis: University of Minnesota Press, 2000.

Ainsztein, Reuben. *Revolte gegen die Vernichtung. Der Aufstand im Warschauer Ghetto*. Berlin: Schwarze Risse Verlag, 1993.

Albury, William R., and George M. Weisz. "The Attempt on the Life of Reinhard Heydrich, Architect of the 'Final Solution': A Review of His Treatment and Autopsy." *Israel Medical Association Journal* 16, no. 4 (2014): 21216.

Aly, Götz. *Endlösung. Völkerverschiebung und der Mord an den Europäischen Juden.* Frankfurt: Fischer Taschenbuch, 2014.

Aly, Götz, and Susanne Heim. *Vordenker der Vernichtung. Auschwitz und Die Deutschen Pläne für eine Neue Europäische Ordnung.* Hamburg: Hoffmann und Campe, 1991.

Anderson, Stanford. "People in the Physical Environment: The Urban Ecology of Streets." In *On Streets,* edited by Stanford Anderson, 1–12. Cambridge, MA: MIT Press, 1986.

Arani, Miriam Y. "Die Fotografien der Propagandakompanien der deutschen Wehrmacht als Quellen zu den Ereignissen im besetzten Polen 1939–1945." *Zeitschrift Für Ostmitteleuropa-Forschung* 60, no. 1 (2011): 1–49.

Baberowski, Jörg. *Räume der Gewalt.* Frankfurt: S. Fischer Verlag, 2015.

Becker, Maximilian. *Mitstreiter Im Volkstumskampf: Deutsche Justiz in den Eingegliederten Ostgebieten 1939–1945.* Berlin: De Gruyter, 2014.

Benjamin, Walter. *Berliner Chronik/Berliner Kindheit Um Neunzehnhundert.* Edited by Burkhardt Lindner and Nadine Werner. Vol. 11. Werke und Nachlaß. Berlin: Suhrkamp, 2018.

Benjamin, Walter. *Rundfunkarbeiten.* Edited by Thomas Küpper and Anja Nowak. Vol. 9. Werke und Nachlaß. Berlin: Suhrkamp, 2017.

Bergman, Eleonora, Katarzyna Czerwonogóra, Konstanty Gebert, Vera Hannush, Helise Lieberman, Magdalena Matuszewska, and Aleksandra Sajdak, eds. *1,000 Years of Jewish Life in Poland: A Timeline.* San Francisco: Taube Foundation for Jewish Life and Culture, 2011.

Bethke, Svenja, and Hanna Schmidt Holländer. "Lebenswelt Ghetto: Raumtheorie und interpretatives Paradigma als Bereicherung für Die Erforschung jüdischer Ghettos im Nationalsozialismus." In *Ghetto: Räume und Grenzen im Judentum,* 17:35–51. PaRDeS Zeitschrift der Vereinigung für Jüdische Studien e.V. Potsdam: Universitätsverlag Potsdam, 2011.

Birdsall, Carolyn. *Nazi Soundscapes. Sound, Technology and Urban Space in Germany, 1933–1945.* Amsterdam: Amsterdam University Press, 2012.

Birn, Ruth Bettina. *Die Höheren SS- und Polizeiführer: Himmlers Vertreter im Reich und in den Besetzten Gebieten.* Düsseldorf: Droste, 1986.

Blomley, Nicholas. "Law, Property, and the Geography of Violence: The Frontier, the Survey, and the Grid." *Annals of the Association of American Geographers* 93, no. 1 (2003): 121–141.

Blunt, Alison. "Cultural Geography: Cultural Geographies of Home." *Progress in Human Geography* 29, no. 4 (2005): 505–515.

Boehm, Philip. "Introduction." In *Words to Outlive Us: Eyewitness Accounts from the Warsaw Ghetto,* edited by Michał Grynberg, translated by Philip Boehm, 1–13. New York: Metropolitan Books, 2002.

Bourdieu, Pierre. "Physischer, Sozialer und Angeeigneter Physischer Raum." In *Stadt-Räume,* edited by Martin Wentz, translated by Bernd Schwibs, 25–34. Frankfurt: Campus Verlag, 1991.

Broszat, Martin. *Nationalsozialistische Polenpolitik 1939–1945*. München: Deutsche Verlags-Anstalt, 1961.

Browning, Christopher. *Die Entfesselung der "Endlösung." Nationalsozialistische Judenpolitik 1939–1942*. Berlin: List Verlag, 2006.

Browning, Christopher. "Nazi Ghettoization Policy in Poland: 1939–1941." *Central European History* 19, no. 4 (1986): 343–368.

Buggeln, Marc, and Michael Wildt. "Lager im Nationalsozialismus. Gemeinschaft und Zwang." In *Welt der Lager: Zur "Erfolgsgeschichte" Einer Institution*, edited by Bettina Greiner and Allan Gramer, 166–202. Hamburg: Hamburger Edition, 2013.

Calmore, John O. "Racialized Space and the Culture of Segregation: 'Hewing a Stone of Hope from a Mountain of Despair.'" *University of Pennsylvania Law Review* 143, no. 5 (1995): 1233–1273.

Certeau, Michel de. *The Practice of Everyday Life*. Translated by Steven F. Rendall. Berkeley: University of California Press, 1988.

Chalmers, Beverly. "Jewish Women's Sexual Behaviour and Sexualized Abuse during the Nazi Era." *Canadian Journal of Human Sexuality* 24, no. 2 (2015): 184–196.

Chapman, Tony. "Spoiled Home Identities: The Experience of Burglary." In *Ideal Homes?: Social Change and the Experience of the Home*, edited by Tony Chapman and Jenny Hockey, 133–146. New York: Routledge, 1999.

Charlesworth, Andrew. "The Topography of Genocide." In *The Historiography of the Holocaust*, edited by Dan Stone, 216–252. London: Palgrave MacMillan, 2004.

Clarke, David B., Marcus A. Doel, and Francis X. McDonough. "Holocaust Topologies: Singularity, Politics, Space." *Political Geography* 15, no. 6/7 (1996): 457–489.

Cobel-Tokarska, Marta. *Desert Island, Burrow, Grave. Wartime Hiding Places of Jews in Occupied Poland*. New York: Peter Lang, 2018.

Cole, Tim. "Geographies of Ghettoization: Absences, Presences, and Boundaries." In *Hitler's Geographies: The Spatialities of the Third Reich*, edited by Paolo Giaccaria and Claudio Minca, 266–281. Chicago: University of Chicago Press, 2016.

Cole, Tim. "Ghettoization." In *The Historiography of the Holocaust*, edited by Dan Stone, 65–87. London: Palgrave MacMillan, 2004.

Cole, Tim. *Holocaust City: The Making of a Jewish Ghetto*. New York: Routledge, 2003.

Cole, Tim. *Holocaust Landscapes*. London: Bloomsbury, 2016.

Cole, Tim. *Traces of the Holocaust. Journeying In and Out of the Ghettos*. London: Continuum, 2011.

Colombijn, Freek. "The Production of Urban Space by Violence and Its Aftermath in Jakarta and Kota Ambon, Indonesia." *Ethnos* 83, no. 1 (2018): 58–79.

Cresswell, Tim. "Place." In *The SAGE Handbook of Human Geography*, edited by Robert Lee, Noel Castree, Rob Kitchin, Victoria Lawson, Anssi Paasi, Chris Philo, Sarah Radcliffe, Susan M. Roberts, and Charles W. J. Withers, Vol. 1, 3–21. London: SAGE, 2014.

Cywiński, Piotr M. A., Piotr Setkiewicz, and Jacek Lachendro. *Auschwitz from A to Z. An Illustrated History*. Oświęcim: Auschwitz-Birkenau State Museum, 2013.

Czarnowski, Thomas V. "The Street as a Communications Artifact." In *On Streets*, edited by Stanford Anderson, 207–212. Cambridge, MA: MIT Press, 1986.

Czech, Danuta. *Kalendarium der Ereignisse im Konzentrationslager Auschwitz-Birkenau 1939–1940*. Hamburg: Rowohlt, 1989.

Dembowski, Peter F. *Christians in the Warsaw Ghetto: An Epitaph for the Unremembered*. Notre Dame: University of Notre Dame Press, 2005.

Desbois, Patrick. *The Holocaust by Bullets: A Priest's Journey to Uncover the Truth behind the Murder of 1.5 Million Jews*. New York: St. Martin's Griffin, 2008.

Dilts, Andrew. "Revisiting Johan Galtung's Concept of Structural Violence." *New Political Science* 34, no. 2 (2012): 191–194.

Długoborski, Wacław, and Franciszek Piper. *Auschwitz 1940–1945. Central Issues in the History of the Camp*. Oświęcim: Auschwitz-Birkenau State Museum, 2000.

Döblin, Alfred. *Berlin Alexanderplatz*. München: Deutscher Taschenbuchverlag, 2011.

Duncan, James S., and David Lambert. "Landscapes of Home." In *A Companion to Cultural Geography*, edited by James S. Duncan, Nuala C. Johnson, and Richard H. Schein, 382–403. Hoboken: Blackwell, 2004.

Duńczyk-Szulc, Anna. "Reinterpreted." In *Dispersed Contact. Photographs from the Ringelblum Archive Reinterpreted*, 48–59. Warsaw: Jewish Historical Institute, 2019.

Dünne, Jörg, and Stephan Günzel, eds. *Raumtheorie: Grundlagentexte aus Philosophie und Kulturwissenschaften*. Berlin: Suhrkamp, 2006.

Dylewski, Adam. *Ruda, Córka Cwiego: Historia Żydów Na Warszawskiej Pradze*. Sękowa: Czarne, 2018.

Dynner, Glenn, and François Guesnet. "Introduction." In *Warsaw: The Jewish Metropolis. Essays in Honor of the 75th Birthday of Professor Antony Polonsky*, edited by Glenn Dynner and François Guesnet, 1–16. Leiden: Brill, 2015.

Dziewulski, Stanisław, and Stanisław Jankowski. "The Reconstruction of Warsaw." *Town Planning Review* 28, no. 3 (1957): 209–221.

Ellis, William C. "The Spatial Structure of Streets." In *On Streets*, edited by Stanford Anderson, 115–132. Cambridge, MA: MIT Press, 1986.

Engel, David. "What's in a Pogrom? European Jews in the Age of Violence." In *Anti-Jewish Violence: Rethinking the Pogrom in East European History*, edited by Jonathan Dekel-Chen, David Gaunt, Natan M. Meir, and Israel Bartal, 19–37. Bloomington: Indiana University Press, 2011.

Engelking, Barbara. *Holocaust and Memory. The Experience of the Holocaust and Its Consequences: An Investigation Based on Personal Narratives*. Edited by Gunnar S. Paulsson. Leicester: Leicester University Press, 2001.

Engelking, Barbara, and Jacek Leociak. *The Warsaw Ghetto: A Guide to the Perished City*. Translated by Emma Harris. New Haven: Yale University Press, 2009.

Epsztein, Tadeusz. "Photographs in the Ringelblum Archive." In *Dispersed Contact. Photographs from the Ringelblum Archive Reinterpreted*, 42–47. Warsaw: Jewish Historical Institute, 2019.

Epsztein, Tadeusz. "Structure and Organization of the Ringelblum Archive and Its Catalog." In *The Warsaw Ghetto: Oyneg Shabes—Ringelblum Archive. Catalog and Guide*, edited by Robert Moses Shapiro and Tadeusz Epsztein, 1–22. Washington, DC: United States Holocaust Memorial Museum, 2009.

Fidelis, Malgorzata. "'Participation in the Creative Work of the Nation': Polish Women Intellectuals in the Cultural Construction of Female Gender Roles, 1864–1890." *Journal of Women's History* 13, no. 1 (2001): 108–125.

Foucault, Michel. "Of Other Spaces." *Diacritics* 16, no. 1 (1986): 22–27.

Foucault, Michel. "Space, Power and Knowledge." In *The Cultural Studies Reader*, edited by Simon During, 134–141. New York: Routledge, 1993.

Foucault, Michel. "Von anderen Räumen." In *Raumtheorie: Grundlagentexte Aus Philosophie und Kulturwissenschaften*, edited by Jörg Dünne and Stephan Günzel, translated by Michael Bischoff, 317–329. Berlin: Suhrkamp, 2006.

Friedman, Filip, and Gerszon Taffet, eds. *Zagłada Żydostwa Polskiego/Extermination of Polish Jews*. Łódź: Wydawnictwa Centralnej Żydowskiej Komisji Historycznej przy C.K. Żydów Polskich, 1945.

Friedman, Philip. "The Jewish Ghettos of the Nazi Era." *Jewish Social Studies* 16, no. 1 (1954): 61–88.

Füssel, Marian. "Tote Orte und Gelebte Räume: Zur Raumtheorie von Michel De Certeau S. J." *Historical Social Research/Historische Sozialforschung* 38, no. 3 (2013): 22–39.

Galtung, Johan. "Violence, Peace, and Peace Research." *Journal of Peace Research* 16, no. 3 (1969): 167–191.

Gebert, Konstanty. "Reading the Palimpsest." In *Jewish Space in Contemporary Poland*, edited by Erica T. Lehrer and Michael Meng, 223–237. Bloomington: Indiana University Press, 2015.

Geiss, Imanuel, and Wolfgang Jacobmeyer, eds. *Deutsche Politik in Polen 1939–1945. Aus dem Diensttagebuch von Hans Frank, Generalgouverneur in Polen 1939–1945.* Düsseldorf: Leske Verlag, 1980.

Giaccaria, Paolo, and Claudio Minca. "For a Tentative Spatial Theory of the Third Reich." In *Hitler's Geographies: The Spatialities of the Third Reich*, edited by Paolo Giaccaria and Claudio Minca, 1–44. Chicago: University of Chicago Press, 2016.

Giaccaria, Paolo, and Claudio Minca, eds. *Hitler's Geographies: The Spatialities of the Third Reich*. Chicago: University of Chicago Press, 2016.

Giaccaria, Paolo, and Claudio Minca. "Life in Space, Space in Life: Nazi Topographies, Geographical Imaginations, and Lebensraum." *Holocaust Studies* 22, no. 2–3 (2016): 151–171.

Gieseking, Jen Jack, William Mangold, Cindi Katz, Setha Low, and Susan Saegert. "Editors' Introduction and Suggestions for Further Reading: Section 9 The Social Production of Space and Time." In *The People, Place, and Space Reader*, edited by Jen Jack Gieseking, William Mangold, Cindi Katz, Setha Low, and Susan Saegert, 285–288. New York: Routledge, 2014.

Gigliotti, Simone. "A Mobile Holocaust? Rethinking Testimony with Cultural Geography." In *Hitler's Geographies: The Spatialities of the Third Reich*, edited by Paolo Giaccaria and Claudio Minca, 329–347. Chicago: University of Chicago Press, 2016.

Gilbert, Martin. *Atlas of the Holocaust*. Oxford: Pergamon Press, 1989.

Goldberg, Amos. "The History of the Jews in the Ghettos: A Cultural Perspective." In *The Holocaust and Historical Methodology*, edited by Dan Stone, 79–100. Oxford: Berghahn Books, 2012.

Goldberg, Amos. "Rumor Culture among Warsaw Jews under Nazi Occupation: A World of Catastrophe Reenchanted." *Jewish Social Studies: History, Culture, Society* 21, no. 3 (2016): 91–125.

Gong, Catherine. *George's Kaddish. For Kovno and the Six Million*. Edited by Michael Berenbaum. Bloomington: Xlibris, 2009.

Grbin, Miloje. "Foucault and Space." *Sociološki Pregled* 49, no. 3 (2015): 305–312.

Grime, Keith, and Grzegorz Węcławowicz. "Warsaw." In *Urban Problems and Planning in the Developed World*, edited by Michael Pacione, 258–291. New York: Routledge, 2013.

Grundmann, Karl. "Plan der Stadt Warschau." In *Führer Durch Warschau*. Krakau: Buchverlag Deutscher Osten, 1942.

Gutman, Israel. "Introduction." In *Das Tagebuch des Adam Czerniaków: Im Warschauer Getto 1939–1942*, by Adam Czerniaków, vii–xxiii. München: Beck'sche Reihe, 2013.

Gutman, Israel, and Michael Berenbaum. *Anatomy of the Auschwitz Death Camp*. Bloomington: Indiana University Press, 1998.

Gutman, Yisrael (Israel). *The Jews of Warsaw 1933–1943: Ghetto, Underground, Revolt*. Bloomington: Indiana University Press, 1989.

Gutschow, Niels. *Ordnungswahn: Architekten Planen im "Eingedeutschen Osten" 1939–1945*. Berlin: Birkhäuser, 2001.

Gutschow, Niels, and Barbara Klain. *Vernichtung und Utopie: Stadtplanung Warschau 1939–1945*. Hamburg: Junius Verlag, 1994.

Gutterman, Bella. *Fighting for Her People: Zivia Lubetkin, 1914–1978*. Translated by Ora Cummings. Jerusalem: Yad Vashem, 2014.

Hagen, Joshua. "Parades, Public Space, and Propaganda: The Nazi Culture Parades in Munich." *Geografiska Annaler. Series B, Human Geography* 90, no. 4 (2008): 349–367.

Harshav, Barbara. "Introduction." In *Kazik. Memoirs of a Warsaw Ghetto Fighter*, by Kazik (Simha Rotem), vii–x. Edited and translated by Barbara Harshav. New Haven: Yale University Press, 1994.

Heinemann, Isabel, and Patrick Wagner. "Introduction." In *Wissenschaft—Planung—Vertreibung. Neuordnungskonzepte und Umsiedlungspolitik im 20. Jahrhundert*, edited by Isabel Heinemann and Patrick Wagner, 7–21. Stuttgart: Franz Steiner Verlag, 2006.

Helpland, Kenneth I. *Defiant Gardens. Making Gardens in Wartime*. San Antonio: Trinity University Press, 2006.

Hilberg, Raul. *Die Vernichtung der Europäischen Juden*. Vols. 1–3. Frankfurt: Fischer Taschenbuch, 1994.

Hilberg, Raul. "The Ghetto as a Form of Government." *Annals of the American Academy of Political and Social Science* 450 (1980): 98–112.

Hock, Nikita. "Making Home, Making Sense: Aural Experiences of Warsaw and East Galician Jews in Subterranean Shelters during the Holocaust." *Transposition* 2 (2020).

Hubbard, Phil, Rob Kitchin, and Gill Valentine, eds. *Key Thinkers on Space and Place*. London: SAGE, 2004.

Hughes, Kirsty. "A Behavioural Understanding of Privacy and Its Implications for Privacy Law." *Modern Law Review* 75, no. 2 (2012): 806–836.

Hutchison, Ray. "Racialization." In *Encyclopedia of Urban Studies*, 310–313. London: SAGE, 2010.

Jacobs, Jane. "'The Uses of Sidewalks: Safety' from the Death and Life of Great American Cities (1961)." In *The City Reader*, edited by Richard T. LeGates and Frederic Stout, 149–153. New York: Routledge, 2015.

Jakimyszyn, Anna. "The Jewish Community in Kraków and Kazimierz and the Jewish Communal Authorities in the Light of Internal Sources (16th–18th Centuries)." *Mesto a Dejiny* 1, no. 1–2 (2012): 57–67.

Kajczyk, Agnieszka. "Nalewki: Stories from a Non-existent Street." In *Nalewki: Opowieść o Nieistniejącej Ulicy/Stories from a Non-existent Street*, edited by Agnieszka Kajczyk, 26–34. Warsaw: Emanuel Ringelblum Jewish Historical Institute, 2018.

Kapralski, Sławomir. "Battlefields of Memory. Landscape and Identity in Polish-Jewish Relations." *History and Memory* 13, no. 2 (2001): 35–58.

Karwowska, Bożena, and Anja Nowak, eds. *The More I Know, The Less I Understand: Young Researchers' Essays on Witnessing Auschwitz*. Oświęcim: Auschwitz-Birkenau State Museum, 2017.

Kassow, Samuel D. "Introduction." In *The Warsaw Ghetto: Oyneg Shabes-Ringelblum Archive. Catalog and Guide*, edited by Robert Moses Shapiro and Tadeusz Epsztein, xv–xxiv. Washington, DC: United States Holocaust Memorial Museum, 2009.

Kassow, Samuel D. "Introduction." In *Those Nightmarish Days: The Ghetto Reportage of Peretz Opoczynski and Josef Zelkowicz*, by Peretz Opoczynski and Josef Zelkowicz, vii–iii. Edited by Samuel D. Kassow. Translated by David Suchoff. New Haven: Yale University Press, 2015.

Kassow, Samuel D. *Who Will Write Our History? Rediscovering a Hidden Archive from the Warsaw Ghetto*. London: Penguin Books, 2007.

Katsh, Abraham Isaac. "Introduction." In *Scroll of Agony: The Warsaw Diary of Chaim A. Kaplan*, by Chaim A. Kaplan, 9–17. Edited and translated by Abraham Isaac Katsh. Bloomington: Indiana University Press, 1999.

Klee, Ernst. *Das Personenlexikon zum Dritten Reich: Wer war was vor und nach 1945.* Hamburg: Nikol Verlag, 2016.

Klemperer, Victor. *Lingua Tertii Imperii.* Leipzig: Reclam Verlag, 1980.

Knowles, Anne Kelly, Tim Cole, and Alberto Giordano, eds. *Geographies of the Holocaust.* Bloomington: Indiana University Press, 2014.

Kogon, Eugen. *Der SS-Staat. Das System der Deutschen Konzentrationslager.* München: Heyne Verlag, 2012.

Kozlowski, Nina, and Christian Prunitsch. "Czerniaków, Adam: Dziennik Gettawarszawskiego." In *Kindlers Literatur Lexikon,* edited by H. L. Arnold, 1–2. Stuttgart: J. B. Metzler, 2020.

Krahmann, Elke. "The State Monopoly on Collective Violence and Democratic Control over Military Force." In *States, Citizens and the Privatisation of Security,* 21–50. Cambridge, UK: Cambridge University Press, 2010.

Kunze, Donald. "The Topography of Fear: Architecture's Fourth Walls and Inside Frames." In *Architecture and Violence,* edited by Bechir Kenzari, 175–198. New York, Barcelona: Actar, 2011.

Lange, Karl. "Der Terminus 'Lebensraum' in Hitlers 'Mein Kampf.'" *Vierteljahrshefte Für Zeitgeschichte* 13, no. 4 (1965): 426–437.

Langegger, Sig. *Rights to Public Space: Law, Culture, and Gentrification in the American West.* London: Palgrave Macmillan, 2017.

Lefebvre, Henri. *The Production of Space.* Translated by Donald Nicholson-Smith. Hoboken: Blackwell, 1991.

Lehnstaedt, Stephan. "Jewish Spaces? Defining Nazi Ghettos Then and Now." *Polish Review* 61, no. 4 (2016): 41–56.

Lehnstaedt, Stephan. *Okkupation im Osten. Besatzeralltag in Warschau und Minsk 1939–1944.* München: R. Oldenbourg Verlag, 2010.

Leociak, Jacek. *Biografie Ulic. O żydowskich ulicach Warszawy: Od narodzin po Zagładę.* Warsaw: Dom Spotkań z Historią, 2018.

Leociak, Jacek. *Doświadczenia graniczne: Studia o dwudziestowiecznych formach eeprezentacji.* Warsaw: Instytutu Badań Literackich PAN, 2009.

Leociak, Jacek. "From Żydowska Street to Umschlagplatz." Unpublished typescript. Warsaw, 2016.

Leociak, Jacek. "Literature of the Personal Document as a Source in Holocaust Research (a Methodological Reconnaissance)." *Holocaust Studies and Materials: Journal of the Polish Center for Holocaust Research* 1 (2008): 31–53.

Leociak, Jacek. *Text in the Face of Destruction. Accounts from the Warsaw Ghetto Reconsidered.* Warsaw: Jewish Historical Institute, 2004.

Levi, Primo. "The Grey Zone." In *The Drowned and the Saved,* translated by Raymond Rosenthal, 31–71. London: Abacus, 2013.

Levine, Madeline G. "Home Loss in Wartime Literature: A Typology of Images." In *Framing the Polish Home: Postwar Cultural Constructions of Hearth, Nation, and Self,* edited by Bożena Shallcross, 97–114. Athens: Ohio University Press, 2002.

Lewiński, Jerzy. "The Death of Adam Czerniaków and Janusz Korczak's Last Journey." In *Jewish Life in Nazi-Occupied Warsaw*, edited by Antony Polonsky, 224–252. Oxford: Littman Library of Jewish Civilization, 2008.

Lifton, Betty Jean. "Introduction: Who Was Janusz Korczak?" In *Ghetto Diary*, by Janusz Korczak, vii–xxx. New Haven: Yale University Press, 2003.

Line, Maria. "Introduction." In *Aufzeichnungen Aus dem Warschauer Ghetto: Juli 1942 Bis April 1943*, by Eugenia Szajn-Lewin, 7–8. Leipzig: Reclam Verlag, 1994.

Lipphardt, Anna, Julia Brauch, and Alexandra Nocke. "Introduction: Exploring Jewish Space an Approach." In *Jewish Topographies*, edited by Anna Lipphardt, Julia Brauch, and Alexandra Nocke, 1–23. New York: Routledge, 2008.

Lipsitz, George. "The Racialization of Space and the Spatialization of Race: Theorizing the Hidden Architecture of Landscape." *Landscape Journal* 26, no. 1 (2007): 10–23.

Löw, Andrea, and Markus Roth. *Das Warschauer Getto: Alltag und Widerstand im Angesicht der Vernichtung*. München: Beck'sche Reihe, 2013.

Lynch, Kevin. *The Image of the City*. Cambridge, MA: MIT Press, 1960.

Madanipour, Ali. *Public and Private Spaces of the City*. New York: Routledge, 2003.

Madryas, Cezary, Arkadiusz Szot, and Leszek Wysocki. "Upgrading Old Masonry Interceptor Sewers to Modern Sewerage Standards." In *Underground Space: The 4th Dimension of Metropolises*, edited by Jirí Barták, Ivan Hrdina, Georgij Romancov, and Jaromir Zlamal, 1919–1924. Boca Raton: CRC Press, 2007.

Mai, Uwe. *"Rasse und Raum": Agrarpolitik, Sozial- und Raumplanung im NS-Staat*. Paderborn: Ferdinand Schöningh, 2002.

Majer, Diemut. *"Non-Germans" under the Third Reich: The Nazi Judicial and Administrative System in Germany and Occupied Eastern Europe, with Special Regard to Occupied Poland, 1939–1945*. Lubbock: Texas Tech University Press, 2013.

Mantho, Robert. *The Urban Section: An Analytical Tool for Cities and Streets*. New York: Routledge, 2014.

Marshall, Stephen. *Streets and Patterns*. New York: Routledge, 2004.

Martyn, Peter J. "The Undefined Town within a Town. A History of Jewish Settlement in the Western Districts of Warsaw." In *The Jews of Warsaw*, edited by Antony Polonsky, 17–45. Polin: Studies in Polish Jewry 3. Liverpool: Liverpool University Press, 2004.

Massey, Doreen. "On Space and the City." In *City Worlds*, edited by Doreen Massey, John Allen, and Steve Pile, 157–170. New York: Routledge, 1999.

Massey, Douglas S., and Nancy A. Denton. "Hypersegregation in U.S. Metropolitan Areas: Black and Hispanic Segregation along Five Dimensions." *Demography* 26, no. 3 (1989): 373–391.

McClain, Linda C. "Inviolability and Privacy: The Castle, the Sanctuary, and the Body." *Yale Journal of Law and the Humanities* 7, no. 1 (2013): 195–241.

McMahon, Laura. "Home Invasions: Phenomenological and Psychoanalytic Reflections on Embodiment Relations, Vulnerability, and Breakdown." *Journal of Speculative Philosophy* 28, no. 3 (2014): 358–369.

Mehta, Vikas. *The Street: A Quintessential Social Public Space*. New York: Routledge, 2013.

Meng, Michael. "Muranów as a Ruin. Layered Memories in Postwar Warsaw." In *Jewish Space in Contemporary Poland*, edited by Erica T. Lehrer and Michael Meng, 71–89. Bloomington: Indiana University Press, 2015.

Michman, Dan. *The Emergence of Jewish Ghettos during the Holocaust*. Translated by Lenn J. Schramm. Cambridge, UK: Cambridge University Press, 2011.

Michman, Dan. "Judenräte, Ghettos, 'Endlösung': Drei Komponenten einer antijüdischen Politik oder separate Faktoren?" In *Der Judenmord in den eingegliederten polnischen Gebieten 1939–1945*, edited by Jacek Andrezej Młynarczyk and Jochen Böhler, 167–176. Osnabrück: fibre, 2010.

Michman, Dan. "Why Did Heydrich Write the *Schnellbrief*? A Remark on the Reason and on Its Significance." Edited by David Silberklang. Translated by Naftali Greenwood. *Yad Vashem Studies* 32 (2004): 433–447.

Miller Lane, Barbara. *Architecture and Politics in Germany, 1918–1945*. Cambridge, MA: Harvard University Press, 1968.

Miron, Guy. "'Lately, Almost Constantly, Everything Seems Small to Me': The Lived Space of German Jews under the Nazi Regime." *Jewish Social Studies: History, Culture, Society* 20, no. 1 (2013): 121–149.

Musial, Bogdan. *Deutsche Zivilverwaltung und Judenverfolgung im Generalgouvernement: Eine Fallstudie Zum Distrikt Lublin 1939–1944*. Wiesbaden: Harrassowitz Verlag, 1999.

Nałkowska, Zofia. "The Adults and Children of Auschwitz." In *Medallions*, translated by Diana Kuprel, 45–49. Evanston: Northwestern University Press, 2000.

Nałkowska, Zofia. *Medallions*. Translated by Diana Kuprel. Evanston: Northwestern University Press, 2000.

Neumann, Boaz. *Die Weltanschauung des Nazismus: Raum—Körper—Sprache*. Translated by Markus Lemke. Göttingen: Wallstein, 2010.

Nowak, Anja. "Spatial Configurations of the Concentration Camp: The Inside and the Outside." In *Geograficzne przestrzenie utekstowione*, edited by Bożena Karwowska, Elżbieta Konończuk, Elżbieta Sidoruk, and Ewa Wampuszyc, 371–386. Białystok: University of Białystok Publishing House, 2017.

Ofer, Dalia. "Gender Issues in Diaries and Testimonies of the Ghetto: The Case of Warsaw." In *Women in the Holocaust*, edited by Dalia Ofer and Lenore J. Weitzman, 143–167. New Haven: Yale University Press, 1998.

Ofer, Dalia, and Lenore J. Weitzman. "Introduction: The Role of Gender in the Holocaust." In *Women in the Holocaust*, edited by Dalia Ofer and Lenore J. Weitzman, 1–23. New Haven: Yale University Press, 1998.

Ofer, Dalia, and Lenore J. Weitzman, eds. *Women in the Holocaust*. New Haven: Yale University Press, 1998.

Paulsson, Gunnar S. "Evading the Holocaust: The Unexplored Continent of Holocaust Historiography." In *Remembering for the Future*, edited by John K. Roth,

Elisabeth Maxwell, Margot Levy, and Wendy Whitworth, 302–318. London: Palgrave Macmillan, 2001.

Paulsson, Gunnar S. *Secret City. The Hidden Jews of Warsaw, 1940–1945*. New Haven: Yale University Press, 2002.

Pentlin, Susan. "Introduction." In *The Diary of Mary Berg: Growing Up in the Warsaw Ghetto*, by Mary Berg, xv–xxxii. Edited by S. L. Shneiderman. Oxford: Oneworld, 2006.

Person, Katarzyna. "Sexual Violence during the Holocaust—The Case of Forced Prostitution in the Warsaw Ghetto." *Shofar: An Interdisciplinary Journal of Jewish Studies* 33, no. 2 (2015): 103–121.

Person, Katarzyna. *Warsaw Ghetto Police. The Jewish Order Service during the Nazi Occupation*. Translated by Zygmunt Nowak-Soliński. Ithaca, NY: Cornell University Press, 2021.

Petersen, Hans-Christian. *Bevölkerungsökonomie—Ostforschung—Politik. Eine Biographische Studie Zu Peter-Heinz Seraphim (1902–1979)*. Osnabrück: fibre, 2007.

Pető, Andrea, Louise Hecht, and Karolina Krasuska, eds. *Women and the Holocaust: New Perspectives and Challenges*. Warsaw: Instytut Badań Literackich PAN, 2015.

Piątek, Grzegorz. *Sanator: Kariera Stefana Starzyńskiego*. Warsaw: W.A.B., 2016.

Piper, Franciszek. "The Political and Racist Principles of the Nazi Policy of Extermination and Their Realization at KL Auschwitz." In *Auschwitz: Nazi Death Camp*, edited by Franciszek Piper and Teresa Świebocka, 11–20. Oświęcim: Auschwitz-Birkenau State Museum, 1996.

Polonsky, Antony. "Introduction." In *A Cup of Tears: A Diary of the Warsaw Ghetto*, by Abraham Lewin, 1–54. Edited by Antony Polonsky. Translated by Christopher Hutton. London: Fontana, 1988.

Popitz, Heinrich. *Phänomene der Macht*. Heidelberg: J. C. B. Mohr, 1992.

Popitz, Heinrich. *Phenomena of Power: Authority, Domination, and Violence*. Edited by Andreas Göttlich and Jochen Dreher. Translated by Gianfranco Poggi. New York: Columbia University Press, 2017.

Raithel, Thomas, and Irene Strenge. "Die Reichstagsbrandverordnung: Grundlegung der Diktatur Mit den Instrumenten des Weimarer Ausnahmezustands." *Vierteljahrshefte Für Zeitgeschichte* 48, no. 3 (2000): 413–460.

Razac, Olivier. *Barbed Wire: A Political History*. New York: The New Press, 2002.

Reemtsma, Jan Philipp. *Trust and Violence*. Princeton: Princeton University Press, 2012.

Reich, Walter, ed. *Hidden History of the Kovno Ghetto*. Washington, DC: United States Holocaust Memorial Museum, 1997.

Rodov, Ilia M. *The Torah Ark in Renaissance Poland: A Jewish Revival of Classical Antiquity*. Vol. 23. Jewish and Christian Perspectives Series. Leiden: Brill, 2013.

Rosenkranz, Shmuel. "Memoir of Janek Kostanski." In *Janek. A Gentile in the Warsaw Ghetto*, by Jan Kostański, 9–10. Melbourne: Puma Press, 1998.

Rossi, Aldo. *The Architecture of the City*. Translated by Diane Ghirardo and Joan Ockman. Cambridge, MA: MIT Press, 1984.

Rössler, Mechthild. "Applied Geography and Area Research in Nazi Society: Central Place Theory and Planning, 1933–1945." In *Hitler's Geographies: The Spatialities of the Third Reich*, edited by Paolo Giaccaria and Claudio Minca, 182–197. Chicago: University of Chicago Press, 2016.

Roszkowski, Wojciech, and Jan Kofman, eds. *Biographical Dictionary of Central and Eastern Europe in the Twentieth Century*. New York: Routledge, 2008.

Roth, Markus. *Herrenmenschen: Die deutschen Kreishauptleute im besetzten Polen—Karrierewege, Herrschaftspraxis und Nachgeschichte*. Göttingen: Wallstein Verlag, 2009.

Rubinstein, Avraham, Danuta Dombrowska, and Stefan Krakowski. "Warsaw." In *Encyclopaedia Judaica*, 2nd ed., edited by Michael Berenbaum and Fred Skolnik, 20:666–675. New York: Macmillan Reference USA, 2007.

Rupnow, Dirk. "The Invisible Crime: Nazi Politics of Memory and Postwar Representation of the Holocaust." In *The Holocaust and Historical Methodology*, edited by Dan Stone, 61–78. New York: Berghahn Books, 2012.

Rypson, Piotr. "What Do Those Images Want from Us ?" In *Where Art Thou? Exhibition Catalog*, edited by Paweł Śpiewak, 119–159. Warsaw: Jewish Historical Institute, 2020.

Schafer, Murray E. *The Soundscape: Our Sonic Environment and the Tuning of the World*. Rochester: Destiny Books, 1977.

Schneersohn, Isaac. "Foreword." In *The Vanished City: Everyday Life in the Warsaw Ghetto*, by Michel Mazor, 3–5. Translated by David Jacobson. New York: Marsilo, 1993.

Schroer, Markus. *Räume, Orte, Grenzen. Auf dem Weg Zu Einer Soziologie des Raumes*. Berlin: Suhrkamp, 2012.

Sennett, Richard. "The Jewish Ghetto in Venice." In *The Foreigner: Two Essays on Exile*, by Richard Sennett, 1–44. London: Notting Hill Editions, 2017.

Shallcross, Bożena. "Introduction: Home Truths. Toward a Definition of the Polish Home." In *Framing the Polish Home: Postwar Cultural Constructions of Hearth, Nation, and Self*, 19. Athens: Ohio University Press, 2002.

Shapiro, Robert Moses. "Translator's Preface." In *The Warsaw Ghetto: Oyneg Shabes-Ringelblum Archive. Catalog and Guide*, edited by Robert Moses Shapiro and Tadeusz Epsztein, xiii. Washington, DC: United States Holocaust Memorial Museum, 2009.

Shapiro, Robert Moses, and Tadeusz Epsztein, eds. *The Warsaw Ghetto: Oyneg Shabes–Ringelblum Archive. Catalog and Guide*. Washington, DC: United States Holocaust Memorial Museum, 2009.

Siemens, Christof. "Die Menschenerniedrigungsmaschine." *Die Zeit*, May 27, 1994.

Sloane, Jacob. "Introduction." In *Notes from the Warsaw Ghetto: The Journal of Emmanuel Ringelblum*, by Emanuel Ringelblum, ix–xxvii. Edited and translated by Jacob Sloane. New York: Schocken Books, 1974.

Sofsky, Wolfgang. *Die Ordnung des Terrors. Das Konzentrationslager.* Frankfurt: S. Fischer Verlag, 1993.

Soja, Edward W. *Postmodern Geographies: The Reassertion of Space in Critical Theory.* London: Verso, 1989.

Springer, Simon, and Philippe Le Billon. "Violence and Space: An Introduction to the Geographies of Violence." *Political Geography* 52 (2016): 1–3.

Stone, Dan. "Holocaust Spaces." In *Hitler's Geographies: The Spatialities of the Third Reich,* edited by Paolo Giaccaria and Claudio Minca, 45–62. Chicago: University of Chicago Press, 2016.

Stone, Dan. "Introduction." In *The Holocaust and Historical Methodology,* edited by Dan Stone, 1–8. New York: Berghahn Books, 2012.

Strathern, Andrew, and Pamela J. Stewart. "Introduction: Terror, the Imagination, and Cosmology." In *Terror and Violence: Imagination and the Unimaginable,* edited by Andrew Strathern, Pamela J. Stewart, and Neil Whitehead, 1–39. London: Pluto Press, 2005.

Strobl, Ingrid. *Die Angst kam erst danach. Jüdische Frauen im Widerstand 1939–1945.* Frankfurt: Fischer Taschenbuch, 1998.

Strobl, Ingrid. "Preface." In *Das Ghetto Kämpft: Warschau 1941–43,* by Marek Edelman, 9–25. Translated by Ewa and Jerzy Czerwiakowski. Berlin: Harald Kater Verlag, 1999.

Strobl, Ingrid. *"Sag nie, du gehst den letzten Weg." Frauen im bewaffneten Widerstand gegen Faschismus und deutsche Besatzung.* Frankfurt: Fischer Taschenbuch, 1989.

Struk, Janina. *Photographing the Holocaust: Interpretations of the Evidence.* New York: I. B. Tauris, 2005.

Sundstrom, Ronald R. "Race and Place: Social Space in the Production of Human Kinds." *Philosophy and Geography* 6, no. 1 (2003): 83–95.

Sydnor, Charles. "Reinhard Heydrich—Der 'Ideale Nationalsozialist.'" In *Die SS: Elite Unter dem Totenkopf. 30 Lebensläufe,* edited by Ronald Smelser and Enrico Syring, 208–219. Paderborn: Ferdinand Schöningh, 2000.

Szarota, Tomasz. *Warschau unter dem Hakenkreuz.* Translated by Claudia Makowski and Ryszard Makowski. Paderborn: Ferdinand Schöningh, 1978.

Taylor, Robert R. *The Word in Stone: The Role of Architecture in the National Socialist Ideology.* Berkeley: University of California Press, 1974.

Thompson, Larry von. "Friedrich-Wilhelm Krüger—Höherer SS- und Polizeiführer Ost." In *Die SS: Elite Unter dem Totenkopf. 30 Lebensläufe,* edited by Ronald Smelser and Enrico Syring, 320–331. Paderborn: Ferdinand Schöningh, 2000.

Thompson Fullilove, Mindy. *Root Shock: How Tearing Up City Neighborhoods Hurts America, and What We Can Do about It.* New York: New Village Press, 2016.

Till, Karen E. "Wounded Cities: Memory-Work and a Place-Based Ethics of Care." *Political Geography* 31 (2012): 3–14.

Trotha, Trutz von. "Zur Soziologie der Gewalt." *Soziologie der Gewalt. Kölner Zeitschrift für Soziologie und Sozialpsychologie Sonderheft* 37 (1997): 9–56.

Ubertowska, Alexandra. "'Masculine'/'Feminine' in Autobiographical Accounts of the Warsaw Ghetto: Comparative Analysis of the Memoirs of Cywia Lubetkin and Icchak Cukierman." In *Women and the Holocaust: New Perspectives and Challenges*, edited by Andrea Pető, Louise Hecht, and Karolina Krasuska, 161–179. Warsaw: Instytut Badań Literackich PAN, 2015.

Van Pelt, Robert Jan, and Carroll William Westfall. *Architectural Principles in the Age of Historicism*. New Haven: Yale University Press, 1993.

Vasiliev, Irina, Scott Freundschuh, David M. Mark, G. D. Theisen, and J. McAvoy. "What Is a Map?" *Cartographic Journal* 27, no. 2 (1990): 119–123.

Veerman, Philip E. "In the Shadow of Janusz Korczak—The Story of Stefania Wilczynska." *Melton Journal* 23 (1990): 8–15.

Wasser, Bruno. *Himmlers Raumplanung im Osten. Der Generalplan Ost in Polen 1940–1944*. Basel: Birkhäuser Verlag, 1993.

Waxman, Zoë. "Transcending History? Methodological Problems in Holocaust Testimony." In *The Holocaust and Historical Methodology*, edited by Dan Stone, 143–157. New York: Berghahn Books, 2012.

Waxman, Zoë. *Women in the Holocaust: A Feminist History*. Oxford: Oxford University Press, 2017.

Weber, Max. *Politik Als Beruf*. Leipzig: Reclam Verlag, 2017.

Węgrzynek, Hanna. "Illegal Immigrants: The Jews of Warsaw, 1527–1792." In *Warsaw. The Jewish Metropolis. Essays in Honor of the 75th Birthday of Professor Antony Polonsky*, edited by Glenn Dynner and François Guesnet, 19–41. Leiden: Brill, 2015.

Westin, Alan. "The Origins of Modern Claims to Privacy." In *Philosophical Dimensions of Privacy: An Anthology*, edited by Ferdinand David Schoeman, 56–74. Cambridge, UK: Cambridge University Press, 1984.

Weszpiński, Paweł E. "Borders Before the Great Liquidation Action." In *The Warsaw Ghetto: A Guide to the Perished City*, by Barbara Engelking and Jacek Leociak. New Haven: Yale University Press, 2009.

Weszpiński, Paweł E. "Distribution of Jews in Warsaw According to the Census of 9 December 1931." In *The Warsaw Ghetto: A Guide to the Perished City*, by Barbara Engelking and Jacek Leociak, 16. New Haven: Yale University Press, 2009.

Weszpiński, Paweł E. "Present Structure of Streets and Remains of Buildings in March 2001 against the Old Plan of the City." In *The Warsaw Ghetto: A Guide to the Perished City*, by Barbara Engelking and Jacek Leociak. New Haven: Yale University Press, 2009.

Weszpiński, Paweł E. "Residual Ghetto after the Liquidation Action." In *The Warsaw Ghetto: A Guide to the Perished City*, by Barbara Engelking and Jacek Leociak. New Haven: Yale University Press, 2009.

Weszpiński, Paweł E. "Social Life." In *The Warsaw Ghetto: A Guide to the Perished City*, by Barbara Engelking and Jacek Leociak. New Haven: Yale University Press, 2009.

Wienert, Annika. *Das Lager Vorstellen: Die Architektur der Nationalsozialistischen Vernichtungslager*. Berlin: Neofelis Verlag, 2015.

Wiesel, Elie. "Introduction." In *On Both Sides of the Wall*, by Vladka Meed, 3–8. Translated by Steven Meed. New York: Holocaust Library, 1999.

Winckler, Emily. "A Language Lost: The Holocaust's Impact on Yiddish Language and Literature." In *The More I Know, The Less I Understand: Young Researchers' Essays on Witnessing Auschwitz*, edited by Bożena Karwowska and Anja Nowak, 181–193. Oświęcim: Auschwitz-Birkenau State Museum, 2017.

Winter, Yves. "Violence and Visibility." *New Political Science* 34, no. 2 (2012): 195–202.

Wolf, Gerhard. "The East as Historical Imagination and Germanization Policies of the Third Reich." In *Hitler's Geographies: The Spatialities of the Third Reich*, edited by Paolo Giaccaria and Claudio Minca, 93–109. Chicago: University of Chicago Press, 2016.

Wolter, Heike. *"Volk ohne Raum"—Lebensraumvorstellungen im geopolitischen, literarischen und politischen Diskurs der Weimarer Republik*. Münster: LIT Verlag, 2003.

Wulf, Joseph. *Das Dritte Reich und seine Vollstrecker*. Berlin: Ullstein, 1984.

Żbikowski, Andrzej. "Antisemitism, Extortion against Jews, Collaboration with Germans and Polish-Jewish Relations under German Occupation." In *Inferno of Choices. Poles and the Holocaust*, edited by Sebastian Rejak and Elzbieta Frister, 182–235. Warsaw: Oficyna Wydawnicza RYTM, 2011.

Zeldowicz, Ludmilla. "Personal Notes on Stanislaw Adler." In *In the Warsaw Ghetto, 1940–1943: An Account of a Witness*, by Stanisław Adler, xi–xviii. Jerusalem: Yad Vashem, 1982.

Zieleniec, Andrzej J. L. "Henri Lefebvre: The Production of Space." In *Space and Social Theory*, 60–97. London: SAGE, 2007.

Zimmerer, Jürgen. "In Service of Empire: Geographers at Berlin's University between Colonial Studies and Ostforschung (Eastern Research)." In *Hitler's Geographies: The Spatialities of the Third Reich*, edited by Paolo Giaccaria and Claudio Minca, 67–92. Chicago: University of Chicago Press, 2016.

Media and Internet Sources

"About Nalewki Street Talks dr Rafał Żebrowski." Jewish Historical Institute, 2014. https://www.jhi.pl/en/articles/about-nalewki-street-talks-dr-rafal-zebrowski,117.

Amnesty International. "Amnesty International Report 2020/21. The State of the World's Human Rights." amnesty, April 7, 2021. https://www.amnesty.org/en/documents/pol10/3202/2021/en/.

Bergman, Eleonora. "'Following the Markers.' Jewish Warsaw: Past and Present." POLIN Museum of the History of Polish Jews, n.d. https://warsze.polin.pl/en/przeszlosc/terazniejszosc/teraz-eleonora-bergman.

bs. "Stefan Starzyński—prezydent, który poświęcił życie dla stolicy." ["Stefan Starzyński—the President Who Dedicated His Life to the Capital."] Polskie Radio, October 27, 2021. https://www.polskieradio.pl/39/156/Artykul /909881,Stefan-Starzynski-%E2%80%93-prezydent-ktory-poswiecil-zycie -dla-stolicy.

"The Construction of the Camp." Auschwitz-Birkenau Memorial and Museum, 2021. http://auschwitz.org/en/history/auschwitz-ii/the-construction-of -the-camp.

Deutsches Militärisches Karteninstitut Warschau. "Plan der Stadt Warschau, 1941." Mapster, n.d. http://igrek.amzp.pl/1755218.

Gordon, Justin. "The Ghetto Mail Man: Warsaw Ghetto." The Journey: The Holocaust through the Letters and Cards of the Victims, 2014. http://www .holocaustjourney.com/ghetto-postman-warsaw-ghetto/.

Hen, Jozef. "'Walking in a Non-Existent City.' Jewish Warsaw: Past and Present." POLIN Museum of the History of Polish Jews, n.d. https://warsze.polin.pl/en /przeszlosc/terazniejszosc/jozef-hen.

Hersonski, Yael. A Film Unfinished. Oscilloscope Laboratories, 2010. 1 h 29 min.

"History." Auschwitz-Birkenau Memorial and Museum, 2021. http://auschwitz.org /en/history/auschwitz-ii/the-construction-of-the-camp.

"'Holocaust—Jewish Warsaw.' Jewish Warsaw: Past and Present." POLIN Museum of the History of Polish Jews, n.d. http://warsze.polin.pl/en/przeszlosc/wojna /podsumowanie.

Jagielski, Jan. "Three Synagogues." Jewish Historical Institute, 2013. https://www .jhi.pl/en/articles/three-synagogues,13.

Jewish Historical Institute. "Central Jewish Library," n.d. https://cbj.jhi.pl/.

Jewish Historical Institute. "English Translations of the Ringelblum Archive," 2021. https://www.jhi.pl/en/oneg-shabbat/projects/english-translations -ringelblum-archive.

Jewish Historical Institute and Association of the Jewish Historical Institute. "Warsaw Ghetto Photography." DELET, n.d. https://delet.jhi.pl/en/library /fotografie-archiwum-ringelbluma.

Josem, Jayne. "Obituaries: Janek Kostanski. Heroic Saviour of the Warsaw Ghetto." The Sidney Morning Herald, February 18, 2011. https://www.smh.com.au/national /heroic-saviour-of-the-warsaw-ghetto-20110217-1ay70.html.

Krupski, Jan, and Roman Janusiewicz. "Commercial Cartography in Poland." International Cartographic Association, 2001. https://icaci.org/files/documents /ICC_proceedings/ICC2001/icc2001/file/f08011.pdf.

Ksiaznica-Atlas. "Plan of the Capital City of Warsaw." Urban Media Archive, n.d. https://uma.lvivcenter.org/en/maps/34553.

Majewski, Jerzy S. "Uzbiegu Bagna, Wielkiej, Świętokrzyskiej." ["At the Confluence of the Bagno, Wielka and Świętokrzyska Streets."]. Wyborcza, 2001. https:// warszawa.wyborcza.pl/warszawa/1,34880,460903.html.

Mémorial de la Shoah. Musée, Centre de Documentation. "Les Photographes." Regards sur les Ghettos, n.d. https://regards-ghettos.memorialdelashoah.org /photographes/cusian.html.

Motte, Robin de la. "D44: WaterTime Case Study—Warsaw, Poland." WaterTime, 2005. http://www.watertime.net/wt_cs_cit_ncr.html#Poland.

Muzeum Powstania Warszawskiego/Warsaw Rising Museum. "Mieczysław Bil-Bilażewski." Muzeum Powstania Warszawskiego, n.d. https://www.1944.pl/en /photo-library/collection/mieczyslaw-bil-bilazewski,121.html.

Muzeum Powstania Warszawskiego/Warsaw Rising Museum. "Photo Library." Muzeum Powstania Warszawskiego, n.d. https://www.1944.pl/en/photo -library.html.

Muzeum Treblinka. "The Nazi German Extermination and Forced Labour Camp (1941–1944)." Muzeumtreblinka, 2021. https://muzeumtreblinka.eu/en /informacje/commemoration/.

Piper, Franciszek. "The Topography of the Camp." Auschwitz-Birkenau Memorial and Museum, 2005. http://auschwitz.org/en/history/kl-auschwitz-birkenau/the -topography-of-the-camp/.

POLIN Museum of the History of Polish Jews. "A Unique Discovery—Photographic Film with Images of the Warsaw Ghetto Uprising." POLIN Museum of the History of Polish Jews, 2023. https://polin.pl/en/news/2023/01/16 /unique-discovery-photographic-film-images-warsaw-ghetto-uprising.

Polish Center for Holocaust Research. "Warsaw Ghetto Database." New, 2022. https://new.getto.pl/en/Atlas-of-the-ghetto.

Romik, Natalia. "Hiding Places. The Architecture of Survival." Miejsce, June 2020. http://miejsce.asp.waw.pl/english-hiding-places-the-architecture -of-survival/.

Saidel, Rochelle G. "Vladka Meed 1921–2012." Jewish Women's Archive, 2009. https://jwa.org/encyclopedia/article/meed-vladka.

Shachar, Guy. "Feeling/Filling Void—Warsaw/Muranów Architecture Project—Phase Two." Multidisciplinary View of the World, 2014. https://guyshachar.com /en/2014/warsaw-architecture-project-phase-2/.

Starzyński, Stefan. "Jedno z Radiowych Przemówień Stefana Starzyński—Archiwum Polskiego Radia, Wrzesień." ["One of the Radio Broadcasts of Stefan Starzyński—Archive of the Polish Radio Station, September 1939."] Polskie Radio, 2011. https://www.polskieradio.pl/39/156/Artykul /909881,Stefan-Starzynski—prezydent-ktory-poswiecil-zycie-dla -stolicy.

Szwarcman-Czarnota, Bella. "'A Closed Book.' Jewish Warsaw: Past and Present." POLIN Museum of the History of Polish Jews, n.d. https://warsze.polin.pl/en /przeszlosc/terazniejszosc/bella-szwarcman-czarnota.

Teunissen, Harrie. "Topography of Terror: Maps of the Warsaw Ghetto." Siger, 2011. http://www.siger.org/warsawghettomaps/.

Webb, Chris. "Adam Czerniakow Diary Extracts. The Aktion to Confiscate Furs from the Ghettos in Poland." Holocaust Research Project, 2008. http://www.holocaustresearchproject.org/economics/furs.html.

Weinhold, Andreas. "Zum Umgang mit Fotografien aus der Zeit des Holocaust im Geschichtsunterricht." Yad Vashem, n.d. https://www.yadvashem.org/de/education/newsletter/5/photos-in-the-holocaust.html#footnoteref6_jl2qjqp.

Yad Vashem. "Clearing the Ruins of the Ghetto." Voices from the Inferno: Holocaust Survivors Describe the Last Months in the Warsaw Ghetto, 2022. https://www.yadvashem.org/yv/en/exhibitions/warsaw_ghetto_testimonies/gesia_camp.asp?WT.mc_id=wiki.

"Zagadka śmierci prezydenta Starzyńskiego." ["The Riddle of President Starzyński's Death."] *Polskie Radio*, 2011. https://www.polskieradio.pl/39/1240/Artykul/468203,Zagadka-smierci-prezydenta-Starzynskiego.

Zonszajn, Mosze. "Ulica Dzika-Zamenhofa." ["Dzika-Zamenhofa Street."] Varshe, 2011. http://varshe.org.pl/teksty-zrodlowe/o-miejscach/28-ulica-dzika-zamenhofa2.

INDEX

Anja Nowak received her PhD from the University of British Columbia, Vancouver. She published a monograph on Theodor W. Adorno's aesthetics (*Elemente einer Ästhetik des Theatralen in Adornos Ästhetischer Theorie*, 2012), co-edited the new critical edition of Walter Benjamin's radio broadcasts (*Werke und Nachlass* 9, 2017, with Thomas Küpper) and a collection of student essays on Auschwitz (*The More I Know the Less I Understand*, 2017, with Bożena Karwowska). She works as a freelance writer, researcher and educator in Frankfurt, Germany.

For Indiana University Press

Sophia Hebert, Assistant Acquisitions Editor

Brenna Hosman, Production Coordinator

Kathryn Huggins, Production Manager

David Miller, Lead Project Manager/Editor

Bethany Mowry, Acquisitions Editor

Pamela Rude, Designer

Stephen Williams, Marketing and Publicity Specialist